Anacreon Redivivus

RECENTIORES: LATER LATIN TEXTS AND CONTEXTS

Poetry and the Cult of the Martyrs: The Liber Peristephanon *of Prudentius*
   by Michael Roberts

Dante's Epistle to Cangrande
   by Robert Hollander

Macaronic Sermons: Bilingualism and Preaching in Late-Medieval England
   by Siegfried Wenzel

Writing Ravenna: The Liber Pontificalis *of Andreas Agnellus*
   by Joaquín Martínez Pizarro

Anacreon Redivivus: *A Study of Anacreontic Translation in Mid-Sixteenth-Century France*
   by John O'Brien

Anacreon Redivivus
A Study of Anacreontic Translation in Mid-Sixteenth-Century France

John O'Brien

Ann Arbor

THE UNIVERSITY OF MICHIGAN PRESS

Copyright © by the University of Michigan 1995
All rights reserved
Published in the United States of America by
The University of Michigan Press
Manufactured in the United States of America
⊗ Printed on acid-free paper

1998 1997 1996 1995   4 3 2 1

A CIP catalog record for this book is available from the British Library.

Library of Congress Cataloging-in-Publication Data

O'Brien, John, 1954–
    Anacreon redivivus : a study of Anacreontic translation in mid-sixteenth-century France / John O'Brien.
       p.   cm. — (Recentiores : later Latin texts and contexts)
    Includes bibliographical references (p.   ) and index.
    ISBN 0-472-10617-1 (hard : alk. paper)
    1. Anacreon—Parodies, imitations, etc. 2. Greek poetry—Translations into Latin (Medieval and modern)—History and criticism. 3. Translators and translating—France—History—16th century. I. Title. II. Series: Recentiores.
PA3865.Z5027   1995
884'.01—dc20   95-34523
                                                                         CIP

To my parents

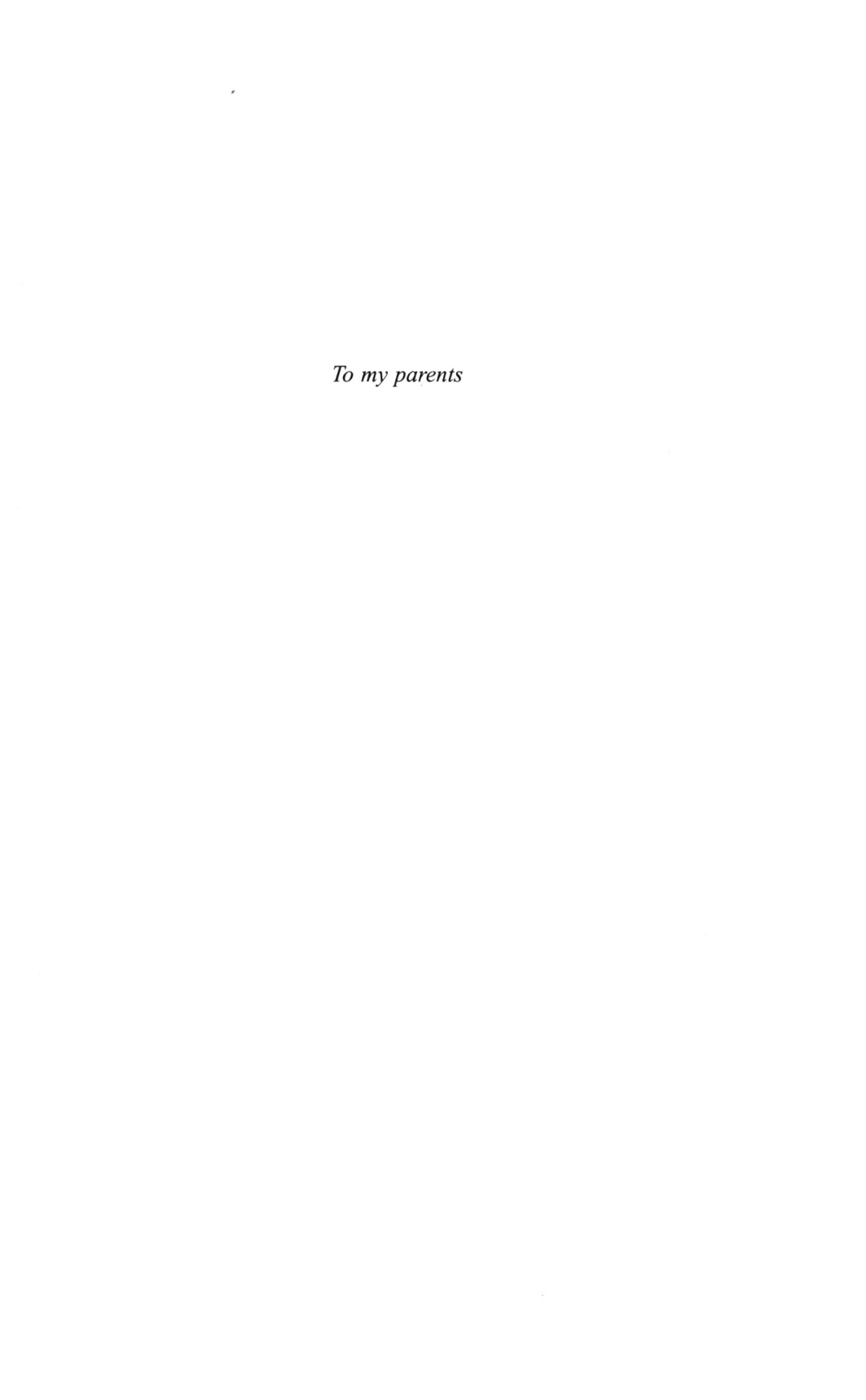

Contents

Abbreviations	ix
Introduction	1
Chapter 1. Transmitting the Classics I: Philology, Exegesis, and the *Anacreon* of 1554	5
Chapter 2. Transmitting the Classics II: Translation	49
Chapter 3. The Virtues of the Commentary: Translation and Textual Criticism in Estienne	91
Chapter 4. Words and Voices in Elie André	125
Chapter 5. Neo-Latin into French: Ronsard from the *Livret de Folastries* to the *Continuations des Amours*	155
Chapter 6. Inspiration, Metamorphosis: Belleau's *Odes d'Anacreon Teien*	201
Translating "Anacreon": Reflections in Conclusion	241
Appendix: Concordance of Estienne's *Editio Princeps* with Selected Modern Editions of the Anacreontea	247
Bibliography	251
Index	271

Abbreviations

Editions

1554	*Anacreontis Teij odae. Ab Henrico Stephano luce and à Latinitate nunc primùm donatae.* Edited by Henri Estienne. Paris: Henri Estienne, 1554.
1556	*Anacreontis Teii antiquissimi poëtae lyrici Odae, ab Helio Andrea Latinae factae, ad clariss. virum Petrum Montaureum Consiliarium, & Bibliothecarium Regium. Nec si quid olim lusit Anacreon, Deleuit aetas.* Paris: Robert Estienne and Guillaume Morel, 1556.
Lm.	*Pierre de Ronsard: Oeuvres complètes.* 20 vols. Edited by Paul Laumonier; Raymond Lebègue and Isidore Silver. Paris: Hachette; Droz; Didier, 1914–75.
M.-L.	*Oeuvres poétiques de Remy Belleau.* Edited by Charles Marty-Laveaux. 2 vols. La Pléiade Françoise. Paris: Lemerre, 1878. Page references are to this edition, but the text is quoted from the new standard edition of the *Odes d'Anacreon Teien* by John O'Brien and Keith Cameron. Paris: Champion, forthcoming.

Other Works of Reference

LS	*A Latin Dictionary.* Edited by Charlton T. Lewis and Charles Short. Many editions. Oxford: Clarendon Press.

LSJ	*A Greek-English Lexicon.* Edited by H.G. Liddell and R. Scott. Revised by H. Stuart Jones and R. McKenzie, with a "Supplement 1968." Oxford: Clarendon Press, 1973.
OCD	*The Oxford Classical Dictionary.* Edited by N.G.L. Hammond and H.H. Scullard. 2d ed. Oxford: Clarendon Press, 1978.
OLD	*The Oxford Latin Dictionary.* Edited by P.G.W. Glare. Oxford: Clarendon Press, 1982.
Pauly-Wissowa	*Paulys Real-Enzyklopädie der klassischen Altertumswissenschaft.* Edited by G. Wissowa; W. Kroll et al. Stuttgart: Metzler; Druckenmüller, 1894–1972.
TGL	*Thesaurus Graecae Linguae, ab Henrico Stephano constructus.* Edited by C.B. Hase, G. Dindorf, and L. Dindorf. 8 vols. Paris: Firmin Didot, 1831–65.
TLL	*Thesaurus Linguae Latinae.* Leipzig: Teubner, 1900–.

Introduction

> Par la grâce naïve, par l'inspiration spirituelle et tendre, par l'émotion voluptueuse et philosophique à la fois qui animent ses pièces légères, le génie d'Anacréon se rapproche du génie français, tel surtout que nous le retrouvons dans nos vieux rimeurs.[1]

> This confusion of the copy with the original speaks ill for the literary judgment of the scholars of the 16th and 17th Centuries.[2]

Edmonds' comment was of its age. The pseudo-Anacreontic poetry known as the Anacreontea has only recently seen a renewal in the scholarly or critical interest that it enjoyed over the course of three centuries after its discovery. A new critical edition by Martin West, Campbell's new Loeb translation replacing Edmonds, and above all Patricia Rosenmeyer's study of the Anacreontea, *The Poetics of Imitation,* have done much to remedy the neglect into which this poetry had fallen.[3] All these editions and books concentrate on the Anacreontea as products of a classical or classicizing age. None deals with the reception

---

1. Charles A. Sainte-Beuve, "Anacréon, *Odes,* traduites en vers français avec le texte en regard, par M. Veissier-Descombes," in *Oeuvres,* vol. 1, *"Premiers Lundis," début des "Portraits littéraires,"* ed. Maxime Leroy, Bibliothèque de la Pléiade (Paris: Gallimard, 1956), 218.

2. J.M. Edmonds, trans. and ed., *Elegy and Iambus,* vol. 2, *Being the Remains of all the Greek Elegiac and Iambic Poets from Callinus to Crates excepting the Choliambic Writers, with the Anacreontea,* Loeb Classical Library (London: Heinemann; New York: Putnam, 1931), 2, preface to Anacreontea, 1.

3. Martin L. West, *Carmina Anacreontea,* 2d ed., (Leipzig: Teubner, 1993); David Campbell, trans. and ed., *Greek Lyric,* vol. 2, *Anacreon, Anacreontea, Choral Lyric from Olympus to Alcman,* Loeb Classical Library (Cambridge, Mass.: Harvard University Press; London: Heinemann 1988); Patricia A. Rosenmeyer, *The Poetics of Imitation: Anacreon and the Anacreontic Tradition* (Cambridge and New York: Cambridge University Press, 1992); and for a brief study of sympotic motifs in this poetry, see Martin L. West, "The *Anacreontea,"* in *Sympotica: A Symposium on the "Symposion,"* ed. Oswyn Murray (Oxford: Clarendon Press, 1990), 272–76.

of the Anacreontea at the moment of their publication in 1554. Yet Renaissance writers were no less enthusiastic about the Anacreontea. Indeed if the sixteenth century had to vote on the issue, it would unanimously vote with Sainte-Beuve. Only one scholar, the Italian Francesco Robortello, raised his voice in dissent at the general acclaim that "Anacreon"[4] received on publication in 1554; and the gist of Robortello's complaint—that Estienne had tried to pass off as authentic the compositions of "some witless Greek"—could be taken as woundingly true but reads like personal rancour against Estienne himself.[5] Matters should perhaps have been set straight by the publication of Fulvio Orsini's *Carmina novem illustrium feminarum,*[6] in which he sets aside the Anacreontea, correctly recognizing that Anacreon is authentically preserved only in the fragments occurring in Athenaeus, Apollodorus, Stobaeus, and other compilers of anthologies, compendia, or dictionaries. But by 1568, the publication date of his edition, Orsini's initiative was too late and his voice a lone one. "Anacreon" was well established and his diffusion ensured.

One prime factor in this diffusion is known to Sainte-Beuve: the Anacreontea, in France at least, reinforce a strain already present in indigenous poetry. But—crucially—they do so by grafting this strain onto a familiar classical stem locatable in the Greek Anthology and Catullus (as evidenced above all in the Italian neo-Catullan tradition). Equally well, by 1554, the date of the publication of the Anacreontea, Greek studies had gained sufficient momentum—notably though not exclusively from the initiative of Jean Dorat—to ensure understanding and acceptance of what Anacreontic poetry had to offer. Having access in Paris to a printing press, as well as contacts in the spheres of humanism and vernacular poetry, Estienne was thus able to introduce his work directly into the classicizing currents of the Pléiade, some of whose members had been instructed by Dorat. Had "Anacreon" been published ten years earlier, his reception would have been no less generous, but his assimilation and diffusion, in vernacular culture at any rate, less rapid than was possible under Ronsard's patronage: the subsequent vernacular *essor* in the "ode légère" is directly attributable to Ronsard's Anacreontic experiments in the decisive years 1554–56. At the same time, a Neo-Latin audience is not

---

4. Throughout I use "*Anacreon*" for the pseudo-Anacreontic poetry ascribed to his name; Anacreon for the authentic lyric poet. (A concordance of Estienne's *editio princeps* with selected modern editions is in the appendix.)

5. See Francesco Robortello, *Francesci Robortelli Utinensis, De arte sive ratione corrigendi antiquorum libros disputatio* (1557), in Gaspar Schoppe, *De arte criticâ.* . . . (Amsterdam: Pluymer, 1662), 103.

6. Fulvio Orsini, *Carmina novem illustrium feminarum . . . et lyricorum.* . . . (Antwerp: Plantin, 1568).

neglected: Estienne's commentary and partial translation that accompany the Greek text of the *editio princeps* are followed shortly afterward by André's full translation of the poems work through a medium, Latin, that seeks to ensure familiarity to those not totally versed in Greek. Since Latin was moreover the *lingua franca* of the European scholarly community, "Anacreon" can be read by more than just the home market.

The existence of Neo-Latin translations by Estienne and André is a salutary reminder that translation is in the first instance a response to the need for immediate understanding in a wider public. The appeal of the Anacreontea was not to be confined to a small number of elite poetic practitioners. Yet to say that audiences are not totally conversant with Greek is to present a historical and not an aesthetic argument; it argues a lack of access to the learning of Greek rather than a lack of sophistication in the reading audience. Indeed, the demands that Anacreontic translators make on their readers implicitly demonstrate the opposite. Translation is not, then, restricted to a pedagogical exercise; and the choice of it as a focus for critical study is not the choice of a secondary phenomenon impatiently awaiting the imitations whose strongest single representative is probably Ronsard. In Ronsard above all, translation will make sufficient appearance to illustrate amply something of the ambiguous nature constantly governing its relation with imitation.

Far from being passively informative, translation has options of its own to propose, as the theoreticians of the genre underline by the diversity and richness of their approaches. The arguments over literal and nonliteral translation are the source of a series of wide-ranging reflections.[7] Imagery is equally varied: imagery of paths and tracks symbolizes the translator's following of his chosen author; imagery of reflection bears on the idea of representation itself; imagery of internalization describes the intellectual capacity of the translator himself, his ability to match successfully source and target language. One image that receives no overt theoretical attention, but is nonetheless central to the study of translation, is more truly a metaphor: the notion of trans-lation itself actively involves a spatial or spatiotemporal metaphor, a carrying across of the Greek author from one country to another, from one literary context to another, a *translatio studii* or a *translatio poesis*[8] operated on a writer whose new context is sensibly different from his context of origin. George Steiner

---

7. An excellent detailed examination of such theoretical positions is available in Glyn P. Norton's *The Ideology and Language of Translation in Renaissance France and Their Humanist Antecedents,* Travaux d'Humanisme et Renaissance, no. 201 (Geneva: Droz, 1984).

8. The term *translatio poesis* is that of Albert Py, *Imitation et Renaissance dans la poésie de Ronsard,* Histoire des idées et critique littéraire, no. 228 (Geneva: Droz, 1984), 9.

puts this idea at its simplest and most succinct: "If culture depends on the transmission of meaning across time—German *übertragen* carries the exact connotations of translation and of handing down through narrative—it depends also on the transfer of meaning in space."[9] Anacreontic translation will have to devise strategies for the re-creation, if not the creation, of meaning. It must engage in the attempt to convert and convey transferred senses, an attempt that itself resurrects the long-standing problem of aligning *res* or *sententia* with *verba*.

In the light of the controlling metaphor of transfer, this study will be concerned with the manner in which the Anacreontea are accommodated to a French setting; the objective is closer to *Rezeptions-* than to *Textgeschichte*. The idea of conveyance and the mobility it implies is certainly appropriate to the tentative nature of translation, particularly in its theoretical aspects, which are frequently difficult to resolve into a fixed set of conventions, a matrix of determined constants. The mobility is also appropriate to the nature of the cultures, Neo-Latin and vernacular French, that translate "Anacreon." Differences in literary heritage or audience expectation within these two cultures cannot obscure the collaborations, friendships, and influences passing between them. More than that, a common range of translative techniques emerges, whether devised independently or adapted by one culture from the other, as a way of preserving the elasticity of the translation, its unfinished, always-in-motion nature, while allowing the contemporary translator to gain a purchase on the material of sufficient strength to give a passable account of it to the reader. A study of translations of "Anacreon," then, though in the first place dictated by historical circumstances (translations of "Anacreon" precede imitations), affords a particularly fruitful vantage point from which to view the interplay between two literary cultures handling the same texts and producing solutions that are as individual as they are similar, and whose strength is arguably their partiality. How, in the two years following their publication, translators deal, separately and collectively, with the Anacreontea, the shape they give their translation, is the subject of this inquiry.

---

9. George Steiner, *After Babel: Aspects of Language and Translation* (London: Oxford University Press, 1975), 31.

CHAPTER 1

Transmitting the Classics I: Philology, Exegesis, and the *Anacreon* of 1554

The 1554 *Anacreon* is the *editio princeps* of its author and the first publishing adventure of its editor, Henri Estienne.[1] The poems did not appear alone but were supported by a partial translation into Latin and a selective commentary. In format, Estienne's edition is typical of the French humanist editorial enterprise of the 1550s and before. In content, however, it is far from being an unobtrusive addition to the humanist philological canon. And in order to gauge the nature of Estienne's undertaking, it will be important to give a brief overview of the French tradition of philology and exegesis practiced during the 1550s.

1

One of the boldest and most substantial of hypotheses in recent years concerning Renaissance philology is that of Anthony Grafton.[2] Grafton argues persuasively that Italian and French philology reveal individually the guiding influence of Politian in their respective allegiance to *recensio* and exegesis (combined with *emendatio*). Italian *recensio*, Grafton says, is symbolized by the person of Pier Vettori, the Florentine humanist whose contacts with such contemporaries as Faerno, Agustín, and Orsini reveal a communal interest in

---

1. Opinions differ as to whether Henri Estienne published the book himself: Olivier Reverdin opts for Henri's uncle, Charles, while Elizabeth Armstrong suggests Henri himself, using the *grecs du roi* of Guillaume Morel (see "Les rapports d' Henri Estienne avec les membres de sa famille restés ou redevenus catholiques," in *Henri Estienne,* Cahiers V.-L. Saulnier, no. 5 [Paris: Presses de l'E.N.S. de Jeunes Filles, 1988], 45; and that same text, 23).

2. Grafton, *Joseph Scaliger: A Study in the History of Classical Scholarship,* vol. 1, *Textual Criticism and Exegesis,* Oxford Warburg Studies (Oxford: Clarendon Press, 1983). The complementary volume has now appeared: *Joseph Scaliger: A Study in the History of Classical Scholarship,* vol. 2, *Historical Chronology,* Oxford Warburg Studies (Oxford: Clarendon Press, 1993).

the assessment and disciplined recording of manuscript witnesses to the classical text.[3] If Politian's legacy to Italy is a devotion to *recensio,* his presence in France, according to Grafton, strengthens the exegetical tradition, and, at least in part, owes its impact to Jacques Toussain who had contributed to the 1518–19 edition of Politian's works.[4] Grafton picks out the principle of *divinatio* (conjecture) in the resolution of *cruces* (corrupt passages) as the peculiarly French contribution to the history of classical scholarship.[5] The major exponent of this principle is Toussain's pupil, Dorat, the importance of whose philological work is also highlighted by Pfeiffer.[6]

What stands out from Grafton's account is French classical scholarship's growing awareness of a sense of autonomy, of the possibility of an independent contribution to philology. One area in which this independence was plainly operative was in the use of Greek sources to elucidate Latin authors. Although this penchant is not peculiar to the French tradition, the object the *Quellenforschung* (study of sources) serves takes on distinctive shape in at least some sections of French tradition in the 1550s. As representative of the trend recognizing Latin writers as literary heirs to the Greeks, we may take Muret. In his *Variae Lectiones* (published from 1559 onward, but composed earlier), he persistently returns to a detailed exposition of the borrowings of one Roman poet, Horace. So, for example, on the use of "equitavit" in *Carmina* 4.4.44:

> Audaci sane metaphora usu videtur Horatius, cum Euro vento equitandi verbum tribuit. notus est enim ille versiculus:
> *Per Siculas equitavit undas*
> neque unquam id, ut opinor, sine veterum exemplo ausus esset. sed meminerat, Euripidem quoque eodem modo locutum esse de Zephyro. itaque fecit more suo, ut, persequendis Graecorum vestigiis, τὸ τῆς λέξεως καινόν τε καὶ ξενικὸν quaereret, seque quam longissime a trita & plebeja loquendi consuetudine abduceret. quo in genere plane singularis fuit: neque, me quidem judicio, Graecas loquendi formas Latinorum poëtarum quisquam vel frequentius, vel fidentius, vel felicius imitatus est. Locus autem ille Euripidis, quem dico, ita scriptus est in Phoenissis [211]:

---

3. Grafton, *Joseph Scaliger,* vol. 1, chapter 2, "Poliziano's Followers in Italy, 1500–1560," 45–70.

4. Grafton, *Joseph Scaliger,* vol. 1, chapter 3, "Poliziano's Legacy in France, 1500–1570," 71–100; 73 for Toussain and Politian.

5. Grafton, *Joseph Scaliger,* 1:83.

6. Notably in Rudolf Pfeiffer, "Dichter und Philologen im französischen Humanismus," *Antike und Abendland* 7 (1958): 73–83.

Ζεφύρου πνοιαῖς ἱππεύσαντος ἐν οὐρανῷ.[7]

[Horace seems to be using a bold metaphor indeed, when he attributed the word *riding* to the wind Eurus. The verse is well known: "he rode over the Sicilian waves." He would never have dared do this, in my opinion, without ancient precedent. But he remembered that Euripides also spoke of Zephyrus in the same way. And so he carried out his normal practice of seeking "strange, new diction" by following the paths of the Greeks and distancing himself as far as possible from hackneyed common idiom. In this respect he was certainly unique: in my view, nobody else among the Latin poets imitated Greek forms of speech more frequently, more faithfully, or more successfully. Here is the line in Euripides's *Phoenissae* I am referring to: "Zephyrus riding in heaven on the breezes."]

Muret asserts elsewhere that his demonstration of Horace's dependence on the Greeks is a central feature of his undertaking in the *Variae Lectiones:*

Cum multa & in his libris & in aliis loquendi genera notaverim, quae Horatius a Graecis poëtis mutuatus est, videor mihi convenienter instituto meo consuetudinique facturus, si plura etiam notare perrexero.[8]

[Since both in these books and in others I have noted many turns of phrase that Horace borrowed from Greek poetry, it seems to me that I would be consistent with my purpose and practice if I continue to note even more instances.]

He foresees a twofold result of this inquiry: first, that his spirit of inquiry may prove of interest to others engaged in the line of same study; and secondly,

... utile puto esse iis, qui pangendis versibus laudem aliquam sibi parare in animo habent, pernoscere, quomodo veteres Latini poëtae Graecos loquendi modos in Latium invexerint: ut ipsi quoque, illorum exemplo, in eodem illo peregrinitatis aucupio elaborent.[9]

---

7. *M. Antonii Mureti Opera omnia, ex MSS. aucta et emendata, cum brevi annotatione Davidis Ruhnkenij,* 4 vols. (Leiden: Luchtmans, 1789), 2.1.10:18–19. For further references to Horace, see also 2:115–16, 170–72, 272, 301–2, 412.
8. Muret, *Opera omnia,* 2:115.
9. Muret, *Opera omnia,* 2:115. For citation of this passage in a related context, see Carlotta Dionisotti, "Hellenismus," in *The Vocabulary of Teaching and Research, 1350–1550,* ed. O. Weijers (forthcoming).

[. . . I think it is useful to those who intend to gain fame for themselves by composing poetry to know how the old Latin poets imported Greek expressions into Latium: so that they themselves, following their example, may take pains to seek out this foreign quarry.]

To the plain statement that Horace imitates his predecessors, Muret adds a more specific point: this classical precedent can aid modern writers to do likewise. Elsewhere he shows that he has in mind a particular group of poets when he speaks of modern imitators following in Horace's footsteps. In the preface to his *Iuvenilia* of 1553, Muret comments with admiration on the recent upsurge of poetry and poets in France:

Qui se vernaculo nostro sermone poëtas perhiberi volebant, perdiu ea scripsere, quae delectare modò ociosas mulierculas, non etiam eruditorum hominum studia tenere possent. Primus, vt arbitror, PETRVS RONSARDVS cùm se eruditissimo viro IOANNI AVRATO in disciplinam dedisset, eóque duce, veterum vtriusque linguae poëtarum scripta, multa & diligenti lectione triuisset, transmarinis illis opibus sua scripta exornare aggressus est: cuius postea exemplum insecuti I. ANTONIVS BAIFIVS, I. BELLAIVS, aliíque permulti, breui tempore tantos fecere progressus, vt res vel ad summum peruenisse iam, vel certè haud ita multo pòst peruentura esse videatur.[10]

[Those who wanted to be called poets in our vernacular tongue have long written works that can only delight women with nothing to do and cannot hold the attention of scholars. In my view, Pierre de Ronsard was the first to begin adorning his writings with these foreign spoils, when he had been educated by the very learned Jean Dorat and under his guidance had familiarized himself with the works of the ancient Greek and Latin poets by long and careful reading. His example was then followed by Jean-Antoine de Baif, Joachim du Bellay, and very many others. They made so much progress in such a short time that success seems to have been assured, or if not it very soon will be.]

A striking feature of this passage is that Ronsard has transferred the "transmarinum" to a new context. It is noticeable that Muret uses precisely the same

---

10. *M.A. Mureti Iuuenilia* (Paris: Veuve Maurice de la Porte, 1553), 8–9.

term of Horace's linguistic borrowings in the *Variae Lectiones*[11] and greatly approves of this "following in the tracks of the Greeks." It is, moreover, a fact that Ronsard conceived of his poetic production in the 1550 *Odes* as vindicated precisely by the precedent of Horace.[12] To be sure, we have not far to search for the reason for the shared standpoint of Muret and Ronsard; the former was not only in contact with the Coqueret group before his escape to Italy in 1554, but his lectures at the Collège Lemoine had tangible results, in the poetry of Ronsard at least.[13] As one who helped guide certain members of the Pléiade along classical lines, Muret's endorsement of vernacular poetry reveals the point at which the work of the lecturer coincides with that of the scholar.

Viewed in a general way, Muret emphasizes, then, the benefits that can accrue from the comparative study of literature. Indeed, it was in collections of *variae lectiones, adversaria,* or *castigationes* such as those of Muret, rather than in critical editions, that advances were being made in this study in the France of the 1550s. One particular practitioner of this genre was Jean Brodeau, otherwise known for his important edition of the Greek Anthology published in 1549. Six years later, he issued his first six books of *Miscellanea,* a collection that swelled to ten books in Gruter's *Lampas* of 1604. The title of Brodeau's work is significant: it recalls that of Politian's great philological enterprise, and not by accident. Indeed, Baptista Sapinus prefaces the work with an explicit statement that Brodeau is following in the tradition of Politian and the Italians,[14] then he adds the rider that Brodeau cannot be compared with

---

11. Muret, *Opera omnia,* 2:115: "quiddam transmarinum, neque in Romanorum consuetudine positum" (Venice 1559 et seq.); and 272: "transmarini saporis aliquid . . . in his Horatii versibus" (Antwerp 1580 et seq.). The twenty years separating these two statements are a measure of the consistency of Muret's views.

12. Lm. I, 44: "j'allai voir les étrangers, & me rendi familier d'Horace, contrefaisant sa naive douceur. . . ."; and 45: ". . . m'acheminant par un sentier inconnu, & monstrant le moien de suivre Pindare, & Horace. . . ." On Horace's position in France, see Raymond Lebègue, "Horace en France pendant la Renaissance," *Humanisme et Renaissance* 3 (1936): 141–64, 289–308, 384–419.

13. For Muret and his teaching, see Isidore Silver, *The Intellectual Evolution of Ronsard,* vol. 1, *The Formative Influences* (St. Louis: Washington University Press, 1969), chapter 3, "Ronsard and the Humanists: Marc-Antoine de Muret (1526–85)," 64–92, especially section 1: "Muret and the Brigade," 64–68, and section 5: "Muret's Teaching in Paris," 80–88; Mary Morrison, "Ronsard and Catullus: The Influence of the Teaching of Marc-Antoine de Muret," *Bibliothèque d'Humanisme et Renaissance* 18 (1956): 240–74; and Julia Haig Gaisser, *Catullus and His Renaissance Readers* (Oxford: Clarendon Press, 1993), 147–51 (151–68 for Muret's commentary on Catullus).

14. *Ioannis Brodaei Turonensis Miscellaneorum libri sex.* . . . (Basel: Oporinus, [1555]), 5. Sapinus specifically names Alexander Neapolitanus and Caelius Rhodiginus, as well as Politian. Brodeau is also mentioned in Grafton, *Joseph Scaliger,* 1:80, 262 n. 50.

them in stature.[15] Since Sapinus has already expounded upon the difficulties involved in finding a patron and a publisher for this volume (pp. 3–4), this disclaimer has something of the anxiously formal about it: it serves to explain away, rather than to explain. If Brodeau criticizes, Sapinus asserts, it is not out of any venomous intention but out of a clear perception of their faults—something which, he continues, in no way detracts from their standing:

> Neque uerò haec à me dicta existimet candidus lector, quasi persuadere uelim, Brodaeum Politiano, caeterisque quorum doctrina communi gentium & temporum consensu probata est, anteponendum.[16]

[The sincere reader should not think that I have said this as though I wish to convince him that Brodeau should be preferred to Politian and others whose learning has been proven to the general satisfaction.]

Despite these prefatory remarks, the challenge offered by Brodeau to his predecessors is apparent enough. It seems to demonstrate that Politian was regarded as something of a modern father figure, a major precursor in the field of critical annotations, in which Brodeau was now seeking to make his mark. Brodeau's attacks are directed at the *Variae Lectiones* of Pier Vettori, who advocated and practiced his master Politian's method of manuscript recension. In particular, the Frenchman criticizes the Italian's remarks on Cicero, an author on whom Vettori had devoted much time and energy, publishing his *Epistulae, Philosophica,* and *Rhetorica* in 1536–37. In chapter 5 of his first book, Brodeau ironically shows that if Cicero is condemned, on the same view Diodorus Siculus, a scholiast to Homer, Seneca, Lactantius, and Servius, must likewise be condemned (p. 11), and he ends with an exasperated outburst against the Italians:

> Est autem omnino ridiculum, quòd eiusdem libri [*Var. lect.* lib. 2] cap.12. trancheae, Gallicae penitus uocis, atque ipsi quidem, ut apparet, incognitae, ut quae uallum non significet, etymum Graecum reddat Victorius. Hanc autem cum exprimere nequeant Itali, trinceam balbutientes nominant.[17]

[It is utterly ridiculous that in chapter 12 of the same book Vettori translates a Greek word by *tranchea,* a thoroughly French word (but

---

15. Brodeau, *Miscellanea,* 5–6.
16. Brodeau, *Miscellanea,* 6.
17. Brodeau, *Miscellanea,* 12.

apparently unknown to him), seeing that it does not mean "rampart." Since the Italians cannot express this term, they babblingly call it "trincea."]

Elsewhere, Brodeau takes Vettori to task on the basis of wide-ranging source material. Vettori had quoted both Greek and Latin in support of his claims in the *Variae Lectiones,* but Brodeau seeks to surpass him on this point.[18]

By criticizing the method of Politian in its modern embodiment of Vettori and by in particular his criticism of Vettori's use of parallel sources, Brodeau essentially demonstrates the direction of French scholarship during the mid-1550s. A similar critical rationale is discernible in the work of Adrien Turnèbe. His *Adversaria* first appeared in two volumes in the years 1564–65 (though composed some time before their date of publication). By the year 1580, they had been expanded into three folio volumes comprising thirty books. The contents of these volumes—which run to nearly one thousand printed pages—are an abundant wealth of exposition and explanation of difficult or obscure points in classical poetry and prose. Most frequently, the discussion centers on a word or phrase drawn from one or a number of authors; parallels are cited to illuminate the context, and the argument moves rapidly from one context to another. One way of understanding Turnèbe's collection would be to look again at Vettori's *Variae Lectiones.* These similarly deal with the Greek sources of Latin texts, though in a less sustained way than Turnèbe. Vettori focuses on Latin texts with a view to elucidation in such a way that the text is secured by a select range of parallel sources. Not infrequently, this leads to a reasoned rejection of the vulgate in favor of a reading contained in a better—that is, historically assessed—manuscript. This was a lesson learned from Politian, but it relates to the text alone—exegesis is not considered to be part of the critic's business, in *variae lectiones* at least. Turnèbe's writing has some obvious links with that of Vettori. His *Adversaria* are constructed along the same lines; they follow the same tradition. Indeed, when Joseph Scaliger called this collection an "abortivus foetus," it was not "for its content, in which he found much to admire, but because it continued the Italian fashion of *Adversaria* promoted by Politian and Vettori."[19] Certainly, Turnèbe never explains the possible validity of making Greek and Latin parallels—he never relates his technique to a broader view of things in the same way that Muret

---

18. Cf. Brodeau, *Miscellanea,* 46–47, taking Vettori to task over Cicero's reference to the plant "aristolochia."

19. Leighton D. Reynolds and Nigel G. Wilson, *Scribes and Scholars: A Guide to the Transmission of Greek and Latin Literature,* 3d ed. (Oxford: Clarendon Press, 1991), 173–74.

does. And after the youthful challenge of Brodeau, he must come as something of a disappointment: his philological style relies more on the established, less on the innovative. That, moreover, Reynolds and Wilson can cite his work as an instance of the Italian style persisting in French *castigationes* form is a measure of the extent to which an anti-Italian style was already developing in the 1550s.

But in certain ways, Turnèbe goes beyond what Vettori did or would have wished to do. The Frenchman's work is characterized by a willingness to practice emendation by deriving readings from an old manuscript (*emendatio ope codicum* [emendation using manuscripts])[20]—in one case at least, that of Plautus, his collation is of prime importance[21]—and perhaps above all, by an insistent use of Greek material to substantiate his claims. Turnèbe's interest in the comparative study of Greek and Latin literature is more than the personal interest of a professor of Greek and director of the Royal Press: for the milieu in which he works, Turnèbe represents no more than the norm. This becomes all the clearer if the previously mentioned features are set beside the activities of Muret and Brodeau, whereas Vettori by contrast chose to emphasize the investigation of the manuscript tradition nearly at the expense of all else. A further significance of Turnèbe's philology may be suggested: his technique here recalls that of the teacher, fleshing out into printed form the substance of his remarks in the lecture hall.[22] There is, as yet, no historical evidence to indicate when Turnèbe composed his *Adversaria,* but their bulk is such that a number of years would have been necessary. Whatever the length of time involved, he would also have been teaching and it is difficult to believe that there is no correlation between Turnèbe's teaching and his writing. Even if this only partly accounts for the *Adversaria,* it does explain the emphasis placed on

---

20. Cf. Sebastiano Timpanaro, *La genesi del metodo del Lachmann,* 2d ed. (Padua: Liviana, 1985), 9–10: "I grandi filologi francesi del Cinquecento sentirono tutti, dal Turnebus al Lambin, al Daniel, al Pithou, l'esigenza di ricercare codici antichi e di utilizzarli per le loro edizioni." This statement also applies in a general way to volumes of *variae lectiones.* To say which is not to suggest that in either case French humanists used manuscripts in a strictly conceived historical manner: all too frequently, no chronological criteria are given by which the age of manuscripts might be verified; though they may indeed have had some broad notion of the age of their exemplars (see on this point Patricia E. Easterling, "Before Palaeography: Notes on Early Descriptions and Datings of Greek Manuscripts," *Studia Codicologica* 124 [1977]: 179–87, for examples of distinctions between minuscule and uncial hands).

21. See W.M. Lindsay, *The Codex Turnebi of Plautus* (1898; reprint, Hildesheim: Olms, 1972), 9–13, for examples of Turnèbe's citation of this manuscript.

22. Turnèbe's relationship with Ronsard and the Pléiade is examined in Pierre de Nolhac, *Ronsard et l'humanisme,* Bibliothèque de l'Ecole des Hautes Etudes, no. 227 (1921; reprint, Paris: Champion, 1966), 152–54. A new book on Turnèbe's work as a humanist is shortly to be published by John Lewis.

the study of comparative literature. Where Turnèbe is both profuse and diffuse, Muret is selective in his treatment of critical sources. The same tendency toward interpretation is broadly present in Turnèbe, but it is restricted to the form of critical *castigationes*. That for him is its rightful place; he only selectively introduces it into his editions (for example, in his Cicero), as Muret was to do uniformly in his work of the mid-1550s onward and as Estienne was to do in his *Anacreon*.

2

In the years preceding the publication of the 1554 *Anacreon,* Henri Estienne had spent three years journeying through Europe, "visiting scholars and inspecting manuscripts."[23] The clearest account he gave of the discovery of "Anacreon" is in the prefatory letter to Giovanni della Casa, dedicatee of a selection of Greek bucolic poetry Estienne published with Paolo Manuzio in 1555 and reprinted a year later in Paris:

> Quod autem ad Anacreontis odas attinet, quas me Latinas reliquis meis additurum pollicitus tibi fueram, sic habeto. Quum earum exemplaria duo in manus meas peruenissent: quorum vnum, Ioannis Clementis Britanni (cui viro Grẹcae literae quantum debeant, dici vix potest) beneficio consecutus essem: alterum deinde post longam peregrinationem ex Italia Lutetiam reuersus, mecum attulissem: feci vt haec duo exemplaria, quorum neutrum per se satis poterat, operas, vt ita dicam, mutuas traderent. non multo verò pòst adhibita quanta maxima adhiberi à me potuit diligentia, illas in hominum venustiorum gratiam edere non recusaui. Vt autem etiam Graecae linguae ignaris commodarem, easdem Latinas factas cum Graecis copulaui: non omnes quidem . . . sed eas tantummodo, quae vt integerrimae, ita etiam elegantissimae videbantur, & è quarum plurimis apud aliquem antiquum auctorem deprompta testimonia reperiebantur.[24]

---

23. James Hutton, *The Greek Anthology in France and in the Latin Writers of the Netherlands to the Year 1800,* Cornell Studies in Classical Philology, no. 28 (Ithaca: Cornell University Press, 1946), 128. For the length of the journey, begun around 1547, see Léon Feugère, *Essai sur la vie et les ouvrages d' Henri Estienne suivi d'une étude sur Scévole de Sainte-Marthe* (Paris: Delalain, 1833), 48, 49, and n. 1; and Silver, *The Formative Influences,* 107–8.

24. *Moschi, Bionis, Theocriti, elegantissimorum poetarum idyllia aliquot, ab Henrico Stephano Latina facta.* . . . (Paris: Robert Estienne, 1556), sig. Aij[r].

[Regarding the odes of Anacreon that I had promised you I would add to my other works in Latin translation, this is how matters stand. Two manuscripts came into my hands. I had obtained the first through the favor of the Englishman John Clement (it is scarcely possible to say how much Greek literature owes to him). The second I had brought with me on my way back to Paris from Italy after a long journey. I made these two manuscripts, neither of which was adequate on its own, help each other out. Soon afterward, having shown the utmost possible care, I was not reluctant to publish the odes to please the cultured. Moreover, in order to oblige even those who were ignorant of Greek, I linked those odes translated into Latin with the Greek—not all of them, just those that seemed both most complete and most elegant, and for most of which evidence could be found and produced in some ancient author.]

Two manuscripts are in question. The first was lent by John Clement, who spent the years 1550–53 in self-imposed religious exile in Louvain.[25] Estienne passed through Louvain in 1551 on his way back from England.[26] The Anacreontea are contained in an appendix to the tenth-century manuscript of the Greek Anthology, a *codex unicus* subsequently held in Heidelberg, then divided and bound in two unequal parts. The Anacreontea, bound in the smaller part, now resides in Paris (= Par. Graec. Supp. 384), with the Greek Anthology in Heidelberg (= Cod. Pal. 23).[27] In his 1566 edition of the Anthology, Estienne reiterates his indebtedness to Clement's manuscript,[28] while his apograph of the Anacreontea, coinciding with the poems as contained in the Palatine manuscript, is preserved in Leiden and extensive report of it is given

---

25. West, *Carmina Anacreontea*, vii–viii.

26. See Valentin Rose, ed., *Anacreontis Teii quae vocantur συμποσιακὰ ἡμιάμβια*. . . . , 2d ed. (Leipzig: Teubner, 1876), preface [iii]; Carl Preisendanz, ed., *Carmina Anacreontea e Bybl. Nat. Par. Cod. Gr. Suppl. 384.* . . . (Leipzig: Teubner, 1912), preface vi. Estienne mentions his own return from England via Louvain in *Athenagorae Atheniensis Philosophi Christiani apologia pro Christianis.* . . . ([Geneva]: Henri Estienne, 1557), [190].

27. The wanderings of the Anacreontea and the Anthology are recounted by Rose, *Anacreontis Teii*, [iii]–iv; Preisendanz, *Carmina Anacreontea*, viii, x–xiii; more recently Rosenmeyer, *The Poetics of Imitation*, 3 n. 4; and Alan Cameron, *The Greek Anthology from Meleager to Planudes* (Oxford: Clarendon Press, 1993), 178–201. For John Clement's books, see A.W. Reed, "John Clements and His Books," *The Library*, 4th ser., no. 6 (1926): 329–39.

28. *Florilegium diuersorum epigrammatum ueterum, in septem libris diuisum, magno epigrammatum numero & duobus indicibus auctum* ([Geneva]: Henri Estienne, 1566), sig. ss. ii^v; cited by Rose, *Anacreontis Teii*, [iii]; Preisendanz, *Carmina Anacreontea*, [v]–vi; West, *Carmina Anacreontea*, vii.

by modern editors.²⁹ Rose affirmed, and Preisendanz denied, that Estienne had sight of the complete Palatine manuscript.³⁰ Preisendanz held that it was inherently unlikely that John Clement would have been fortunate enough to gain the whole Anthology, which he asserted had in any case already been divided into its present two unequal sections during the thirteenth or fourteenth century.³¹ Without mentioning the arguments of Rose and Preisendanz, the most recent Teubner editor, Martin West, comes down in favor of the hypothesis that Clement did possess the full Anthology, concluding baldly, "hinc igitur Stephanus Anacreontea cepit" (it was from this that Estienne took the Anacreontea).³²

What all the editors are agreed on is the total lack of evidence for a second manuscript of the Anacreontea. Certainly no evidence from an additional manuscript source is recorded in Estienne's extant papers: his Anacreontic apograph corresponds to the Palatine collection only. The strange factor in this affair is that Estienne is adamant about the existence of this manuscript. In the prefatory letter to the bucolic selection already quoted, he describes his exemplar as of Italian provenance and emphasizes that each exemplar must supplement the other, neither being sufficient alone to constitute a sound text. Estienne repeats this information, in rather greater detail, in his preface to his 1554 *Opuscula* of Dionysius of Halicarnassus. Dedicating the edition to Pier Vettori, he says that difficulties have arisen in the production of the *Anacreon*, which would already have been issued

> ... nisi me uana spes tenuisset, fore ut ad duo eius exemplaria, quae diuersis in locis non sine immenso labore inuenire mihi contigit, tertium accederet. Nam ex duobus his alterum in membranis, alterum in cortice arboris scriptum erat: illud, confusum, & alicubi non satis emendatum: hoc, adeò antiquum, ut in singulis uerbis litera aliqua oculos fugeret. ut taceam, adeò diuersam fuisse elementorum formam à nostris, ut prius an posset legi, cogitandum fuerit, quàm an posset intelligi.³³

---

29. Rose, *Anacreontis Teii*, iv–v; Preisendanz, *Carmina Anacreontea*, viii–x; West, *Carmina Anacreontea*, vii n. 4. The apograph is contained in Cod. Voss. Gr. Qu. 18.
30. Rose, *Anacreontis Teii*, [iii], vi; Preisendanz, *Carmina Anacreontea*, vii.
31. Preisendanz, *Carmina Anacreontea*, viii.
32. West, *Carmina Anacreontea*, viii.
33. *Dionysii Halicarnassei responsio ad Gn. Pompeij epistolam, in qua ille de reprehenso ab eo Platonis stylo conquerebatur. Eiusdem ad Ammaeum epistola.* (Paris: Charles Estienne, 1554), sig. *6ʳ⁻ᵛ.

[... had I not had the vain hope of a third manuscript being added to the two exemplars of *Anacreon,* which I happened to find in different places with considerable effort. Of these two, one was written on parchment, the other on papyrus?: the former muddled and insufficiently correct, the latter so old that in individual words some letter or other was hard to make out. In short, the shape of the letters was so different from ours that consideration would have to be given to whether it could be read at all, let alone understood.]

Estienne makes further references to the exemplar on papyrus in the course of his commentary. Of the very first ode, for example, he notes:

In altero exemplarium, nimirum in eo quod in libro, id est cortice, scriptum reperi, primum locum occupat haec oda.[34]

[In the second of the two manuscripts—I mean the one I found written on, that is, papyrus tree rind—this ode is placed first.]

And again a little later on the lemma Λέουσι χάσμ' ὀδόντων:

In cortice propemodum fugiebat oculos hoc verbum χάσμα sed in altero exemplari facilè legebatur.[35]

[In the papyrus this word *mouth* was almost illegible, but in the other copy it was easy to read.]

This last example bears out what Estienne likewise says in the preface to the Dionysius: the exemplar written on papyrus is "so old that some letter or other was hard to make out." Despite Estienne's reiterated assertions, editors have remained skeptical about the existence of this second exemplar. West summarizes the matter in a terse statement: "codicisque alterius nec vola nec vestigium est" (there is neither hide nor hair of the second manuscript),[36] while Pfeiffer speaks simply and unambiguously of a *codex unicus* discovered in Italy.[37] Estienne leaves the matter in greater vagueness still by inferring nothing about the relative dependence or independence of the witnesses involved in

---

34. 1554.65.
35. 1554.65.
36. West, *Carmina Anacreontea,* vii.
37. Rudolf Pfeiffer, *History of Classical Scholarship from 1300 to 1850* (Oxford: Clarendon Press, 1976), 107.

his *recensio:* his epithet "antiquum" for the exemplar "in cortice arboris scriptum" gives no firm indication of the age of the two manuscripts.[38]

Such imprecision on Estienne's part excited attention, not to say roused passions, in one quarter at least. This was from the Italian humanist, Francesco Robortello, who in 1557 published *De arte sive ratione corrigendi antiquorum libros disputatio,* in which Estienne is criticized, though not by name.[39] Robortello's terms of reference are familiar, the critic's aim being "pristino nitori veteres restituere scriptores" (to restore the ancient writers to their original condition),[40] and corrupt passages are to be emended "aut conjecturâ, aut ex veterum librorum, qui manuscripti sunt, aut impressi, scriptione" (by conjecture or by readings from old manuscripts or printed books).[41] It is encouraging to find the critic having recourse to manuscripts, but in context it does not represent their independent assessment. Indeed, the fact that they are placed on a par with printed editions demonstrates the force of the *lectio recepta*—so that Robortello's words signify little more than *emendatio ope codicum.* The interest of the book is, however, greater than these remarks might give us cause to believe. Robortello concentrates principally on Latin paleography and first distinguishes minuscule and uncial scripts that he labels "Lombardic." He even links Lombardic script to a point in time, calculating its prevalence from the year A.D. 700 until Charlemagne drove the Lombards out of Italy. Manuscripts written in this hand can easily be distinguished from others, he says, since they are written on parchment.[42]

The central body of this treatise is concerned with *emendatio ope ingenii* (emendation using one's intelligence). Robortello is careful to emphasize the care with which emendation must be exercised and he usefully summarizes three ways in which manuscripts may confirm our findings: "notione antiquitatis, notione scriptionis antiquae, notione locutionum, & verborum antiquorum" (by indication of age, by indication of ancient script, by indication of ancient expressions and words).[43] Once again, it is noteworthy that manuscripts are viewed as supplementing a technique innate to the critic. Robortello does not suggest, in this section or the previous one, that the critic should return

---

38. Note that Estienne hopes to find yet a third codex, according to the *Opuscula* preface. The hope was not realized and it is not mentioned elsewhere.
39. Francesco Robortello, *De arte.* A longer examination of Robortello's work is to be found in Edward J. Kenney, *The Classical Text: Aspects of Editing in the Age of the Printed Book,* Sather Classical Lectures, no. 44 (Berkeley: University of California Press, 1974), 29–35.
40. Robortello, *De arte,* 99.
41. Robortello, *De arte,* 100.
42. Robortello, *De arte,* 101.
43. Robortello, *De arte,* 106.

to manuscripts in order to establish a *prima facie* case based on direct evidence; had he done so, a progressively historical attitude toward the whole manuscript tradition would have been inevitable. This in turn leads Robortello to consider the question of *fides* (fidelity), a term that, in its context, indicates an attitude toward the verification of sources. Robortello has his own view of *fides*. He directs particular criticism against "quisquiliae" (rubbish) or "nugae" (nonsense), which appear to mean readings manifestly false or absurd.

The larger implications of Robortello's position on *fides* and the question of sources are readily seen in his attack on Estienne's *Anacreon*. At the beginning of his treatise, Robortello reprimands the editor's claim to have had exemplars "in cortice . . . descripti": "Quare perridiculus est is, qui nuperrime, editis quibusdam insulsi hominis Graeci lusibus, Anacreontis odas esse scribit, hoc utens argumento, quòd in cortice essent descripti" (therefore that man is most ridiculous who, publishing the trifles of some witless Greek, very recently entitled them "The Odes of Anacreon," using the argument that they were written down on papyrus).[44] When he returns to the attack toward the end of the book, his overall weapon is *fides*. Robortello states as a principle that:

> In primis verò in emendatione librorum requiritur FIDES, ut ne fucum faciat ullum, ut ne lectori imponat. Si dixerit, se in manuscriptis libris invaenisse *[sic]*, quod ipse excogitarit, possit fortasse decipere imperitos: at peritis, necesse est, ut se deridendum praebeat.[45]
>
> [The paramount requirement for emending manuscripts is fidelity, so that he does not practice deceit and inflict it on the reader. If he says that he found in manuscripts what he thought up himself, he may perhaps deceive the unwary; but he will inevitably expose himself to ridicule by the experts.]

Robortello's point about *fides* is important and his choice of Politian and Vettori (among other names, not all of them Italians) as embodiments of this critical quality is a mark of the editorial discrepancies still prevalent between scholars. Robortello returns to the attack a little later, when he mocks the imagery of resurrection that Estienne applies to "Anacreon" in his preface:

---

44. Robortello, *De arte,* 103. For "cortex" and "cortex arboris" meaning "papyrus," see Kenney, *The Classical Text,* 31, and particularly Montaigne's *Journal de voyage,* of a manuscript in the Vatican Library: "J'y vis aussi un lopin de l'ancien papyrus, aù il y avait des caractères inconnus: c'est une écorce d' arbre." Of Chinese paper, Montaigne comments: "Ils tiennent que c'est la membrane de quelque arbre." (*Michel de Montaigne: Journal de voyage*) ed. Fausta Garavini, Collection Folio [Paris: Gallimard, 1983], 212.)

45. Robortello, *De arte,* 119.

Nunc exstiterunt, (si diis placet,) qui excitant ab inferis Anacreontas, Halicarnasseos. Brevi etiam revixisse audietis Sappho illam, & Menandrum: ne dubitate. Exstiterunt, inquam, qui manuscriptos libros citant, nec tamen proferunt, qui sint, ubi sint, cujus notae sint. Ecquis scit, an somnia illa sint, an quisquiliae, meraeque nugae? Quae tandem igitur his est habenda fides?[46]

[Now there have been people (can you believe it?) who summon up from the underworld Anacreons and Dionysiuses of Halicarnassus. Shortly you will even hear that the famous Sappho and Menander have come back to life: have no doubt about it. There have been people, I say, who appeal to manuscripts yet do not mention what they are, where they are, or to whom they are known. Does anyone know whether these are dreams, or rubbish and pure nonsense? What trust can be placed in these things?]

Robortello was not the last critic to question Estienne's editorial integrity.[47] In principle, his own integrity is praiseworthy. It is the expression of a standard to which scholars thought they should aspire; and, it seems, they thought consciously, for the pin-pointing of Politian and Vettori as examples of successful editorial policy is the advocacy of a critical tradition with which the potential editor could fruitfully align himself. In practice, however, it must be said, Robortello does not represent a complete embodiment of his own *fides*. As Kenney has pointed out,[48] he recorded inaccurately the sources of his *Aelian,* which appeared in 1552, five years before this present statement of principle. Whether or not he intended to mislead is not in question. But the fact that he could do so at a time when Vettori had been urging the exact recording of manuscripts is a salutary warning not to see progress in textual matters as a continuous line uninterrupted by problems. Broad distinctions often break down in the face of individual idiosyncrasies.

---

46. Robortello, *De arte,* 119–20.
47. Cf. the controversy that arose over R.Y. Tyrrell's use of the term "mendacissimus" to describe Estienne's work on Euripides. E.B. England, "H. Stephens's *vetustissima exemplaria,*" *Classical Review* 8 (1894): 196–97, defended Estienne, in which he was supported by Arthur Tilley, "Henri Estienne," *Classical Review* 8 (1894): 251. Tyrrell replied ("The *Bacchae* of Euripides," *Classical Review* 8 [1894]: 294–96), withdrawing the term "mendacissimus," but still holding "the belief that Stephens' *vetustissima exemplaria* had no existence" (ibid., 294). A further defense of Estienne as editor is found in K. Sintenis, "Zur Ehrenerklärung für H. Stephanus," *Philologus* 1 (1846): 134–42.
48. Kenney, *The Classical Text,* 33.

That Robortello's objections had so little impact on the fortunes of the Anacreontea is a testimony at once against Robortello's own character[49] and in favor of the popularity and rapid dissemination that the collection enjoyed in France. *A fortiori*, Fulvio Orsini's *Carmina novem illustrium feminarum . . . et lyricorum*, published in 1568, had even less impact.[50] This edition received nothing like the recognition it deserved in its own time, especially since Orsini's insight is that the authentic Anacreon is preserved only in fragmentary form. He anticipates later suspicions about the spuriousness of the Anacreontea by according them no place at all in his edition.[51] His own statement of principle reads:

> Ex Anacreontis autem carminibus, ea tantum edenda curauimus, quae nos in veterum scriptorum, quos ipsi legerimus, monumentis citata obseruauimus.[52]

> [From the poetry of Anacreon, we have had published only those pieces that we have seen quoted in the works of the ancient writers that we have ourselves read.]

What, therefore, Estienne includes in his appendix of Anacreontic fragments without risking the question of the relationship between these fragments and the poems he publishes, Orsini takes as his text. In layout, his edition resembles a proto-*PMG*. For Anacreon, as for the other lyric poets, he gives first verse tributes to the poet,[53] then the fragments in verse, followed by fragments and *testimonia* found in prose writers.[54] Later he records his sources: the lemma is followed by its provenance, designated by book and chapter, and the relevant part of the source is usually cited for purposes of contextualization.[55] Orsini recognizes that a mastery of sources is an essential complement to a mastery of the text itself, and a full view of the author can only be gained by bringing to

---

49. Cf. Michael Baumann, *Die Anakreonteen in englischen Übersetzungen: Ein Beitrag zur Rezeptionsgeschichte der anakreontischen Sammlung*, Studien zum Fortwirken der Antike, no. 7 (Heidelberg: Winter, 1974), 24 n. 48: "Robortellos notorische Streitsucht mag mitverantwortlich dafür sein, daß seine Bedenken nicht allzu ernst genommen wurden."

50. The best study of Orsini remains Pierre de Nolhac, *La bibliothèque de Fulvio Orsini: Contributions à l'histoire des collections d'Italie et à l'étude de la Renaissance*, Bibliothèque de l'Ecole des Hautes Etudes, no. 64 (Paris: Vieweg, 1887).

51. Two pieces only overlap, the Anacreontic odes 15 and 17 (= Orsini, *Carmina*, 130–31), which he admits since they are preserved in Gellius (so *Carmina*, 320).

52. Orsini, *Carmina*, [*6ᵛ].

53. Orsini, *Carmina*, 123–29.

54. Orsini, *Carmina*, 143–52.

55. Orsini, *Carmina*, 320–28.

the text as wide a range as possible of firsthand witnesses. Orsini's reading is impressively broad: the *testimonia* include in their ranks Athenaeus and Hephaestion (both prominently), Maximus of Tyre, Aelian, Plutarch, the scholia to Aristophanes and Apollonius of Rhodes, as well as Pausanias and Strabo, Stephanus and Ammonius.

In his preface to his patron Cardinal Alessandro Farnese, Orsini comments on his method:

> haec autem quę nos in praesentia damus, cuiusmodi sint, iudicabunt ij, qui ea cum scriptorum codicibus, è quibus deprompta sunt, contulerint. nec enim vno, aut altero, sed pluribus manuscriptis exemplaribus in huiusmodi fragmentorum collatione vsi sumus, nec è vulgatis tantum scriptoribus, sed de non editis etiam pleraque descripsimus.[56]

> [The nature of our present material will be judged by those who compare them with the manuscripts of the writers from whom we extracted it. In a collation of fragments of this kind, we used not one or two manuscripts but several, and we took the majority not just from published writers but from unpublished authors too.]

The emphasis on manuscript usage here is crucial. Even though Orsini does not indicate the quality of the manuscripts employed, the range of his research suggests that his text does not rest on whatever manuscript is simply to hand.[57] Such a view naturally colors Orsini's position on emendation. By his own admission, Estienne performed emendation on his Anacreontic text through a process of intelligence supported by recourse to manuscripts—not a uniquely French attitude, but one common enough there, especially with the emphasis on the first of these components. Orsini also believes in the correction of the vulgate, where this vulgate is corrupt, by recourse to the largest number of available witnesses. This is *emendatio ex codicum auctoritate* (emendation based on manuscript authority), but where the passage in question has been emended, the source of the emendation must be given each time: such is the nature of his *fides,* a *fides* that would be recognizable to Robortello. It represents the primacy of the witness, to which are subordinated the critical discriminations brought into play by *ingenium.*

---

56. Orsini, *Carmina,* *3r–v.
57. Cf. Kenney, *The Classical Text,* 4, on the confusion caused by the printing of texts from manuscripts that were humanist copies or simply available to hand.

The comparison of Estienne's editorial practice in 1554 with Orsini's fourteen years later is not, however, being undertaken in order to reproach Estienne. He is, in effect, dealing with a completely different set of texts from Orsini. Moreover, Estienne's own taste for textual source hunting becomes more pronounced over the years, so that his 1560 edition of the Greek lyric poets will move more steadily in that direction. This new edition will accord larger admission to the authentic Anacreontic fragments, but will not for all that renounce belief in the primacy of the Anacreontea. What a comparison between Estienne and Orsini does throw up, and throw up sharply, is the centrality of *emendatio ingenii auxilio* (emendation with the help of one's intelligence)—*divinatio* (conjecture), in fact—in the *editio princeps* of pseudo-Anacreon. Almost no page of Estienne is without conjectural emendations, sometimes carried out with the help of manuscripts *(codicum ope)*, but more often the product of intuition alone. *Divinatio* above all is not susceptible to the patient exposition of the kind Orsini is able to give his source material. By its very nature, *divinatio* involves a qualitative leap from *crux* to solution. In this light, Robortello's objections to Estienne and his method amount to the suspicion that Estienne is using an appeal to manuscript authority to cover readings derived from his own divinatory powers. *Fides,* in Robortello's view, requires strict respect for critical procedure. Orsini would fall squarely within Robortello's criteria; Estienne, in 1554, would not. Inasmuch as this quarrel reflects national differences in approach to textual criticism (and with so many personalities in the field, it is difficult to systematize completely), Estienne shows a preference for *divinatio* that Grafton had identified as a typical French characteristic.

3

However, to restrict consideration of the *Anacreon* to questions of manuscript recension alone would be to do Estienne less than justice. Of at least equal prominence is the space he devotes to exegesis in his commentary. In particular, the commentary demonstrates remarkable affinities with the views that Muret puts forward about literary transmission. For Muret, the transmission is from Greece to Rome, focused on the person and work of Horace; then in turn named French vernacular writers transfer the "transmarinum" to their own setting. The stages are clear and the notion of transmission itself constitutes the onward dynamic, the *translatio studii.* In Estienne, a prime instance of just the same phenomenon is his extensive commentary on Horace in ode 31.[58] The

---

58. 1554.76–79. The passage is also quoted in Grafton, *Joseph Scaliger,* 1:79.

central principle of organization here is literary theft—a mimetic technique shared by all writers, according to Estienne.

Estienne begins with the observation that Horace imitated ("imitatus est") the phrase θέλω θέλω μανῆναι (I want, I want to go mad) in *Carmina* 2.7.25–28 ("quem Venus arbitrum / dicet bibendi? non ego sanius / bacchabor Edonis: recepto / dulce mihi furere est amico" [Whom shall Venus make the master of our drinking? I'll rave as wildly as the Edonians. It is pleasant for me to go mad now that a friend has been regained]) and 3.19.18–19 ("insanire iuvat: cur Berecyntiae / cessant flamina tibiae?" [To behave madly is my pleasure. Why should the notes of the Berecynthian pipe cease?]). He then compares the Anacreontic ode 39 (1554.35–36) and the supposititious ode Ὁ δραπέτας μ' ὁ χρυσός (1554.52–53) with *Carmina* 1.26.1–3. From this prelude, Estienne moves on to comment as follows on his next set of examples:

haec verò maioris sunt momenti, in quibus apertius imitatur vel potius interpretatur nostrum poetam. (1554.76)

[of greater importance are those passages in which he openly imitates, or rather translates, our poet.]

The instances will exemplify Horatian *interpretatio* ("translation") of "Anacreon"; and translation is classified as open allusion, a palpable transfer of linguistic resources in contrast to more allusive (and elusive) forms to be discussed later. Moreover, in a broader sense, *interpretatio* might also serve as a correlative description ("interpretation") of this present passage in the commentary, a way of marking Estienne's deployment of critical resources in order to analyze "Anacreon." From this point of view Estienne's next critical move might be classified as a form of *contaminatio,* for, still devoting his attention to the legacy of "Anacreon," he now extends the scope of his investigations. Yet, increasingly, his quoted instances are taken from the fragments of the true Anacreon rather than from the Anacreontea; "Anacreon" has been displaced by Anacreon as Estienne's focus of interest. Indeed, the paucity of examples drawn directly from the Anacreontea is striking—only two, placed initially, compared with five from the authentic author. Thus Horace's lines on Lyde—

quae velut latis equa trima campis
ludit exsultim metuitque tangi,
nuptiarum expers et adhuc protervo
    cruda marito.

(*Carm.* 3.11.9–12)]

[who like a three-year-old filly frolics over the broad plains and fears to be touched, having no experience of marriage and still not ripe for an eager husband]

—are shown to have an Anacreontic analogue, but in the original Anacreon:

πῶλε Θρηικίη, τί δή με
λοξὸν ὄμμασι βλέπουσα,
νηλεῶς φεύγεις, δοκεῖς δέ
μ' οὐδὲν εἰδέναι σοφόν;[59]

[Thracian filly, why do you look at me askance and pitilessly flee, thinking that I have no skill?]

Alongside this well-known Anacreontic *locus* in Horace, Estienne adduces two additional *loci:* Chloe as the frightened deer (*Carm.* 1.23), imitated from Anacreon's νεβρὸν νεοθηλέα γαλαθηνὸν;[60] and *Carmina* 1.27—

Natis in usum laetitiae scyphis,
pugnare Thracum est. tollite barbarum
    morem, verecundumque Bacchum
sanguineis prohibere rixis.

[To fight with cups designed for pleasure is a Thracian habit. Set aside such barbarous customs and protect law-abiding Bacchus from bloody brawls.]

—Horace's version of

ἄγε δηῦτε μηκέτ' οὕτω
πατάγῳ τε κἀλαλητῷ
σκυθικὴν πόσιν παρ' οἴνῳ
μελετῶμεν, ἀλλὰ καλοῖς
ὑποπίνοντες ἐν ὕμνοις.[61]

[Come now, let us practice no more Scythian drinking with clattering and cries over our wine; let us drink slowly amid beautiful festive songs.]

---

59. 1554.76; Greek text: 1554.57–58; Page, *Poetae melici graeci* (Oxford: Clarendon Press, 1962), 417.
60. 1554.76–77; Page, *Poetae melici graeci*, 408.
61. 1554.77; Greek text: 1554.56; Page, *Poetae melici graeci*, 356(b).

The drift away from "Anacreon" then becomes more marked still:

Caeterùm vel ex his aestimare possumus quàm multa ex nostro poeta mutuatus sit Horatius: quae paterent omnibus, si quemadmodum huius, ita & illius opera extarent. quanquam satis notum est plura hunc ex Alcaeo, quam ex vllo alio transcripsisse: quod nec ipse dissimulat. (1554.77)

[We can gauge even from these passages how much Horace borrowed from our poet. This would be obvious to everybody if the works of Anacreon were extant in the same way that the works of Horace are. Nonetheless it is quite well known that Horace transcribed more from Alcaeus than from any other. He himself does not conceal this.]

Like Anacreon, Alcaeus is a lyric poet, from a genre that Horace shares; as with Anacreon, certain of Alcaeus's fragments are published by Estienne along with the Anacreontea. Thus the absence in Horace of palpable thefts from "Anacreon" is covered first by moving to the authentic Anacreon and then by introducing Alcaean influence[62] and finally bewailing the loss of the greater part of the Alcaean corpus: "nam si haec omnia ἀποσπασμάτια inter Horatij odas latere deprehendimus, quid si corpus integrum huius Graeci poetae extaret?" (for if we can discover all these fragments hiding among Horace's odes, what would happen if the whole corpus of this Greek poet were extant? 1554.77). This *ex silentio* argument might with greater pertinence have been applied to the question of Anacreontic authenticity. But by substituting Alcaeus and Horace for "Anacreon" and Horace, Estienne unconsciously disguises the embarrassing paucity of references to the text that he took to be Anacreon. What emerges with particular clarity is the way in which this passage constantly modifies its own terms of reference: the initial connection between the Anacreontea and Horace is transformed into one between Horace and Anacreon (Horace becomes the dominant term); and this in turn is replaced by Horace and Alcaeus and almost immediately by Alcaeus and Horace (Alcaeus is the dominant term), reaching its climax in the "quid si corpus integrum huius Graeci poetae

---

62. The parallels established by Estienne between Horace and Alcaeus are 338.1–2, 5–6 Lobel-Page and *Carm.* 1.9.1–8; 332 L.-P. νῦν-πώνην and *Carm.* 1.37.1–2; 342 L.-P. and *Carm.* 1.18.1–2; 347.1–2 L.-P. and *Carm.* 3.29.18–20; 346.1 L.-P. and *Carm.* 3.21.23–24. Two further Alcaean inspirations are mentioned without their Greek counterparts: *Carm.* 1.10 (= 308 L.-P.) and *Carm.* 1.14 (= 326 L.-P.). These Alcaean examples are all contained on 1554.77–78. They correspond to the following fragments in the 1554 *editio princeps:* 338 L.-P. = 1554.61; 332 (no entry); 342 (no entry); 347 = 1554.61; 346 = 1554.61.

extaret?" where Alcaeus is virtually the representative of Greek lyric poetry in general.

Since Estienne then proceeds to instance Pindaric allusion in Horace's work,[63] it seems clear that Horace himself has ceased to be a term of comparison and has become the principal subject of critical inquiry. In the culmination of the passage, Horace acts in fact as a metaphor for a form of mimesis for which Estienne reworks standard terminology:

> Denique Horatius multa ex ijs quos nominauimus poetis aliisque aperte transfert: quae autem aliunde ita mutuatur, vt sua tamen velit videri, ea ita in varias formas commutat, vt vix ab eo cuius sunt, si adsit, agnosci possint. & hoc est honestè furari. (1554.78)

> [In short Horace openly transfers many passages from those poets we have mentioned and others. Moreover this material from elsewhere that he thus borrows, in order to make it nevertheless seem his own, he transmutes it into such a variety of forms that it could scarcely be recognized by its author, if he were present. And this is honest theft.]

Horace is a preeminent, though by no means unique, example of this principle of literary theft or plagiarism. Major Greek writers, Estienne says, are exponents of the same scheme:

> Ipse enim Homerus ex Orpheo & Musaeo multa furatus est: ex Homero vicissim fere omnes multo plura. (1554.78–79)

> [For Homer himself stole a lot of material from Orpheus and Musaeus: in turn nearly everybody stole much more from Homer.]

The pattern continues: among the tragedians, Euripides stole from Homer and his successors, and Sophocles from Euripides. Comic poets illustrate comparable principles. And Estienne concludes:

> Ita igitur furari turpe non est: sed furti conuinci, hoc verò longè est turpissimum. Nam & apud Lacedemonios, qui cautè furari potuerat, impunitus abibat: qui in furto deprehensus erat, loris cedebatur. Nec iniuria, meo quidem iudicio. nam, Quam quisque nouit artem, in hac se exerceat. At qui in furto deprehenditur, imperitus est artis quam profitetur. (1554.79)

---

63. A single, if celebrated, instance is given: *O.* 2.1 ff. and *Carm.* 1.12 (1554.78).

[So it is not shameful to steal. But it is far more shameful to be convicted of theft. Among the Spartans, anybody able to steal secretly escaped unpunished; the person who was caught stealing was whipped. Not unjustly, in my opinion, for Whatever art a person knows, let him practice that. Anyone who is caught stealing is unskilled in the art he professes.]

As a view of literary history, the notion of theft links all writers in a diachronic chain through a shared technique of mimesis. The predecessor exists embodied in fragmented form in the successor, constituting his network of reference, his subtextual grid. The past subsists as hidden allusions, quotations, and references, and so it bears witness to Horace's words about Anacreon that André sets as his epitaph for the title page to his 1556 translation: "Nec si quid olim lusit Anacreon, Deleuit aetas" (nor has time destroyed what Anacreon once sang in merriment, *Carm.* 4.9.9–10). This model of literary history would also serve as a model of reading and writing. For to draw "Anacreon" back into the light—to use the conventional statement from the 1554 title page—could be said to match the reader's necessary perception of *allusio* implicit in Estienne's phrase "aperte transfert":[64] the openness of the transfer can only be apparent, the hidden Anacreontic subtext made plain, and the past discerned, if the reader recognizes the allusion. And such reader recognition must occur despite the "varias formas" into which the subtext has been transposed ("commutat")—forms so radical that they mean for Estienne the dismantling and re-erection of references in a transformed context. If the writer, in order to avoid a conviction for theft, must transpose his material with a sufficient degree of inflection and nuance, then the corresponding activity is that of the reader able to perceive the changes that have been rung. The reader seeks out the hidden fragments in exactly the same way as Estienne unearthing subliminal Alcaean allusions in Horace (". . . haec omnia ἀποσπασμάτια inter Horatij odas latere deprehendimus . . . ," 1554.77). To read is to locate and reintegrate the fragmentary ("dispersè aliqua eius dicta collocasse," 1554.78).

These points may in turn be related to questions of imitation and translation also raised in the course of the passage. The notions occur, in the form of verbs, during discussions of Horace's reaction to Anacreon and Alcaeus. This whole section of commentary begins with Estienne's candid admission that just as Horace has imitated Anacreon, so he himself has translated by recourse to Horace ("ex ipso Horatio sum interpretatus," 1554.76). Horace has openly

---

64. Note also the actual occurrence of the verb "alludo": Horace "videri possit allusisse" to Alcaeus 346 L.-P. in *Carm.* 3.21.23–24 (1554.78).

imitated or rather translated "Anacreon" (1554.76). Further on, Alcaean passages in Horace are characterized by the assertion that "Horatius non imitetur Alcaeum, sed ita eum interpretatur vt verbum verbo reddat" (Horace does not imitate Alcaeus but construes him in such a way as to translate him word for word, 1554.77). The first instances given are Alcaeus 332 Lobel-Page—

νῦν χρὴ μεθύσθην, καί τινα πὲρ βίαν πώνην

[now is the time to get drunk, to drink with all one's strength]

—and Horace *Carmina* 1.37.1–2—

Nunc est bibendum, nunc pede libero
  Pulsanda tellus.

[now is the time for drinking, now is the time to stamp the ground freely.]

Next, Alcaeus 342 L.-P.—

μηδ' ἒν ἄλλο φυτεύσῃς πρότερον δένδριον ἀμπέλω

[plant no tree in preference to the vine]

and Horace *Carmina* 1.18.1–2—

Nullam, Vare, sacra vite prius severis arborem
circa mite solum Tiburis et moenia Catili.

[Varus, plant no tree in preference to the sacred vine around the mellow soil of Tibur and the walls of Catilus.]

And finally Estienne gives the longest example, Alcaeus 347 L.-P.—

τέγγε πνεύμονας οἴνῳ, τὸ γὰρ ἄστρον περιτέλλεται·
ἀ δ' ὥρα χαλέπα, πάντα δὲ δίψαισ' ὑπὰ καύματος.

[Steep your lungs in wine, for the star is turning round. The season is hard, and everything is thirsting from the heat.]

—and Horace *Carmina* 3.29.18–20—

> iam Procyon furit
> et stella vesani Leonis,
> sole dies referente siccos.

[Already Procyon rages and the star of furious Leo, as the sun brings back the season of drought.]

Of these instances, only the first two would count as word-for-word translations; even here the allusions contained in Tibur and the walls of Catilus show cultural and geographical acclimatization of the kind commonly associated with nonliteral versions. This in itself gives some idea of the degree of imprecision attendant upon the distinctions made in the course of the passage. Each example tends to be treated impressionistically rather than according to hard-and-fast rules as to the nature of imitation and translation. The passage yields a number of fluctuating values for which it is consequently difficult to offer precise definition. This fact can be seen in the diverse terminology of transfer and transmutation that acts as a subsidiary vocabulary to the more distinct notions of imitation and translation. Horace has borrowed a number of passages from "Anacreon" ("mutuatus," 1554.77) and several from Pindar (1554.78). He has transcribed more from Alcaeus than from any other poet ("transcripsisse," 1554.77) and has adapted passages from the Greek poet ("expressisse quaedam Alcaei," 1554.78). In *Carmina* 1.9, Horace has taken ("sumptum," 1554.77) not only the beginning but very possibly the whole ode from Alcaeus, just as elsewhere he has followed him ("sequitur," "secutus," 1554.78).

These supporting terms, which present a fluid rather than a rigid conceptual scheme, foreshadow the dense closing sentences where concepts follow each other rapidly and with mounting intensity: open transfer, then change, then radical transformation almost to the point of unrecognizability, and finally the notion of theft. Theft itself straddles the line between imitation and translation. Inasmuch as it derives from reflection on the work of Horace, its most natural field of application would be the imitative one, in the form of allusion: Estienne has in fact been concerned with little else in the entire course of this exposé. Yet, as humanist translations will demonstrate, such an assumption cannot stand without qualification. Indeed, Estienne's own comment (one of several throughout the commentary) that he has translated ode 31 by the use of Horace (1554.76) is a preliminary adumbration of a phenomenon of which a flavor is given at the climax of this section. Here Estienne is arguing, as an analogy for his literary position, that to be caught red-handed in the commission of theft rightly brought punishment in Sparta:

> Nec iniuria, meo quidem iudicio. nam, Quam quisque nouit artem, in hac se exerceat. At qui in furto deprehenditur, imperitus est artis quam profitetur.
>
> (1554.79)

[Not unjustly, in my opinion. For, Whatever art a person knows, let him exercise that. Anyone who is caught stealing is unskilled in the art he professes.]

The provocative challenge "Quam quisque nouit artem, in hac se exerceat" summarizes and exemplifies a number of distinctions and principles. It is itself a quotation, a blatant form of *allusio,* resited from its home in Cicero, *Tusculan Disputations,* 1.41.[65] Yet as Cicero acknowledges there, the phrase is a Greek proverb ("Bene enim illo Graecorum prouerbio praecipitur" [that Greek proverb teaches a good lesson]), found most famously in Aristophanes *Vespae* 1431: ἔρδοι τις ἣν ἕκαστος εἰδείη τέχνην. Cicero's line is thus itself a translation into Latin iambics of a line from Greek comedy. As such, it represents an addition to the string of translations and imitations Estienne has provided, with a switch from Horace to Cicero. Like the previous translations and imitations, which it concludes and caps, it is a Latin equivalent of what was originally a Greek expression. Unlike its companions, however, the corresponding Greek is in this case absent, not quoted: the reader must depend on his or her own perceptual apparatus to recognize first the line's proverbial status, then the fact that it is an allusion to Cicero, and finally that it is a translation from the Greek.

These renewed acts of widening recognition are analogous to the progressive stages of the line's transmission from one literary context to the next. Muret's term "transmarinus" would be the appropriate one to evoke in order to speak of the appearance of Cicero's translated line in a French humanist commentary: the journey overseas from Greece to France once more passes by way of a particular Latin intermediary accorded, like Horace, special favor in the Renaissance. To revert to Estienne's language—a complementary language of transcription and carrying over—the line has been openly transferred but its pristine Greek form changed into Latin apparel—not, however, to such

---

65. *Ciceronis poetica fragmenta,* ed. Antonio Traglia, Testi per Esercitazioni Accademiche, no. 1 (Rome: Gismondi, 1950), fasciculus prior, no. 42. The Latin line exists in adapted form in Horace *Ep.* 1.14.44 and Propertius *Carm.* 2.1.46.

a degree that it is scarcely recognizable (a major criterion for "honestè furari"). In other words, the quotation treads, perilously but boldly, the frontier between "honestè furari" and "furti conuinci," for it ostentatiously calls attention to itself by its typographical format but leaves no obvious and automatic hints as to the density of the allusions it compactly conceals or the multiplicity of conceptual areas it illustrates.

Two processes may thus be discerned at work in this critical passage from Estienne's commentary. It operates principally by a form of metonymnic contiguity, whereby the relationship of a writer to his intertext (here Horace to his Greek lyric predecessors) is explored through the substitution of Alcaeus and later Pindar for "Anacreon" as tokens of those predecessors. In many cases, the instances Estienne provides, especially from Alcaeus, are taken from the ἀποσπασμάτια accompanying the Anacreontea in the *editio princeps*. In the closing lines, however, Horace's assimilation of the composite strata of Greek lyric is broadened into a generalized metaphor that establishes an antithesis ("honestè furari" versus "furti conuinci") as a criterion for judging this process of assimilation. What is likewise apparent is that the metaphor of theft could also serve as a metaphor for reading this very passage, a means of summarizing Estienne's charting of the imitative motion between the Anacreontea and Anacreon to Horace, and from Horace back to Alcaeus and Pindar. The metaphor of theft thus works on two levels, as an image of any author's relationship to his or her precursors, and as a description of the process also characteristic of this humanist commentary, which is open to the same laws of displacement and transfer discernible in the notion of *imitatio* it discusses. The commentary extrapolates from the known to the unknown and domesticates the new Greek text by discovering within it familiar features, even though they are in fact alien to it.

The critical position elaborated over the question of "honestè furari" receives further substantial confirmation in the Greek preface to the *editio princeps*. In a moderately lengthy development, Estienne strikes the contrasts between the diction of Pindar and that of Sappho and Anacreon:

ἄλλος γὰρ ἄλλῳ καρδίην ἰαίνεται, φασίν. αὐτίκα γοῦν τοῦ Πινδάρου ἄλλοι μὲν τὸ ἀξιωματικὸν καὶ μεγαλοπρεπὲς τῶν μελῶν ἄγανται, ἄλλοι δὲ τὸ αὐστηρὸν καὶ ἀκόμψευτον τῆς συνθέσεως αὐτοῦ, καὶ τὸ τῶν ἐννοιῶν δυσπαρακολούθητον ἀποτρέπονται. (1554.*2ʳ)

[Different people enjoy different things, as the saying goes. For example some enjoy the augustness and magnificence of Pindar's poetry, while others shrink from the austerity and plainness of his diction and the difficulty of following his thought.]

Who are these people? Estienne asks. They are φιλόμουσοι (lovers of the Muses), not φιλόπονοι (lovers of toil), he replies:

οἱ γὰρ τοιοῦτοι ἢ Σαπφοῖ τῇ καλῇ, ἢ Ἀνακρέοντι τῷ σοφῷ ἥδιον ἂν ἐντύχοιεν, ὧν τοῖς μέλεσι πᾶσαι χάριτες ἐπανθοῦσι, καὶ ὧν ἡ γλαφυρὰ καὶ ἀνθηρὰ σύνθεσις τὰς εὐφώνους μόνον καὶ λείας καὶ μαλακὰς τῶν λέξεων ἀποδέχεται καὶ παρ' οἷς σαφῆ καὶ στρογγύλα καὶ ἀκριβῶς ἕκαστα τῶν ὀνομάτων ἀποτετόρνευται. (1554.*2r–v)

[Such people would gladly encounter beautiful Sappho or skillful Anacreon, in whose poetry all charms are displayed, and whose smooth and flowery composition admits only melodious, smooth, and soft phraseology, and in whose poetry each word is clear, compact, and precisely turned.]

As a restatement of Estienne's critical position, the preface might serve as a valuable adjunct to what has already emerged from Estienne's discussion of "honestè furari." But these sentences represent far more than that. More strikingly and adventurously than the bravado of "Quam quisque nouit artem, in hac se exerceat," they are themselves instances of "honestè furari," for they shape a critical vocabulary out of the rhetorical works of Dionysius of Halicarnassus. Certain works by Dionysius had been published by Henri Estienne's father, Robert, in 1547;[66] Henri had had some part in their preparation.[67] In 1554, he himself was to publish further essays by Dionysius.[68]

The key to Estienne's characterization of Pindar is contained in the word αὐστηρόν (austere), one of Dionysius' three λέξεις, or stylistic types. In *De*

---

66. Dionysius of Halicarnassus, *Dionysii Halicarnassei De compositione seu orationis partium apta inter se collocatione, ad Rufum.* . . . (Paris: Robert Estienne, 1547). The contents of this volume are (i) *De compositione;* (ii) *Ars rhetorica;* (iii) *Epistula ad Ammaeum ii;* (iv) the critical essays on Lysias and Isocrates.

67. Feugère, *Essai sur . . . Henri Estienne,* 48, claims that Henri had collated the manuscripts of Dionysius for his father's edition. He quotes from Henri's edition of Athenagoras in support of this view. But he overstates the position. Estienne merely says: "Memini certè, dum pater meus excuderet Dionysii Halicarnassei historiarum volumen, vsos nos exemplari in quo idem acciderat" (*Athenagorae . . . apologia pro Christianis,* 195, "idem" refers to dittography). Note that Henri is specifically speaking about Dionysius' histories, not the rhetorical works, but it is plausible to postulate some degree of involvement on his part in the preparation of the rhetorical works also.

68. Dionysius of Halicarnassus, *Dionysii Halicarnassei responsio ad Gn. Pompeij epistolam.* The contents of this volume are (i) *Epistola ad Pompeium;* (ii) *Comparatio Herodoti cum Thucydide;* (iii) *Epistula ad Ammaeum i;* (iv) *De praecipuis linguae Graecae autoribus elogia.* All references to Dionysius will be confined to the works represented by these two publications of the Estiennes.

compositione verborum 21, Dionysius formally names these types as a prelude to detailed individual discussion: αὐτὰς . . . καλῶ τὴν μὲν αὐστηράν, τὴν δὲ γλαφυράν [ἢ ἀνθηράν], τὴν δὲ εὔκρατον (I call the first of them austere, the second smooth or flowery, and the third well blended).[69] The central terms of reference are set for Estienne. His task is further facilitated by the following section of *De compositione verborum,* where Dionysius' analysis of the austere style centers on Pindar and Thucydides as primary instances of this class. The characteristic rhythms of the austere style are ἀξιωματικοὺς καὶ μεγαλοπρεπεῖς (august and magnificent); its periods are emphatically not γλαφυραί (smooth); it is ἥκιστ' ἀνθηρά (anything but flowery), but rather μεγαλόφρων, αὐθέκαστος, ἀκόμψευτος, τὸν ἀρχαισμὸν καὶ τὸν πίνον ἔχουσα κάλλος (aristocratic, plainspoken, unadorned, with a beauty glowing with old-world charm). Later in the same section, Thucydides' style is said not to have λείας . . . τὰς ἁρμονίας οὐδ' ἔστιν εὐεπὴς καὶ μαλακὴ (smooth arrangement, nor is it harmonious and soft); and it is from other Dionysian *Opuscula* dealing equally with Thucydides that Estienne borrows the term δυσπαρακολούθητος (hard to follow) and applies it to the difficulty of Pindar's thought.[70]

In his description of Pindar, Estienne thus transfers a homogeneous Dionysian vocabulary and incorporates its principal features in the concentrated argument of his sentence. He follows the same tactic in dealing with Sappho and "Anacreon." Indeed, Estienne's expression γλαφυρὰ καὶ ἀνθηρὰ σύνθεσις is as much a marker to the Dionysian subtext as was αὐστηρόν, since it is with this phrase that Dionysius opens his section on his second type of style (*Comp.* 23). It is in the nature of the smooth or florid style that εὐφωνά τε εἶναι βούλεται πάντα τὰ ὀνόματα καὶ λεῖα καὶ μαλακὰ καὶ παρθενωπά (it requires all its words to be melodious, smooth, soft, and feminine). Its principal exponents are Anacreon and Sappho, with Sappho singled out by Dionysius for detailed analysis: her poetry is shown to exhibit εὔρους τις ἡ λέξις καὶ μαλακὴ (flowing and soft language). Onto this Dionysian vocabulary, Estienne grafts a final clause of quite different provenance. Σαφῆ καὶ στρογγύλα καὶ ἀκριβῶς ἕκαστα τῶν ὀνομάτων ἀποτετόρνευται (each word is clear, compact, and precisely turned) is Socrates' description of the orator Lysias (*Phdr.* 234 e).[71]

---

69. *Dionysii Halicarnassei opuscula,* ed. Hermann Usener and Ludwig Radermacher, 2 vols. (Leipzig: Teubner, 1899–1929), vol. 2.
70. *Pomp.* 3, *Am. ii,* 15.
71. The expression is also partly quoted by Plutarch *Moral.* 45a, *De recta ratione audiendi.* Note furthermore that στρογγύλος is also Dionysius' constant description of Lysias' style: e.g., *Lys.* 6, 9, 13.

In the light of Socrates' subsequent remarks about orators and oratory, the expression is less than complimentary. Estienne recontextualizes it and in so doing gives it positive inflection and shading, as support for Dionysius' already favorable assessment of the smooth style.

This last example, from Plato, may perhaps provide additional elucidation of the interrelation of open transfer, radical reshaping, and honest theft. The quotation from Plato is quite unlike the Dionysian vocabulary alongside which it stands. To use Dionysius is to use an inherited language of criticism and Estienne's adaptation of it allows it to function on the level of allusion in a way perfectly in keeping with the tenor of Dionysius' essays. The allusions are a shorthand, activating acquaintance with a set of closely argued values. The sentence from Plato is, by contrast, a direct quotation out of harmony with, or indeed working against, Plato's larger purposes in the *Phaedrus*.[72] In Estienne, the nature of this quotation's origin is never in any doubt; the openness of the transfer is never concealed. Nonetheless, Plato's transmitted words are submitted to reevaluation; to a permutation not of form but of analytical intention and design. As with "Quam quisque . . . ," Socrates' comment on Lysias is so verbally accurate as to be only half integrated into the neighboring verbal texture. Yet such integration is, in an immediate sense, more successfully achieved than with "Quam quisque . . .": the quotation from Plato is not cast in obtrusive proverbial shape, nor is the line of argument broken up by typographical setting. It is also more tightly accommodated to the nature of the argument in hand. It has greater particularity of application than the inevitably looser fitting, more neutral tonality of the proverb, and in this its coincidence with the Dionysian term στρογγύλος aids considerably.

In spite of Estienne's avowed insistence on radical reshaping as the *sine qua non* for "honestè furari," his own critical practice does not always bear him out as one might expect. It does not follow from this that his statement is made in polemical bad faith or that he can be automatically charged with theft. For one thing, much of the preface does contain allusions of a less immediately discernible nature, imported from a variety of contexts (not always critical contexts and by no means all from Dionysius) to illuminate the topic of "Anacreon." When collected together, these fuse into an entity different from the fragments that compose it. Again, Estienne's own theory in ode 31 is more flexible, less straightjacketed than its concluding notion of utter transformation might sug-

---

72. Similar observations could be made about the phrase ὧν τοῖς μέλεσι πᾶσαι χάριτες ἐπανθοῦυσι, applied positively to the style of "Anacreon" and Sappho by Estienne. It is based on τῷ Ἰσοκράτει χάριτες ἐπήνθουν in *Comp.* 19, where Dionysius is making a concession about Isocrates amid his general disapproval of the Isocratic school of oratory.

gest. Estienne himself acknowledges that Horace virtually translates as well as imitates his models, so that honest theft and radical transmogrification cannot be the prerogative of imitation alone. Finally, the inclusion in the preface of substantial quotation alongside reworked allusion points to a tolerance not only of composite imitation but of critical *contaminatio,* a willingness to allow different authors to shape analytical thought and a willingness to admit varying classes of critical terminology: allusion, direct quotation, borrowing, calque. In such an atmosphere, while notions of transformation and reshaping do invaluable work in underlining the changes implied by imitation and translation and entailed by cultural transmission, nonetheless not everything depends on a total dissolution of the constraints of form, which would give a decided preference to the more extreme of imitative exercises. On the strength of the present example, changed intentions count for as much as changed forms.

Critical *contaminatio* and analytical "honestè furari" also emerge elsewhere in Estienne's commentary, in places where there is equally an attempt to forge a language suitable for Anacreontics. The pertinent observations here center on ode 11:[73]

Εἴτ' εἰσὶν, εἴτ' ἀπῆλθον. Mira est ἀφέλεια τοῦ λόγου in hoc poeta: vt hîc vides in verbo ἀπῆλθον. In nullum certè melius quàm in hunc illud Fabij quadrare possit, Esse in hoc quandam iucunditatem inaffectatam, sed quam nulla affectatio consequi possit. Vnde & Horatius verè de ipso pronunciauit, Qui persępe caua testudine fleuit amorem Non elaboratum ad pedem. Quotquot ergo dulcedini & suauitati orationis studuerunt, huius tanquam optimi magistri, vestigia ita secuti sunt, vt ne à verbis quidem eius discedere voluerint. Ac ne longe abeam, hoc verbum ἀπῆλθον eo sensu passim apud illos reperies: sed in pręsentia mihi ex multis vnus ille locus succurrit [*A.P.* 5.28], —ὅτε σοῦ τὸ πρόσωπον ἀπῆλθε Κεῖνο τὸ τῆς λύγδου βάσκανε λειότερον.

["Whether they are there or whether they are gone." The simplicity of diction in this poet is wonderful, as you can see here in the phrase "they are gone." No one better than this poet could fit Quintilian's description: "There is in him a delight without affectation but which no affectation could follow." Hence Horace too spoke truly about Anacreon: "he who on his hollow lyre often sang plaintively of love in simple strains." Students of sweetness and charm in language followed in his footsteps as the best teacher, so much so that they did not wish to deviate even from

---
73. Commentary: 1554.68; Greek text: 1554.11–12.

his words. To return to the point, you will find this phrase "they are gone" in this sense everywhere in their works. One passage among many that supports my claim in the present instance is "When they faded, those looks of yours smoother than marble, you witch."]

This is a passage very plainly characterized by imitative *contaminatio*. Ἀφέλεια (simplicity) is a term occurring both in Dionysius and in Hermogenes. For Dionysius, ἀφέλεια is the characteristic of the style of Lysias (ἀφελῶς πάνυ καὶ ἁπλῶς [entirely simply and straightforwardly], *Lys.* 8),[74] while with even greater pertinence Hermogenes devotes a whole section to ἀφέλεια in the *Form. or.*, where the term specifically denotes the nature of Anacreontic and bucolic writing (ὡς τὰ πολλὰ ἔχει τῶν Ἀνακρέοντος, καὶ πάλιν τὰ Θεοκρίτου ἐν τοῖς βουκολικοῖς [this is true of most of Anacreon's works and also Theocritus' bucolic poetry]).[75] And again a little later, quoting a saying of Cyrus, King of Persia, Hermogenes asks:

ὁρᾷς ὅσον τὸ ἀφελὲς τῆς γνώμης; καὶ μὴν καὶ τὸ
ἁδύ τι τὸ ψιθύρισμα καὶ ἁ πίτυς, αἰπόλε, τήνα

[Theoc. *Id.* 1.1]

καὶ τὰ πολλὰ τῶν βουκολικῶν, ἵνα μὴ τὰ πάντα λέγω, τοιαῦτά ἐστι. καὶ παρὰ τῷ Ἀνακρέοντι δὲ ὡσαύτως.[76]

[Can you see how simple the thought is? And also in "Sweet is the whispered music of yonder pinetree, goatherd." Most (indeed, one might say all) bucolic poetry is like this. Similarly in Anacreon.]

If one adds these instances to the presence of Dionysius in the preface to *Anacreon*, it seems undeniable that Estienne is referring here to the specific terminology of Greek critical or oratorical writing. We may note that this was not to be the final occasion on which he used ἀφέλεια. In 1555, he was to characterize Greek bucolic in this way:

De me quoque vt fatear, illa ἀφέλεια, quae non exit in ψυχρότητα, & ille sponte nascens miniméque affectatus lepos, sed quem nulla affectatio consequi possit, illud inquam scribendi genus ἀποίητον, & vt ait poeta

---

74. *Dionysii Halicarnassei opuscula*, 1:15.
75. Leonhard von Spengel, ed., *Rhetores graeci*, 3 vols. (Leipzig: Teubner, 1853–56), 2:351.
76. *Rhetores graeci*, 2:352.

ille, non elaboratum, nescio quo modo maxima me semper voluptate affecit.[77]

[In my own case too, to be frank, that simplicity that does not result in frigidity, and that spontaneous and unaffected charm that no affectation could follow, that uncomplicated and as the poet says unstudied manner of writing has always given me indescribable pleasure.]

This appreciation of Greek bucolic style is fully in the tradition of Hermogenes' connecting Anacreon and Theocritus. Moreover it exhibits several critical features in common with the present passage in the "Anacreon" commentary. Quite apart from its own particular points of reference,[78] the comments on bucolic carry in abbreviated form allusions to Quintilian ("Esse in hoc iucunditatem inaffectatam, sed quem nulla affectatio consequi possit," *Inst. or.* 10.1.82)[79] and Horace ("qui persaepe cava testudine fleuit amorem / non elaboratum ad pedem," *Epod.* 14.11–12), which had also appeared in the extract on the Anacreontic ode 11.

In each of these critical passages, therefore, the essential thrust is similar. Two principles dominate them: simplicity ("ἀφέλεια—inaffectatam—non elaboratum" [simplicity—unaffected—unstudied]) and pleasure ("iucunditatam—dulcedini & suauitati" [pleasure—sweetness and pleasantness]). Both are predicated by Estienne of pseudo-Anacreontic diction. The manner of operation of these principles is to travel over the whole range of criticism in a diachronic sense. In so doing, Estienne creates a corresponding synchronic sense of the reach of criticism. *Imitatio* functions as a diachronic feature of all literary production, linking all authors in an extratemporal movement; and it functions as a synchronic movement inasmuch as each succeeding term is metonymic to each previous term: ἀφέλεια, "inaffectatam," and "non elaboratum" are interchangeable terms bearing on the same principal point.

In a sense, this reading overemphasizes the regularity of the process. In reality, since *imitatio* of this kind inevitably involves *contaminatio,* it is functionally impossible to assign all the vocabulary either to a single source or to a source dealing plainly with the characteristics of Anacreontic material. Indeed, only the quotation from Horace's *Epodes* deals directly with Anacreon. At the

---

77. *Moschi, Bionis, Theocriti . . . idyllia aliquot,* sig. Aij^v.
78. Ψυχρότης: Aristotle *Rhet.* 1405b35 ff.; "Longinus" *Sub.* 4.1; Demetrius *Eloc.* 114–27 Spengel. "Lepos": used most notably by Lucretius to describe his own poetry, *Rer. nat.,* 1.28, 934, 4.9. Ἀποίητον: Dionysius of Halicarnassus *Lysias* 8.
79. The *OCT* reads: "illam iucunditatem inadfectatam, sed quam nulla consequi adfectatio possit." Quintilian is speaking about Xenophon.

furthest remove from this is Quintilian's "iucunditatem inaffectatam," originally a comment on the style of Xenophon. Midway between the two stands ἀφέλεια, a term applied by Dionysius to Lysias. *A priori* this suggests the same redirection of critical terminology apparent in the use of Quintilian himself; and a look at the terminology of the bucolic collection where ἀφέλεια is conjoined to ἀποίητον might serve to increase our sense that Dionysius is the source of these terms. On the other hand, to postulate Dionysius as a source for the term ἀφέλεια and hence to make it at one with the homogeneous Dionysian diction of the preface must be offset by the fact that it is Hermogenes who twice expressly applies the term to Anacreon.[80] To some degree also, the terms "dulcedo" and "suauitas" have a similar critical impact, but it is less marked because the defining contexts of these words are broader and less specific than the comparable instances in Greek.[81]

Estienne constantly adapts the terminology he inherits, creating a critical vocabulary for his needs in order to emphasize the twin notions of simplicity and pleasure. The thrust of Estienne's critical enterprise is thus centripetal; it seeks to harness diverse energies not previously brought to bear on the same subject. In so doing it recognizes, for example, the theoretical capacity behind Horace's "non elaboratum," which is here treated as a technical term virtually synonymous with ἀφέλεια and "inaffectata," and it exploits the potential of "honestè furari," now a principle of textual as well as literary criticism. As Estienne explains elsewhere in his commentary in reference to the ancients, " . . . si quid apud illos occurrat, quod in rem nostram sit, ita in vsum nostrum illud vertere, vt non aliunde tamen petitum, sed domi natum videatur" (if anything occurs in their works that is helpful to us, it should be so adapted to our use that it seems to have been an original creation rather than a borrowing, 1554.69): the appropriating move, similar to that of imitation, is literally a move to domesticate ("domi natum"), to assert the presence of critical terminology familiar to the reader from other contexts, but now reworked for other purposes. Displaced from one context to another, from one *locus* to another, the vocabulary of criticism is implicated in the same process of recognition and transformation that characterizes the reader's reaction to *allusio*.

This feature anticipates Estienne's later recognition and explication of a similar device in Horace's own poetic technique: "Denique Horatius multa ex

---

80. The same remarks have equal if not greater pertinence to the case of ψυχρότης which nowhere in classical theory forms a doublet with ἀφέλεια and is indeed, in Aristotle and Demetrius, the antithesis of grandeur.

81. But cf. Cicero *De or.* 3.40.161 ("dulcedo orationis"), *De amicitia* 18.66 ("suavitas . . . sermonum atque morum").

ijs quos nominauimus poetis aliísque aperte transfert: quae autem aliunde ita mutuatur, vt sua tamen velit videri, ea ita in varias formas commutat, vt vix ab eo cuius sunt, si adsit, agnosci possint" (In short Horace openly transfers many passages from those poets we have mentioned and others. Moreover this material from elsewhere that he thus borrows, in order to make it nevertheless seem his own, he transmutes it into such a variety of forms that it could scarcely be recognized by its author, if he were present, 1554.78). The complex process of awareness of *allusio* within a text is brought out by the apparent contradiction of "aperte transfert" followed by "vix ab eo cuius sunt . . . agnosci possint." The parallels between Horatian imitative technique and broader imitative technique as illustrated by the phenomenon of appropriation are indeed striking. In both cases, the initial notion is of transfer ("transfert"/"vertere"), the expropriation of alien material that Muret had also characterized as an act of domestication in reference to Pléiade imitations. Quite apart from this connection, which throws a specifically humanist light on vernacular poetics and suggests a continuity of intellectual outlook, it is clear that no distinction is observed by Estienne between a critical enterprise (how the humanist compiles his commentary) and a poetic enterprise (how Horace treats his predecessors). Differences of genre naturally prevent the total absence of distinctions, but it is the common viewpoint, the features the two processes share, that is paramount. In this connection, Horace can serve as a metaphor not only for the imitative process in poetry but for the imitative process in general. The crucial awareness of *allusio* is defined implicitly as a perception of a specific, albeit a transposed, presence stimulating the reader to recognize and hold in view the original, while appreciating the transformation to which it has been subjected.[82] Thus the apparent contradiction between "aperte transfert" and "vix ab eo cuius sunt . . . agnosci possint" is resolved in the light of the all-important mediating function of transformation or transposition ("commutat").

The distinctions that Estienne makes here about his reader relate also to the type of imitative process concerned. This process is ultimately founded upon an optimistic relationship of imitation with the past. For Estienne himself, the recovery of "Anacreon" is explicitly a return of this author from the dead,

---

82. This definition seems akin to Riffaterre's notion that the reader's pleasure in poetry derives from the perception of clichés or other elements of a common cultural heritage within a text that subjects them to reversal, variation, or a range of other techniques. See Michael Riffaterre, *Essais de stylistique structurale,* ed. Daniel Delas, Nouvelle bibliothèque scientifique (Paris: Flammarion, 1971), chapter 6, "Fonction du cliché dans la prose littéraire," 161–81. For a reply to Riffaterre's theories, see Francis Goyet, "*Imitatio* ou intertextualité? (Riffaterre revisited)," *Poétique* 71 (1987): 313–20.

"Anacreontis Teij odae . . . luce . . . nunc primùm donatae," as the title page claims, thereby indicating both the originality of the humanist's discovery and the fact that the restitution of "Anacreon" is an act of necromancy, a conjuring up of the classical author, a calling him back into the light. This title page image would on its own be no more than a Renaissance cliché, but its implications hold particular importance if the image is translated into the theory of imitation: a powerful impetus to Estienne's disquisition on Horace, "Anacreon" is seen as the origin, the guiding principle to whom Horace is indebted. Accordingly, the oxymoron "honestè furari" summarizes both the inevitability of one's debt to poetic forerunners and the fact that such a debt is not diminishing but enriching. It acknowledges the unbroken sense of literary tradition, yet does not condemn each successor to permanent rehearsals of the similar without ever achieving the same or attaining the eminence of the predecessor.

The theft is an honest one and *renovatio* is possible provided that the successor maintains the necessary balance between the perceptibility of *allusio* to subtexts and the transformation that those subtexts must undergo in order to be accommodated to their new context. If the successor fails to make the *allusio* perceptible, then the rift with the past is complete and no continuity is maintained. If, however, the *allusio* is insufficiently transposed, then no *renovatio* has taken place. *Imitatio,* therefore, depends on transposition to achieve *renovatio,* in order for the contemporary work of art to become a remembering rather than simply a memorial. And the primordiality of these terms is noted by Thomas Greene when he observes that the Erasmian pupil had to produce through memory a reactivation that is also a reformulation. He adds that at the stage beyond verbatim repetition comes "conversion or transposition whereby, for example, an ancient idea is reconceived and rephrased in Christian language."[83] There are clear parallels between this description and Estienne's project in his Anacreontic commentary, except that the reformulation is allowed to act upon itself from within rather than encouraged to seek new terms (Christian terms) from without. The *renovatio* in the case of pseudo-Anacreon takes place precisely in the terms previously enunciated—by activating the allusions inherent in preestablished terminology, but attaching their echoes to a new classical center. This ensures a dynamic sense of the present as well as preserving the values of the past. Nancy Struever puts the point well: "Rhetorical *imitatio,* with its concept of virtuosity as both a command of past techniques which possess continuous sanctions and a sensitivity to the unique

---

83. Thomas M. Greene, *The Light in Troy: Imitation and Discovery in Renaissance Poetry* (New Haven and London: Yale University Press, 1982), 31.

demands of the present situation, provides a model of continuity in change."[84] The effect is not so much to cross-fertilize alien cultures (as a Christian with a classical) as to encourage the classical culture to release its own energies, demonstrate its own resourcefulness, in dealing with an author newly returned from the dead.

Perhaps the full impact of such a dynamics can properly be felt in Estienne's use of the term ἀφέλεια itself. Ἀφέλεια, with its impeccable origins in the Graeco-Roman critical tradition, could possibly be seen as an attempt to discover and defend a term specific to two related types of writing (Anacreontic and bucolic), a term that links together classical criticism and humanist exegesis, and through which the latter inherits and renews the former. From that standpoint, Estienne's use of the term ἀφέλεια could perhaps be portrayed as an equivalent for λεπτότης (lightness),[85] that quality so prized by Alexandrian poets that describes the delicacy of small-scale poetry—a description equally fitting to the Anacreontea and to pastoral. As part of *renovatio,* the usual term λεπτότης is set aside or, more properly, transposed into the unusual ἀφέλεια. Under the action of *imitatio,* Estienne is like Horace, openly transposing ("aperte transfert") an unfamiliar critical term and broadening its scope, its possibility for analytical action. The term arrives redolent of its former context, but its recontextualization emphasizes the *renovatio* effected and the historical distance traveled. Once again it is the similarity of approach, the conformity to a conceptual model, which is striking, between the Latin author and the French humanist.

4

Two sorts of analogue, one classical and the other Renaissance, can be discerned for Estienne's aesthetic position. Of classical views of plagiarism, Russell observes: "κλοπή (*furtum,* plagiarism) was one of the stock themes of

---

84. Nancy Struever, *The Language of History in the Renaissance: Rhetoric and Historical Consciousness in Florentine Humanism* (Princeton: Princeton University Press, 1970), 193.

85. On this term and its associated principles, see representatively Walter Wimmel, *Kallimachos in Rom: Die Nachfolge seines apologetischen Dichtens in der Augusterzeit,* Hermes Einzelschriften, no. 16 (Wiesbaden: Steiner, 1960), Stichwortindex s.vv. λεπτός, "Opfervergleich"; Athanasios Kambylis, *Die Dichterweihe und ihre Symbolik: Untersuchungen zu Hesiodos, Kallimachos, Properz und Ennius* (Heidelberg: 1965), 81, 119, 141 ff.; Mario Puelma Piwonka, *Lucilius und Kallimachos: Zur Geschichte einer Gattung der hellenistisch-römischen Poesie* (Frankfurt am Main: Klostermann, [1949]), Sachregister s.vv. "Kleindichtung," "inflatum," "tumidum," "turgidum." And for a specific example see Erich Reitzenstein, "Zur Stiltheorie des Kallimachos," in *Festschrift Richard Reitzenstein* (Leipzig and Berlin: Teubner, 1931), 23–69.

ancient criticism and formed one of its least intelligent departments."[86] The subject received careful attention in Stemplinger's monograph,[87] complemented by Kroll for Latin literature,[88] as well as in Ziegler's thorough article in Pauly-Wissowa.[89] Plagiarism itself affected the very notion of mimesis, since classical *imitatio* and *furtum* alike rely on the same principle of indebtedness, so that "das tendenziöse *furtum* wird stets mit *imitari, mutuari, sequi, trahere, transferre* u.a. umschrieben."[90] As the shadowy stepbrother of *imitatio, furtum* is particularly susceptible of overturning the reworked *allusio*, which might itself be defined as recontextualized quotation. Stemplinger's list suggests the misalliances, the failures of imitative contact into which *furtum* can draw the reader and the writer. *Furtum* is *imitatio* directly possessed rather than obliquely repossessed, offering as one's own something that is another's and so betraying that fundamental principle of processing that is the core of *allusio*. *Furtum* is, as it were, the most blatant and literal of transfers *(transferre)*, a carrying across that attempts to deceive and that might constitute the least satisfactory, if most common, definition of the characteristic work of translation.

In its purely classical form, then, *imitatio* carries within itself a negative self-image whose deceptive nature scrambles the careful technical transactions on which *imitatio* relies. *Furtum* implies a duplicity that *imitatio* wishes to eradicate; yet what distinguishes these otherwise similar processes is the degree of occultation practiced on the reader. Quotation is the test case for *imitatio* as well as for *furtum*. "Confessed borrowings were not κλοπή."[91] Plagiarism is not only unconfessed borrowing but unacknowledged quotation. By definition, it is a series of such unacknowledged quotations, drawn from one or several sources. Imitation will tolerate quotation, but not on a large scale; its habitual frame of reference is allusive, which implies the distancing and reperception of an original. In imitation, allusion is creation of the subtext by reference and in contrast to which the successor defines his position; in

---

86. Donald A. Russell, ed., *"Longinus": On The Sublime*, corrected ed. (Oxford: Clarendon Press, 1970), 117 *ad* 13.4; cf. Russell, *De imitatione*, in *Creative Imitation and Latin Literature*, ed. David West and Tony Woodman (Cambridge: Cambridge University Press, 1979), 11–12.

87. Eduard Stemplinger, *Das Plagiat in der griechischen Literatur* (Leipzig and Berlin: Teubner, 1912).

88. Wilhelm Kroll, *Studien zum Verständnis der römischen Literatur* (Stuttgart: Metzler, 1924), chapter 7, "Originalität und Nachahmung," 139–84.

89. K. Ziegler, Pauly-Wissowa 20: cols. 1956–97, s.v. "Plagiat."

90. Stemplinger, *Das Plagiat*, 168; similarly Ziegler, Pauly-Wissowa 20: col. 1959, s.v. "Plagiat."

91. Russell, *"Longinus,"* 117, citing Cicero *Brutus* 76, Seneca *Suas.* 3.7.

plagiarism, subtext becomes text without redefinition, but equally with attempted concealment from the reader. Therein lies the most important distinction of attitude between plagiarism and imitation. Both rely on concealment to some degree. *Imitatio* based on *allusio* only half conceals its debt; indeed, without the reader's perception that subtextual reading is pertinent and necessary, *allusio* is useless. Reader perception is stimulated by the surface text's cues, allowing the reader the crucial work of holding in view the finished product before him and the original it reshapes. In *furtum,* the concealment of the original attempts to be total. If reader perception is allowed its full play, the deception will be brought to light: perception must therefore be accorded no room for maneuver.

Estienne's own attitude toward this classical tradition itself stands out as a reworking, an imitation rather than a simple copying. In the light of classical theory about plagiarism, his paradoxical contribution is to evolve the oxymoron "honestè furari" as a description of an action more extensive than and so not identical with the idea of confessed borrowing. Plagiarism is honest, Estienne believes, when it is undetected, in other words when concealment is successful because of the transmutation the borrowing has undergone. The transmutation he describes is radical—transmutation to the point of unrecognizability. This startling statement has two effects. First, it clearly separates "honestè furari" from its opposite, which is characterized by detection of the borrowing, that is, by its lack of concealment, its lack of transmutation; so that, though two areas are covered by a single term, "furari," there is no functional or conceptual confusion between them. Second, the criterion of unrecognizability, of total absorption and assimilation, could with greater ease and significance be taken to be a manifesto for *contaminatio,* as being the most obviously available literary feature by which multifarious fragments of classical discourse can be fitted side by side without necessary reference to their context of origin. Estienne's description is, however, too brief for the plain assertion that it pertains to *contaminatio* alone. *Contaminatio* is certainly the major feature of his own practice as a translator, but not in such a way as to exclude allusive reference to ancestral subtexts, which pure *contaminatio* obviates, but which Estienne is at pains to disclose in Horace's practice. Moreover, the sole example Estienne appears to provide of borrowing—"Quam quisque . . ."—is all too clearly a quotation, a "confessed borrowing" advertised as such by its typographical marking off. In sum, then, Estienne's theory is sufficiently elastic to accommodate a number of senses. But the general urge to transformation is clear, and it shows up sharply as an individual reapplication of a classical worry about plagiarism and imitation when compared with

Pigman's statement that "borrowing, and its unscrupulous cousin, theft, like culling flowers, are frequent images of nontransformative imitation or following."[92] In the light of this statement, Estienne works against a norm, against a theoretical assumption.

The norm itself is discernible in other Renaissance writers: Estienne is not unique in propounding a version of literature as theft. Such ideas are extraordinary in humanist editorial practice of the period, but not in humanist circles as a whole. Such affinities may well be parallels rather than sources, but they are not likely to be fortuitous or coincidental. Muret, for one, partly covers the same area with the same fundamental notion of transmission or transfer in relation to Horace, though without Estienne's distinctive vocabulary. By contrast, a poem by Jean Dorat treats of precisely the same topic in similar terms to Estienne. For Dorat, too, literary theft is a permissible form of imitation, the origins of which can be traced back to the ancients. Writing to Antoine Valet, he maintains that even the poets of antiquity were thieves:

Autolyci fures, sequitur sua quemque iuuentus,
   Orphaeus, Musaeus, fur & Homerus, erant.
Fur erat Hesiodus, clypeum furatus Achillis.
   Herculis est, olim tegmen Achillis erat.
Ipsas quinetiam furatur uterque Sibyllas,
   Séque Sibyllinis ornat vterque modis.
Néve putes, mendax quia semper Graecia, Graecos
   Furaces Latiis vatibus esse magis.
Ennius ipse pater magnum furatur Homerum,
   Maeonides alter visus & inde sibi est.
Ennium vt ante omnes, alios sic denique cunctos
   Virgilius furtis per sua scela *[sic]* modus.[93]

[Orpheus, Musaeus, and Homer, one after the other, were the thieves of Autolycus. Hesiod was a thief too: he stole the shield of Achilles. Once it protected Achilles; now it is Hercules'. Indeed, both Homer and Hesiod stole from the very Sibyls and each adorned himself with the Sibyls' verses. Do not think that because the Greeks always lie, the Greeks were greater thieves than the Latin poets. Father Ennius himself stole from

---

92. G.W. Pigman, "Versions of Imitation in the Renaissance," *Renaissance Quarterly* 33, no. 1 (1980): 5 n. 8.

93. *Ioannis Aurati Lemovicis poetae et interpretis regij Poëmatia* (Paris: Linocer, 1586), part 2, 157. The passage is quoted by De Nolhac, *Ronsard et l'humanisme*, 21 n. 2; and Grafton, *Joseph Scaliger*, 1:78.

mighty Homer and thought of himself as a second Maeonides. As all had previously stolen from Ennius, so Virgil unscrupulously stole from all other poets.]

The program sketched here is strikingly similar to Estienne's, with the addition of the sibylline oracles on which Homer and Hesiod are said to have drawn. The transmission from Greece to Rome is made via Ennius, the father of Latin epic, to devolve finally on Virgil whose eclectic mimesis serves as a focus in much the same way that Horace had for Estienne. Dorat states the literary lineage but gives no detailed exemplification as to what theft means in practice. Authors stand in undifferentiated relationship, tied together by the transhistorical process of theft. This theory of transmission of classical texts works against our received notion or even our expectations. Transmission is normally portrayed as a diachronic, historical act; handing on is a handing down, with all the cultural adaptation and change this entails. But by regarding all writers as implicated in a synchronic activity, Dorat is setting up a notion close to intertextuality. There is a constant layering of the text through the incorporation of predecessors; and the text is textured, woven out of this assimilation of models and traditions. Whether this assimilation is a large-scale adherence to a single model or a more concentrated attention to set pieces and fragments, Dorat does not specify, and his words allow both views. In relating the work of specific authors to each other, he gives the impression of substantive incorporation; yet the sole instance he supplies—Hesiod's *Scutum* deriving from Homer's shield of Achilles (*Il.* 18.478 ff.)—is an anthology piece, readily excerpted and reworked. Nor, since he regards integration as normative, does Dorat make any additional qualification based on the latency or otherwise of the thieving act, as Estienne does through his antithesis "honestè furari" and "furti conuinci."

More tantalizing still, but potentially just as fruitful and indeed more striking, is the possibility of uncovering the influence of Vida's *De arte poetica*.[94] His sketch of the genealogy of literature in book 1 recalls vividly those of Estienne and Dorat, albeit with fewer examples and greater circumstantial detail. Vida's revered model is Virgil (1.208) and Virgil's illustrious Greek ancestor is Homer (1.135 ff.). Both of these are unashamedly representatives of epic, the preeminent poetic genre in Vida's eyes (1.33–38). Unsurprisingly, therefore, Vida's other representative and intermediary from Homer to Virgil is Ennius (1.155–57). The scheme Homer—Ennius—Virgil is also apparent in Dorat but is too schematic to constitute any proof of affiliation between him

---

94. *The "De arte poetica" of Marco Girolamo Vida*, ed. Ralph G. Williams (New York: Columbia University Press, 1976). Williams bases his text on the edition of 1527.

and Vida. By contrast, the literary tradition as outlined by Vida here does underscore the peculiarity of the lineage envisaged by Estienne and Dorat and hence draws these two closer together.

Where Vida bulks perceptibly larger on the imitative horizon is in the developed precept of theft or dissimulation that occupies a central section of book 3 of the *De arte poetica;* a precept enacted as well as described by his own theft of Virgilian diction. Vida's exhortation to the prospective pupil—

Ergo agite o mecum securi accingite furtis
Una omnes, pueri, passimque avertite praedam.

(3.243–44)

[Therefore, my students, do as I do: undertake your thefts confidently and carry off your plunder from all sides.]

—is preceded by the warning that theft should entail dissimulation:

Quum vero cultis moliris furta poetis,
Cautius ingredere, & raptus memor occule versis
Verborum indiciis, atque ordine falle legentes
Mutato. nova sit facies, nova prorsus imago.
Munere (nec longum tempus) vix ipse peracto
Dicta recognosces veteris mutata poetae.

(3.217–22)

[When you undertake thefts from elegant poets, tread warily and do not forget to hide your plunder by varying the words; hoodwink your readers by altering the word order. Let everything have a new appearance, a new look. When this task is completed (it is not a long job), you yourself will hardly recognize the altered words of the ancient poet.]

The argument bears on microcontext rather than on macrocontext: a change of word order or word form. The results of such concealment are such that the thief himself will be unable to recognize the altered words of the ancient poet. Estienne had made the equally hyperbolical assertion that the theft must go undetected even to the original creator of the words. The act of detection is the object of Vida's following remarks. Some authors, he says, commit their thefts openly, purposely inviting detection (3.223–25). In those cases, either they have made no change to the word order but have endowed the stolen words with a different significance,[95] or they have improved their predecessors' data in a spirit of ambitious rivalry (3.225–30). The first instance extends the microcontext of altered forms to a macrocontext: the selfsame words have different signifiers according to the signifying chain in which they are placed. Imitation plays on similarity of form and disparity of meaning, a phenomenon accentuated by the *aemulatio,* which, in Vida's categorization, must blatantly advertise its theft in order to display the alterity of its own vision as equal or indeed superior to the model.

The momentum generated by Vida's examples eventually widens the gap between subtext and surface text, by making of the successor not a belated parasite but rather, in the boldest cases, a peer, a champion of literary independence, a protagonist of imitative progress. Through classifying reworked quotation and *aemulatio* within the confines of theft, Vida makes allowance for the direct but reperceived presence of the source text within the host text (quotation) or for a shifting of interest from source text to host text *(aemulatio).* Hence, Vida is able to distinguish a true acculturation of lexis—the contextualized reshaping of vocabulary for other purposes—from straightforward plagiarism or unworked quotation. In Estienne such distinctions are far from clear. "Furti conuinci" appears to exclude self-aware quotation; but "Quam quisque . . ." is precisely that. Possibly Estienne is attacking a crude plagiarism that transfers rather than transforms; in contrast, his development of ἀφέλεια and the related rhetoric of evaluation is exactly in line with his own (and Vida's) observations about the purposeful transformation of an inherited vocabulary. In Vida, dissimulation is permitted to ally itself with its opposite in order to achieve perception of the changes worked by imitation. This alliance is something that the stated antagonisms of Estienne's version of theft will not tolerate, but it does nonetheless emerge from the actual examples he provides.

Estienne's theory of honest plagiarism constitutes, then, a particular variant on an idea familiar from other quarters in the Renaissance. Naturally, the image of theft has sufficient common currency to have been developed independently by Estienne; with his Parisian background, though, it is tempting to give greater weight to the Dorat parallel. There is, as it happens, a certain amount of evidence to tie Dorat in with the Estiennes. Pierre de Nolhac stated quite unequivocally that Dorat "était lié avec les Estienne,"[96] while Silver noted that in 1538 Dorat had written a long poem in honor of Robert Estienne, Henri's father.[97] Furthermore, conjectures by Dorat appeared in Henri Estienne's 1566

---

95. Vida acknowledges this as his own preferred practice: 3.257–58.
96. De Nolhac, *Ronsard et l'humanisme,* 108.
97. Silver, *The Formative Influences,* 111 n. 82.

Poetae Graeci principes heroici carminis.[98] In a rather broader sense, moreover, other circumstantial evidence points to the influence of Parisian critical attitudes in the 1554 *Anacreon*. To invoke Grafton's criterion, Estienne's propensity to exegesis is strongly marked. The whole discussion of Horace leading to the principle of honest theft is simply the most extensive instance of Estienne's constantly renewed endeavors to forge an analytical language appropriate to Anacreontics. Other instances, if shorter, are no less impressive and demonstrate not just close familiarity with Greek critical writing but an ability to reshape this heritage into an intellectual instrument. To that extent, such passages exactly match the notion of "honestè furari" the ode 31 commentary develops: as Muret might have put it, there is an active transfer of the "transmarinum" into a new setting where that same "transmarinum" will be renewed.

Despite their apparent dissimilarities, Muret's "transmarinum" and Estienne's "honestè furari" cover essentially the same phenomenon. In both cases an image of spatiotemporal transfer is prominent. In both cases a powerful stimulus is provided by observation of a major Latin writer, Horace, modeling himself upon Greek antecedents. With Muret, this brings an awareness of the value of Greek sources in the elucidation of Latin authors, an awareness that shows itself clearly in his approach to writing *variae lectiones*. For Estienne, it nourishes primarily a view of classical composition but can also provide insights into the nature of reading classical texts: to read is to perceive allusion, to be aware of the subtextual dialogue that a text enters upon with its precursors. Subtextual reading, the counterpart of allusive writing, is not, moreover, the prerogative of imitation alone but could equally well apply to translation.

Decidedly, the 1554 *Anacreon* is a product of a particular historical moment. Just how fleeting this moment could be is shown by the nature of Estienne's subsequent editions of pseudo-Anacreon. In 1556, the Greek preface disappears, to be replaced in 1560 by a translation of it into Latin, so that the distinctive Dionysian vocabulary of the *editio princeps* is lost. If in 1556 the commentary maintains its position, in 1560 and again in 1566 even this is supplanted by a series of critical *castigationes*. Henceforward, Estienne's career will take him deeper into the territory of textual criticism.

---

98. See the example in Grafton, *Joseph Scaliger,* 1:84.

CHAPTER 2

Transmitting the Classics II: Translation

In the course of the previous chapter, a method of writing and reading emerged with rich implications for the study of translation and imitation. Reading the writings of the ancients was, in that case, synonymous with subtextual reading, a reading of the submerged strata of allusions that constitute the poem in translation as well as in imitation. It is now necessary to set Estienne's remarks into the broader context of humanist and vernacular theories of translation before linking these to the Anacreontea and so finally allowing some overall pattern to emerge. In view of the considerable secondary literature that Renaissance translation theory has excited, the following account makes no attempt to be exhaustive but highlights certain features of the debate pertinent later to a study of translations of the Anacreontea.

1

Ancient theory gave an important role to translation within the framework of oratorical training. Translation is a propaedeutic through which the orator seeks to exercise *copia* as a way of increasing the capacity and efficacy of his own *memoria*. Both of these elements are in turn a necessary preliminary to *pronunciatio,* the orator's technique of delivery. As a translator himself, as well as a theoretician of oratory, Cicero plays a dominant role in shaping critical terminology and attitudes of lasting influence.[1] Of particular strategic importance among Ciceronian material on translation is the *De optimo genere oratorum,* translations of speeches by Aeschines and Demosthenes of which only the

---

1. Cicero's influence on French translation theory has been carefully studied by Glyn P. Norton, "Translation Theory in Renaissance France: Etienne Dolet and the Rhetorical Tradition," *Renaissance and Reformation* 10 (1974): 1–13, especially 4–5, and *Ideology and Language,* general index, s.v. "Cicero." For the wider context, see Marc Fumaroli, *L'âge de l'éloquence: Rhétorique et "res literaria" de la Renaissance au seuil de l'époque classique* (Geneva: Droz, 1980).

preface survives; the work is now acknowledged to be pseudo-Ciceronian. The author's explanation of his task nevertheless repays careful scrutiny:

> Converti enim ex Atticis duorum eloquentissimorum nobilissimas orationes inter seque contrarias, Aeschinis et Demosthenis; nec converti ut interpres, sed ut orator, sententiis isdem et earum formis tamquam figuris, verbis ad nostram consuetudinem aptis. In quibus non verbum pro verbo necesse habui reddere, sed genus omne verborum vimque servavi. Non enim ea me adnumerare lectori putavi oportere, sed tamquam appendere.[2]

> [I have translated the most notable speeches of the two most eloquent Attic orators, Aeschines and Demosthenes, which were delivered against each other. I did not translate them like a translator, but like an orator, preserving the same ideas and figures of speech, but in words suited to our usage. In so doing, I did not think it necessary to translate word for word, but I preserved the general style and force of the language. I did not consider that I ought to count them out to the reader, but to balance like for like.]

"Cicero" makes two distinctions regarding the connection between translation and oratory. In the first place, the oratorical objective in his translation is uppermost. As a professional orator, not a translator *(interpres),* he seeks formal equivalents for the ideas *(sententiae)* and appropriate figures of speech *(figurae),* insofar as these suited his purposes. As a natural consequence, it follows that his is not a word-for-word translation (the domain of the *interpres* mentioned earlier?). Instead, "Cicero" appeals to a less readily quantifiable task, that of rendering the "genus omne verborum vimque." And he points up the contrast between literal and nonliteral versions by the metaphors of the final sentence: first, translation is a matter not of counting words out *(adnumerare)* but of weighing them *(appendere).* By looking not to the words but to their abstract configuration, their "genus omne . . . vimque," pseudo-Cicero sets up moreover a contrast between word and expression, *verbum* and *sententia* or *res,* that will become a staple of later classical as well as Renaissance theories of translation. Second—reading on from this—the author emphasizes that carrying over of the "genus omne verborum vimque" between languages re-

---

2. "Cicero," *De optimo genere oratorum,* 5.14; cf. 7.23: "expressero virtutibus utens illorum omnibus, id est sententiis et earum figuris et rerum ordine." On the spuriousness of this work, see Michael D. Reeve, "De optimo genere oratorum," in *Texts and Transmissions: A Survey of the Latin Classics,* ed. Leighton D. Reynolds (Oxford: Clarendon Press, 1983), 100–102.

quires, practically speaking, a series of reemphases. The new rendering will necessitate some measure of reformulation, of altered focus or changed intensity. Often enough, reemphasis of this kind will entail compensation; the translation compensates for the transition between languages or poetic genres by establishing an analogous lexicon or metrical or structural scheme. A characteristic idiom or structural device can be reproduced without the necessity for these constants to inhere in exactly the same words. As "Cicero" says, the thought pattern and rhetorical figures that convey it (as distinct from the words) are susceptible to reproduction: idiom is re-created as an effort of figuration or at a wider level of structural effect. Thus, the author of *De optimo genere oratorum* is demonstrating that translation requires full attention to *elocutio,* a domain traditionally embracing figures as well as words.

The importance of this pseudonymous treatise is not lost on succeeding generations. In particular, it recurs in the context of biblical translation, a sphere that had long debated issues of literalism and inspiration.[3] Here, it is Jerome who plays a decisive role through his famous letter "Ad Pammachium de optimo genere interpretandi." Jerome not only alludes to the pseudo-Ciceronian work in the title to his letter but also quotes from it while defending himself against attacks on his abilities as a translator. Jerome appeals to the practice of "Cicero":

Ego enim non solum fateor, sed libera uoce profiteor me in interpretatione Graecorum absque scripturis sanctis, ubi et uerborum ordo mysterium est, non uerbum e uerbo sed sensum exprimere de sensu. Habeoque huius rei magistrum Tullium, qui Protagoram Platonis et Oeconomicuum Xenofontis et Aeschinis et Demosthenis duas contra se orationes pulcherrimas transtulit. Quanta in illis praetermiserit, quanta addiderit, quanta mutauerit, ut proprietates alterius linguae suis proprietatibus explicaret, non est huius temporis dicere. Sufficit mihi ipsa translatoris auctoritas qui ita in prologo earundem orationum locutus est: . . .[4]

---

3. Cf. Werner Schwarz, *Principles and Problems of Biblical Translation: Some Reformation Controversies and Their Background* (Cambridge: Cambridge University Press, 1955), and Jerry H. Bentley, *Humanists and Holy Writ: New Testament Scholarship in the Renaissance* (Princeton: Princeton University Press, 1983).

4. *Saint Jérôme: Lettres,* ed. and trans. Jérôme Labourt (Paris: Belles Lettres, 1953), 3, letter 57, section 5. For Jerome's place in the history of translation, see Rolf Kloepfer, *Die Theorie der literarischen Übersetzung,* Freiburger Schriften zur romanischen Philologie, no. 12 (Munich: Fink, 1967), 28 ff., and more particularly Eugene F. Rice, *St. Jerome in the Renaissance* (Baltimore and London: Johns Hopkins University Press, 1985).

[I not only confess but profess unreservedly that in translating from Greek—except for Holy Scripture, where the very order of the words is a mystery—I translate not word for word but idea for idea. In this matter, my model is Cicero, who translated Plato's *Protagoras*, Xenophon's *Oeconomicus*, and the two magnificent speeches delivered by Aeschines and Demosthenes against each other. What he omitted in these speeches, what he added, what he changed, in order to explain the idioms of the first language by the idioms of his own, this is not the time nor the place to say. I need only appeal to the translator who spoke thus in the prologue to these speeches: . . .]

The previously quoted passage from the *De optimo genere oratorum* ("Converti enim . . .") then follows. Jerome next proceeds via the standard quotation about translation from Horace's *Ars poetica* ("nec uerbum uerbo curabis reddere fidus / interpres," vv. 133–34) to citing his own preface to his translation of Eusebius' *Chronicon,* where once again problems of rendering had been resolved by recourse to nonliteralness:

Accedunt hyperbatorum anfractus, dissimilitudines casuum, uarietatis figurarum, ipsum postremo suum et, ut ita dicam, uernaculum linguae genus: si ad uerbum interpretor, absurde resonant.[5]

[In addition, there were the problems caused by hyperbata, the dissimilarity of the cases, the divergency of the rhetorical figures, and ultimately the *je ne sais quoi* of the language, which is special to it and inherent. If I translate literally, they sound absurd.]

Jerome's instances of what nonliteralism means are changes of figures after the manner that "Cicero" specifies as his own practice. In addition, he formalizes the implicit "Ciceronian" antinomy of *verba* against *sententia* into sense-for-sense against word-for-word—a formula later to become a theoretical commonplace.

Taken along with pseudo-Ciceronian pronouncements, the precepts of *De optimo genere oratorum* have, then, a discernible historical thread. In effect, they emphasize the virtues of nonliteralism by way of concentrating on *res* (provisionally the content of the piece), at the expense of *verba* (provisionally the words of the piece, conducive to style but not coincidental with it). The questions that the Ciceronian position raises are the subject of further con-

---

5. Saint Jerome, *Lettres,* letter 57, section 5.

troversy in the French Renaissance. In 1540, the year in which Dolet published his *La maniere de bien traduire,* the Benedictine Joachim Périon brought out a collection of Aristotelian material. As Norton points out, the work is a series of commentaries on Cicero's translation of Aristotle's *Nicomachean Ethics.*[6] Its very title (assuming, but not mentioning, Jerome's precedent) looks back to the pseudo-Ciceronian work: *De optimo genere interpretandi Commentarij.* Indeed Périon makes his position amply clear in his preface; and of the rich discriminations it offers about the nature of translation,[7] one passage may be isolated:

Nunc enim ex his paucis quae commemoraui satis est intelligi id quod nobis propositum fuit, si disertè quod è graeco interpretari uelimus, haec duo tenenda esse necessario: unum, ut uerbum ex uerbo exprimendum non putemus: alterum, ut graeca cum latinis maximè Ciceronis eiusdem generis ferè coniungamus. Quae duo qui negliget, is non solum indisertè, sed barbarè etiam multa dicat necesse est.[8]

[Now these few remarks are enough to make our plan clear—if we wish to translate from Greek fluently, these two principles are crucial: first, that we should not believe in a word-for-word translation; second, that we should couple Greek with Latin in the manner of Cicero. Anybody who neglects these two principles is bound to express himself not only without eloquence but also without culture.]

Despite its ostensible Ciceronian tendencies, Périon's project is in fact a fundamental misunderstanding of Cicero. Périon shares with his elected model the dispensation from literalism in translation. However, to judge *Latinitas* by the language of Cicero alone is nowhere a stated objective of Cicero himself. Indeed, Cicero's own statements on the matter place greater emphasis on the figuration of the piece than on its supporting vocabulary, so highlighting by contrast the rigidity of Renaissance Ciceronianism of which Périon is a representative. Ciceronianism will not allow for the shifts between languages, the changes in linguistic climate, that "Cicero" himself recognizes in the subordi-

---

6. Norton, *Ideology and Language,* 217.
7. Norton, *Ideology and Language,* 217–21, offers the most perceptive analysis.
8. *Ioachimi Perionii Benedict. Cormoeriaceni De optimo genere interpretandi . . . Commentarij* (Paris: De Colines, 1540), sig. [Aiiij^r]. Current critical interest in Périon and his Ciceronianism may be gauged from his appearance in the following works: Grafton, *Joseph Scaliger,* 1:74–75; Norton, *Ideology and Language,* 217–21; Charles B. Schmitt, *Aristotle and the Renaissance* (Cambridge, Mass., and London: Harvard University Press, 1983), 72–76.

nate role he attaches to linguistic expression. On the strength of his statements in the *De optimo genere oratorum,* "Cicero" himself is anti-Ciceronian. Périon puts his trust in something that "Cicero" expressly denies—the possibility of an equivalence between two disparate contexts. Further, Périon holds that the language conditions of Cicero can be reestablished and that, it seems, through the crucial intermediary of the Latin orator, any source text can be repossessed, "eradicating the space of estrangement which otherwise separates us from that text."[9] A thoroughly Ciceronian position could match alien *res* with strictly Ciceronian *verba*. Nowhere else is there, in potential at least, so startling a dissociation between *res* and *verba* nor so firm an assurance that the matching of the two can nonetheless be accomplished.

Périon's translations of Aristotle caused something of a stir, as can be judged from the responses they provoke. One humanist with his own version of Aristotle to propose was Jacques Louis d'Estrebay (Strebaeus), who engaged in an exchange of polemical pamphlets with Périon over the latter's translation of Aristotle's *Politics*.[10] D'Estrebay's translation of this work bears instructive comparison with Périon's attitude toward his task. D'Estrebay begins with an assessment of the previous translations of the work made by Leonardo Bruni and Lefèvre d'Etaples, who "in errorem depulsi, ab Aristotelis sententia viáque deflexissent" (propelled into error, deviated from Aristotle's thought and path).[11] The basis of this corruption of Aristotelian *sententia* is grammatical or cultural error.[12] D'Estrebay then summarizes his position and states the rationale that guides his translation:

> Itaque summopere contendi vt ea restituerem, quae mihi deprauata videbantur: fecíque diligentia vt locos ferè mille ducentos emendarem, vnde Aretinus ille & Iacobus Stapulensis non videntes impressa sui ducis vestigia aberrassent. Exemplaria Graeca quae venerunt in manus, correxi. nullum enim mendis librariorum vacabat. Partem locorum notaui: partem quae deprehendi facile potest, adscribendum libello minimè duxi. Praeterea faciendum erat, vt omnia verbis Latinis, propriis & compositis

---

9. Norton, *Ideology and Language,* 219.

10. Schmitt, *Aristotle,* 76–77, and Kees Meerhoff, *Rhétorique et poétique au XVIe siècle en France: Du Bellay, Ramus et les autres* (Leiden: Brill, 1986), 49–64. D'Estrebay is referred to approvingly by Barthelemy Aneau: see *Le Quintil Horatien* in Francis Goyet, ed., *Traités de poétique et de rhétorique de la Renaissance* (Paris: Livre de Poche, 1990), 197: "la lecture ou écriture du bon Rhétoricien maître Jacques Loys."

11. *Aristotelis Stagiritae Politica ab Iacobo Lodoico Strebaeo à Graeco conuersa* (Paris: Roigny, 1549), A.ii.r.

12. D'Estrebay, *Aristotelis . . . Politica,* A.ii.r.

exprimerentur, ne barbara ac inusitata foeditatem, improbria obscuritatem, incondita confusionem gignerent.[13]

[Thus my greatest concern was to restore those passages that I thought corrupt. I worked carefully to emend about one thousand two hundred passages, in which Bruni and Lefèvre d'Etaples, not seeing the footprints of their leader [Aristotle], went wrong. I corrected the Greek exemplars that came to hand, for none was without the errors of copyists. I have noted some of the passages; others that can readily be understood, I did not think it necessary to put down. The important thing was to express everything in proper, orderly Latin, in case the barbarous and the unusual should give rise to ugliness, the perverse to obscurity, and the disorderly to confusion.]

Faced with predecessors who are also rivals, the editor's task is not just that of the critic but more specifically that of the textual critic; he proves the inadequacy of previous translations by restoration of defective manuscript tradition. Restoration is made largely on the strength of *divinatio*. In other respects, D'Estrebay displays an alarming lack of historical method: his Greek exemplars are simply those "that came to hand," they bear extensive scribal corruption, and no dating evidence is provided for them. Elsewhere in D'Estrebay's work as a translator, there are substantial references to what seem now to be standard classical authorities for humanist translations: in his translation of Xenophon's *Oeconomicus* of 1553, he invokes Cicero and Saint Jerome to support a conception of translation and its requisite style different from that of Périon:

> Adde quòd in conuertendis graecis, quia rebus & uerbis aliorum seruiendum est, nec tam liberè fluit oratio, nec locos amoenos tam sequitur, quàm si alueum pronum, dulcesque uoluptates sibi delegisset. Id apertè demonstrat oratio M. Ciceronis qua res Platonis de uniuersitate prosequitur. Quàm fuerit humilis ac demissus in hoc uertendo Xenophontis oeconomico, testatur diuus Hieronymus in praefatione quam scriptam reliquit in Eusebij Cęsariensis chronica: Noster, inquit, Tullius Platonis integros libros ad uerbum interpretatus est: & cùm Aratum iam Romanum hexametris uersibus edidisset, in Xenophontis oeconomico lusit. In quo opere ita saepe aureum illud flumen eloquentię quibusdam scabris & turbulentis obicibus retardatus, ut qui interpretatum nesciunt à

---

13. D'Estrebay, *Aristotelis . . . Politica,* A.ii.ᵛ.

Cicerone, dicta non credant. Difficilè est enim alienas linguas insequentem, non alicubi excidere. Arduum, ut quae in aliena lingua bene dicta sunt, eundem decorum in translatione conseruent. Haec ille.[14]

[Additionally, in translating Greek, since one must be subservient to the thoughts and words of others, one's language does not flow so freely nor does it find itself in such beautiful surroundings as when it can procure for itself a rushing torrent and sweet delights. This is clearly demonstrated by the discourse of Cicero accompanying Plato's "De universitate." How humble and unassuming he was in translating Xenophon's *Oeconomica* is witnessed by Saint Jerome in his preface to Eusebius' *Chronicon:* "Cicero translated the complete works of Plato word for word; and when he had published a Latin translation of Aratus in hexameters, he amused himself with Xenophon's *Oeconomica*. In this work, that golden flow of eloquence is so often impeded by rough obstacles that anyone who does not know that it is a translation by Cicero would not believe it. It is difficult for anyone tackling foreign tongues not to slip up somewhere. It is hard for what is well expressed in a foreign language to preserve the same propriety in translation." This is what Jerome says.]

The major difficulty in translation is for D'Estrebay capturing the *res* and the *verba* to which the translator is bound. To be sure, the impossibility of transferring *verba* with any degree of success or adequacy to the *decorum* of the original is first and foremost a practical difficulty encountered in translation. But it also represents a topos of humanist translation theory, a statement that relativizes the sweeping confidence of Renaissance Ciceronians that Cicero's *verba* can be isolated from their *res* and applied without obstacle in any translative context. The awareness of specificity of context and the problems of re-creating the classical *res* with Renaissance *verba* are defended by reference to Cicero himself, as recorded by Jerome.

D'Estrebay's objections to Périon are thus based on a number of converging fronts: textual criticism, questions of stylistic *decorum,* problems of matching *res* and *verba*. Nonetheless, despite his polemical brushes with Périon, D'Estrebay remains implicit rather than outwardly explicit in his critique. Far more direct and also more probing in his attack was Denys Lambin, a renowned

---

14. *Xenophontis philosophi et historici clarissimi Opera, quae quidem Gręcè extant, omnia, partim iam olim, partim nunc primùm, hominum doctissimorum diligentia, in latinam linguam conuersa* (Basel: Isingrinius, 1553), 239.

editor of classical texts whose connections with Ronsard are well attested.[15] In his 1571 lecture *De utilitate linguae Graecae*,[16] he gives an account of a confrontation between himself and Périon that took place in the early 1550s,[17] when both he and Périon belonged to the circle of the Cardinal de Tournon.[18] Donato Giannotti reported that Périon's Aristotle translation had met with Vettori's disapproval as being "aliquanto longius à verbis Aristotelis, atque adeò ab ipsa mente, ac sententia" (rather too far away from Aristotle's words, and indeed from his intention and meaning).[19] Lambin's charges are more precise. He accuses Périon of confusing the styles of Plato and Aristotle: Plato's style is "grandis, fusus, vber, amplus, elatus, & à poëtica locutione breuissimo distans" (sublime, flowing, copious, abundant, exalted, and only a hairsbreadth away from poetic diction), whereas Aristotle's is "exilis, pressus, contractus, breuis, angustus, humilis, & ad docendum, quàm ad mouendum, aptior" (spare, concise, compact, brief, succinct, low, and more suited to imparting a lesson than moving the heart).[20] Périon has translated Aristotle as though he were Plato. The distinctions that Lambin draws are manifestly related to rhetorical type, as is signaled by the use of "grandis" and "humilis."[21] He does not directly criticize Périon's Ciceronianism, though he does express doubts as to whether Cicero drew on the *Nicomachean Ethics* for the composition of the *De amicitia,* as Périon maintains in his own defense.[22]

---

15. See Silver, *The Formative Influences,* 253–56, quoting Laumonier and De Nolhac on Lambin's role as Ronsard's counselor or tutor in the study of Greek philosophy; Henri Potez' transcription of Lambin's correspondence from MS. Par. Lat. 8647 in "Deux années de la Renaissance (d'après une correspondance inédite)," *Revue d'Histoire Littéraire de la France* 13 (1906): 458–98, 658–92 (495–98 for correspondence with Ronsard); Grafton, *Joseph Scaliger,* 1:75, 80–82; and for a further investigation of this quarrel, John O'Brien, "Translation, Philology, and Polemic in Denys Lambin's 'Nicomachean Ethics' of 1558," *Renaissance Studies* 3, no. 3 (1989): 267–89.
16. *Dionys. Lambini, litterarum Graecarum doctoris, et earundem Latini interpretis regii, De utilitate linguae Graecae, & recta Graecorum Latinè interpretandorum ratione, oratio* (Paris: Bienné, 1572).
17. Lambin, *De utilitate linguae Graecae,* 18: "viginti ferè ab hinc annos." See also Schmitt, *Aristotle,* 77–78, for Lambin's translation of Aristotle's *Nicomachean Ethics.*
18. On which, see Michel François, *Le Cardinal François de Tournon: Homme d'état, diplomate, mécène et humaniste (1489–1562),* Bibliothèque des Ecoles Françaises d'Athènes et de Rome, no. 173 (Paris: De Brocard, 1951).
19. Lambin, *De utilitate linguae Graecae,* 19.
20. Lambin, *De utilitate linguae Graecae,* 20.
21. A little further on, Lambin describes Aristotle's style as "genus orationis subtile, contractum, pressum, & limatum, cuiusmodi genus ad docendum aptissimum est" (*De utilitate linguae Graecae,* 20).
22. Lambin, *De utilitate linguae Graecae,* 21–22.

The quarrel did not end there. In 1558, Lambin produced his own translation of the *Nicomachean Ethics*. He reiterates in its preface his criticism of Périon's version, more fully though in practically the same terms as are set out in the later *De utilitate linguae Graecae*. By contrast with Périon's cultivation of a rigidly Ciceronian approach, Lambin outlines a rationale that combines philology with exegesis:

> Primùm Aristotelis sententiam quàm apertissimè & fidelissimè potui, oratione latina expressi: deinde orationis genere usus sum humili, presso, subtili, tenuiter limato, & ad docendum quàm maxime accommodato: Tùm optima & emendatissima exemplaria non solum typis excusa, uerumetiam manu scripta conquisiui, exploraui, consului: lectionis uarietatem diligenter consideraui, eamque in meis annotationibus eo consilio proposui, ut tu lector erudite de ueritate, & (ut ita dicam) germanitate scripturae iudicares: Postremò multos locos partim ueterum codicum fide ac testimonio fretus, partim coniectura quadam ductus emendaui.[23]

> [First of all, I rendered Aristotle's meaning into Latin prose as clearly and faithfully as I could. Next I used the type of style that is low, compact, precise, lightly polished and best suited to imparting a lesson. Then I sought out, looked for and consulted the finest and most error-free exemplars, both printed editions and indeed even manuscripts. I gave careful thought to variant readings and set them down in my notes, with the intention that you, learned reader, might judge the truth and as it were the authenticity of the reading. Finally, I emended many passages partly by relying on the trustworthiness and witness of ancient manuscripts, partly induced by some conjecture.]

Lambin's Aristotle is a product of his years in Italy, as these criteria demonstrate: textual criticism works concurrently with the translator's enterprise, a typically French reliance on "coniectura" as the remedy for textual *cruces* is juxtaposed with scrupulous attention to manuscript evidence ("ueterum codicum fide"), and Lambin is careful in his editions to give the provenance of the manuscripts he consults. Lambin's commentary similarly bears the marks of the transnational scholarship behind the editorial criteria elaborated firmly

---

23. *Aristotelis De moribus ad Nicomachum libri decem. Nunc primùm è Graeco & Latinè & fideliter, quod vtrunque querebantur omnes praestitisse adnuc neminem, à Dionysio Lambino expressi* (Venice: Valgrisi, 1558), [*6ᵛ]–[*7ᵛ]. A Parisian edition was published in the same year by Jean Foucher.

and succinctly in the preface.[24] Among French scholars, Muret wrote a complementary letter to the reader explaining the necessity of a new translation. He also acted as a textual referee whose opinion Lambin consulted and reports in the course of the controversy. Adrien Turnèbe is also frequently cited. Among Italian scholars, Ludovico Corrado plays the principal role, with Vettori held in reserve as much for disagreement as for agreement.

The evidence of scholarly activity that Lambin plentifully supplies shows an entirely different attitude toward the evolution of the text of Aristotle and hence of translation. Lambin does not work within a formal theoretical exposition of translation. Rather, his view of translation derives from a scrupulous attention to critical method in textual matters: it is an extension—albeit an important extension—of his concern for a better text. Indeed, that Lambin continued to devote the major part of his endeavors to the editing of texts is a clear indication that his interest in translation is not to be divorced from his work as a textual critic. Where Lambin differs from Périon is in his appreciation of a historical text. He has recourse to manuscript authority combined with intuitive divination in order to repair whatever damages the *textus receptus* has undergone. Périon's translation is frozen in a particular historical moment and is thereby effectively ahistorical, since he regards Cicero as capable of utilization in any place or time. Moreover, specifically unlike Cicero himself, Périon pays strict allegiance to words: Périon's refusal to venture outside the circumference of Ciceronian diction is in emphatic distinction to Cicero's own views on the relative status of words and his recommendation that they should be "ad nostram consuetudinem aptis" (adapted to our idiom). For Lambin, the injunction to translate accurately is not enough: he adds the imperative to do in accordance with a certain rhetorical style, the *genus humile*. The focal point is not an author but a style. Lexical restrictions do not operate, lexis being in any case subordinate to textual criticism. As an exercise in its own right, translation has determined stylistic requirements, a principle of *decorum* that Périon has violated. As an offshoot of textual criticism, it becomes an activity in which textual criticism can rightfully have a part. Thus the translator-critic must collate printed and manuscript sources, set down variant readings for his audience's consideration, and finally emend corrupt passages.

In its choice of criteria for the promotion of translation, Lambin's *Aristotle* is not just an updating of Périon's work in the same area. It can also be read as a challenge to Italian scholarship under the leadership of Vettori—a proof that

---

24. In a note to *Nic. Eth.* 2.7.1 (*De moribus*, 306), Lambin names his principal coadjutors and gives evidence to suggest that the preparation of the edition went back at least to 1555.

French scholars are capable of more than unmotivated antirational qualitative leaps characteristic of *divinatio*. Similarly Lambin makes considerable progress in the deployment of Greek sources. Comparisons between Latin and Greek had formed part of Périon's project, in virtue of Cicero's preferences. When he engages in the same process, Lambin undertakes more systematic research and joins together exegesis and textual criticism. In so doing, Lambin and his generation, which reaches its height in the 1560s, move away from the centralization of a Ciceronian model as a stylistic criterion of humanist translation and toward a larger perspective whose dominant motif is the concern with textual criticism. In Lambin, as earlier in Estienne, this concern is vastly stimulated by his stay in Italy. Yet at the same time, this concern is also shaped by an indigenous French tradition of exegesis, as well as by an understanding of the importance of Greek models in the establishment of Latin idiom or topoi. Estienne and Lambin thus parallel and complete the more allusive and succinct version of the same position outlined fragmentarily in Muret's use of Greek sources in his *Variae Lectiones*.

Alongside the Ciceronian position stands the related influence of Quintilian, who had himself exploited and capitalized upon Cicero's support of translation in oratorical training.[25] Like Cicero, Quintilian advocates primarily the translation of poetry, a point that is not lost in subsequent Renaissance vernacular debates over the virtues of translation. His most important pronouncements come in book 10 of the *Institutio oratoria,* where his stated objective is that the prospective orator should gain for himself "copia rerum ac uerborum" (10.1.5). The comprehensive reading program that Quintilian elaborates as a means of gaining such *copia* includes the very opposing speeches of Demosthenes and Aeschines previously translated by Cicero (10.1.22). In the later and crucial section on translation (10.5), Quintilian prefaces his remarks with the explanation "Vertere Graeca in Latinum ueteres nostri oratores optimum iudicabant" (our old orators considered it an excellent thing to translate Greek into Latin)[26] and among the examples he gives are Cicero's translations of Xenophon and Plato. Quintilian, like Cicero before him, finds two sorts of advantage in this exercise. First, the variety of Greek authors will encourage students to make best use of their native language ("hos transferentibus uerbis uti optimis licet: omnibus enim utimur nostris" [in translating them, we may use the best words available, for all we use are our own], 10.5.3). Second, because of the discrepancies between Greek and Latin systems of figuration, translation will stimulate an independent thinking out of rhetorical figures (10.5.3).

---

25. See Norton, "Etienne Dolet," 3–6, and *Ideology and Language,* 192–96.
26. *Inst. or.* 10.5.2.

But Quintilian goes further: under the same category he includes paraphrase, paraphrase of poetry being of particular value to the orator (10.5.4). The degree to which paraphrase is more than just bare interpretation is underscored when Quintilian goes on to warn:

Neque ego paraphrasin esse interpretationem tantum uolo, sed circa eosdem sensus certamen atque aemulationem. (. . .). Nam neque semper est desperandum aliquid illis quae dicta sunt melius posse reperiri, neque adeo ieiunam ac pauperem natura eloquentiam fecit ut una de re bene dici nisi semel non possit.[27]

[I do not want paraphrase to be simply interpretation; it should rival and vie with the original in respect of the same thoughts. (. . .). For it is not out of the question that we may find a better means of expressing what has already been said. Nature did not make eloquence so poor and meager that there is only one perfect expression for any topic.]

Paraphrase here shows its true colors as a variety of imitation[28]—not a subservient medium, but a contentious one. It is a commonplace of translation that in the transfer from one translative space to another, meaning is unavoidably subject to a degree of alteration. A pessimistic account of such textual dealings would view alteration as a distortion of meaning, the impossibility of reproducing the same signifying patterns over time within a dissimilar context. Quintilian's paraphrase is a far more optimistic image of this same transaction: his paraphrase does not reproduce or even re-create meanings but produces rival meanings as a result of the superabundance of nature. The possibilities for expression are not restricted to those proposed by the source text; the young orator has the right, or the duty, to seek out rival versions that improve upon the model. Translation, in at least one of its major forms, involves dialogic rivalry and not dialogic submissiveness. The words of the original are accordingly not hallowed and untouchable, to be carried over into the new context with the minimum damage, and they have only relative importance when compared with the production of new meanings or insights. Thus Quintilian explicates "Cicero's" image of weighing rather than counting words by pushing nonliteral versions to the point at which an exchange between source and host texts becomes an ambitious supplanting of the data of the original by the data of the paraphrase, alien words bearing compatible senses. Quintilian here maximizes

---

27. *Inst. or.* 10.5.5.
28. For a thorough account of these issues, see Arno Reiff, *Interpretatio, imitatio, aemulatio: Begriff und Vorstellung literarischer Abhängigkeit bei den Römern* ([Düsseldorf]: n.p., 1959).

the dichotomy between sense-for-sense and word-for-word translation and outlines a scheme whereby verbal variety and linguistic resourcefulness are encouraged in the production of specific meanings for a specific context. Yet rivalry with the source text requires recognition that the source text is being rivaled with. As a consequence, the paraphrase exists in a curious state of complicity and independence—independent in its capacities for reordering meaning, yet bound by the desirability for change to be acknowledged, for its all-but-parallel existence to be known by derivation from its proposed model.

This interplay of the constructed and the free receives a further impetus during the Renaissance, in the form of Erasmus' *De copia rerum ac verborum* of 1512. Just as Périon was directly to take up Cicero, so Erasmus harks back to Quintilian's directive to achieve "copia rerum ac verborum," both in his title and in the method he advocates. The details of the Erasmian method have attracted considerable attention in recent years and do not need extensive exposition here.[29] The most important consideration for our purposes is that Erasmus enhances the position of translation as a means of increasing the writer's verbal expertise. In the opening chapters of his treatise *De copia*, he pursues the path traced out by Cicero and Quintilian by assertions such as the following:

> Praeterea in enarrandis autoribus, in vertendis ex aliena lingua libris, in scribendo carmine, non parum adiumenti nobis attulerit. Siquidem in iis, nisi erimus his instructi rationibus, saepenumero reperiemur aut perplexi, aut duri, aut muti denique.[30]

> [Besides, describing writers in detail, translating books from a foreign language, writing a poem will be of no small assistance to us. Since, unless we are instructed in these methods, we shall frequently be found bewildered, or uncultured, or in short speechless.]

> Ad haec, vertendis Graecis auctoribus non mediocriter augebimus sermonis copiam, propterea quod haec lingua rerum verborumque ditissima est.[31]

---

29. The impetus was supplied by Robert R. Bolgar, *The Classical Heritage and Its Beneficiaries* (Cambridge: Cambridge University Press, 1954), e.g., 273–75, 297–98, 320 ff., and taken up most particularly by Terence Cave, *The Cornucopian Text: Problems of Writing in the French Renaissance* (Oxford: Clarendon Press, 1979).

30. Desiderius Erasmus, *De copia verborum ac rerum*, ed. Betty I. Knott, vol. 1.6 of *Opera omnia Desiderii Erasmi Roterodami* (Amsterdam and New York: North-Holland, 1988), 34.

31. Erasmus, *De copia*, 34.

[To this end, in translating Greek authors, we shall substantially increase our word power, especially as this language is richest in words and things.]

A further proposal that Erasmus classifies under the general heading of *copia* recalls a feature already seen in Quintilian:

Magnopere iuuabit et illud, si eum locum qui maxime videbitur scatere copia ex auctore quopiam aemulemur, et eum nostro Marte vel aequare vel etiam superare contendamus.[32]

[This will also give very great pleasure, if we copy that passage that most seems to abound in abundance in some author, and if we strive either to equal him by our own exertions or even to surpass him.]

As one critic notes apropos of Erasmus' aesthetic, "we find . . . what might well be called the typical formula of the development of most Renaissance poets."[33] This comment hints at the change in sphere of application that the rhetorical idiom of Cicero and Quintilian has undergone. In all cases, translation is expressly a method of increasing word power prior to the exercise of independent faculties of composition. Translation is a technique not simply for collecting suitable material (a purpose equally well served by a chapbook) but more crucially for the coherent deployment of such material so as to supplant any potentially mechanical device of *amplificatio* by a dynamic of multiplicity. In Erasmus' hands, this dynamic receives considerable enlargement of emphasis. Of great consequence for translation is the thinking out of alternative versions that Erasmus especially encourages, so that any particular thought can be given multiple expression unrestricted by the constraint to find a single adequate linguistic form for each concept.[34] In practical terms, this fosters a high degree of variant, emphasizing lexical mobility and the susceptibility of individual renderings to be supplanted by others.

Erasmus' method both accounts for and exploits the shifts that take place between original and translation. This dynamic model allows such discontinuities and inadequacies to become stimuli to productivity; the emphasis is

---

32. Erasmus, *De copia,* 34.
33. E. Jacobsen, *Translation, a Traditional Craft: An Introductory Sketch with a Study of Marlowe's "Elegies,"* Classica et Medievalia, Dissertationes, no. 6 (Copenhagen: Gyldendal, 1958), 115.
34. For a study of an Erasmian example, see Terence Cave, "Copia and Cornucopia," in *French Renaissance Studies 1540–70: Humanism and the Encyclopedia,* ed. Peter Sharratt (Edinburgh: Edinburgh University Press, 1976), 52–69, especially 55–57.

less on finding the correct expression or the right word than on discovering a number of overlapping possibilities that refract the original without coinciding with it in any direct or straightforward way. The appropriate image to evoke for Erasmus' method would be Quintilian's circling senses rather than a line moving directly between two given points, the source language and the target language. With Erasmus' remodeling of Quintilian's recommendations, translation has a means to combat the fluctuations in sense and idiom between languages without inducing a sense of its own inadequacy. If a translation does fail, this can be ascribed to the translator's lack of *copia,* his failure to discover the compensations to which he may justly have recourse, or to his inability to manipulate the weightings (to use pseudo-Cicero's term) in language or meter that the exercise of translation must involve.

If the devices of Latin rhetoric had already, by Erasmus' time, entered the common pool of poetic resources, Erasmus nevertheless has a distinctive formulation to propose. Although in effect he maintains the theoretical constants of translation as handed down from Quintilian and Cicero and envisages no role for translation not previously envisaged by the Latin rhetorical tradition, the clear merit of his system is that translation finds a home within the overall framework of imitation of the ancients nourished by an active concept of *copia.* Above all, this support for translation as a compositional device for building the writer's *facilitas* and *memoria* ensures its diffusion in the sphere of vernacular poetry among whom he had so unmistakable an influence.

The numerous images proposed by the Latin rhetorical tradition for avoiding plodding literalism constitute a series of resources, well understood by translators even if not always openly acknowledged in vernacular theoretical expositions of translation's role. Where we do find more direct emergence of the intersecting traditions of Cicero and Quintilian is in the simple argument against word-for-word translation. The argument is a topos of French Renaissance translation theory. It occurs in Dolet's *La maniere de bien traduire d'une langue en aultre* of 1540, where literalism is held to be a fault proceeding from "pauvreté et deffault d'esprit."[35] Dolet goes on to say that

---

35. *La maniere de bien traduire,* in Bernard Weinberg, *Critical Prefaces of the French Renaissance,* Northwestern University Studies, Humanities Series, no. 20 (Evanston: Northwestern University Press, 1950), 82. For secondary literature on vernacular translation, see most significantly, Paul H. Larwill, *La théorie de la traduction au début de la Renaissance (d'après les traductions imprimées en France entre 1477 et 1527)* (Munich: Wolf, 1934); Raymond Lebègue, "Les traductions en France pendant la Renaissance," in *Association Guillaume Budé, Actes du Congrès de Strasbourg, 20–22 avril 1938* (Paris: Belles Lettres, 1939), 362–77; Norton, *Ideology and Language,* "Etienne Dolet," and "Translation Theory in Renaissance France: The Poetic

[ung bon traducteur] faira en sorte, que l'intention de l'autheur sera exprimée, gardant curieusement la proprieté de l'une et l'aultre langue.[36]

Dolet acknowledges a "proprieté" in all language that he does not doubt the capacity of translation to convey. For Dolet, the key to success lies in the perfect command that his translator has over both source and target languages. Translation depends first and foremost on the translator's own assimilation of the "proprietés, translations en diction, locutions, subtilités, et vehemences" (p. 81) peculiar to each language. Dolet's ideal translator is instinctively able to adjust source language to target language and enjoys an extraordinary degree of intellectual perception that allows him to penetrate through to the core, the "proprieté," of his chosen languages. Translation for Dolet seizes spirit over letter in an act that corresponds to the internalization of languages. Language has an inner core and an outer shell, in the same way as a human being.

Where this image of internalization and consequently translative competence recurs as a bulwark against literalism, it is subject to greater qualifications. Sebillet's *Art poétique françois* of 1548 includes a eulogy for the translator based on precisely this image of inward conception:

> Et vrayement celuy et son oeuvre meritent grande louenge, qui a peu proprement et naïvement exprimer en son langage, ce qu'un autre avoit mieus escrit au sien, aprés l'avoir bien conceu en son esperit.[37]

Once again, the creative *locus* is the "esperit" of the writer, to which an authentic translation responds by its "propre" and "naïf" expression. But although Sebillet's translator must, like Dolet's, be in perfect control of his medium,[38] these sentences recognize that there are two distinct languages upon

---

Controversy," *Renaissance and Reformation* 11 (1975): 30–44; Monique Nemer, "La traductionau XVIe siècle: Contrôle et transformation du discours," *Cahiers de l'U.E.R. Froissart* 2 (1977):30–44; Isidore Silver, *The Intellectual Evolution of Ronsard*, vol. 2, *Ronsard's General Theory of Poetry* (St. Louis: Washington University Press, 1973), chapter 5, "Creative Imitation and the Renewal of the European Literary Tradition in France," section 3: "Translation and Imitation," 130–40; Luce Guillerm, *Sujet de l'écriture et traduction autour de 1540* (Paris: Aux Amateurs de Livres, 1988); Valerie Worth, *Practising Translation in Renaissance France: The Example of Etienne Dolet* (Oxford: Clarendon Press, 1988); Paul Chavy, *Traducteurs d'autrefois, Moyen Age et Renaissance: Dictionnaire des traducteurs et de la littérature traduite en ancien et moyen français, 842–1600* (Paris: Champion, 1988).

36. *La maniere de bien traduire,* in Weinberg, *Critical Prefaces of the French Renaissance,* 82.

37. Thomas Sebillet, *Art poétique françois,* ed. Félix Gaiffe, revised and updated by Francis Goyet, Société des textes français modernes (Paris: Nizet, 1988), 188.

38. Sebillet, *Art poétique françois,* 189.

which the translator must work. By contrast with Dolet, Sebillet does not envisage the passage from one language into another as a matter of preserving two types of "propriété," that of the source language and that of the target language. Quite the contrary, his attack on word-for-word literalism is accompanied by the injunction to ensure that fidelity to the original is not to the detriment of vernacular expression:

> ... ne jure tant superstitieusement aus mos de ton auteur, que iceus delaissés pour retenir la sentence, tu ne serves de plus prés a la phrase et propriété de ta langue, qu'a la diction de l'estrangére.[39]

The studied balances of Dolet's translator turn into an awareness that two languages may be rival systems of communication; and the target language, so frequently conceived of as a subservient vehicle, has rights that will be violated if its "phrase et propriété" are not respected by the translator. Sebillet's translator is one keenly aware of the potential diminishments and subtractions that one language can impose on another, keenly aware of the gaps between languages—gaps across which Dolet's master translator had traveled with ease.

This perception of the disjunctive, seesaw relationships between languages is accentuated in Sebillet's image of the mirror. Since the author of the original work cannot appear in the translated text, Sebillet says, the translation must be his mirror:

> La dignité toutesfois de l'auteur, et l'enargie de son oraison tant curieusement exprimée, que puis qu'il n'est possible de représenter son mesme visage, autant en montre ton oeuvre, qu'en représenteroit le miroir.[40]

The metaphor of internalization characteristic of Dolet and also occurring in Sebillet is now transferred from inner "esperit" to outer reflection. This new image is an ostensibly innocent one, the perfect reflection of the original work by the translation. But as Terence Cave points out,[41] such flawless replication carries with it its own ambiguities and unresolved problems. The translation stands in for the original. But it is a partial and incomplete simulacrum, not characterized by the plenitude of the original: a mirror is inevitably a selective reflection of what is placed in front of it, as Sebillet's restrictive clause "autant

---

39. Sebillet, *Art poétique françois*, 188–89.
40. Sebillet, *Art poétique françois*, 190.
41. Terence Cave, *The Cornucopian Text*, 57, to which this present discussion is due.

... que" ambiguously underlines. The simulacrum remains just that, never able to encompass and reproduce the totality entrusted to it.

Sebillet's choice of image and emphasis disrupts the stable metaphor of psychological hierarchies expressive of the steady transfer from translator to translation and guarded by the control that the translator exercises over his own and his source language. Earlier, Sebillet himself espouses this image; but the rephrasing of the image allows ambiguities to appear, cracks in the harmonious transfer between different media and from consciousness to execution. The disquiet emerging from Sebillet's images of translative activity is given a greater airing in Peletier du Mans' *Art poëtique* of 1555.[42] Peletier's express advocacy of translation is modified by his awareness that it is being called upon to perform an impossible task. This idea surfaces when Peletier follows Dolet and Sebillet in condemning word-for-word literalism:

Suiuant notré propos, les Traduccions dé mot a mot n'ont pas gracé: non qu'elés soęt contré la loę de la Traduccion: męs seulémant pour ręson qué deus langués ne sont jamęs uniformés en frasés. Les concepcions sont comunés aus antãdémans de tous hommés: męs les moz e manierés dé parler sont particuliers aus nacions.[43]

Dolet's code of practice had taken it for granted that translation was universally feasible, unfettered by local constraints, unimpeded by lexical discriminations that individual languages throw up. While adopting largely the same standpoint, Sebillet had realized that source language and target language cannot be equally promoted: the charge that "diction de l'estrangére" should not take precedence over the "phrase et propriété" of one's own language throws up a discrepancy. Peletier expands on this view: only thought ("concepcions") is universal, whereas its expression is national. There are no rules, as Dolet would wish to maintain, that codify the expression of one language by another. Peletier divides *res* from *verba* in a manner that at one and the same time gives the practice of translation greater liberty and sets greater obstacles in its path. Greater liberty, since translation is now allowed to find its own level of conduct, not held back by its original, but, as in Erasmus' model of generous expansion or Quintilian's image of *aemulatio*, stands alongside rather than under its model, is equal rather than inferior. Greater obstacles, since transla-

---

42. Jacques Peletier du Mans, *Art poëtique*, ed. André Boulanger, Publications de la Faculté des Lettres de l'Université de Strasbourg, no. 53 (Paris: Belles Lettres, 1930). An edition in modern French is provided by Francis Goyet, ed., *Traités de poétique et de rhétorique de la Renaissance* (Paris: Livre de poche, 1990).
43. Peletier du Mans, *Art poëtique*, 109–10.

tion is never entirely possible, always potential, never realized: there is no prevailing metalanguage that will enable the permeability of one language and another. A nation is a unit not identical with any other and thus isolated within its linguistic frontiers. National expressions of meaning and international expressions of meaning do not and cannot coincide. As Peletier wistfully says:

> Puis, pansèz quelé grandeur cé seroęt de voęr uné sécondé Langué repondré a touté l'elegancé de la prémieré: e ancor auoęr la sienné propré.[44]

It is a vision of the perfect congruence and the perfect distinctiveness of target language and source language. Yet as he tellingly concedes, this project "né sé peùt fęré."[45] Foreign and native, Art and Nature remain unbreachable antinomies:

> ... quand a ceux qui totalement se uouent et adõnent a une langue peregrine (i'entens peregrine pour le respect de la domestique), il me semble qu'il ne leur est possible d'atteindre à cette naïue perfection des anciens nõ plus qu'a l'art d'exprimer Nature, quelque ressemblance qu'il i pretende.[46]

By taking one strand of French vernacular theory of translation—the antiliteralism topos—it is possible to see how theoreticians confront problems of transfer from one medium to another. The very notion of transfer is a spatial one, indicating a distance to be traveled, textual spaces to be crossed. The metaphor may nonetheless remain inactive, as in the case of Dolet, for whom translation is susceptible to a high degree of codification that in turn reduces the distance between source and target languages. In Sebillet and Peletier, however, the metaphor is to varying degrees active. Both writers emphasize the difficulties inherent in maintaining the "propriété" of two languages concurrently. In addition, Sebillet's image of the mirror, with its ambiguous associations of selective or even distorted reproduction, and Peletier's concept of linguistic isolation serve to heighten our sense of the pitfalls besetting the translative enterprise. Or at least these are pitfalls of translation viewed as a type of imitation, since for Sebillet and Peletier alike, translation falls automat-

---

44. Peletier du Mans, *Art poëtique*, 111.
45. Peletier du Mans, *Art poëtique*, 111.
46. Peletier du Mans, preface to his translation of Horace's *Ars poetica* (1545 edition), in *Art poëtique*, 228–29.

ically under this heading.[47] It is Peletier who gives greater substance to this argument:

> La plus vṛẹé especé d'Imitacion, c'ẹ̀t dé traduiré: Car imiter n'ẹ̀t autré chosé que vouloẹr fẹré cé qué fẹ̀t un autré: Einsi qué fẹ̀t lẹ Traducteur qui s'assẹruìt non seulémant a l'Inuantion d'autrui, mẹs aussi a la Disposicion.[48]

On this optimistic view, translation is a transparent vehicle capable of displaying ideas ("Inuantion") and their order of appearance ("Disposicion") and so encompassing two major categories of composition. Peletier makes bolder claims still:

> E bien souuant ceus qui sont inuanteurs, sé mẹtét au hazard dé viuré moins qué les Traducteurs: d'autant qu'uné bonné Traduccion vaut trop mieus qu'uné mauuẹsé inuancion. Dauantagé, les Traduccions quand ẹlés sont bien fẹtés, peuuét beaucoup anrichir uné Langué. Car le Traducteur pourra fẹré Françoẹsé une bẹlé locucion Latiné ou Grecqué: e aporter an sa Cite, auẹc le poẹs des santancés, la majeste des clausés e elegancés dé la langué etrangeré.[49]

At the purely microcontextual level of the phrase, translation has the ability to enhance that vernacular, and the favorable image of spatial transfer in "aporter an sa Cite" supports not an umbrella assertion that the "integrité" or "propriété" of the translation is capturable but a modest yet firm confidence that the "majeste des clausés e elegancés dé la langué etrangeré" can be displayed in translated form. If the translator cannot attain the "naïue perfection des anciens" (*ed. cit.*, pp. 228–29), he can at least give some hint of it. Whatever difficulties attend their translation theory, Sebillet still translates Euripides' *Iphigenia* (1549) and Peletier Horace's *Epistula ad Pisones* (1545). Translation relies on the willingness to attempt transfer in the knowledge that it may never be entirely possible.

A coherence of view emerges from these Renaissance theoreticians that is largely at odds with Du Bellay's reflections on the whole subject of imitation.[50]

---

47. Sebillet, *Art poétique françois*, 190: "la version n'est rien qu'une imitation"; Peletier du Mans, *Art poëtique*, 105.
48. Peletier du Mans, *Art poëtique*, 105.
49. Peletier du Mans, *Art poëtique*, 106–7.
50. Joachim du Bellay, *La deffence et illustration de la langue françoyse*, ed. Henri Chamard, Société des textes français modernes (1948; reprint, Paris: Didier, 1970).

His strictures against translation are too widely known to require exhaustive exposition here.[51] Du Bellay's preference for imitation is given most potent expression in the celebrated image of "innutrition" (to use Faguet's term), a metaphor of consubstantiation through which the imitator transforms himself into his model:

> Immitant les meilleurs aucteurs Grecz, se transformant en eux, les devorant, & apres les avoir bien digerez, les convertissant en sang & nouriture, se proposant, chacun selon son naturel & l'argument qu'il vouloit elire, le meilleur aucteur, dont ilz observoint diligemment toutes les plus rares & exquises vertuz, & icelles comme grephes . . . entoint & apliquoint à leur Langue.[52]

While belonging to a recognized subdivision of imitative images,[53] Du Bellay's metaphor can more particularly be viewed as a twofold rewriting of motifs common to the tradition of translation theory. On one hand, as an image of internal adjustment to an alien language, it is not just analogous to but more far-reaching than Dolet's imperative of flawless linguistic command.[54] The perfect reduplication of the past in the present is now made possible by the fact that the contemporary author transforms himself into the living organism of the classical author. Sebillet's image of the reflecting mirror had been a larger form of this idea, operating as an optimistic symbol of perfect coalescence, of translation's power to capture the past or the original. Yet there the resemblance ends. For Du Bellay, translation is no longer viewed as the form of imitation. His strategic splitting of translation from imitation is perhaps the most provocatively famous facet of his work, and it moves directly against the working assumptions of such theoreticians as Sebillet and later Peletier.

But the terms of his attack need to be carefully considered. In 1.5 of *La deffence et illustration,* for instance, Du Bellay warns about the difficulties of

---

51. Among the prolific literature on Du Bellay and the *Deffence,* note particularly Grahame Castor, *Pléiade Poetics: A Study in Sixteenth-Century Terminology and Thought* (Cambridge: Cambridge University Press, 1964), index, s.v. "Du Bellay"; Cave, *The Cornucopian Text,* 60–76; Margaret Ferguson, *Trials of Desire: Renaissance Defenses of Poetry* (New Haven: Yale University Press, 1983), chapter 2, "Joachim du Bellay: The Exile's Defense of His Native Language," 18–53; Greene, *The Light in Troy,* 189–96; Norton, *Ideology and Language,* 290–302, particularly 298.

52. Du Bellay, *La deffence et illustration,* 42–43.

53. Cf. Pigman, "Versions of Imitation in the Renaissance," 5, 7, and especially 8 n. 13 for a large collection of examples of the digestive metaphor for imitation.

54. One notes that immediately prior to this passage (*La deffence et illustration,* 41) Du Bellay condemns translators who do not have perfect knowledge of the original.

translating poetry, especially in the case of rhetorical figures (preservation of which was an express feature of pseudo-Cicero's undertaking as a translator). Translation is not "suffisant" because it cannot render such figures "sans les quelz tout oraison & poëme sont nudz, manques & debiles."[55] He then continues:

> ... je ne croyray jamais qu'on puisse bien apprendre tout cela des traducteurs, pour ce qu'il est impossible de le rendre avecques la mesme grace dont l'autheur en a usé: d'autant que chacune Langue a je ne scay quoy propre seulement à elle, dont si vous efforcez exprimer le naif en une autre Langue, observant la loy de traduyre, qui est n'espacier point hors des limites de l'aucteur, vostre diction sera contrainte, froide, & de mauvaise grace.[56]

And again a little later:

> Celuy donques qui voudra faire oeuvre digne de prix en son vulgaire, laisse ce labeur de traduyre, principalement les poëtes, à ceux qui de chose laborieuse & peu profitable, j'ose dire encor'inutile, voyre pernicieuse à l'acroissement de leur Langue, emportent à bon droict plus de molestie que de gloyre.[57]

Enlarging and refining Chamard's extrapolations about Du Bellay's preferences,[58] Margaret Brady Wells and Glyn Norton[59] have justifiably pointed out that the object of Du Bellay's recriminations is not translation as such but "traduction," word-for-word translation. Du Bellay is reiterating the antiliteralism theme recurrent in vernacular poetry but also fitting the theme into a larger hierarchy that moves through the graded functions of "traducteur," "translateur," "paraphraste," and finally "imitateur."[60] Where the "traducteur" and "traduction" play a restricted role, of use only as pedagogical instruments, the

---

55. Du Bellay, *La deffence et illustration*, 36.
56. Du Bellay, *La deffence et illustration*, 36.
57. Du Bellay, *La deffence et illustration*, 41–42.
58. Du Bellay, *La deffence et illustration*, 60 n. 2, repeated by Robert J. Clements, *Critical Theory and Practice of the Pléiade*, Harvard Studies in Romance Languages, no. 18 (1942; reprint, New York: Octagon Books, 1970), 264.
59. Margaret Brady Wells, "What Did Du Bellay Understand by 'Translation'?" *Forum for Modern Language Studies* 16 (1980): 175–85; Norton, "The Poetic Controversy."
60. For these distinctions, see particularly Wells, "Translation," 176.

"translateur" and the "paraphraste," for Du Bellay as for Quintilian, "may be loosely construed . . . as limited functions of a higher imitative ideal."[61]

In an age when terminology fluctuated and distinctions on the basis of such fluctuating terminology were easily liable to misinterpretation, it is unsurprising that Du Bellay's scheme met with hostility. For one thing, the scheme is itself subject to some conceptual confusion on Du Bellay's part, with the gradations neither carefully marked nor formally expounded.[62] The distinctions will become fully apparent only with the appearance of the less dogmatic *épître-préface* to Du Bellay's 1552 translation of book 4 of the *Aeneid*.[63] Opponents of Du Bellay's scheme could be led to emphasize his terminology variously. A representative of this is Guillaume des Autelz, who, two years after the appearance of *La deffence et illustration*, objected to Du Bellay's disparagement of translation and to his use of "imitation" as a description of the desirable type of poetic exercise:

> En premier lieu ie ne suis pas de l'auis de ceux, qui ne pensent point que le François puisse faire chose digne de l'immortalité de son inuention, sans l'imitation d'autrui: si c'est imiter desrober vn sonnet tout entier d'Arioste, ou de Petrarque, ou vne ode d'Horace, ou ilz n'ont point de proprieté, mais comme miserables emphyteotaires reconnoissent tout tenir auecques redeuance des Seigneurs directz, & ne different en rien des translateurs qu'ilz mesprisent tant, sinon en ce qu'ilz laissent ou changent ce qu'il leur plait: quelque immodeste plus librement diroit ce qu'ilz ne peuuent traduire.[64]

Des Autelz' central point is the charge that an overlap exists in practice between a certain type of imitation cultivated by Du Bellay and the genre of translation that he rejects. But in order to make this point, Des Autelz couples "translateurs" and "traduire" without recognizing the further distinctions that

---

61. Norton, "The Poetic Controversy," 36.

62. For Du Bellay's confusion, cf. Castor, *Pléiade Poetics*, 67–68, and particularly Norton, "The Poetic Controversy," 37, who untangles the threads. Wells, "Translation," 178, gives the crucial difference between "traduire" and "translater."

63. For this, see Wells, "Translation," 179–80.

64. *Replique de Guillaume des Autelz, aux furieuses defenses de Louis Meigret.* . . . (Lyon: De Tournes and Gazeau, 1551), 58–59. On this work, see Margaret M.L. Young, *Guillaume des Autelz: A Study of His Life and Work*, Travaux d'Humanisme et Renaissance, no. 48 (Geneva: Droz, 1961), 79.

they hold for Du Bellay.[65] For Du Bellay, there might indeed be some overlap between the activities of the "translateur" and the imitator; but in that case he could not classify the activity of the former as "traduire."[66]

In addition to its clarification of critical terms, Du Bellay's 1552 translation of Virgil also provides the translator with guidance of a more practical nature. For his work is evidence of exactly that degree of adjustment of target to source language that shows Du Bellay coming to terms with the practice of translation after the tradition of Cicero or Jerome. Such adjustments entail for Du Bellay an art of compensation,[67] a maneuver well recognized in translation and that in itself denies any absolute status to the words of the original: meaning is not automatically deposited in the words but is in some way transcendent to them and (more importantly) can be recovered in the target language. In short, compensation exalts *res* over *verba,* in much the same way that is counseled by Du Bellay's contemporaries when they urge the translator to seize the *sens, sentence,* or *intention* of his chosen source text. Crucially, however, Du Bellay's compensation is the privilege of the "translateur," not the "traducteur,"[68] who has far greater restrictions on his liberty than his counterpart. As an exponent of translation, then, Du Bellay is undoubtedly closer to the practice of his contemporaries than *La deffence et illustration* might give reason to expect. Nonetheless, this attribution of compensation to the task of the "translateur" maintains the distinctions that Du Bellay elaborates in embryonic form in 1549 and that now place the "translateur" closer to the "imitateur."

Starting with a nucleus idea—the search for equivalence between two languages—the responses to and treatments of this issue encounter a fundamental distinction affecting not just translation but all verbal representation. This distinction is formulated most commonly in the classical period as a discrepancy between *verba* and *sententia* or *res.* Their permanent rift discloses itself subsequently and paradoxically in later theories such as those of Sebillet

---

65. For a further contemporary reaction, again reviewing Du Bellay's terminology in a different light, see Sebillet's preface to his 1549 translation of *Iphigenia,* where, alluding to Du Bellay, he mocks "celuy qui se vante d'avoir trouvé ce qu'il ha mot a mot traduit dés autres" (Weinberg, *Critical Prefaces of the French Renaissance,* 143). For the Du Bellay of 1552, invention ("trouvé," cognate with the Latin *invenire*) would no doubt be the partner of "translater," not "traduire."

66. How far Du Bellay was out of line with current terminological assumptions is clear from Wells, "Translation," 176 and n. 5, where it is shown that from 1541 onward "traduction" came to be preferred to "translation" as the standard description of translation.

67. Wells devotes part of her article (181 ff.) to an instance of compensation in Du Bellay's *Virgil.* Compensation (or "restitution") plays a similarly important role in Steiner's theory of translation: *After Babel,* 395 ff.

68. So Wells, "Translation," 179.

and Peletier as a belief in the wholeness of meaning countermanded by statements or metaphors undermining or problematizing that belief. But in response to the problem, a number of preferences are asserted among theoreticians of translation. One group recognizes the loss necessitated in the translative act but combats the deficiency by evolving countering factors described as an act of calculating balances (pseudo-Cicero) or of compensation (Du Bellay). Again, along with classical rhetoricians, Du Bellay and Erasmus view translation as a useful propaedeutic, a cultivatable preliminary to independent discourse, whether poetic or oratorical. Other Renaissance theorists—Sebillet, Peletier, Des Autelz—directly qualify translation as a manifestation of just such an independent discourse, in other words as a manifestation of imitation. Their authority might be Quintilian, for whom translation marshals an argumentative force, competitive with or even adversarial to the poem with which it is paired. In essence, these debates are concentrated on a spatial aspect of translation, in that they concern the passage of translation between surface and surface. Lambin's opposition to Périon has a correspondingly temporal aspect, with diction as the property of a single authority and historical period being contrasted with a view based solely on the *decorum* appropriate to the author in hand. Erasmus prefigures Lambin's position by his anti-Ciceronian belief in a necessary acclimatization or updating of imitative technique: account must be taken of the changes wrought by the downward diachronic transmission of diction. The mutability of words as they are registered with apparent ease upon ostensibly equivalent typographical planes is to be imputed to the uneven emphases they receive according to time and place. Hence the French Renaissance view of translation elicits the two understandings of the term— translation as transfer from one space to another and translation as transmission from one time to another—which are then set either in opposition or in conjunction. The practice of translation is situated at their intersection, which is also their point of harmony or of variance.

2

These questions of temporal and spatial transfer that are at the heart of French humanist and vernacular theories of translation must now be further related to the Anacreontea themselves. It will therefore be necessary to give some account of the type of poetry that the Anacreontea represent.

As Brioso Sánchez and Rosenmeyer have demonstrated,[69] the Anacreontea

---

69. Máximo Brioso Sánchez, *Anacreontea: Un ensayo para su datación* (Salamanca: Cole-

can be divided into chronological blocks, beginning with odes composed in the second century B.C. and stretching through to Byzantine times, a period that saw a surge in Anacreontic composition.[70] West for his part establishes four bands, in which he sees a progressive falling away from Ionic dialect and the strict use of hemiambia and anacreontics to a growth of anaclasis and metrical and linguistic license.[71] Interestingly enough, West remarks that this first group are "carmina satis lepida, neque ita multum ab Hellenistico distantia spiritu" (quite charming poems, not very far removed from the Hellenistic spirit).[72] In so doing, West identifies what may be termed Alexandrianism in the Anacreontea.[73] In using this term, it needs to be firmly emphasized that it is not a statement about the dating of the poems. It is in the first instance a statement about the perception of what Anacreon's odes were or meant. Anacreon was, of course, a member of the canon of nine lyric poets established by the Alexandrians;[74] and in the light of Alexandrian interest in predecessors, Bergk held that imitations of the Anacreontic manner were only to be expected:

Es ist nich unwahrscheinlich, dass man schon in der alexandrinischen Zeit solche Anakreontische Lieder dichtete, lebt doch diese Periode vorzugsweise von der Nachahmung der Alten; so gut wie Theokrit Knabenlieder im Stile des Alkäus verfasste, so gut konnten andere an den Sänger von Teos sich anlehnen; jedoch die Lieder in Anakreontische Manier, welche wir besitzen, reichen nicht so hoch hinauf, sie gehören erst der römischen Zeit an.[75]

---

gio Trilingue de la Universidad, 1970); Rosenmeyer, *The Poetics of Imitation*, 123–25. A review of the different attempts to date the Anacreontea is provided by Campbell, *Greek Lyric*, 2:10–18, notably 16–18.

70. See Theodor Nissen, *Die byzantinischen Anakreonteen*, Sitzungsberichte der Bayerischen Akademie der Wissenschaften, philosophisch-historische Abteilung, no. 3 (Munich: Verlag der Bayerischen Akademie der Wissenshaften and Beck), 1940.

71. West, *Carmina Anacreontea*, xvi–xviii. On the meter of the Anacreontea, see West, *Carmina Anacreontea*, xiv–xvi, and *Greek Metre* (Oxford: Clarendon Press, 1982), 166–69; Edmonds, *Elegy and Iambus*, 2:6–17; Campbell, *Greek Lyric*, 2:7–10; Johann Sitzler, "Zu den Anakreonteen," *Wochenschrift für klassische Philologie* 1913: cols. 853–58.

72. West, *Carmina Anacreontea*, xvi.

73. For a discussion of the term "Alexandrian" and the related concept "Hellenistic," see most succinctly Rudolf Pfeiffer, "The Future of Studies in the Field of Hellenistic Poetry," *Journal of Hellenic Studies* 75 (1955): 70.

74. See, e.g., Rudolf Pfeiffer, *History of Classical Scholarship from the Beginnings to the End of the Hellenistic Age* (Oxford: Clarendon Press, 1968), 205.

75. Theodor Bergk, *Griechische Literaturgeschichte*, 2 vols. (Berlin: Weidmann, 1883), 2:347–48.

At a more "personal" level, Sitzler emphasizes that the carefree hedonism of the Anacreontea was, indeed, associated with the character of the poet Anacreon proper:

> Der allgemeine Charakter der Anacreontea erinnert eher an die alexandrinische Zeit und noch spätere Perioden der griechischen Litteratur als an die lebensfrische Poesie Anakreons, die Liebe und heiteren Lebensgenuß atmete und ihre Figuren keck aus dem Leben herausgriff, während die Verfasser der Anacreontea ihre dichterische Begeisterung künstlich erregen.[76]

In addition to this confusion of authorial *persona* and a poet's character, one also notes that the Anacreontic odes were generically analogous to epigram in their short length, their lyrical nature, and their treatment of love motifs:

> En lisant les épigrammes alexandrines, on est tout d'abord frappé du nombre des épigrammes érotiques. [. . .] l'amour est, dans la littérature alexandrine, le lien commun de tous les genres poétiques depuis les épopées jusqu'aux épigrammes, devenues des espèces de pièces lyriques analogues aux odes d'Anacréon.[77]

The parallels evoked here also recur, revealingly enough, in Estienne's commentary, which may be taken as symptomatic of French Renaissance reactions to the Anacreontea. For the simple fact is that the parallels most central to the arguments he advances about pseudo-Anacreontic literary usage are drawn from Alexandrian authors (largely from the Greek Anthology) and from Latin writers with known Alexandrian influence, such as Ovid and Tibullus.[78] The noticeable absence in Estienne's commentary is that of the Greek lyric poets—there is comparatively little substantive reference to Pin-

---

76. Jakob Sitzler, *Anthologie aus den Lyrikern der Griechen*, vol. 2, *Die melischen und chorischen Dichter* (Leipzig: Teubner, 1898), 38.

77. Auguste Couat, *La poésie alexandrine sous les trois premiers Ptolémées (342–222 av. J.-C.)* (Paris: Hachette, 1882), 173. Pfeiffer, "The Future of Studies in the Field of Hellenistic Poetry," 73, labels Hellenistic epigrams "the lyric poetry of the time." Parallels between the Anacreontea and the epigrams of the Anthology are expressly noted by F.G. Welcker, "Anacreon," review of *Anacreontis carminum reliquiae*, by T. Bergk, *Rheinisches Museum für Philologie* 3 (1835): 302–3.

78. Among the exhaustive literature on the subject of the Alexandrian heritage in Rome, one may note the following: Wendel V. Clausen, "Callimachus and Roman Poetry," *Greek, Roman, and Byzantine Studies* 5 (1964): 181–96, and "Catullus and Callimachus," *Harvard Studies in Classical Philology* 74 (1970): 85–94; James E.G. Zetzel, "Re-creating the Canon: Augustan Poetry and the Alexandrian Past," *Critical Inquiry* 10, no. 1 (1983): 83–105; G.O. Hutchinson, *Hellenistic Poetry* (Oxford: Clarendon Press, 1988), 277–354, with bibliography on 360–61.

dar, Sappho, or Alcaeus.[79] To ascribe (restrictively) such parallels and echoes simply to the limitations of Estienne's comparative reading at the time is to miss the point. If his comments on θέλω θέλω μανῆναι (I want, I want to go mad) had, as it were, implied a vertical relationship between subtexts and surface texts, this accumulation of instances can by the same token be dispersed along a horizontal spectrum, so that "Anacreon" is made to react to a succession of texts, all purportedly representing his literary legacy. No historical deductions are made on the basis of the philological investigation to which the poet is subjected: there is never any suspicion on Estienne's part, at this stage, that the absence of true lyric parallels betokens larger problems for the authenticity of the text. Exegesis outweighs philological inquiry. *Imitatio,* at such points, is of greater intrinsic importance than *recensio.*

The *editio princeps* of pseudo-Anacreon contains numerous examples of Estienne's preference for explanations based on *imitatio* rather than *recensio.* The following instance is drawn from ode 22 (1554.70; Greek text: 1554.18–19) *ad* Ἐγὼ δ' ἔσοπτρον εἴην (would I were a mirror):

Extat epigramma Διονυσίου σοφιστοῦ [*A.P.* 5.83], in quo ludit eodem fere modo quo hic. initium eius est hoc,

Εἴθ' ἄνεμος γενόμην, σὺ δέ γε στείχουσα παρ' αὐγὰς
Στήθεα γυμνώσαις, καί με πνέοντα λάβοις.
Εἴθε ῥόδον γενόμην ὑποπόρφυρον, ὄφρα.&c. Sic apud Theocritum [*Id.* 3.12 f] vouet quidam pastor—εἴθε γενοίμαν Ἁ βομβεῦσα μέλισσα, καί ἐς τεὸν ἄντρον ἱκοίμαν. Sic in quodam Scholio [1554.58], Εἴθε λύρα καλὴ γενοίμην ἐλεφαντίνη, Καί με καλοὶ παῖδες φοροῖεν διονύσιον ἐς χορόν. Εἴθ' ἄπυρον καλὸν,&c.[80] Ouidius mittens anulum ad amicam, tandem ait [*Amores* 2.15.9–11],

O vtinam subito fieri mea munera possem,
    Artibus AEaeij, Carpathiique senis.
Tunc ego te cupiam dominae tetigisse papillas. &c.

[There is an epigram of Dionysius the Sophist in which he plays in almost the same way. Its opening is as follows: "Would that I might

---

79. The sole exception to this statement is Estienne's exposé on ode 31. Even here the instances relate more properly to Horace than to "Anacreon."

80. For a discussion of these passages and their relationship to Anacreon, see Richard Reitzenstein, *Epigramm und Skolion: Ein Beitrag zur Geschichte der alexandrinischen Dichtung* (Giessen: Ricker, 1893), 93 and n. 2.

become the wind and that you, walking in the sunlight, would bare your breast and receive my breath. Would that I might become a crimson rose, so that" etc. A shepherd in Theocritus makes the following wish: "Would that I might become the buzzing bee and come into your cave." So too in a drinking song: "Would that I might become a beautiful ivory lyre and the beautiful boys carried me to the dance of Dionysus." Ovid sending a ring to his girlfriend ends by saying: "Would that I could become my own gifts to you, by the magic of Circe or Proteus. Then I would wish you to touch my mistress' breasts."]

Here, as frequently, the exposition follows chronological order and the movement of imitation—in this case the imitation of a topos—is traced with close attention to the evidence. Examples of this kind underline the extent to which *divinatio* and the feeling for exegesis supplant strict textual reporting: textual concerns are shown to form part of an overall picture with an emphasis on exegesis dominated by a concern for *imitatio*. Particularly significant from this point of view are the occasions on which Estienne inserts translation into the imitative sphere. Ode 28 displays this process:[81]

Περὶ λυγδίνῳ τραχήλῳ. Verti, colla laeuia, secutus hos versus, ex lib. 7. Graec. Epigrammatum [= *A.P.* 5.28],—ὅτε σοῦ τὸ πρόσωπον ἀπῆλθε Κεῖνο τὸ τῆς λύγδου βάσκανε λειότερον. Quo in libro etiam hoc carmen habes [= *A.P.* 5.48], Δειρὴ λυγδινέη καὶ στήθεα μαρμαίροντα.

["Around the neck of white marble." I have translated this, "smooth neck," following these lines from book 7 of the Greek Anthology: "When your looks had faded, your looks smoother than marble, you witch." In the same book you have this poem: "Neck of white marble and dazzling breasts."]

Here the Greek model is paramount. Its value, once again, lies not in deductions about dating to which it might have led but in its role as evidence of the imitative process active in Alexandrian writers. Thus the conclusions of twentieth-century scholarship about Alexandrian rewriting of distant predecessors are already anticipated in Estienne, though without formal conclusions.

---

81. Commentary: 1554.73; Greek text: 1554.24.

The same remarks would, of course, also cover Latin writers. Estienne's commentary on ode 11 is a particularly rich instance of intertextual activity.[82] It begins with a recognition that the ode has a sibling in an epigram by Palladas (*A.P.* 11.54); but his special comments are reserved for the Anacreontic phrase τὰ τερπνὰ παίζειν in the poem's penultimate line:

Quod dixit Anacreon τὰ τερπνὰ παίζειν, latius à Pallada explicatum est, sed ita tamen vt vim verborum non expresserit. Horatius eodem ferè modo dixit [*Carm.* 3.12.1], Amori dare ludum. Ouidius hoc vocat [e.g., *A.A.* 2.389] Ludere. Ego verti, Vacare amoribus iocísque, secutus quendam ipsius Horatij versum [*Ep.* 1.6.65], quem ex Mimnermo transtulit [frag. 1 West].

[When Anacreon said "to play games," this was more broadly explained by Palladas, yet in such a way that he has not expressed the force of the words. In much the same way Horace said "to play the game of love." Ovid calls this "to play." I have translated the expression as "to have time for fun and games," following a line of the selfsame Horace, which he took over from Mimnermus.]

This is intertextual activity at its most intense and it operates at a number of levels. Palladas, Horace, and Ovid are all implicitly taken to be imitators; and Palladas' failure is a failure to encapsulate *verba* as well as *res*. The Horatian model is preferred; and its importance lies not only in the happy similarity of its phraseology to that of "Anacreon" ("eodem ferè modo") but in its determining role in Estienne's own translation: the translator here is engaged in the same enterprise as the poet, and the identity of this enterprise is highlighted by attributing the phrase to Mimnermus. The twists and turns of the argument— from "Anacreon" to epigrammatist to Latin elegist and then to Latin lyric poet and Greek elegist—underline the overlapping, ambiguous nature of the disciplines involved. What distinction exists between "verti" and "transtulit"? Nothing indicates the subserviency of translation, which is deeply implicated in the same mimetic process as imitation; nothing evokes more suggestively the complex interdependency of imitation and translation. Estienne grasps the principles linking the two domains and organizes his thought around the contrast between Palladas' amplification, which misses the "vim verborum," and the approved imitators, who reach their target by recourse to another source (Mimnermus in the case of Horace and Estienne himself). The Latin imitators

---

82. Commentary: 1554.68; Greek text: 1554.12.

are all preferred because of their capacity to handle *allusio:* as Estienne will stipulate in his lengthy reflection on Horace, their *allusio* is sufficiently transformed to hold the status of true *renovatio*. And so "amori dare ludum," "ludere," and "vacare amoribus iocísque" have recognizable similarities and subtle modifications. They repeat, and do not repeat, their given model and each other.

Thus, paradoxically enough, even though the Anacreontea were held by the Renaissance to be the product of a more distant historical period, the thematic instances that Estienne draws show that the poems could be read in the light of Alexandrian ideals and Alexandrian literary products. Several reasons may account for this antihistorical intuition, which is not necessarily exceptional in Estienne as it may at first glance appear; it is not enough to identify Estienne as unrepresentative of broader cultural awareness. In particular, the Greek Anthology was widely known and intensively imitated, as James Hutton showed long ago.[83] The link with the Anthology occurs, first, since two Anacreontic poems (odes 15 and 17) are preserved in the Anthology as *A.P.* 11.47 and 48 and, second, since epigrams attributed to Anacreon are printed in Estienne's ἀποσπασμάτια.[84] From that standpoint, Estienne's analogies with epigram read as the product of empirical observation. What distinguishes Estienne is not his analogies as such but the fact that he abstracts from the analogies a potentially totalizing paradigm that will account for the imitative status of allusion. More generally still, the role of the Latin heirs of Alexandrian poetry, and notably Catullus, is equally decisive for the Renaissance view of "Anacreon." Many Catullan poems are epigrams or epigrammatic in character; in general, his poetry shows a preference for short pieces on the Alexandrian model, of a sort that would provide a sense of familiarity to the reader of Anacreontic poetry, even where Catullus himself is not directly evoked. Catullus' historical reception plays an additionally weighty role.[85] Such Italian or Italian-based exponents as Pontano and Marullo initiate the trend to which Secundus' *Basia* add a decisive contribution, since their exploitation of a theme drawn from Catullus 5 could easily be seen to harmonize with certain

---

83. In his two books *The Greek Anthology in France,* and its earlier companion, *The Greek Anthology in Italy to the Year 1800,* Cornell Studies in English, no. 23 (Ithaca: Cornell University Press), 1935.

84. 1554.59–60. Both epigrams are held to be spurious by Denys L. Page, ed., *Further Greek Epigrams* (Cambridge: Cambridge University Press, 1981), 124.

85. See Gaisser, *Catullus and His Renaissance Readers,* and Mary Morrison, "Catullus in the Neo-Latin Poetry of France before 1550," *Bibliothèque d'Humanisme et Renaissance* 17 (1955): 365–94, especially 393 for the conclusion that "sustained imitations, or adaptations of whole poems are rare," whereas "the influence of his style is very great."

erotic themes in the Anacreontea. Finally, given the Alexandrian or Alexandrian-inspired concentration on imitations of predecessors, the existence of comparable Hellenistic material would confirm an imitative principle, rather than point to a flaw in the Renaissance historical perception of "Anacreon's" identity.

A first definition of the Anacreontea as "Alexandrian," then, appeals to their historical mode of reception in the Renaissance as represented here by Estienne. Yet such "Alexandrianism" is not always directly perceived as in Estienne but is frequently mediated through those Latin authors who were the heirs of the Alexandrian poets—so Catullus, Propertius, Tibullus, Ovid. Quite apart from his appreciation of Greek and Roman Alexandrianism in general, Estienne's treatment of such Alexandrianism is of particular interest since he is able to go one step further and fit his own translation into this diachronic imitative scheme. His Neo-Latin translation can thus demonstrate the same compositional devices that classical Latin poetry understood and developed. Foremost among such devices, as Estienne's discussion of ode 31 made clear, is *allusio*. Awareness of *allusio* is fully present in what Estienne has to say about the possibility of referring "honestè furari" to translation as well as to imitation. This possibility is now confirmed and translation is allotted an active role in the use of *allusio*.

As Estienne appreciates, *allusio* is a central feature of Latin Alexandrianism in respect of their Greek predecessors. In Alexandrian poetry proper, the principle is no less central. Herter dealt with Callimachus' Homeric allusions in an essay that remains the best methodological introduction to this feature of Alexandrian writing; Giangrande, developing Pasquali's term, dubs Alexandrian literature as a whole an *arte allusiva* and has studied its effect over a range of Hellenistic genres.[86] Yet, most characteristically, *allusio* does not appear directly in Alexandrian poetry. As Giangrande emphasizes elsewhere, "imitation was compulsorily accompanied by variation in Alexandrian poetry."[87] *Allusio* as an integral part of *imitatio* is coupled with *variatio,* in a way that would incidentally also define Estienne's view of allusive "honestè furari":

---

86. Hans Herter, *Kallimachos und Homer: Ein Beitrag zur Interpretation des Hymnos auf Artemis,* in *Kleine Schriften,* ed. E. Vogt (Munich: Fink, 1975), 371–416; Giuseppe Giangrande, "*Arte Allusiva* and Alexandrian Epic Poetry," *Classical Quarterly,* n.s., 17 (1967): 85–97, and "Gli epigrammi alessandrini come arte allusiva," *Quaderni Urbinati di Cultura Classica* 15 (1973): 7–31. For Pasquali, see the reference in Giangrande, "*Arte Allusiva,*" 85 n. 1.

87. Giangrande, review of *Recherches sur le poème Mégara,* by T. Breitenstein, *Classical Review,* n.s., 18 (1968): 164. *Variatio,* in the present study, will thus be understood as the partner of *allusio* and the reverse of *repetitio.* It is not used to signify merely "variety" (ποικιλία), which nonetheless is a rightful goal of translation, for it is a species of *copia.*

allusio signals that imitation is taking place, *variatio* that it is a question not of simple quotation but of rewriting—a question of transposition rather than just transfer. In the Greek Anthology (to name a genre perceived as akin to the Anacreontea), Walther Ludwig finds the justification for *variatio* in a display of learning:

> Das dritte ausschlaggebende Motiv für die Variationsfreudigkeit der hellenistischen Epigrammatiker aber dürfte in der zu dieser Zeit allgemein herrschenden Kunstauffassung zu suchen sein, im poeta doctus-Ideal, im anspielungsreichen Dichten für literarische Kenner.[88]

Ludwig proceeds to instance several works by Hellenistic poets that can be seen to perform reciprocal variations:

> Ebenso wie Kallimachos ein Vergnügen daran hatte, in Arats Phainomena die hesiodischen Züge und die Nachklänge der homerischen Sprache zu entdecken, oder wie er selbst in seinen Iamben als Hipponax redivivus aufzutreten liebte, so konnte auch Asklepiades von Fall zu Fall an berühmte Muster erotischer und sympotischer dichtung, z.B. Alkaios, Sappho, Ibykos oder Pindar, anknüpfen; und ebenso wie Apollonios mit Theokrit in der Gestaltung der Hylassage konkurrierte, konnte der Archeget des erotischen Epigramms seinerseits von seinen Freunden und Nachfolgern imitiert und variiert werden.[89]

Ludwig couples three elements of particular interest and importance: "imitiert," "variiert," and the earlier "konkurrierte." *Variatio,* in other words, is a particular technique stimulated by the general principle of *imitatio* and extending as far as *aemulatio*. By this scheme, the model not only will be rewritten but will subsist exclusively in its rewritten form, which has autonomous validity. The extreme point of this principle is reached when the model has vanished or is dispersed throughout a number of tributary poems that substitute for the original. The dispersal is without any possibility of reintegration; what hence-

---

88. Walther Ludwig, "Die Kunst der Variation im hellenistischen Liebesepigramm," in *L'épigramme grecque,* Entretiens sur l'Antiquité classique, no. 14 (Vandoeuvres-Geneva: Fondation Hardt, 1968), 302. See also Sonya L. Tarán, *The Art of Variation in the Hellenistic Epigram,* Columbia Studies in the Classical Tradition, no. 9 (Leiden: Brill, 1979); and on epigram and symposium, see Giangrande's collection of material in "Sympotic Literature and Epigram," also in *L'épigramme grecque,* 93–177.

89. Ludwig, "Die Kunst der Variation," 302.

forth claims fundamental attention is the imitative copy, now in fact a new poem that strives to emulate its predecessor.

Now this holds implications for the status of translation. For *variatio* is not merely a device contained within the sphere of imitation. If the way back from complex variation to original is blocked by the degree of transmutation that the original undergoes, then the observed distinctions between original and translation, between "primary" and "secondary," can likewise be thrown out of alignment by the systematic mimicking of devices of the "primary" text by the "secondary." Translative mimesis under the stimulus of *variatio* displaces the original. In that it involves a constant realignment to what Greene conveniently terms the *mundus significans,* the signifying potentialities particular to any culture,[90] translation cannot simply be a *repetitio* of the source text. Speaking in respect of the novel, Peter Brooks offers remarks with pertinence for this issue in translation:

> Is repetition sameness or difference? To repeat evidently implies resemblance, yet can we speak of resemblance unless there is a difference? Without difference, repetition would be identity, which would not usually appear to be the case, if only because the chronological context of the repeated occurrence differs from that of the "original" occurrence (the "original" is thus a concept that puts repetition into question). In this sense, repetition always includes the idea of variation in time, and may ever be potentially a progressive act.[91]

Brooks's reflection is crucial in its acknowledgment of the temporal modifications of a spatial activity and the resulting reevaluation to the principles of "identity," "resemblance," and "repetition." If "repetition in the text" (in this case, the Anacreontic text) is to fulfill itself as "a return, a calling back" of the Greek author,[92] there can be no simple *translatio studii,* no *repetitio* without corresponding reactivation. Saussure wrote of the production of meaning out of the differential relations existing between the individual component elements of language *(parole)* and not intelligible outside the total linguistic

---

90. Greene, *The Light in Troy,* 20: ". . . *mundus significans,* a signifying universe, which is to say a rhetorical and symbolic vocabulary, a storehouse of signifying capacities potentially available to each member of a given culture."

91. Peter Brooks, *Reading for the Plot: Design and Intention in Narrative* (Oxford: Clarendon Press, 1984), 124.

92. The quoted terminology is from Brooks, *Reading for the Plot,* 125.

system that is language *(langue)*.⁹³ As theoretical accounts of the translative text, *allusio* and *variatio* are, in an extended sense, instances of just such differential relations. *Allusio* relies upon the reader's powers of perception in order to establish the dialogue with a text's antecedents upon which Renaissance translation, and not just Anacreontic tradition, will rely. But without *variatio, allusio* cannot activate that renovation that is Greene's *mundus significans* and Erasmus' desirable acclimatization. At the same time, *variatio* depends upon *allusio* for the degree of deviation from the original phraseology to be measurable. Neither term can easily be attributed prior status when one is evaluating their role in translation; *allusio* occurs just as frequently in varied guise as it does in its own right.

More radically, Derrida speaks of "espacement," the displacement of a text through space that prevents this text from ever being entirely identical with itself.⁹⁴ In this sense, *repetitio* and *variatio* play out Derrida's perception. For the awareness that the text must differ from itself is an imitative as well as a historical necessity that, in its most acute form, aggravates the successor's sense of his own shortfall in achievement. As a means of combating such a shortfall, the successor attempts to turn the fractured loss of identity into a virtue by insisting upon *variatio* as an intrinsic component of successful writing. Shifted meanings, displaced senses, the constant shading of the text are evidence not of failure but of a recreative, manipulative facility for which Horace could in some sense be construed as Estienne's symbol. *Allusio* can then be understood as the attempt to maintain continuity with the past, despite the refraction imposed by time. Through *allusio,* the predecessor's presence as voice in the successor's text need no longer be perceived as demonstrating by contrast the paucity of the successor's response but rather as a stimulus to a continual rewriting that constitutes a dialogic relationship with the subtext in that the terms of the relationship between subtext and surface text are never fixed in one mode. Thus while *allusio* enjoins awareness of the diachronic imitative thread linking all writing (and supremely exemplified by Estienne from the work of Horace), *variatio* makes allowance for the passage of time.

---

93. Ferdinand de Saussure, *Cours de linguistique générale* (1915; reprint, Paris: Payot, 1972), 36–39.

94. See "La différance," in *Tel Quel: Théorie d'ensemble (choix),* Points (Paris: Seuil, 1968), 48, 50, 59, and passim. For Derrida's own interest in translation itself, see the "Table ronde sur la traduction," in *L'oreille de l'autre: Otobiographies, transferts, traductions,* Textes et débats avec Jacques Derrida, ed. Claude Lévesque and Christie V. McDonald (Montreal: VLB, 1982), 125–212, and "Des tours de Babel," in *Difference in Translation,* ed. Joseph F. Graham (Ithaca and London: Cornell University Press, 1985), 209–48.

Two additional techniques are also possible. First, if *allusio* is to multiple subtexts rather than to a single model, the result is known as *contaminatio*, a feature by no means confined to Alexandrian poetry but exemplified within it.[95] *Contaminatio* is accordingly a Renaissance version of polyvocality exploited either as a controlled semiosis susceptible to systematic elucidation or as a sportive play of texts and allusions that do not willingly settle into a single set of clearly defined readings. More frequently than an uncoordinated series of random evocations, however, *contaminatio* defines a broad level of response, which in the sphere of translation becomes an approximate rather than an equivalent lexicon. Second, on occasion this dialogue involves the refining of the reader's perceptual apparatus to the point at which *allusio* is so severely diminished as to reconstitute the text/subtext relationship in terms of *aemulatio*. At this point, the *variatio* is so strong, the displacement so marked, that it becomes impossible to acknowledge subtexts in anything more than a general sense, which compels the recognition on our part that the etiological link between text and subtext works more to the advantage of the surface text than had previously been allowed.

A further definition of Alexandrianism would refer, therefore, to a discernible body of literary techniques employed in Hellenistic times but also applicable, it may be argued, to the Renaissance reaction to the Anacreontea. It is Estienne's commentary that provides initial and powerful support for this view, especially in the parallels it draws or perceives with the prominent Alexandrian genre of epigram. Such techniques are in the first instance the privilege of Neo-Latin literary culture, where *allusio* can easily be activated through the historical resonances of words, their previous use in defined and recollectable literary contexts. As with the pronouncements of Renaissance theoreticians on the subject of translation considered above, such criteria as *allusio, variatio,* and *contaminatio* imply a spatiotemporal dialogue with literary forerunners. These criteria also have affinities with current theories of historical belatedness. Thomas Greene's reading of Renaissance intertextuality is characteristic of this latter approach: "In the literature of the Renaissance, intertextuality has to be analyzed as an interplay between stabilizing etiologies and a destabilizing

---

95. Francis Cairns, *Tibullus: A Hellenistic Poet at Rome* (Cambridge: Cambridge University Press, 1979), 42: "*contaminatio* is a characteristic Hellenistic and post-Hellenistic literary technique." For further investigation of the phenomenon, see Wilhelm Kroll, *Studien zum Verständnis der römischen Literatur,* chapter 9, "Die Kreuzung der Gattungen," 202–24; and Philippe-Ernest Legrand, *Etude sur Théocrite,* Bibliothèque des Ecoles Françaises d'Athènes et de Rome, no. 79 (Paris: Fontemoing, 1898), chapter 5, section 2: "Le caractère livresque du recueil: La confusion des genres," 413–36.

perception of disjuncture."[96] Greene follows Garin in arguing persuasively for a Renaissance sense of anachronism, of its own painful separation from an admired classical past.[97] It could be said that the concepts of *allusio* and *variatio* revolve around the same dilemma, which is embodied most forcefully in the Ciceronian debate. For the Ciceronians, *allusio* is synecdochic in the most automatic of senses, and *variatio* is an impossibility since it opens the revered predecessor's idiom to an unacceptable degree of manipulation. The Ciceronians purchase historical continuity at the expense of imitative diversity; they establish an imitative priority, an unshakable *auctoritas* in place of imitative polyvocality. But in Estienne's conception, *variatio*—the necessary difference between the predecessor and the successor—allows for the passage of time in ways that do not deny the vitality of the original model; *variatio* is not destructive (as Ciceronians might contend) but productive of *renovatio*, that renewal of classical texts that is an opening up of new perspectives.

In many of his observations on "Anacreon," Estienne seeks to bring out the underlying rhetorical principles that allow the opening up of an etiological passage, allow continuity to be visibly established. The gulf between past and present is obviated by discerning lines of concord not only between authors of distinctly different historical periods but also between translation and imitation as exercises: these various areas are all linked by the shared techniques of *allusio* and *variatio*. Imitative sequences are traced diachronically, in the form of unofficial literary histories; resemblances and disparities are recorded and accounted for. Concurrently, Estienne also elides or submerges possible distinctions between imitation and translation. It is often superfluous to ask what distinctions are or might be, because he is not interested in answering this question. His terms of reference are quite different. He forgets or collapses old distinctions, while emphasizing points of convergence, the places at which translation most resembles imitation. So the commentary to ode 11 does not distinguish between "ego verti" and "Horatius transtulit"; this affinity is further strengthened by setting Horace in the same allusive relation to Mimnermus as Estienne to Horace. The gap between past and present is acknowledged, but exploited as a stimulus to *renovatio* rather than as a lament on irretrievability. Estienne marshals the resources that will allow the gap to be bridged, multi-

---

96. Greene, *The Light in Troy*, 30.
97. A neat short account of this position is U. Peter Burke, *The Renaissance Sense of the Past*, Documents of Modern History (London: Arnold, 1969). A specific case study with reasoned bibliography appended is to be found in G.W. Pigman, "Imitation and the Renaissance Sense of the Past: The Reception of Erasmus's *Ciceronianus,*" *Journal of Medieval and Renaissance Studies* 9, no. 2 (1979): 155–77 (bibliography: 156 n. 4).

plies the means of reception, the methods of assimilation by taking as representative of these means and methods the *allusio-variatio* dyad, operative within the general principles of *imitatio,* itself covering the spheres of translation and imitation.

Estienne can be taken as a prime representative of the mission upon which all the translators of the Anacreontea in the years 1554–56 are engaged. *Allusio, repetitio, variatio,* and *contaminatio* constitute a historically derived scheme underscoring the sympathies of contemporary Renaissance writers with literary devices discernible in Alexandrian literature. To say which is to place Renaissance translators in touch with an appreciable intellectual tradition but not to assume that the problems of translation can be solved by mechanical application of a theoretical scheme, or to assume that such a scheme has identical manifestation in each of its exponents. The devices themselves will vary substantially between Neo-Latin and the vernacular. *Contaminatio,* for example, a standard resource of Neo-Latin translation or imitation indifferently, is more easily established in vernacular imitation than in vernacular translation, though both Ronsard and Belleau will provide ingenious evidence of the attempt to construct a "contaminated" poetic form. More fundamentally still, an analogous distinction exists as to what counts as *allusio*. The weight of historical use behind the inherited Neo-Latin vocabulary builds an echoic density that allows, if required, precision of reference to the constitutive subtexts of the Neo-Latin translation. Indeed, constitutive subtexts may, at their least percussive, simply be a "contaminated" deployment of verbal forms without more specific references. In other words, the subtextual readings that Neo-Latin can command may, in Gisèle Mathieu-Castellani's language, be synecdochic or elliptical. In the first case, the subtext is the part standing for the whole, "le fragment résiduel d'un discours étranger, convoqué par bribes, renvoyant à l'ensemble où il prend sens."[98] In the second, "l'allusion est en rapport avec un non-dit situé ailleurs, dans un contexte étranger, restant à l'état de virtualité":[99] the accreted meanings of the word remain latent, submerged rather than actualized and pertinent to an understanding of the translation. Vernacular *allusio* has to be differentiated from quotation or borrowing as a trope that "met en jeu le rapport de ce qu'on *dit* à ce qu'on *veut dire* mais qu'on *ne dit pas,* et dont il faut postuler la présence à l'horizon du discours tenu."[100] In contradistinction, quotation represents a "déjà-dit" in respect to which allu-

---

98. Gisèle Mathieu-Castellani, "Intertextualité et allusion: Le régime allusif chez Ronsard," *Littérature* 55 (1984): 30.
99. Mathieu-Castellani, "Intertextualité et allusion," 30.
100. Mathieu-Castellani, "Intertextualité et allusion," 29.

sion is a "non-dit," no more than "une citation incomplète."[101] Equally well an allusion is not a borrowing, since allusion is elliptical and enigmatic. Thus:

> Dans le régime allusif, le texte porte inscrit en filigrane un motif . . . , et ce motif absent, virtuellement présent, a le statut d'un code autorisant un décodage du message.[102]

In the field of translation such additional lexical aids to orientate the reader's response are perfectly possible, though once again with essential differences between the Neo-Latin and vernacular cultures. In essence, distinctions of the kind elaborated by Mathieu-Castellani are not always apparent in humanist Latin translation. Although borrowing (particularly Greek loan words or calques) is distinguishable enough from allusion, quotation and allusion are closer together. Quotation seems to be a stabler form of allusion, its presence being ascertainable through intensive allusion to a specific subtext. Even then, the quotation is most usually in the form of individual words rather than phrases, the latter being normally disbarred by the restrictions of meter.

Where Neo-Latin translation depends on an intensified occurrence of reference coupled with an awareness of the subtext's pertinence to the topic in hand, vernacular subtextual reference is less automatically established without the addition of interpretative elements, since allusion depends to a large degree on perceptibility. In vernacular imitation proper, the choice of interpretative elements is not circumscribed by the restrictions that translation imposes.[103] In vernacular translation, the most notable tendency is for a degree of amplification of the original, a feature that Larwill notes to be in the interest of clarity:

> Ces procédés d'insistance, de répétition, d'amplification par voie d'équivalents, loin d'être des travers personnels à tel ou tel traducteur, nous sont apparus comme des auxiliaires de la clarté. Consacrés par un long usage, on en est venu peu à peu à les considérer comme des éléments du beau langage. Ceci est si vrai qu'ils ont fini par être codifiés.[104]

Such amplifications are, in fact, but a small part of a spectrum of comparable devices that Du Bellay himself exploits in his translations of Virgil and that

---

101. Mathieu-Castellani, "Intertextualité et allusion," 28. For quotation, note especially Antoine Compagnon, *La seconde main ou le travail de la citation* (Paris: Seuil, 1979).
102. Mathieu-Castellani, "Intertextualité et allusion," 28.
103. Mathieu-Castellani, "Intertextualité et allusion," 31–36, inspects the range of devices put to use by Ronsard in his treatment of allusions to fables.
104. Larwill, *La théorie de la traduction,* 52.

critics label as compensations.[105] Displacements and rearrangements of emphasis are the practical consequences of that weighing of words that pseudo-Cicero takes as axiomatic in his own translations of the Greek orators.

In the last analysis, what all Neo-Latin and vernacular translators share is the endeavor to match *verba* to *res,* to turn traducement into a virtue, as Valesio has it.[106] This had been the concern of classical theoreticians, and it is constantly voiced by Renaissance theorists in their appeals to seize the "sentence" or "sens" (the *sententia*) rather than the words of a passage.[107] All these are essentialist arguments entailing a substance/accidence relationship between *res* and *verba* and so implying that *verba* are secondary or subordinate to *res*. If theoreticians insist on this hierarchy, it is because translation is preeminently a domain in which the hierarchy is held to be especially problematical. A reductive view of translation's work would hold that every attempt at translation is but partially successful as an elucidation of the source language and never definitive as an interpretation of *res*. In a more positive light, however, translation's gloss on the original is not so much an inadequate account of an evasive object as a recreative faculty of the target language. It is the means by which the target language achieves a measure of creative independence of its source text.

Nonetheless, here as elsewhere, the lines are once again not as clear-cut as this description might suggest. A Renaissance translation may partake of both these tendencies, which are fundamentally those of fidelity and autonomy. This ambiguous interplay of fidelity and autonomy corresponds to that between translation and imitation as aesthetic categories or, at another level, that between *verba* and *res*. These parallels are intended not to suggest that these polarities are simply symmetrical duplications of each other but to emphasize that their function is to discredit the facile establishment of norms or unswerving classifications by which traditional divisions may be unfailingly known. Translation invites its practitioners to perform a continual reassessment of familiar categories. Thus while concerns with *res* and *verba* are common to all translators of pseudo-Anacreon, the solutions they propose remain, in large measure, individual. Reacting against the straightforward putting into practice

---

105. See Wells, "Translation," 179–81.
106. Paolo Valesio, "The Virtues of Traducement: Sketch of a Theory of Translation," *Semiotica* 18, no. 1 (1976): 1–96.
107. In addition to the theoreticians examined previously, see the collection of statements on "sentence" or "sens" in Jean Porcher, "La *Théologie Naturelle* et les théories de la traduction au XVIe siècle," in *Oeuvres complètes de Michel de Montaigne,* ed. A. Armaingaud, vol. 10, *La "Théologie Naturelle" de Raymond Sebon, II* (Paris: Conard, 1935), 460–61.

of a theoretical scheme, they propose individual modifications of a shared standpoint and data, and so they confirm Meschonnic's dictum: "Le lieu de la pratique et de la théorie, pour la traduction de tout texte, est le lieu de sa pratique."[108] In order to examine the particularities of Anacreontic translative practice, we may begin *da capo* and proceed to formalize the contacts between Estienne's translation and his commentary.

---

108. Henri Meschonnic, *Pour la poétique,* vol. 2, *Epistémologie de l'écriture, poétique de la traduction,* Le Chemin (Paris: Gallimard, 1973), 313.

CHAPTER 3

The Virtues of the Commentary: Translation and Textual Criticism in Estienne

In his first major revision of the Anacreontic text in 1560, Estienne explains the reasons for the discrepancies in translation between his own version of the text and that of his contemporary Elie André:

> Iam verò ad Anacreontem quod attinet, cur meas in illas emendationes hîc annotauerim, dicam. Quum poetam illum in lucem primò edidi maiusculis characteribus, vnà etiam meam interpretationem edendam curaui, sed earum duntaxat odarum quae vt venustiores, ita etiam ab omni labe erant puriores. Simul verò meas de corruptis aliquot locis coniecturas adiunxi, quarum bonam in illa mea interpretatione partem sequutus eram. Quoniam autem Elias Andreas (qui suam versionem aliquot post meam mensibus edidit, sed omnium odarum) non eandem vbique lectionem sibi sequendam proposuit, atque hinc fit vt interdum illius interpretatio cum mea non consentiat, meas illas quas dixi coniecturas hîc annotare necesse habui, quibus mea versio astipulatur. Dissentiunt tamen interpretationes nostrae aliquando etiam ubi alioqui in lectione consentimus.[1]

[As far as Anacreon is concerned, let me say why I have recorded here my emendations on the odes. When I first brought out this poet in larger format, I had it published together with my translation, but it was a translation only of those odes that were free from errors as well as

---

1. *Pindari . . . Caeterorum octo lyricorum carmina* ([Geneva]: Henri Estienne, 1560), 429–30. As Estienne points out in this passage, his translation of the Anacreontic odes is selective. He translates odes 1–5, 9, 11, 12, 14–17, 19, 20, 23, 26, 28, 29, 31, 33–35, 37, 40, 43–47, 53, 55.

charming. At the same time I appended my conjectures on some corrupt passages; I had followed a large number of these conjectures in my translation. Now since Elie André—who published his complete translation of the odes a few months after mine—decided on following readings that were not at every point identical to my own (this is why his translation differs from mine at times), I thought it necessary to record here those conjectures with which my version concurs. However, our translations sometimes differ even when we otherwise agree on the reading.]

His explanation formalizes as a difference between two translators and two translations something that had already been apparent in his short note to the reader preceding the commentary in the *editio princeps:*

Feci itaque non inuitus vt quae vertendo hoc poeta, tanquam aliud agens, obseruarem, ea in commentariolum redigerem: quo tum meae interpretationis alicubi rationem tibi redderem: tum etiam in locis difficilioribus labore meo tuum aliqua ex parte subleuarem.[2]

[And so I have willingly put together in a short commentary the jottings I made while translating this poet, so as to justify my translation to you and also, by my toil, to lighten your task a little in the more difficult passages.]

The difference is, in the last analysis, a matter of attitude toward the interrelation of text, translation, and commentary. For Estienne, it would seem, a major concern for the commentary is to provide a justification and rationale for the translation. The commentary is not a purely philological medium, or rather it is an exegetical as well as a philological medium.[3] The corollary of this position is that the translation can be used to propagate the findings of philology, to disseminate textual readings. In this sense, the translation is an adjunct to the

---

2. 1554.64.
3. For critical interest in the Renaissance commentary, see August Buck and Otto Herding, eds., *Der Kommentar in der Renaissance,* Deutsche Forschungsgemeinschaft, Kommission für Humanismusforschung, Mitteilung 1 (Bonn and Bad Godesberg: Boldt, [1975]); Gisèle Mathieu-Castellani and Michel Plaisance, eds., *Les commentaires et la naissance de la critique littéraire: France, Italie, XIVe–XVIe siècles* (Paris: Aux Amateurs de Livres, 1990); Michel Jeanneret, "La lecture en question: Sur quelques prologues comiques du seizième siècle." *French Forum* 14, no. 3 (1989): 279–89, "Préfaces, commentaires et programmation de la lecture: L'exemple des *Métamorphoses,*" in Mathieu-Castellani and Plaisance, *Les commentaires et la naissance de la critique littéraire,* 31–39, "Commentary on Fiction, Fiction as Commentary," *The South Atlantic Quarterly* 91, no. 4 (1992): 909–28.

commentary and the Greek text, a means for advancing scholarship. Thus at one level the typographical separation of text, translation, and commentary in Estienne loses the visual impact of "encadrement"—a fragment of text surrounded by a block of commentary. At another level, nonetheless, the stated interdependency of commentary and translation, philology and exegesis, ensures a reciprocal enrichment between distinct areas.

Within Estienne's *editio princeps* itself, there is ample evidence for the interdependency of translation and commentary. Consider the opening of ode 20 (1554.95), for instance:

NIOBEN stetisse dicunt
Saxum ad fluenta Troiae.

[The story goes that Niobe was turned into a stone and stood by the rivers of Troy.]

"Stetisse" is the translation's counterpart to Estienne's choice of reading given in the commentary: Ἡ Ταντάλου ποτ' ἔστη ... Non puto poetam aliter scripsisse quàm ἔστη ("Tantalus' daughter once stood." I do not think the poet wrote anything other than "stood," 1554.70). Or again, the famous rejection of Gyges and other tyrants in favor of a life dominated by drinking ends (1554.15):

Μὴ νοῦσος ἤν τις ἔλθῃ,
Λέγῃ σε μὴ δεῖ πίνειν.

[lest some disease were to come along and say that you must not drink.]

This passage already represents a correction of the λέγει of the *textus receptus* into λέγῃ. The commentary pushes this process even further: "legendum videtur," Estienne writes, "aut μηδὲ πίνειν, aut μὴ "τι πίνειν pro μὴ ἔτι [...]" (it seems the reading should be either "no longer drink" or "drink no more" for "drink no longer," 1554.69). The translation opts indirectly for the second of these solutions (1554.94):

Ne si quis opprimat te
Morbus, repentè dicat,
Ohe satis bibisti,

[lest some disease surprises you and suddenly says, "Stop! You have drunk enough."]

Here "satis" represents an approximation for μὴ ῍τι πίνειν. Or again, the received text of line 25 of ode 3 runs (1554.4):

τόδε τόξον ἐστί μοι νῦν

[this bow is mine]

Estienne comments (1554.66–67):

Si pro ἐστὶ, legamus εἴ τι, interpunctio esse debet post τόξον, non post verbum πειράσωμεν. vt sit, πειράσωμεν τόδε τόξον, εἴ τι μοι νῦν βλάβεται, &c.

[If instead of "is," we read "if," the punctuation ought to come after "bow," not after the verb "let us try." So that the sentence becomes, "let us try out this bow, to see if it is at all damaged."]

And the translation presses home the point (1554.87):

Probemus, inquit, arcum,
An laesus imbre neruus.

["Let us try the bow," he said, "to see whether the string has been damaged by water."]

A particular variant on this scheme is for the translation to bear both the *textus receptus* and its emendation. Thus the *textus receptus* of ode 9, line 31 reads (1554.10): Καὶ δεσπότην Ἀνακρέοντα (and my master Anacreon). Estienne regards the proper name as an interpolated gloss and proposes the emendation ἐμοῖσι (1554.68). His translation nevertheless adopts both possibilities (1554.90–91):

Sin fortè pota salto,
Pennis Anacreonta
Herum meis obumbro.

[But if perchance I dance drunkenly, I shade my master Anacreon with my wings.]

The instances examined above reveal very plainly the close associations between the Greek text, the Latin translation, and the commentary. The critical conclusions arrived at by the application of *divinatio* are supported and eventually disseminated by the translation. Thus the results of an active intelligence are reflected in the translation and the emphasis lies on the fact of validating certain textual reasons rather than on the choice of vocabulary used to convey these reasons. In such cases, the commentary is in the forefront of attention and it is seen to exercise control over the accompanying translation. Its virtue, it would appear, is to function as a theoretical justification for the text appended to it—a common occurrence, as Glyn Norton has observed.[4]

These are straightforward, restricted instances of the threads tying translation to commentary. More substantial cases (which support and extend the argument I have sketched here) are available in the exegesis accompanying crucial poems in the Anacreontic collection. The very opening translation is representative:

CANTEM libens Atridas,
Cantem libénsque Cadmum:
Sed barbiti mihi vnum
Nerui sonant amorem.[5]

[I want to sing of the Atreidae, I want to sing of Cadmus; but my lyre strings will sing only of love.]

Its controlling trope is *recusatio,* not seldom associated in Hellenistic times with small-scale composition and its rejection of the long poem or of epic.[6] Its consequently programmatic characteristics are underlined by Estienne himself

---

4. Glyn P. Norton, "*Fides interpres:* A Philological Contribution to the Philosophy of Translation in Renaissance France," in *Neo-Latin and the Vernacular in Renaissance France,* ed. Terence Cave and Grahame Castor (Oxford: Clarendon Press, 1984), 241. Norton speaks of "the capacity of philology as an exercise (and with it, translation) to reflect on itself."

5. 1554.85.

6. The work of Callimachus is the *locus classicus* for this theme, discussed by major critics. Representatively, one may cite P. Fraser, *Ptolemaic Alexandria,* 3 vols. (Oxford: Clarendon Press, 1972), 1:625, 641–42, 749, 754 ff., 2:1058–59 nn. 287 ff.; Pfeiffer, *History of Classical Scholarship from the Beginnings to the End of the Hellenistic Age,* 136–37, and *Aetia* frag. 1; Puelma Piwonka, *Lucilius und Kallimachos,* 138–39; Wimmel, *Kallimachos in Rom,* 39 n. 1, 83–84. Elroy T. Bundy, "The 'Quarrel between Kallimachos and Apollonius' Part I: The Epilogue of Kallimachos's 'Hymn to Apollo'," *California Studies in Classical Antiquity* 5 (1972): 39–94, examines the rhetoricity of the *recusatio* in Callimachus, emphasizing that the rejection of epic is an aesthetic topos rather than an autobiographical statement. The same point is made by Mary R. Lefkowitz ("The Quarrel between Callimachos and Apollonius," *Zeitschrift für Papyrologie und Epigraphik* 40 [1980]: 1–19, who argues that autobiographical information cannot simply be extrapolated either from programmatic topoi in poetry or from the *vitae* of classical writers.

when he reveals his choice of this ode to begin the collection and cites in support partial manuscript evidence:

> In altero exemplarium, nimirum in eo quod in libro, id est cortice, scriptum reperi, primum locum occupat haec oda: & rectè, meo quidem iudicio. Proponit enim in hac versuum suorum argumentum: ídque, lepido vtens commento, quo se quodammodo excusare velle videtur.[7]

> [In the second of the two manuscripts—I mean the one that I found written on tree rind, that is, on papyrus—this ode is placed first: and rightly so, in my judgment, because the poet sets out in it the argument of his poetry and does so by using a charming fiction by which he seems to want to excuse himself in a way.]

The deliberate change in the sequence of the poems and the favoring of one kind of textual evidence over another testify to an intentionality on Estienne's part that he displaces into an intentionality, real or supposed, on the author's part. Once again Estienne shows a willingness to allow exegetical to take precedence over textual criteria: the recording of manuscript evidence is subordinated to an exegetical vision based, it transpires, on imitation.

Indeed, Estienne makes this point plain by the allusions to Ovid's *Amores* that immediately follow in the commentary (1554.65). The similarities perceived by the editor between the present Anacreontic ode and the opening poem in *Amores* book 1 already suggest the imitative faculty at work and *a posteriori* validate imitation as exegetical principle, since rejection of the epic is a well-established programmatic topos in Latin elegy.[8] First of all Estienne perceives (invents) a resemblance, albeit of a general kind, with the Ovidian text:

> Arma graui numero uiolentaque bella parabam
>   edere, materia conueniente modis.
> par erat inferior uersus; risisse Cupido
>   dicitur atque unum surripuisse pedem.[9]

---

7. 1554.65.

8. See R. Müller, *Motivkatalog der römischen Elegie: Eine Untersuchung zur Poetik der Römer* (Zürich: Juris, 1952), 47–57, 62 ff., 66, 68, s.v. "Ablehnung des Epos." Rosenmeyer, *The Poetics of Imitation*, 96–106, provides a useful examination of the *recusatio* theme in the Anacreontea as well as in Hellenistic literature generally.

9. *Am.* 1.1.1–4.

[I was preparing to write about wars and violent battles in serious vein, with the subject matching the meter. The second line was complete, when Cupid reportedly laughed and stole away one foot.]

In other poems, Ovid specifies the topics rejected, as, for example, in *Amores* 3.12.15 f., an instance equally cited by Estienne as parallel for the opening of the Anacreontic poem. So too the Greek Χαίροιτε λοιπὸν ἡμῖν Ἥρωες at the close of the poem has its counterpart for Estienne in *Amores* 2.1.35–36—

. . . heroum clara ualete
nomina: non apta est gratia uestra mihi;

[farewell, famed names of heroes: your favor is not suitable for me.]

—and Estienne's translation follows suit:

Heroes ergo longum
Mihi valete posthac.
Nam barbiti mihi vnum
Nerui sonant amorem.

[Farewell, then, heroes, henceforth; for my lyre strings sing only of love.]

In the dominant trope, the opening, and the close, Estienne anchors his reordered text not only through an exegetical commentary but also through an allusive translation. The upshot of the interaction of the two is almost a theory of lexis, as the middle section of the translation abundantly illustrates:

Sed barbiti mihi vnum
Nerui sonant amorem.
Mutata nuper à me
Chelys, fidésque cunctae:
Iámque Herculis labores
Canebam: at illa contrà
Sonabat vsque amores.

[But my lyre strings sing only of love. I recently changed the lyre—the whole instrument; and I was going to sing of the labors of Hercules. But in response the lyre kept singing of love affairs.]

Metonyms and synonyms for the lyre abound. Yet it is the term "chelys" that is reactivated by the commentary's discussion of imitative parallels and that resumes its obtrusive Ovidian tonality.[10] Ovid now appears as the presiding genius of this opening translation, an authoritative confirmation for what might otherwise remain a Neo-Latin rhapsody of nouns after the style of Ravisius Textor. Ovid's strategic positioning in the commentary allows Estienne to present a coherent reading of the Anacreontic poem in translation, perceived as a restatement of a known literary idiom. Operating a reversal of actual historical relationships, Estienne's observations on this poem thus act as a rhetorical *hysteron proteron,* establishing retrospectively an act of transmission between Anacreontic "source" and Ovidian "inheritance" of precisely the kind postulated in the case of Horace in ode 31. And when Estienne translates ode 1, Ovid acts as the same focus for an imitative dynamics, usurping or extending the place equivalently occupied by Horace elsewhere. In the transfer from commentary to text or vice versa, imitation can be reformulated around a variable center: Ovid here, Horace in ode 31, others again elsewhere.

Within the confines of this translation, therefore, Estienne establishes a number of strategic points. By maximizing the number of possible substitutions for lyre, he emphasizes the range of diction through which his translation will be filtered while nonetheless favoring Ovid as source of imitative interest. Ovid's presence itself thus stands within a complex of intersecting issues. It suggests primarily the practice of imitation; it entertains a synecdochic relationship with non-Ovidian diction as equally illustrated by the translation, in that it represents one branch of lexis; and because of the close links between translation and commentary, it illustrates the degree to which manuscript evidence and textual reading can be modified or manipulated by Estienne to reflect exegetical requirements. Ovidian overtones suggest the centripetal convergence of the paradigmatic and the syntagmatic. On the other hand, this is to ignore the undeniable plurality of metonyms occupying the center of the poem, a plurality that is itself indicative, at the microcontextual level of individual words, of that liking for *variae interpretationes* that is a type of *variatio.*[11]

---

10. Or rather pseudo-Ovidian: *Epist. Sappho* 181 is the sole Augustan instance supplied by *TLL,* s.v. "chelys," 1005.77–78. The word becomes current with Seneca and particularly Statius.

11. Estienne's fondness for *variae interpretationes* can be corroborated by a look at the textual and explanatory notes at the back of his 1566 edition of the Greek Anthology. Here he offers a Latin translation of a six-line epigram by Agathias Scholasticus (*A.P.* 6.76). Of the final distich, however, Estienne supplies no fewer than fifty alternative renderings (*Florilegium diuersorum epigrammatum ueterum, in septum libros diuisum* . . . , sigs. [rr.iv.ᵛ]–ss.i.ʳ) Estienne comments on his motives as follows: "Caeterùm ad accendendum iuuenum studium, meam epigrammatis huius interpretationem, & postremi insuper distichi alias quinquaginta varias interpretationes (verbis quidem certè diuersas, sed sensu easdem) placuit adscribere" (sig. [rr.iv.ᵛ]).

Exemplified in this opening translation, the principle of constantly rewriting subtexts and hence redefining one's relationship to one's inherited literary tradition can be amply illustrated from the cluster of translations dealing with the "komos" and "somnia amoris" topoi. The first of the two poems on the rose is a case in point. Its thematics are frequent in Renaissance literature.[12] In Estienne its elegiac components are immediately perceptible, particularly in midpoem:

Roseis puer Cytheres
Caput implicat coronis,
Charitum choros frequentans.
Agedum ergo me corona
Pater ô Lyaee, templis
Modulans tuis vt adstem.[13]

[Aphrodite's boy twines crowns of roses round his head, when visiting the choirs of the Graces. Well then, crown me, father Lyaeus, that I may stand in your temple playing the lyre.]

It is "caput implicat coronis" that compresses the greatest number of references, Tibullan (*Carm.* [3].6.64), Virgilian (*Aen.* 4.148, 7.135–36), and above all Ovidian ("coronas sertaque . . . implicitura comas," *Fast.* 5.219–20; "se violave rosave / implicet," *Met.* 12.410–11). Yet however precise the verbal echoes, the more general informing subtext seems to be none of these. Its identity is clarified by André's translation, which in earlier lines reads: "Foliis rosa decoris / Caput vndique impediti / Age molle rideamus."[14] The middle line here indicates the reference, crucial to both translations, to Horace's *Carmina* 1.4.5–10:

iam Cytherea choros ducit Venus imminente Luna,
　　iunctaeque Nymphis Gratiae decentes
alterno terram quatiunt pede, dum gravis Cyclopum
　　Vulcanus ardens visit officinas.
nunc decet aut viridi nitidum caput impedire myrto

---

12. Cf. Henri Weber, *La création poétique au XVIe siècle en France de Maurice Scève à Agrippa d'Aubigné* (Paris: Nizet, 1955), chapter 5, "La poésie amoureuse de la Pléiade: Etude de thèmes," 231–398, especially section 7: "L'image de la rose et le thème de la fleur qui se fane," 333–56. The section covers a broad spectrum of Neo-Latin as well as vernacular examples of the theme.
13. 1554.89.
14. 1556.9.

aut flore terrae quem ferunt solutae.

[Already Cytherean Venus is leading the dances, with the moon overhead, and the fair Graces linked with the Nymphs tread the ground with alternate steps, while fiery Vulcan visits the mighty forges of the Cyclops. Now one should crown one's handsome head either with green myrtle or with a flower from the unfettered earth.]

The other references now become easily intelligible. Estienne's "puer Cytheres" recalls the Horatian "Cytherea," "Charitum choros" supplants "Gratiae," and both are preludes to the narrator's own involvement in the Horatian dance:

Roseis comásque sertis
Redimitus, atque pulchra
Comitante me puella,
Choreas & ipse ducam.

[Wreathed in rose garlands and with a beautiful girl for company, I too shall lead the dance.]

"Choreas . . . ducam" is Horace's "choros ducit," corresponding as a conclusion to André's "pedibus solum lacessam,"[15] itself looking back to "terram quatiunt pede." In both translations, the final words appear to close their respective poems without reference to the Horatian "pallida mors" that interrupts the Graces' harmonious dance. The appearance is, however, deceptive. If André's closing line looks back to the rhythmical step of the goddesses, it equally recalls death's brutish interruption: "pallida Mors aequo pulsat pede" (*Carm.* 1.4.13). Estienne's narrator is allowed to end with his leading the dance; yet this activity itself is precariously threatened by mortality, as in the translation immediately preceding (ode 4, 1554.88), where the narrator views dancing with distinct self-irony: "Etenim priusquam ad Orci / Rapiar nigri choreas, / Volo dissipare curas" (in fact, before I am carried off to the dances of black Orcus, I want to dispel my cares, 1554.88). Both poems maintain the dialogue with their predecessors beyond formal closure; and the irony of the reference, already implicit in the Greek, is actualized by the specificity of the subtext to which the translations allude.

Possibly the most striking feature of this Estienne translation, by contrast

---

15. 1556.10.

with André's, is its degree of departure from the Horatian subtext: it is André who provides the most direct of *allusiones* to the rewritten predecessor, rather than Estienne, whose "Folijs rosam decoram / Capiti reuincientes, / Calices iocemur inter" (wreathing our heads in beautiful rose leaves, let us make merry over cups of wine, 1554.89), followed by "caput implicat coronis," both indicate divergence from Horace. One immediate consequence of this is that the perceptible *variatio* in Estienne's translation is increased. "Capiti reuincientes" is not a failed opportunity to anchor the text to a Horatian referent; it is an attempt to appeal to a perception of historical change, to measure the distance between a specific poetic diction historically located and a contemporary idiom of translation in which *contaminatio* instigates dialogue of more than one kind. Thus Horatian allusion is juxtaposed, in Estienne, with instances of ordinary prose usage: "sociemus," "sertis redimitus" (for which compare Cicero *Cat.* 2.5.10: "sertis redimiti"). *Allusio* and *variatio,* then, if often complementary, can equally well polarize the text. The urge to *variatio* is particularly strongly felt, since its net product is the expansion of Latinity because of the capacity to form new linguistic collocations. "Capiti reuincientes" and "caput implicat coronis" are the emblems of this heuristic expansive movement. As *variae interpretationes* that are closer to each other than their Greek counterparts (Κροτάφοισιν ἁρμόσαντες and Στέφεται καλοῖς ἰούλοις, 1554.5), they are engaged in what may be termed a linguistic *amplificatio* of the Latin language, moving outward from a shifting center. Moreover, in terms of Estienne's theory of imitation expounded in the commentary, the use of *variatio* distances the *allusio* and so reindividualizes the possibility of the *allusio*'s otherness, its obtrusiveness.

Such obtrusiveness becomes a feature of translation's idiom when this idiom is read in continuous sequence. For *amplificatio* does not simply depend on the forging of new collocations, it can depend also on the revival of archaisms or *hapax legomena:* the desire to expand diachronically on Latin is accompanied by the urge to maintain it whole, as a synchronic unit. A simple example of this phenomenon is given by ode 44 (1554.106), one of several "somnia amoris." The narrator dreams of himself as winged yet captured by a leaden-footed Love. He then asks rhetorically: "Sibi somnium quid hoc vult?" (What is the meaning of this dream?). This is the point in the translation that strongly recalls its Ovidian subtexts: such a poem as *Amores* 3.5 supplies the genre, and *Met.* 9.473 the diction: "tacitae quid vult sibi noctis imago?" As with the Horatian example examined earlier, Estienne's line acts as a marker to the subtext, as a signal to the reader that rewriting is taking place. Against this background can be set the small adventure in the common Neo-Latin diminutive ("pedes tenellos"), which recalls contemporary vernacular preference for *mignardise.*[16] Yet the rarity of "tenellus" in classical Latin is immediately reminiscent of its own subtexts, in this case Latin comedy.[17] The allusions are perhaps too sparse or too fleeting to allow absolute certainty. Generically, the Ovidian text as norm would be the natural one to evoke, supported by surrounding contexts. Against this, the comic reference is undeniably obtrusive.[18] If *variatio* works by perceptible deviation from a norm, that norm in this poem is only minimally established; only minimal guidance is given. Is this comedy updated by Ovid, or is Ovid updated by comedy? This is a case where lexical *contaminatio* militates against the integration of diction such as Estienne implicitly recommends under "honestè furari." *Contaminatio* of the kind active in this particular translation ends by the privileging of imitative combination rather than imitative selectivity. The *variatio* that this produces creates renovation only by dispelling any notion of linguistic *proprietas*.

The corpus of Ovidian-inspired translations is extensive and, because Estienne's translations are selective, frequently occupies whole sections in his work. Thus odes 34 and 35 can be taken along with ode 44 (less than two pages later in the printed translation) as examples of this idiom. Ode 35 (1554.103) retells the story of Europa, familiar from *Met.* 2.840f.: the adjective "Sidoniam" indeed acts as a marker to that context, where it similarly serves to introduce the story of the rape of Europa. Estienne's reading metamorphoses the subtext in the same way that the original story itself relies on metamorphoses. The *variatio* centers on the constant substitution of synonymous verbs: "vectat," "tranat aequor," "findit . . . vndas," "tranet fretum." Yet the lexis here is too broad, not sufficiently focused, to permit the unreserved assertion that it is Ovid who is being rewritten. The apparent refusal of contact—unlike André who multiplies the meeting points—may indicate the desire to rewrite to such a degree that the intertext has barely any dialogic role to play. Here again the translation tries to move against its subtext by minimizing the amount of contact with Ovid, despite the familiarity of the allusion. Ode 34 (1554.102–3) works along the same lines. It has nothing *a priori* to link it with Ovid, except the final lines:

---

16. Cf. Ian D. McFarlane, "Reflections on Ravisius Textor's *Specimen Epithetorum*," in *Classical Influences on European Culture, A.D. 1500–1700*, ed. Robert R. Bolgar (Cambridge: Cambridge University Press, 1976), 86; and my chapter 6.

17. "Tenellus": Plautus *Cas.* 110.

18. Importantly, James Hutton notes that "the literary influence of Plautus was greater than the scarcity of translations might suggest" ("The Classics in Sixteenth-Century France," in *Essays on Renaissance Poetry*, ed. Rita Guerlac [Ithaca and London: Cornell University Press, 1980], 215–16 n. 3).

En aspice in corollis,
Rosis decenter alba
Vt lilia implicentur.

[See how beautifully, in garlands, white lilies are entwined with roses.]

Estienne's commentary (1554.79) points out the relevant parallel: "quale rosae fulgent inter sua lilia mixtae" (*Amores* 2.5.37). The parallel, perhaps, remains no more than that. Ovid's status as a subtext remains undecidable, the independence of the translation being more perceptible than the etiological passage from subtext to surface text. The *allusio-imitatio* pair work in these poems in disjunction, the first creating possibilities for reading that are then blocked by the second.[19] *Allusio* creates threads of subtextual significance that *imitatio* refuses to confirm by an increased degree of etiological dependence. The transmutation of the poem's linguistic system has reached the point at which the *variatio* it performs upon previous linguistic phenomena is minimally discernible and yet maximally effective.

These are not simply cases where the Greek mechanically determines the nature of the Neo-Latin translation: the Greek can rarely determine the actual lexis employed in the translation and with it the allusions it bears. Through modulation, the poem achieves a constant transposition of its material. The effect of *variatio* is, indeed, to create a number of linguistic units all rewriting a given theme. Hence, the nucleus idea of the head wreathed with flowers recurs in a variety of contexts, all linguistically similar (usually more so than the Greek), yet all endlessly transposing the forms of which they are composed. *Variatio* will, then, in such contexts be closely allied to the practice of *repetitio:* to that extent, phraseology of this kind expands the dominant structural feature of the opening translation, where *repetitio* combined with antithesis provides the framework through which the *recusatio* is expressed.

In the case of the two *variae interpretationes* already quoted, "Folijs rosam decoram / Capiti reuincientes" and "Roseis comásque sertis / Redimitus" correspond respectively to Στέφεται καλοῖς ἰούλοις (1554.5) and 'Ροδίνοισι στεφανίσκοις / Πεπυκασμενός (1554.6)—where "roseis" is more greatly evocative of Latin elegiac contexts than ῥοδίνοισι, which represents in combination with στεφανίσκοις a self-quotation, since it is the conjunction of two

---

19. Thus the macrocontext operates according to the same principle by which Riffaterre defines stylistic unity in "L'explication des faits littéraires," in *La production du texte* (Paris: Seuil, 1979), 2: "je définis l'unité de style comme une dyade aux deux rôles inséparables dont le premier crée une probabilité et le second frustre cette probabilité [. . .]."

words extant in the real Anacreon (*PMG* 434 and 410). The impression given in the Latin is continued in ode 4 (1554.88), where

Roseas meo corollas
Capiti ferásque odores

[rose garlands on my head, and heady perfumes]

corresponds to

Ἐμὲ μᾶλλον, ὡς ἔτι ζῶ,
Μύρισον, ῥόδοις δὲ κρᾶτα
Πύκασον.[20]

[While I am still living, anoint me and cover my head thickly with roses.]

"Roseas," the exclusively poetic word "corollas," coupled with "odores" (reminiscent, for instance, of Horace *Carm.* 1.5.2: "perfusus liquidis . . . odoribus"): the Augustan quality of the translation is foregrounded. Two final instances: "Hedera comásque cingens" (1554.97) for Κισσοστεφὴς δὲ κεῖμαι (1554.22), "cingo" occurring in numerous poetic contexts;[21] and as a comparison "At poculum ipse gestans / Et has comis corollas" (but waving a goblet and with garlands in my hair, 1554.101) for Ἐγὼ δ' ἔχων κύπελλον / Καὶ στέμμα τοῦτο χαίταις (1554.29).

To these instances could be added others drawn from areas dealing, for example, with the desire for, or the act of, intoxication (a large thematic area). In both areas, the urge to match the copiousness of the original with an equal copiousness in translation is an influential factor: the rich contents of the Latin language can be endlessly displayed either in their original order (an order recognizable from classical Latin poetry) or—perhaps more frequently—in a rearranged order demonstrating the translator's own virtuosity in inventing combinations suitable to the context and the constraints of form and meter. The tendency to invent combinations of itself produces *contaminatio* in that the combination may well employ vocabulary or styles particular to more than one author (rather than common to a genre). Where a combination takes place, the allusions are often too manifold to pinpoint with any finality, and the rewriting

---

20. 1554.5.
21. Cf. Horace *Carm.* 3.25.20: "cingentem viridi tempora pampino," and 30.16: "lauro cingens . . . comam"; Virgil *Aen.* 5.71: "cingite tempora ramis"; Tibullus 2.1.4: "spicis tempora cinge."

they imply is in respect to a general lexis rather than a specific author. Thus to take one of the instances just listed, there is no particular classical context corresponding to Estienne's "hedera comásque cingens": Horace, Virgil, and the Latin elegists use expressions that are analogous but not identical. Insofar as this expression can be said to be a neologistic paraphrase, it seeks to render the Anacreontic κισσοστεφής. Where intertextual pressure is at its greatest, specificity is at its least apparent. This is precisely the problem with the Ovidian intertext in odes 34 and 35: the poems encourage an intertextual reading to which they remain elusive.

One final, extended example may be given of the conjunction and disjunction entailed by *repetitio* and *variatio* in the cultivation of *variae interpretationes*. This involves looking again at the *recusatio* thematics characteristic of ode 1, for this opening poem itself has a number of companion pieces (odes 16 and 31, for instance) equally dealing with this topic. The liminary stance is thus frequently reattempted, involving not the simple repetition but the reshaping of the initial idea. Since it receives extensive treatment in the commentary, ode 31 (1554.101) is a contender for theoretical prominence equal to that of the opening poem. It articulates aesthetic preferences in dramatic form by explicating two functions of the verb μανῆναι—actual madness and the inspired "madness" of drinking.[22] The contribution of the commentary to the elucidation of this poem is immediately to suggest the Horatian subtext from *Carmina* 2.7.26–27: "non ego sanius / bacchabor Edonis: recepto / dulce mihi furere est amico" (I'll rave as wildly as the Edonians. It is pleasant for me to go mad now that a friend has been regained) (1554.76). The poem illustrates the iniquitous effects of "furor" from standard examples of the genre and ends with the rejection of violent "furor" in favor of the "furor" of wine. The thematic rejection, marked each time by the contrastive particle *at,* is mirrored by the shifts in diction, as in:

Olim furebat Aiax,
Ensem Hectoris coruscans,
Septemplicémque parmam.
At poculum ipse gestans
Et has comis corollas,
Non spiculum, nec ensem,
Furere hunc volo furorem.[23]

---

22. For classical definitions of *furere,* cf. particularly Cicero *Tusc.* 3.5.11, citing Athamas, Alcmaeon, Ajax, and Orestes as standard examples.
23. 1554.101.

[Once Ajax went mad, brandishing Hector's sword and sevenfold shield. But waving not a dart or a sword, but a goblet and with these garlands in my hair, I want to go mad with this madness.]

The contrast is a contrast of diction as well as of theme. "Septemplicémque parmam," supported by "coruscans" and "ensem," is Virgilian in tonality. It is, indeed, a variant on the actual phrase "septemplex clipeus" (*Aen.* 12.925), itself a neologism coined to match the Homeric σάκος ἑπταβόειον (*Il.* 7.219–20, 222). Hence the overtly Homeric allusions present in the Anacreontics survive, in Estienne's translation, only as an echo mediated through a Roman successor of Homer. (The innovative nature of the translation is measurable by the absence of any corresponding phraseology in the Anacreontic Greek, where Ajax is simply μετ' ἀσπίδος κραδαίνων [brandishing his shield], 1554.28.) The thematic disputes of the Greek have now been displaced and transferred to questions of diction. Moreover, what was in ode 1 a choice about genre—epic or erotic—has become refocused as a question of madness or inspiration: the "furor" that represented a deviation for the epic or tragic hero is a central necessity for the drink-inspired reveler. The lexical displacement signals an analogous thematic displacement, in that the "furor" and the μανία concerned invite allegorization as erotic frenzy, the links between love and drink being lexically strong.[24]

The translation of this ode displays a further feature of Estienne's theory of imitation. Just as Hellenistic Greek poetry measured its linguistic manipulations against earlier genres, particularly epic, so the lexis of Estienne's translation relocates this practice in respect to the deviation from Virgilian epic diction. The grandeur of the Virgilian enterprise is rejected, with the movement being away from epic to symposium. Epic diction is open to rewriting: the fact that the other celebrated instance of "clipeus septemplex" is in Ovid's *Metamorphoses* (13.2) illustrates the reworking with which such epic diction is handled. The automatic evocation of Ovid through Virgilian diction here supplies a further layer of reference, an instantaneous *contaminatio,* at the very moment of its utterance. Estienne's translation juxtaposes the source and the reworking in a single movement.

In a poem that might be supposed to be the direct counterpart of the theory

---

24. On "furor" and μανία as evoking "amor" and ἐρωμανία, see Giuseppe Giangrande, "Los tópicos helenísticos en la elegía latina," *Emerita* 42 (1974): 6, and Réné Pichon, *Index Verborum Amatoriorum* (1902; reprint, Hildesheim: Olms, 1966), s.v. "furor." The poem is also analyzed by Rosenmeyer, *The Poetics of Imitation,* 82–85.

propounded by the commentary, this theory is represented by the translation in specifically Roman terms (with Homeric epic rather than Alcaean lyric as the shadowy Greek presence), but its restatement only highlights the differences between the poem and its prose counterpart. The movement of imitation is indeed retained in the epic allusions that inform this text, with "septemplex clipeus" representing the passage from Virgil to Ovid and thence to Estienne. But the presentation of the allusions, linked to the thematic structure of the poem, implies the rejection of epic idiom. Thus, whereas the commentary postulates the unbroken handing on of imitative technique, this particular translation modifies that continuity and demonstrates that allusions depend upon their place, their *dispositio,* within each individual poem. Again, where the commentary emphasizes the integrity of diction through the power of *allusio,* this translation implies the rejection of certain types of diction because of the dominant thematic structure. Sympotic poetry entails the revision of epic; "furere hanc volo furorem" can only receive the meaning relevant to the symposiastic genre by a rejection of its epic or tragic associations. In short, these two versions of the theory of imitation, far from being reciprocal reflections, diverge at crucial points. As the values that the commentary propounds are transferred to individual translations, their arrangement opens the theory to a variability not envisaged at the moment of its formulation. This suggests a significant modification of the fit between commentary and translation, theory and practice. Unilinear theory will not account for a plural practice. Thus the gap already existing between *repetitio* and *variatio* can widen into the recognition of this disparity, so that the neat balance that they appear to compose in the production of *variae interpretationes* shifts according to context and their duality is never fully resolved into symmetry.

2

One way of viewing the set of interrelated concepts and techniques at work in Estienne's translation *(allusio, variae interpretationes, contaminatio)* is to say that they all, in various forms, exemplify and explore the problem of the fragment. The whole effect of *variae interpretationes* is, indeed, to offer multiple recall of either different Latin subtexts by different but comparable authors, or different subtexts by the same author. At the level of the translated phrase or word, *variae interpretationes* thus work closely with *allusio* and, if more than one subtext is at play in any given translation, with *contaminatio* also. Observations similar to these could equally characterize the role of the commentary.

By itself, the commentary constitutes a partial manifestation of the literary intertext, filled with representative parallels and *exempla* serving as a grid against which to view both the Greek text and the Latin translation. The commentary anticipates and selectively exemplifies the reader's own perception of the allusions that Neo-Latin translation contains and deploys. Thus attention to the commentary is attention to the intertext; and attention to the intertext is attention to the fragment. At first sight, it appears that the commentary is a series of discrete philological moments partially unified by a theory of imitation ("honestè furari"), whereas the translation is an imitation whose topical composition implies the constant recourse to allusion, quotation, fragments of previous literary texts retrieved and rewritten. Translation and commentary seem complementary modes, composing a harmoniously organized pattern. Yet, as analysis of the translation of ode 31 suggested, this is not always or necessarily the case. For the imitative paradigm of "honestè furari" only partly (and hypothetically) covers the nature of the commentary: whatever the value of such a paradigm, whatever the possibility of integration for the analogies it draws, the commentary's segmented presentation nonetheless places greater emphasis on disconnectedness than on continuity. The most direct consequence of this can be seen in a further body of translations, where Estienne highlights the whole intertext against which a poem is written as a way of illustrating the nature of the literary fragment and its contacts with the commentary on the one hand and techniques of *variatio* and *repetitio* on the other.

A fine illustration of this phenomenon is ode 17 (1554.15–16; translation: 1554.94–95). Its complexity arises from the fact of its survival in several versions with noticeably disparate readings. In the Greek Anthology (*A.P.* 11.47 and 48), it is joined with ode 15, a union that Estienne rejects largely because Aulus Gellius (*N.A.* 19.9) preserves a version of the ode beginning at Τὸν ἄργυρον τορεύσας. The Gellian version indeed proves decisive for this ode, for its readings are compatible with the second half of the poem as it exists in the manuscript. Estienne's printed text reads:

Τί πλειάδεσσι κἀμοὶ,
Τί δ' ἄστρασι Βοώτεω.
Ποίησον ἀμπέλους μοι,
Καὶ βότρυας κατ' αὐτὸ,
Καὶ χρυσέους πατοῦντας
Ὁμοῦ καλῷ Λυαίῳ
Ἔρωτα καὶ Βάθυλλον.

His translation follows suit:

(Nam Pleiades quid ad me,
Quid lucidus Bootes?)
Vitam sed & racemos
Insculpe, cúmque Baccho
Vuas simul prementes
Cupidinem & Bathyllum.

[For what are the Pleiades to me, what is bright Bootes to me? But engrave on it the sprouting clusters of grapes, and Love and Bathyllus pressing the grapes together with Bacchus.]

And Estienne comments:

Τί πλειάδεσσι κἀμοί, Τί δ' ἄστρασι Βοώτεω. Legitur & sic, Τί πλειάδων μέλει μοι, Τί δ' ἀστέρος Βοώτεω. Sed prior lectio magis mihi placet, quòd respondeat superioribus illis, Τί γὰρ μάχαισι κἀμοί. Quo etiam modo dixit alibi [ode 24; 1554.21], Μέθετέ με φροντίδες, Μηδέν μοι καὶ ὑμῖν ἔστω. Sic dixit quidam [A.P. 9.49], Ἔλπις καὶ σὺ τύχη μέγα χαίρετε, τὸν λιμέν' εὗρον. Οὐδὲν ἐμοὶ χ' ὑμῖν. Praeterea lib. 2. Epigramm. Graecorum ita clauditur haec oda [A.P. 11.48], Μὴ στυγνὸν ὠρίωνα. Ἀλλ' ἀμπέλους χλοώσας, Καὶ βότρυας γελῶντας, Σὺν τῷ καλῷ λυαίῳ. Sed melior Gellij lectio, quae consentit cum nostra.[25]

["What have I to do with the Pleiades, what have I to do with the stars of Bootes?" An alternative reading is: "What do I care about the Pleiades, what do I care about the star Bootes?" But I prefer the first reading, in that it corresponds to the earlier line: "What have I to do with battles?" In the same way Anacreon says elsewhere: "Release me, cares; let there be nothing between me and you." Another poet writes: "Adieu, hope and fortune, I have found my haven. There is nothing between me and you." Moreover, in book 2 of the Greek Anthology, this ode has the following ending: "Not hateful Orion, but burgeoning vines and laughing bunches of grapes, together with beautiful Bacchus." But Aulus Gellius' reading is better, since it agrees with our own.]

Estienne's choice devolves on Τί πλειάδεσσι κἀμοί on the grounds of aesthetic neatness and as a result of observing linguistic *repetitio* in these poems. The point is a fair one and Estienne seeks to bolster it with reference to parallel

---

25. 1554.69.

usage, both internal and external. Yet his conclusion is hardly dispassionate, since the alternative reading could have equally legitimate support. What weakens Estienne's argument here most of all is his dismissal of the tradition of the Anthology—a dismissal that has no explanation, though one might perhaps deduce reliance on the "veteres libri" that had been a criterion of Estienne's previous argument in favor of dissociating *A.P.* 11.47 and 48.[26]

In the case of ode 17, the possible subtext is not just a component against which the text reacts: it has become the text. Besides demonstrating the uncertainty and fragmentation to which the Anacreontea are subject, especially given the sometimes cavalier attitude of Estienne's editorial practice ("Sed melior Gellij lectio, quae consentit cum nostra"!), this case reflects fully the impossibility of exercising a reading other than intertextual. The manner in which one version of the text assumes priority without any formal dating or historical appreciation is a further, particularly striking example of difference in intellectual climate and attitude between France and Italy. Beyond that, the passage exhibits to an extraordinary degree the purely differential relations that constitute the text and the corresponding translation. Estienne's printed text, in this light, represents a reading of the textual tradition and our sense of its provisionality is accentuated by the absence of critical distinctions in the commentary itself. Nothing demonstrates more clearly that the printed text can at certain points be broken down into a disaggregated mass of intertextual possibilities dependent upon different critical traditions for their survival and revealing the disparity of these traditions once compared with each other. What emerges from Estienne's analysis of this passage is the undecidability affecting those cases where the evidence is not such as to present an unintelligible reading and so bring *divinatio* into play, and yet where the amount of parallel material is too great to permit the establishment of a literary stemma implicit in Estienne's perception of imitation. As soon as basic principles of this kind become inoperable, the text reveals its readings to be chosen or rejected on the basis of personal preference alone. Moreover, because of the close ties between commentary and translation, the latter is drawn into supporting only one branch of a tangled tradition. In so doing, it indulges on a larger scale Estienne's preference for reflecting through his translation the textual solutions arrived at in the commentary: whereas elsewhere the translation provides the resolution of a crux limited to a single word or phrase, here the crux affects the very stability of the readings over an extensive number of lines.

---

26. 1554.69, lemma: Τὸν ἀργυρον τορεύους.

This translation is an important instance of the way in which the textual etiology created by Estienne can break down if the pressures from the intertext are too great. However capable the commentary is of giving full expression to the diverse textual traditions, the translation must necessarily betray some of these traditions and survive only at the expense of neglecting readings that it cannot possibly represent in print. A translation can absorb glosses (Estienne's can and does); it cannot support contradictory readings. Awareness of divergent traditions does nothing to alleviate the difficulties in the absence of dated witnesses to the text. And this points to a major limitation in the use of translation to mirror textual practice. The printing of a text with an *apparatus criticus*, or a critical commentary or an appendix, has its *raison d'être* in the representation of the diverse traditions that compose the text. Stability is not an end in itself, since the text is constantly subject to revision. In translation, however, the text must be guaranteed a minimum stability in order to focus the reader's attention on the degree of manipulation involved.

Elsewhere, by contrast, the connection between the intertext and text is freer, less cluttered and problematic, as, for example, in ode 12, lemma Τί σοι θέλεις ποιήσω (text: 1554.12; translation: 1554.91–92; commentary: 1554.68–69). Here Estienne notes the *amplificatio* that, according to him, this poem receives at the hands of Agathias Scholasticus (*A.P.* 5.237), and he ends with a theoretical statement of the kind already seen in his dealings with Horace: "Haec obseruatione sunt digna, vt & ipsi discamus cautè imitari veteres, & si quid apud illos occurrat, quod in rem nostram sit, ita in vsum nostrum illud vertere, vt non aliunde tamen petitum, sed domi natum videatur" (this is an important point, in order that we may learn how to imitate the ancients carefully, and if anything occurs in their works that is helpful to us, it should be so adapted to our use that it seems to have been an original creation rather than a borrowing, 1554.69). Estienne's comments on the ode itself are brief, but he appears less concerned with instancing than with affirming the theoretical principle to which the instances, short as they are, give rise.

The call to recognize and follow the intertext is advice that is not just directed toward the potential imitator, *sensu stricto,* but also applicable in a broader understanding to the translator's own activity. This notion, already a familiar one, will bear further exemplification, especially when Estienne seeks to implement the idea by including one of his own translations as intertext. The poem in question is the popular Ἔρως ποτ' ἐν ῥόδοισιν (text: 1554.36–37; translation: 1554.104–5; commentary: 1554.80–81). The commentary establishes the issues:

Antea vidimus vt nonnulli integras odas ex hoc poeta in sua epigrammata transcripserint: vide vt ipse etiam Theocritus ex hac suum Ερωτα κηριοκλέπτην fecerit.²⁷

[We have seen previously that several writers have transcribed whole odes from this poet into their epigrams. Now see how Theocritus too has made out of this poem his "Love the thief of the honeycombs."]

Estienne then quotes his own translation of this pseudo-Theocritean poem so as to afford implicit comparison with his Anacreontic translation. Perhaps the factor most immediately perceptible about Estienne's version of the Anacreontic piece is its emphasis on archaism or rare words:

INTER rosas Cupido
Apiculam iacentem
Non vidit, éstque punctus.
Manúmque sauciatus,
Mox eiulare coepit.
Et cursitans volánsque
Ad candidam Cytherem,
Heu óccidi, óccidi, inquit.²⁸

[Cupid did not see the little bee lying among the roses and was stung. With his hand hurting, he soon began to wail. Flying off to radiant Aphrodite, he said, "Oh, I'm dying, I'm dying . . ."]

"Apiculam," "sauciatus," "eiulare," and "cursitans" all have equivalents in preclassical Latin, for they belong to the diction of Plautus.²⁹ The *proprietas* of using preclassical diction might be situated at a number of levels. First, as a specific support to the *proprietas* of the Anacreontic pieces: since Latin possesses no pristine lyrical diction that might suitably correspond to what Estienne regards as the antiquity of "Anacreon," a heavy veneer of preclassical diction can be defended as a means of creating a sufficiently antiquated diction to correspond to Estienne's views on the date and dialect of his poet.³⁰ Again,

---
27. 1554.80.
28. 1554.104.
29. "Apicula": Plautus *Cur.* 10; "saucio": Plautus *Rud.* 758 (there are also several noncomic uses of this word); "eiulo": Plautus *Aul.* 796, *Mer.* 682; "cursito": Terence *Eu.* 278, Horace *Carm.* 4.11.10.
30. Estienne remarks on the Doric influence in the diction of the poem: 1554.81.

given that this preclassical diction is for the most part the diction of Roman comedy, it sustains a familiarity of tone corresponding to the "lightness" of Anacreontics as a genre and, more centrally, implicitly increases the irony of the piece by subjecting it to the generalized comic associations that this terminology carries in its subtexts (the terminology is generalized because there is no specific comic subtext in which a character is stung). All these features are in turn tributaries of the desire to accomplish a *renovatio* through transposition: the comic transposes the lyric, while comic overtones in the first half of the translation strengthen and renew the irony of the close that these initial lines thereby anticipate. The culmination of this transposition of diction is reached in Cupid's words to Aphrodite:

Heu óccidi, óccidi, inquit,
Vitámque, mater, efflo.[31]

[He said, "Oh, I'm dying, I'm dying; my life is ebbing away, mother."]

Here the repeated verbs of the first line are a comic exaggeration from Terence (*Andr.* 605), the counterpart of the tragic exaggeration of ὄλωλα, ὄλωλα. This phenomenon may properly be termed a transfer, since it corresponds to the most direct of textual itineraries: comic overtones appropriate to the Terentian original are also appropriate to the Anacreontic translations. In the following line, by contrast, we might more suitably speak of a transposition, since what is involved is not merely the displacement of a classical term attested in Cicero—"vitam efflo"—but its inversion also: here in its new context it is made to heighten the irony, since "efflo" is normally associated with the ebbing away of blood.[32] Thus the careful placing of suitable subtexts creates two centers of attention in these lines, two foci for ironic *pointes:* Aphrodite's caustic observations are preceded by Eros' unconscious irony at his own expense.

As well as anticipating the culmination of the piece, these lines also mark a general division between the studied preclassical diction of the opening lines and the unexceptional vocabulary of the remainder; a division that might be symbolized by the standard "vulneravit" (line 11) compared with the rare "sauciatus" (line 4). Contrasts of this kind are more fully exploited in Estienne's translation of pseudo-Theocritus 19, where the more spacious hex-

---
31. 1554.104.
32. Compare the Ciceronian subtext, *Tusc.* 2.24. *ad fin.*

ameter line allows even greater verbal and rhythmic effects.[33] Here, out of the eight-line poem, is the second half, in which Eros questions his mother about the disproportion between the size of the bee and the size of its sting:

> Ostendit digitum: & queritur quòd tantula visu
> Bestia quum sit apis, tantum det acumine vulnus.
> Cui tum subridens mater, Quid? non apis & tu
> Es similis, qui tantillus das vulnera tanta?

[He shows his finger and asks what sort of creature the bee is—so small to look at, but with such a mighty sting. Then smiling at him his mother says, "What? Are you not like the bee, since although you are so small you cause such mighty wounds?"]

"Tantulus" is, from the dictionary's evidence, a "favourite word with Cicero"[34]—entirely classical therefore and supported by the even purer classical "subridens." "Tantillus" has exactly the same sense but is anteclassical and in association with the following "tanta" is perhaps directly reminiscent of an assonantal and alliterative line, such as Milphio's comment on Adelphasium: "monstrum mulieris, tantilla tanta uerba funditat" (a monster of a woman—so tiny yet pouring out such great words) (*Poen.* 273). Here, as in Plautus, "tantillus," while assonantally similar to "tanta," is opposed in sense; the couple "tantillus"/"tanta" echo, moreover, the earlier "tantula"/"tantum," which had been applied to the bee and its wound, and this verbal concision facilitates the ironic transfer of the understanding from the bee to Eros. The ironic *pointe* is supported by the rhythmical features of the final line, which eschews the major caesura so that the break is thrown back to the grammatical pause at "similis" and forward to the bucolic caesura after "das." This divides the line into three units of two-three-two words and articulates into prominence the one word that, midplaced in the sentence, acts as a marker for the poem's lexical manipulations and emphasizes that the two culprits are one: "tantillus."

Aided by the firmer, more spacious structure available in hexameters, Estienne is able to adapt with greater ease the rhythmical aspects of his author. In his commentary on this ode's Anacreontic "parent," he praises such lines as Πονεῖ τὸ τᾶς μέλιττας (the bee's sting hurts): "Habent enim magnam venus-

---

33. The text is quoted from 1554.80–81. The Theocritus translation reappeared in *Moschi, Bionis, Theocriti . . . idyllia aliquot,* sigs. [Biij^v]–[Biiij^r], where it was followed by Estienne's translation of the Anacreontic ode.

34. LS, s.v.

tatem in his versibus huiusmodo articuli" (clauses of this kind have great charm in these lines).[35] Yet it is perhaps in the Theocritus translation that the more delicate interweaving is most in evidence. It exemplifies a predilection for rhythmical patterns corresponding to the marked patterning of the Greek. Κλέπταν . . . κακὰ κέντασε . . . / Κηρίον and σίμβλων συλεύμενον[36] have a wealth of alliterative equivalents, most clearly in "pede pulsat . . . parenti," but also perhaps in "aluearibus: articulos" and "furem/fauos." So too the word order, particularly in lines 6 and 8, echoes the Greek ἁλίκα τραύματα ποιεῖ (line 6)/τραύματα ἁλίκα ποιεῖς (line 8). The concern for verbal and rhythmic harmonics dominates, indeed, the greater adventurousness visible in the Anacreontic ode—the contrasts in diction between the component halves of the poem. The humorous diction of the opening gives way to the picture of Eros whose words ironize him either by subtextual implication or by the polysyllabic pomposity of "minuta serpens/Pennata vulnerauit" dispelled by the bathetic "Apem vocant coloni." And this bathos directly precedes Aphrodite's own deflation of Eros' condition. The same point is made in pseudo-Theocritus, yet the isocola of lines 6 and 8 suggest that polyptoton will be the dominant figure of interest. Indeed, it is against such strongly defined clausulae that Estienne plays off the contrasting diction of the homophonically related "tantula" and "tantillus." (The Greek has polyptoton only: τυτθόν/τυτθός.)

A comparison of these two translations by Estienne demonstrates clearly the *variatio* built into the imitative enterprise. The Anacreontic contrasts are contrasts in types of lexis, all of which assist in ironizing Eros. Rhythm is a rather muted component of such ironies, and despite Estienne's appreciation of the interwoven structure of the Greek, his final lines are less successful than the corresponding lines in the Theocritus translation, where rhythm is dominant: here, indeed, the contrasts and the affinities are all suggested by mellifluous assonantal choices rather than by a fundamental ironization of diction as occurs in the Anacreontic ode. The assonance of these lines, since it takes up and extends the alliterative opening, helps to create a firm rhythmical structure that creates and conveys, rather than simply supports, the meanings of the poem.

To end this section, we may usefully draw its numerous threads together by plotting the interactions of the translation as fragment and of the commentary as intertext within a genre that overtly presupposes the exploitation of space and an emphasis on *variatio*. This genre is ecphrasis (or *descriptio*),[37] a genre

---

35. 1554.81.
36. The Greek text of Theocritus is printed in 1554.80.
37. On ecphrasis, see Heinrich Lausberg, *Handbuch der literarischen Rhetorik: Eine Grundlegung der Literaturwissenschaft,* 2 vols. (Munich: Hueber, 1960), 1: sections 810 and

of which the Anacreontea offer numerous examples. The emphasis in ecphrasis is on the vivid representation of some given object or scene. In odes 28 and 29,[38] this object is the beloved. Precisely in such instances the text as a spatial form, an empty *locus* or habitation is at its clearest. To be sure, this is not solely attributable to a view of the past based on a spatialization of time but is equally well inherent in a genre that depends for its plausibility on what Barthes terms "l'effet de réel."[39] In this case, it is the identification and naming of the bodily parts that performs the function of grounding the description in recognizable reality. The effect is further increased by the deictic illusion directly preceding and indeed triggering the descriptions: "vt edocebo" and "vt te docebo"[40] give the impression of an entity susceptible to exact definition. Because of this fusion between narrative mode and pictorial mode (an example, of course, of *ut pictura poesis*),[41] it is the narrator who effectively acts as "pictor" and the picture to be painted coincides with his prescriptive account of the elements to be included in it. Here, then, the empty *locus* of the poem functions as a canvas to be filled with color; and the colors that the picture receives are the colors of lexis and *elocutio*. Pictorial color is nicely coextensive with narrative color.

As Philippe Hamon rightly points out, two major rhetorical principles regulate the construction of the descriptive mode. On the one hand, "le descriptif peut être d'abord appréhendé comme une tendance du texte à la digression, à l'expansion *(amplificatio)*";[42] on the other hand, "l'hypotypose, sorte d'hyperbole de la description, est ce qui rend 'présent' les choses."[43] These elements combine to subvert any true narrative line by the paratactic juxtaposition of potentially expansible elements designed to make each part of the body as vivid as possible. Hence the tendency for listlike accumulation, which emphasizes parts rather than the whole and threatens to push the constituent elements of the text out of proportion with each other, so that no overall picture

---

1133; and, for its use in Hellenistic poetry, Kenneth J. Dover, ed., *Theocritus: Select Poems* (London: Macmillan, 1971), *ad Id.* 1.29–63.

38. 1554.97–99 and 99–101 respectively.

39. Roland Barthes, "L'effet de réel," in *Le bruissement de la langue* (Paris: Seuil, 1984), 167–74.

40. 1554.97 and 99 respectively.

41. For this notion, see Rensselaer W. Lee, *"Ut pictura poesis": The Humanistic Theory of Painting,* Norton Library, no. 399 (New York: Norton, 1967); Yvonne Bellenger, "Les poètes français et la peinture: La ressemblance comme critère esthétique au XVIe siècle," in *Mélanges Franco Simone,* Bibliothèque Franco Simone, no. 4 (Geneva: Slatkine, 1980), 1: 427–48.

42. Philippe Hamon, *Introduction à l'analyse du descriptif,* Langue, linguistique, communication (Paris: Hachette, 1981), 97.

43. Hamon, *Introduction,* 73.

emerges.[44] However, such accumulation is nonetheless circumscribed by the necessity to name major parts of the body. The poems associate praise of the perfections of the beloved with the practical necessity to conclude when all the major bodily parts have been listed. The natural progression from head to foot characteristic of the *blason*[45] is enforced as a narrative law and reflected by its conventional association with the beginning and the end of the poem and by the subsequent unfolding of the poem according to this association.

Of particular interest in these poems are their final lines. Ode 28, for example, ends by envisaging the possibility that the wax image will gain life; and life is symbolized by the image's capacity to speak, an independent capacity that would not necessarily coincide with the speech of the narrator:

Quid plura? eam ecce cerno.
Loquere credo cera.[46]

[What else? Look, I can see her. I think the wax image is going to speak.]

This particular *descriptio,* then, presents itself as nothing more than a prelude to life, nothing more than a verbal simulacrum to which the ability to speak is the true counterpart. The text attempts to conceal its own autonomous *vox* by appealing to the more important *vox* of the image: the image is lifelike enough to be credited with speech. Yet this subordination of the metalanguage of the description to the language of the living reality is little more than a subterfuge, envisageable only because of the vividness of the narrator's own description: the potentially living reality depends for its efficacy on the supposedly secondary reality of the *descriptio*. In any case, the poem ends without recording any speech on the part of the wax image. And it is the difference between "vt edocebo" and "eam ecce cerno" that itself serves as a symbolic marker for the passage from the textual to the extratextual, as though the referent were dissociable from the rhetoric and diction that act as its vehicle. But this move is itself a rhetorical move, an insistence that the processes of *enargeia* have been

---

44. Cf. Gisèle Mathieu-Castellani, *Les thèmes amoureux dans la poésie française (1570–1600)* (Paris: Klincksieck, 1975), 128 n. 85: "L'unité de la Belle est une unité *morcelée*. Le détail l'emporte sur l'ensemble"; 136, on the rhetoricity and stylization of the portrait as essentially antirealistic.

45. For the *blason,* see Hamon, *Introduction,* 147 ff. (*blason* of Quaresmeprenant from Rabelais, *Quart Livre*); and Dudley B. Wilson, *Descriptive Poetry in France from Blason to Baroque* (Manchester: Manchester University Press; New York: Barnes and Noble, 1967), especially chapter 1, "The Blason," 1–56, and chapter 2, "The Prolongation of the Blason," 57–99.

46. 1554.99.

successful enough to persuade the reader-viewer of the portrait's *vraisemblance*. The assertion of *vraisemblance* is a vindication of the power of *enargeia*, not vice versa; so that the extratextual referent depends for its existence on the success of the *enargeia* that has preceded it. The extratextual is produced by the textual and cannot be divorced from it.

In ode 29, the techniques of the previous poem are taken one step further by the hyperbolical desire to make Bathyllus the source, in comparison to which Apollo's beauty is derivative:

> Sed Apollinem mihi istum
> Refingito in Bathyllum.
> Sin veneris Samum olim,
> Fac Apollinem ex Bathyllo.[47]

[But let this picture of Apollo be remodeled into Bathyllus. If you ever come to Samos, make Apollo out of Bathyllus.]

The final identification of Apollo and Bathyllus is motivated by the previous comparisons with Mars, Venus, Mercury, Pollux, and Bacchus. The recognizable grouping of Olympian deities facilitates the movement from earlier similes to this later implicit metaphor. The recourse to Apollo as the incarnation of male beauty both completes this particular sequence of hyperbolical compliments (based on the stereotyped notion of the beloved as a god or goddess) and attempts to anchor the previous comparisons more securely within a perceptible "reality": note the appeal to sense evidence, intensified by "ecce" supporting "video." Thus although the earlier similes may appear no more than ornamental additions, they in fact fill the twofold purpose of openly establishing the hyperbolical topos of divine beauty and of preparing the shift to metaphorical identification occurring at the conclusion of the poem.

In his commentary, Estienne deals extensively with odes 28 and 29. Imitative parallels are constantly cited. What matters here, however, is less the presence of such parallels than the way in which philological inquiry based on exegesis provides an oddly anachronistic view of the *proprietas* of diction. Thus the lines

> ῞Αμα γλαυκὸν ὡς ’Αθήνης,
> ῞Αμα δ’ ὑγρὸν ὡς Κυθήρης,[48]

---

47. 1554.100–101.
48. 1556.24.

[one eye gray like Athene's, the other languishing like Aphrodite's]

draw from Estienne the comment that γλαυκῶπις 'Αθήνη (gray-eyed Athene) is a Homeric formula; and he continues:

> Quod autem ad ὑγρὸν attinet, verti Paetum, illum secutus versum, qui est inter antiqua diuersorum authorum epigrammata [*Auct. Priap.* 37], Minerua flauo lumine est, Venus pęto.[49]

[As far as the word *languishing* is concerned, I have translated it by "paetus," following that line that is contained in the ancient epigrams of various authors: "Minerva has golden glances, Venus's are languishing."]

In later comments on these poems, Estienne will establish further references, this time on the basis of elegiac echoes;[50] or again there is a Virgilian disquisition on ῥοδινὴν δ' ὁποῖα μῆλον (as rosy as an apple), citing *Aeneid* 8.160 and *Eclogues* 2.51 in order to demonstrate that "lanugo" is the Latin equivalent of χνοῦς (down).[51] Now it is not the fact that Estienne adopts this method at all so much as the implications it holds for translation that are important. Since it is in the nature of the commentary to act as an empty *locus,* a locale or a habitation, having no definite contours of its own but assembling a heterogeneous body of material, its operations are, in this sense, analogous to the instances of *descriptio* that it is glossing; an overall picture in each case is achieved through the accumulation of essentially disjunctive elements for which a unity is asserted through an imitative theory of *elocutio.* In other words, each reading can, within the bounds of the commentary, accrue a considerable amount of comparative material endlessly demonstrating the operations of imitation or suggesting how imitation might work at the level of translation. The textual elucidations contained in the commentary are widely researched. Yet these researches, although conducive to a general theory of imitation, do not necessarily imply homogeneity in their findings. Hence the disparity between findings based on elegiac models and those based on Republican Latin, such as "paetus."

When applied to the accompanying translation, the disparity in diction becomes even more marked. Read as individual units, the translation displays a

---
49. 1554.73.
50. 1554.73–74.
51. 1554.75.

reasonably homogeneous view of imitation. Both Estienne's and André's versions, for instance, exhibit a high degree of elegiac, Ovidian, or Plautine veneer, an attempt, perhaps, to illustrate what Estienne, following Cicero, calls the "venustas" of language. Read according to their *dispositio* within the poem, however, a much broader view of translation emerges—one that juxtaposes the diction of Golden Age Latin poetry with Republican Latin represented by "paetus," with Catullus' "mollicellos" (Estienne uses this as well as André)[52] or with the Silver Age Latin of Pliny (André's "nigresco," for example),[53] some of which had also been actively used by other influential Neo-Latinists.[54] This has a number of consequences. In the first instance, it illustrates how the commentary privileges the unit over the sequence. Commentaries by their nature read parts rather than wholes. Second, since the genre of *descriptio* itself moves by sections, there is no attempt to weld the diction into a whole. The fragmented portrait highlights particularly well the fragmented diction. Indeed, this particular translation illustrates well Barthes' words about the genre of ecphrasis as a whole: "l'*ekphrasis* est un fragment anthologique, transférable d'un discours à un autre."[55] Ecphrasis itself is composed of such brilliant fragments, acting as dense compendia (cultural, semantic, rhetorical) that rivet the narrative line together at many different levels. To that extent, ecphrasis can be seen as a figure for the genre of translation in general. Barthes concludes his discussion of ecphrasis by saying, "Ainsi apparaît une nouvelle unité syntagmatique, le *morceau*";[56] and it is frequently with the fragment that the burden of Estienne's translation rests, rather than with the integrative procedures associated with his commentary.

3

From the evidence of the preceding section, it transpires that the counterpart of Estienne's theory, in the commentary, of imitation as collapsed temporal succession is the spatial image of the poem as an empty *locus,* a locale allowing the constant relocation of lexis. Thomas Greene makes a similar point when he writes in relation to the term *contaminatio,* "History becomes a vast container

---

52. "Paetus": 1554.98; "mollicellos": 1554.97 (André: 1556.25).

53. 1556.25.

54. E.g., Secundus, *Basia* 8.21, 23: "paetulos ocellos," "colla mollicella"; Marullus, *Epig.* 2.32.70: "Iamque nigrescebant prima lanugine malae."

55. Roland Barthes, "L'ancienne rhétorique: Aide-mémoire," in *L'aventure sémiologique* (Paris: Seuil, 1985), 102.

56. Barthes, "L'ancienne rhétorique," 102.

whose contents can be disarranged endlessly without suffering damage."[57] The relationship to the past that this view entails could best be captured in the image of the thesaurus, whose classical sense of treasure-house or storehouse is linked to the idea of lexical productivity through the cognate notion of *copia,* of which indeed thesaurus is a frequent manifestation.[58] Like *copia,* the term *thesaurus* has its roots in rhetorical theory, where it is exploited in connection with the orator's necessary assembling of his materials. For Cicero, and, later, Quintilian, *thesaurus* subsumes *res* as well as *verba* and thus embraces the twin aspects of the orator's task, standing for the wealth of material that is to be the product of his extensive preparation.[59] *Thesaurus* is the equivalent metaphor for the more neutral *copia* and one of its major advantages is to provide a conveniently visual notion of the literary place where, through *inventio,* the orator may "find" his materials. Thus *thesaurus* also covers the realm of topical logic with its emphasis on the availability of material viewed as a series of *loci* or topoi on which the orator can build his argument. (The same idea is also often psychologized as the art of memory, whose role is to establish the combined *res* and *verba* firmly in the mind as a necessary preliminary to discourse.)

Whatever its formal links with the network of oratorical terminology, the thesaurus image has nonetheless autonomous validity. In so far as it presents a synchronic view of the material assembled, it can stand metonymically for the relationship of the Renaissance writer to his or her predecessors—his or her sense of their contemporaneity, their current availability; all previous writing becomes a repository permanently available to succeeding generations. By simple extension of these terms, Neo-Latin translation itself can be said to act as a thesaurus. It consistently preserves lexis in exactly the same way, by acting as an empty container or *locus* receptive to the displacement and relocation of diction, which thereby becomes evidence of the survival of Latinity as a whole. Yet this entails important revisions to the original idea. For one thing, the orator's storehouse had specifically conjugated *res* with *verba,* whereas translation gives priority to *verba,* particularly in the form of allusions that depend upon a perceptible subtext. Since translation submits these subtexts to reworking, the notion of translation as thesaurus will not be coterminous with the oratorical practices of Cicero and Quintilian but involves modification of our understanding of this term, a modification that creates a slippage between two functions and two epochs.

---

57. Greene, *The Light in Troy,* 39.
58. Cf. Cave, *The Cornucopian Text,* 6–7.
59. Cave, *The Cornucopian Text,* 6–7.

At its most optimistic, the image of the thesaurus celebrates exuberantly the miraculous preservation of Latin. The discontinuity separating linguistic and cultural epochs is bridged by the constant reproduction of the distinctive features of the thesaurus image: thus many poems within Estienne's translations thematize the contacts between different linguistic strata and activate disparate authorial echoes latent within the image of the thesaurus as the summation of amassed materials. Nonetheless, Greene's image of history as a container does not allow for selectivity or priority among materials. Selectivity and preference constitute criteria that determine the choice of materials without reference to the overall view of lexis inherent in the notion of thesaurus itself. In particular, the unfolding of the original's riches within a renewed context implies an elaboration that can never be identical with that original. Working within the general framework of *variatio,* the expansion of the original that can be subsumed under the term *amplificatio* suggests a powerful centrifugal motion. This elaboration of the inherited corpus both illustrates ideally the potential capacities of the thesaurus and yet, by the multiple directions it develops, seeks possibly to surpass the actual achievements of the ancients. Thus, perceived as the alternate transmission and renewal of lexis, Neo-Latin translation moves along an axis of *repetitio* and *variatio,* stasis and dynamism, reverence and revolution. For Greene's image to be entirely valid is to underplay the *variatio*-inspired transformations that translation brings into play.

In this context, the very notion of translation as involving transposition might well appear to be a figure for the persistent action of temporal transmission upon the text, since temporal passage involves the prominence of certain lexical elements over others, which are thus displaced and effectively absent from the center of attention. Hence the image of total availability present in the thesaurus is above all theoretical, the symbol of the integrity of the past. In practice, the past is only selectively present. The highlighting, through lexis and the complex tropes of *elocutio,* of certain linguistic areas carries with it the stasis affecting those areas of lexis unvitalized by *renovatio.* As a result, *renovatio* bears on a corpus with potentially ambivalent status: if translation is the representative of the thesaurus, it is necessarily the imperfect representative since it activates a part rather than the whole. In the final analysis, translation is bound to remain a selective fulfillment of the totality for which it stands. Its adumbrations are destined to be partial realizations, versions never attaining definitive status. No one translation can exhaust all the possible variants, allude to all the possible subtexts, create all the opportunities for the dynamics of linguistic release. Indeed, in a curiously paradoxical way, humanist translation depends for its continued existence on the deferral of such a linguistic plenitude. For to attain this plenitude not only would prove the redundancy of translation as a genre but would eliminate any possibility of *renovatio*. Instead, the thesaurus would be actualized, Latin static rather than expansive, retrospective rather than innovative. More important still *repetitio* would suppress *variatio* as a crucial literary process and hence dethrone the endless transformations, the protean multiplicity, on which translation thrives.

In Estienne's hands, Neo-Latin translation is not, then, allotted a merely secondary role, passively repeating or faithfully parading the philological findings of the commentary. While evidence can be adduced for this subordinate view of translation, it ignores the fact that this translation is actively endowed with the capacity to shape distinctive segments of the commentary. Moreover, to the extent that it is itself capable of *renovatio,* the translation equally helps bring about the further *renovatio* of the commentary as a hybrid of philology and exegesis. For, from another angle, the commentary also can be portrayed as the actualization of the thesaurus in a manner parallel to, and possibly more explicit than, the translation. Like the translation, therefore, the commentary is the realization of the notion of the storehouse further reflecting, in however selective a form, the greater storehouse that is the literature of classical antiquity. Indeed, at the most elementary and visual level, the spatial metaphor for the organization of literature emerges most clearly in the actual setting down of the intertext in printed form within the commentary.

Where enacted in specific relation to Estienne's Neo-Latin translation, therefore, "honestè furari" and "furti conuinci" take on an unexpected dimension. In the translation, diction appears as an effect of appropriation in accordance with the commentary's advice that it should not be "aliunde petitum, sed domi natum" (not a borrowing, but an original creation)—an appropriation, in other words, that conceals its alterity. By itself, such advice might be a prescription for imitation alone or for a translation unself-conscious of its origins. In Estienne, by total contrast, the opposite is the case, since the commentary calls attention to the nature of the diction fielded, thus highlighting with particular clarity the direct link to the classical authors. More than that, in his overt statements about choices for translation, Estienne totally bypasses contemporary mediators. Nowhere in the commentary is there any reference to influential Neo-Latin contemporaries or recent predecessors, even though, in reading the translation itself, it is difficult to imagine that none of it had come under the spell of Marullo, Pontano, or Secundus. Nonetheless, in the absence of Anacreontic imitations by Estienne, his translation becomes a means of privileged access to the past, testifying to his desire to keep his sources fresh and clear, to strip away the accretions of historical passage. The individual lexical unit is the place where the past breaks out, shines through. This aspect in itself lays stress on a coruscating diction, in which the choice of an allusive word or phrase can be of prime importance for the reader's awareness of subtext. In Estienne's exercise in translated Anacreontics, "honestè furari" (if understood as lexical importation) is in complicity with its apparent antithesis, "furti conuinci" (if understood as the demand to acknowledge such importation). Or like the lovers in the translation of ode 55 (1554.110), fragments of allusive idiom constitute a "signum," a pointer to the traditions out of which they are composed; and they fire Parthian arrows of recognition at the reader before disappearing once more into the textual hinterland.

CHAPTER 4

Words and Voices in Elie André

"festiuus Anacreon, etiam Latinè loquens"
[merry Anacreon, actually speaking Latin]
—Prefatory epistle to Pierre de Montdoré

Less than a year[1] after the appearance of Estienne's *editio princeps* and partial translation of pseudo-Anacreon, the humanist Elie André (Helias Andreas is his own Latinization of his name) published a complete translated version of the Anacreontic odes.[2] A second edition was published, also in Paris, by Robert Estienne and Guillaume Morel in 1556,[3] but the translation received no further contemporary publication in its entirety.

In order to highlight André's particular approach to Anacreontics, it will be instructive to begin with his translation of the very first ode,[4] a poem that had received extensive notice from Estienne in his commentary.

    CANTARE nunc Atridas,
Nunc expetesso Cadmum:
Testudo verò neruis
Solum refert Amorem.
Mutanda fila nuper
Curo, lyrámque totam.

---

    1. The date of André's dedicatory letter to Pierre de Montdoré is "VIII. Calend. Ianuarias" without indication of year, but the translation was first published in Paris by Thomas Richard in 1555.

    2. On Elie André, see Reinhold Dezeimeris, *De la renaissance des lettres à Bordeaux au XVIe siècle* (1864; reprint, Geneva: Slatkine, 1970), 39 and n. 2, 61 (citing Joseph Scaliger, dedicatory letter to *Lectiones Ausonianae*); and Louis Desgraves, *Elie Vinet, humaniste de Bordeaux (1509–1587): Vie, bibliographie, correspondance, bibliothèque,* Travaux d'Humanisme et Renaissance, no. 156 (Geneva: Droz, 1977), 25. André is the author of a *plaquette* on the death of Henri II and of *Carmen de pace,* both dated to 1559. He had previously been the author of a section of a translation of Theodore of Gaza's Greek Grammar (1551).

    3. All subsequent references will be to this edition.
    4. 1556.5–6.

[First I desire to sing of the Atreidae, then of Cadmus. My lyre strings repeat only love. I recently got the strings changed, and the whole lyre.]

The poet's relationship to his medium, which is also the translator's, ends with the reassertion that a new thematics is being essayed:

Magni valete posthac
Heroës ergo nobis:
Nam barbiti iocosae
Solos canunt Amores.

[Farewell, great heroes, henceforth: for playful lyres sing only of love affairs.]

For the change of course of which *recusatio* is the vehicle and token, "barbitos" might almost serve as the cue, evoking as it does Horace's project to transfer foreign lyric into contemporary Latin idiom.[5] "Barbitos" occurs only here in André; βάρβιτος recurs five times in the Anacreontea.[6] The Horatian overtones are supplemented by the presence of "iocosae," a word used by Horace to refer to his own lyre in *Carmina* 3.3.69: "non hoc iocosae conveniet lyrae" (this is not appropriate for a merry lyre).[7] The poem, with its many synonyms for lyre and strings recalls Latin elegy: "testudo," "nerua," "fila," and "lyra" are all evocative of previous Latin contexts. Such *elocutio* might seem to constitute a pattern of unified, coordinated references, establishing a set of correspondences between the vocabulary of Greek lyric and that of Latin lyric or elegy. A scheme of this kind could produce a coherent reading of this translation in which each reference to the lyre as instrument contains further references to Latin elegy or lyric. And there would be nothing in this view to run counter to the reader's literary expectations.

Yet this view does not account for the lexically most intrusive element in the

---

5. See R.G.M. Nisbet and Margaret Hubbard, eds., *A Commentary on Horace "Odes" Book 1* (Oxford: Clarendon Press, 1975), *ad Carm.* 1.32.3 on "barbitos," a word "never fully naturalized in Latin" and directly recalling Greek lyric poetry (Sappho, Anacreon, Pindar, Bacchylides); and Greene, *The Light in Troy*, 67–72, on Horace's exploitation of Greek idiom.

6. Cf. West, *Carmina Anacreontea*, "Index Verborum," s.v.

7. Cf. *Carm.* 1.6.10: "imbellisque lyrae." Ravisius Textor also combines "iocosa" with "chelys" and "plectrum."

translation, the verb "expetesso." The occurrence of this verb is restricted to Plautus, who himself uses it only a small number of times in the *Miles Gloriosus*.[8] The Plautine item on the one hand and the elegiac vocabulary on the other clamor equally for the reader's attention and neither can be accorded privileged status, since each carries allusions alien to the other. If this poetry is to make an appeal to linguistic authority, it is clear that such an appeal cannot be univocal. Moreover, these instances of *elocutio* function in rather different ways. "Barbitos" is a familiar feature, a feature evocative of a poetic program—and thus entirely appropriate to André's work. There is also the supporting presence of Ovid, who begins his first and second books of *Amores* with poems analogous to that of "Anacreon" here.[9] But whereas these two Latin authors form a compact unit with identifiable thematic connections, the Plautine "expetesso" has none of these programmatic connotations: there is no particular Plautine context of which it is specially representative. Its use, we might say, also constitutes some minor extension of the Latin language: Plautus had not used an infinitival construction after "expetesso"; André, by so doing, innovates.

In this very first translation, then, André adopts the same attitude toward lexis and *elocutio* as Latin elegy had toward its material: the *recusatio* dismisses epic ambitions, and here this dismissal is focused through the motif of the lyre that spontaneously sings of love. This is an evident variation on the motif found in Latin elegy whereby a god (often Cupid) deflects the *carmen* into a new choice of subject matter. In André's translation, this deflection pertains not to the subject matter itself (this is fixed, received rather than created by him) but rather to the deployment of diction. And André indicates the eclectic nature of such diction by the obtrusive and contrasting "expetesso"/"barbitos." Horace is claiming primarily novelty of subject matter, whereas elegy asserts a particular attitude toward diction as well as toward subject matter. The two are not far removed and it might be expected that André would attempt as far as possible to enforce a stylistic uniformity, a *proprietas* of diction, within his translations. This would be entirely consonant with classical appreciations of elegiac style.[10] But this is not the case. Uniformity in diction is allowed to take second place to a preference for a varied

---

8. *Mil.* 959, 1229, 1231.
9. André's translation thus makes the same point as Estienne's.
10. To cite only the most famous, Quintilian's appreciation in *Inst. or.* 10.1.93: "Elegia quoque Graecos prouocamus, cuius mihi tersus atque elegans maxime uidetur auctor Tibullus. Sunt qui Propertium malint. Ouidius utroque lasciuior, sicut durior Gallus."

elocutio. And this opening poem is a demonstration of just such a preference: the topoi of displacement and deflection, the possibility of parallels in the work of Ovid,[11] the Horatian "barbitos" left as a permanent Greek lyric presence in a Latin text, all create a uniformity of impression that is quickly unraveled by "expetesso." "Expetesso" simply cannot be accounted for in the terms that the rest of the poem urges on the reader; the lexis remains diverse. One might argue that "expetesso" and "barbitos" are equally obtrusive, equally distinctive as lexical choices. The difference is that "barbitos" can be accounted for in terms of the general tone of the poem and its translation; "expetesso" resists such accountability. If the poem asserts a choice of nonepic subject matter, the term "expetesso" itself deviates from the otherwise distinctively elegiac formulations that the bulk of the poem espouses. The overall result here is what might be termed a linguistic *concordia discors,* in which the reader's expectation of a final linguistic integration is constantly deferred and the translation continues to act as a signal to the presence of subtexts other than those with the greatest stylistic *proprietas.*

With this initial instance in mind, one can tentatively posit at least two functions of classical Latin lexis in a poem of this sort. On the one hand, a correspondence theory of language emerges in which a lyrical diction in Latin is used to translate a lyrical diction in Greek; on the other hand is a noncorrespondence theory in which a word is chosen on the basis of its rarity or unusualness by an act of linguistic virtuosity on the translator's part. In this latter case, the poem becomes a place where linguistic play is uppermost, a *locus* where the translator tries out diction for its own sake without any reference to the propriety *(proprietas)* or mutual compatibility of such diction within the wider context of the translation; hence the "inappropriateness" of translating Anacreontea by the language of Roman comedy. Just as the lyre consistently deviates from the poet's purpose to sing of epic, martial themes, so the diction of the translation refuses to be assimilated to a consistent linguistic norm, a univocal presentation. Once the pluralizing character of such translations is perceived, it will quickly be seen that the extensive nuanced vocabulary of classical Latin can easily be exploited by a principle of copious proliferation: words can be released into a literary space without any reference to an overall controlling norm. Or rather, the presence of such a norm does not, it would seem, exclude the copresence of the opposite linguistic principle, a principle that allows the spontaneous recourse to any diction, appropriate or not to its context. The most evident of criteria by which to account for a literary

---

11. Recognized, we may remember, by Estienne in his commentary on this poem (1554.65).

project of this kind is an appeal to a notion of lexical profusion, constituting a poetics of *contaminatio*.[12] At the aesthetic level, quite as much as at any other, "Anacreon" is seen to be "festiuus" indeed.

The salient characteristic of the translating processes at work in André's collection can be summarized by the notion of recontextualization. The deflection of poetic material that the opening poem celebrates involves the displacement of terminology from its original setting and its relocation (the translation as a *locus*) within a new setting, where it can be seen to fall into two distinct types: decontextualized diction and contextualized diction. They may be examined, and explained, in turn.

It is a feature of decontextualized diction to build up strata of diction without reference to a controlling (originary) context. It is not that no context is recognizable for these strata but that such contexts do nothing to further the reader's understanding or to enrich the new context within which they now appear. If this diction functions as *allusio*, it does so at a purely ornamental level: the reader is alerted to the presence of an instance or instances of lexis of a particular kind, but the thematic coloring that such instances lend the text may be nonexistent. They are solely the result of *copia* and point to a richly woven surface fabric rather than carrying within them profounder informing meanings. The normal method by which such layers of sedimentation are built up is the constant displacement and incorporation of linguistic material. This persistent displacement builds up layers of vocabulaic sedimentation, frequently recognizable by their lack of compatibility with the other lexical features of their context. Thus a number of poems display an interest in Greek loanwords, such as *machaera, scyphum, cyathus,* and *corymbus*.[13] Comedy is a particularly fruitful source for such vocabulary, since Greek influence there is strong and clear; though elegiac and lyric poetry equally demonstrate a sufficient measure of Hellenism to contribute. Or again, a further stratum is indebted to Catullus and the Catullan tradition: so *codicillos, anhelo, frigerare, mollicellus,* and *suauiari*.[14]

---

12. Greene, *The Light in Troy,* 41, notes that the humanist poet draws on multiple intertexts without anxiety.

13. For instance, "machaera" (ode 31, 1556.29 [twice]); "delicatum / Scyphum" (ode 18, 1556.19), "Affer scyphum" (ode 26, 1556.24); "cyathus" (ode 21, 1556.21), "Cyathi in modum" (ode 39, 1556.36); "nigris . . . corymbis" (ode 26, 1556.24).

14. These instances, together with their counterparts in Catullus himself, are as follows: "codicillos": ode 9, 1556.12 = Cat. 42.11–12; "anhelo": ode 21, 1556.21 = Cat. 63.31; "frigerare": ode 21, 1556.21 = Cat. 61.30; "mollicellus": ode 20, 1556.21 = Cat. 25.10; "suauiari": ode 8, 1556.12 = Cat. 9.9.

In certain cases, a whole translated piece can be built around the deployment of a single instance of lexis or a restricted number of such instances. Such is the case with ode 2, where the eye is attracted by "truces" (line 6) and "lepusculis" (line 4: an example of Neo-Latin interest in diminutives). But it is "parmulis" (line 12) that is the real source of interest, for it is a Horatian *hapax*.[15] As such it requires the reader to acknowledge the deliberate choice of the unusual in place of the usual; a translation is precisely a *locus* where such choices can be displayed as a product of the translator's learning that the reader is invited to savor. The vitality of these Neo-Latin translations, therefore, will depend on the reader's complicity, his ability to recognize and appreciate the *elocutio* displayed. In terms of the whole collection, however, *parmula* does not act as a *hapax,* as it does in Horace; its unusual quality was clearly attractive to André, who uses it four times during the course of his work.[16] Yet gradual acclimatization to this word must be balanced against the fact that its contextualization is minimal. *Parmula* calls attention to itself through its unique occurrence in Latin Augustan literature; it enacts an *allusio* to an author, Horace, but it enacts no *allusio* to the wider poetic context where it appears in Horace's work. In *Carmina* 2.7.10, it will be remembered, Horace recalls his military past and puts it aside in favor of epicurean festivities in the present. Yet none of these undertones is relevant to the understanding of André's translation. Horace as a subtext is evoked by the presence of "parmula," but the status this might imply is subsequently denied because the classical text is not allowed to take up a dialectical relationship with the Neo-Latin text. As a consequence, the connotative aspects of the word *parmula* are severely curtailed. What is important in this particular instance is the ability of the word to "illustrate" the discourse within which it appears. "Parmula" acts as an example of rhetorical *enargeia,* the figure of bright presentation. Yet note that what it presents is only half there: the echoes of the pristine utterance are excluded from the workings of the translation. Engagement and disengagement operate in rapid succession.

A poem that deals in larger linguistic perplexities is ode 40 (1556.36); and it is a prime illustration of what has been termed contextualized diction. The original is known in several versions from pseudo-Theocritus and the Anthology to the Anacreontea.[17] The poem under consideration has, therefore, several peers, all forming a corpus rewriting a single theme. This is André:

---

15. "Relicta non bene parmula," *Carm.* 2.7.10.
16. In addition to the present poem, there are two examples in ode 14 (1556.16–17), one in ode 31 (1556.29).
17. See James Hutton, "Cupid and the Bee," in *Essays on Renaissance Poetry,* 106–31.

Apem rosae Cupido
Non cernit insidentem,
Incautus at ferîtur.
Manúque sauciata
Tenellus eiulauit.
Proinde cùm decoram
Volasset ad Cytheren,
Heus óccidi, óccidi, inquit.

[Cupid does not see a bee lying in wait on a rose. Careless, he is stung. Stung in the hand, the poor tender little thing wailed. Then when he had flown off to beautiful Aphrodite, he said, "Oh! I'm dying, I'm dying."]

The phrase "Tenellus eiulauit," to which can be added "óccidi, óccidi," belongs to the diction of Roman comedy, but despite the obtrusiveness of this diction,[18] no specific subtext is initially evoked that might further inform our reading of the poem: the reader has to await the conclusion of the piece before a larger purpose can be given to this terminology. By contrast, the beginning and end of the poem do deploy diction to more immediately perceptible purpose. The bee of the opening is reposing, κοιμωμένην, in the original, but "insidentem" in Latin, a word signifying not only being settled upon but lying in ambush.[19] This military insinuation plays in with "ferîtur," an otherwise straightforward translation of ἐτρώθη. Cupid flies off to his mother to complain, but her reply is ironical:

At si, inquit illa, fili
Apis perurit ictus,
Quantum putas laborent,
Quos tu feris sagittis?

["But if," she said, "the bee sting burns, how much pain do you think is suffered by those whom you smite with your arrows?"]

Cupid has been dealt the same treatment he metes out to lovers. André points the lesson by using "perurit," a verb occurring in amorous contexts to refer to

---

18. *Tenellus* is rare; the *OLD* gives three examples of its use with respect to human beings, one of which is Plautus *Cas.* 108: "Bellam et tenellam Casinam, conseruam tuam." For *eiulo*, see Plautus *Aul.* 318, 727, 796, *Merc.* 682; for *óccidi,* Plautus *Cas.* 621, Terence *Andr.* 605.

19. For this sense of *insideo*, cf. *TLL*, s.v., 1886.28 ff.; it should be noted that the verb is also *(ut vid.)* the *vox propria* for the action of the bees on flowers: so *TLL*, s.v., 1885.34 ff., citing Virgil *Aen.* 6.707–9 and Pliny *N.H.* 11.18.

the burning pain of love.[20] Here, then, the diction does not contain any particular elegiac referent. It is the general use of the word that is uppermost. In both these instances, the Latin translation extends the scope of the Greek, shapes the reader's response by enlarging the irony with reference to a recognizable corpus of general subtexts. In view of this significant increase in irony, it may even be possible to argue that in retrospect the Plautine and Terentian diction augments the comedy at Cupid's expense: "tenellus" would in that case translate as "poor tender little thing," and "óccidi, óccidi" would be read as comic exaggeration.[21] If so, the linguistic elements of this translation cohere not at the level of a uniform diction—the diction is discernibly polyvocal—but rather at the level of a pervasive irony that at once reinforces and nuances the data of the original.

This translation suggests that *allusio* in André works not by reference to a single lexical principle but by calling on the reader's ability to supply a general context for the diction that is subsequently redeployed within the body of the translation. On occasion the *elocutio* of a poem can be severely restricted so as to present only one or two significant examples around which the poem is then rewritten. The translation of ode 11 will serve to illustrate the point:[22]

> His vocibus procaces
> Me foeminae lacessunt,
> Anacreon senex es,
> Speclo intuere sumpto
> Nullae vt tibi comae sint,
> Vt laeuis insuper frons.

[Bold women provoke me with these words: "You are old, Anacreon. Take a mirror and see that your hair is gone, that your brow is bare."]

Now there is an epigram version of this same poem by Palladas (*A.P.* 11.54) and its wording is indicative of the choice of "procaces . . . lacessunt": ἀποσκώπτουσι (they banter) is Palladas' word. At the very outset the presence of a sibling makes itself felt and changes the neutral λέγουσι (they say) into a tone

---

20. E.g., Ovid *A.A.* 3.543: "sed facile haeremus ualidoque perurimur aestu." In classical Latin, the simple verb *uro(r)* is still more frequent in this sense than in the compound: e.g., Propertius 2.24.8, 3.9.45; Tibullus 1.8.7, 2.4.5–6; Horace *Carm.* 1.6.19, 19.5; Virgil *Ecl.* 2.68.

21. For the reiteration and multiplication of such interjections, cf. Plautus *Mostell.* 1031 ("uicine, perii, interii"), *Aul.* 713 ("Perii, interii, occidi").

22. 1556.14–15. The poems are also compared by Rosenmeyer, *The Poetics of Imitation*, 178–80, who sets their themes in the broader context of Hellenistic poetry.

of reproach that now becomes explicit rather than implicit. To that extent "procaces... lacessunt" can be taken as a prolepsis, a means of channeling the reader's reaction before the criticism itself is voiced. The Anacreontic λέγουσιν (retained as a participle, λέγουσαι, in Palladas) is displaced by its sibling. Ἀποσκώπτουσι, displaced from its home text, sheds its aura of mocking abuse over the Anacreontic translation; yet "procaces... lacessunt" surely seems an excessive means of capturing such mockery. Is it too much to see it as a deliberate adventure in *elocutio?* "Procaces... lacessunt" may refer directly to Cicero *Familiares* 7.13.2, "scio enim te non esse procacem in lacessendo" (I know you are not bold in provoking others): Cicero thus wrote to C. Trebatius Testa and "led to yet another joke at the expense of Trebatius' unwarlike personality."[23] If so, line 4 would prompt a similar observation: "speclo intuere sumpto" evokes *In Pisonem* 71, "tamquam in speculo vitam intueri" (to look at one's life as if in a mirror). The omitted word "initam" would provide by its absence an ironic commentary on the women's words here: what the mirror will reflect are life's ravages, "Anacreon's" white hair, the fact that he is "senex," γέρων.

In this instance, the attention is displaced away from the context in which "procaces... lacessunt" and "speclo intuere" initially appear to their interaction with the hidden subtext. In that respect, "procaces... lacessunt" is terminologically overdetermined, allowing the nuancing of this translation by the sibling readings of the epigram version. This is an extreme instance of incorporating within any given translation terminology whose pristine context is systematically set aside in order for it to be endowed with a different function and to operate in a different sphere. The same principle of overdetermination would also apply to the Ciceronian diction that serves to activate ironies not present in its own contexts of origin but latent elsewhere in the Anacreontic poem. The use of a particular lexis to stimulate reinterpretation of the early part of the translation is deftly handled; it also provides a clear instance of the discrepancy between the minimum and maximum intertextual properties characteristic of redirected terminology.

The poems examined up to this point have centered on the assertion or denial of a quasi-dialogic relationship with their subtext, particular words or phrases delicately evoking contexts that may or may not be accorded a larger role within the framework of the translated poem. The context may be either reasserted within the translation (the original is relevant) or rejected and its

---

23. Cicero, *Epistulae ad familiares,* ed. D.R. Shackleton Bailey, vol. 1, *62–47 B.C.,* Cambridge Classical Texts and Commentaries, no. 16 (Cambridge: Cambridge University Press, 1977), 341.

elements reapplied (the original is irrelevant). What has been termed the deflection of poetic material varies in degree according to the translation.

A further relationship with the subtext is also possible, by which deflection is at its greatest and the relationship with the model or models at its most tenuous. A particular atmosphere appears to be evoked constantly, but the phraseology is ultimately unfamiliar. Ode 8 is an early example of this process:[24]

> Tyrio in tapete noctu
> Facili fruens sopore,
> Hilaratus antè Baccho,
> Mihi cum puellularum
> Grege lusitans videbar
> Celeri volare cursu.

[Enjoying an easeful night's sleep on a Tyrian covering, merry with wine, I seemed to be flying along at great speed, frolicking with a group of young girls.]

Numerous classical equivalents were available for the opening lines and it is interesting that André appears to have disregarded them. For "Tyrio in tapete," we might have expected—more "suitably"—Plautus' "beluata tonsilia tappetia" (*Pseud.* 147). Instead André glances at Catullus' "Tyrio in toro" (61.165) and proceeds to innovate using a combination of materials. Similarly, ἐγκαθεύδειν has a direct Latin equivalent in "indormire" (e.g., Horace *Epod.* 5.69), whereas André chooses a circumlocution emphasizing the easefulness and pleasure of sleep ("facili," "fruens"). Now it is striking that André's stylistic variations on given lexical units cannot simply be ascribed to ignorance of the expressions in question, for in the following lines he shows familiarity with the most precise vocabulary: "puellula" is once more Catullan (61.57, 175, 181), while "lusitans" is Plautine ("lusitent," *Capt.* 1003). Here again it seems likely that the phraseology of these first two lines can be read as a variation on standard terminology.

Compare now the Greek:

> Διὰ νυκτὸς ἐγκαθεύδων
> Ἁλιπορφύροις τάπησι,
> Γεγανυμένος λυαίῳ,

---

24. 1556.11–12; Greek text: 1554.7–8.

Ἐδόκουν ἄκροισι ταρσοῖς
Δρόμον ὠκὺν ἐκτανύειν,
Μετὰ παρθένων ἀθύρων.

[Sleeping by night on purple-dyed coverings, merry with wine, I seemed to be running on the tips of my toes, and sporting with maidens.]

Ἁλιπόρφυρα is a typically Alexandrian allusion to Homeric diction,[25] where the word occurs in the *Odyssey* (6.53, 13.108); while the expression πορφύρεοι τάπετες occurs in Theocritus *Idylls* 15.125. What is interesting is that André has chosen not to reproduce this *allusio* to epic but to call up a response standard in Latin poetry: in addition to Catullan dreams of marriage, the adjective in "Tyrio in tapete" also functions as an index of wealth and luxury, Tyrian dye being particularly costly (cf. Ovid *A.A.* 3.169; Pliny *N.H.* 9.135, 137). In Latin poetry, the adjective is constantly used as a symbol of such wealth.[26] Its appearance here alerts the reader both to a particular diction and to a particular atmosphere—an atmosphere of sensuous luxuriance and ease. Γεγανυμένος is purely Homeric (*Il.* 13.493, 14.504, 20.405). André's solution here is at one with his solution for the succeeding lines: he selects a distinctive lexis, in this case "hilaratus," a rare but classical word occurring in Catullus (63.18) and Cicero (*Fin.* 2.8, *N.D.* 2.102, *Brut.* 44), just as he will subsequently turn to comedy for his solutions to other linguistic problems. It is noticeable, indeed, that each time an epic *vox* occurs in Greek, André adopts corresponding Latin phraseology of equally distinctive origin. Thus ἀθύρων (*Il.* 15.364) is matched by "lusitans," and ἐπεκερτομοῦν (used participally at *Il.* 16.744, 24.649; *Od.* 22.194) by "probra ingerebant," a Livian usage (2.45.10).

André thus handles this poem in a number of distinctive ways. First, where the Greek employs the diction of epic used in the quite different context of lyric, André responds by transposing the text into a version of *mignardise,* deriving, via Neo-Latin contemporaries and antecedents, from the language of Catullus. Second, classical poetic equivalents of Greek phraseology were already existent in Latin and it would have been natural for him to make use of such equivalents. Yet he turns aside and produces his own versions of these expressions. At one and the same time, André displays his own linguistic *copia*

---

25. On this feature of Alexandrian writing, see Giuseppe Giangrande, "Hellenistic Poetry and Homer," *Antiquité Classique* 39 (1970): 46–77, and for Homeric allusions within the Anacreontea, Rosenmeyer, *The Poetics of Imitation,* 151–59.

26. Paul Murgatroyd, *Tibullus I: A Commentary on the First Book of the Elegies of Albius Tibullus* (Pietermaritzburg: University of Natal Press, 1980), *ad.* 1.9.70, gives instances from Propertius and Horace as well as from Tibullus.

by drawing disparate *voces* into a text that looks back primarily to Homer, and he rewrites such standardized phraseology as already exists in Latin. These two processes take place simultaneously, not successively—there is no movement between linguistic levels. Third, all the diction deployed will naturally be linguistically evocative, but in some cases this is much more marked. The outstanding example in this translation is the phrase "Tyrio in tapete," where the adjective constitutes no real attempt to translate ἁλιπορφύροις, but to draw out its implications, to conjure up an atmosphere both lexical and symbolic. It is at such moments as these, supported by the persistent endeavor to rewrite conventional diction, that the translation, by marking its distance from the phraseology of the original, approximates most closely to the techniques of *allusio* and *variatio* characteristic of the Greek.

Elsewhere this compositional technique may be taken to greater lengths. The slight ode 34 exemplifies this process at its most proficient.[27] It opens with an appeal to the girl not to avoid the poet because of his gray hair. The appeal is then reinforced:

Ne verò quòd tuo flos
Aeui renidet ore,
Fastidias amantem.

[Do not despise a lover because the bloom of youth shines on your face.]

The Greek has been shaped in order to allude to Catullan and Ovidian subtexts, one from a Catullan epithalamium ("ore floridulo nitens," 61.186),[28] others from the *Metamorphoses* ("aeui florem," 9.436; "ore renidenti," 8.197). The final lines, by contrast, are a reminiscence of another Ovidian passage, though they do not allow its entry into the text:

Vide vel in coronis
Album rosae implicatum
Vt lilium decens sit.

[See how beautiful is the white lily entwined with the rose in garlands.]

Estienne (1554.79) pointed out the resemblance between this passage and two passages from *Amores:* 2.5.37, "quale rosae fulgent inter sua lilia mixtae"; and

---

27. 1556.32.
28. *Renidet* itself occurs in Catullus 39, a satirical poem on Egnatius' white teeth.

3.3.6, "niueo lucet in ore rubor." At one level, this rewrites the topos—a proverbial topos at that—of the whiteness of lilies.[29] At another, it juxtaposes the rose with the lily, "lilium" with "rosae," and the abiding impression of beauty ("decens") is the result of the juxtaposed combination of colors; thus Ovid's point is André's too, but it is arrived at by a different route. In the process, the "flos" of line 3 is accepted as a metaphor ("flos aeui") in its immediate context, but its literal facets are activated by the comparison with which the poem ends. André establishes at an early point the lustrousness of youth ("renidet"; compare Catullus' "nitens" and Ovid's "fulgent" and "lucet") and allows that lustrousness to pervade the poem by the delicate coloring of the poem's closing lines. Ovidian memories, in other words, are allowed to support the picture without subtracting from the independent play of images upon which André's poem depends.

To this end, parallel metrical positioning helps isolate "puella" and "flos" as a source of interactive interest, the former as the tenor, the latter as the vehicle, a metonymic transformation of long standing.[30] But then the image shifts: "flos" is to be taken with "aeui," a standardized collocation that is the equivalent of the Greek cliché ἥβης ἄνθος, no longer identical with "puella" but nonetheless within the same lexical field—a dead metaphor, in fact.[31] "Renidet" is to be seen as preparatory. As a variant on "fulgent" and "lucet," it helps locate a second sphere of Ovidian influence—the last three lines to which, as it were, it "belongs"; equally, it bears "nitidus" within it, to be placed alongside "album." "Renidet," then, functions as a means of bringing the metaphor "flos" into contact with the apparently deliteralizing elements of the final lines, "album . . . lilium" and "rosae." This process, of course, activates the metaphoricity of "flos" itself. But "renidet" functions only retrospectively, only when the reader considers the relationship of "flos" to "album rosae . . . lilium."

The expression "renidet (ore)," it is clear, is a particularly strong activator of meanings in this translation. Indeed it is able to feed and support two very different readings, a microcontext and a macrocontext, and it is empowered to do so by the subtexts relevant to each case. "Renidet" both prepares and anticipates. Qua preparatory, it alerts the reader to the *variatio* on classical

---

29. Cf. A. Otto, *Die Sprichwörter und sprichwörtlichen Redensarten der Römer* (Leipzig: Teubner, 1890), s.v. "lilium," citing Propertius 2.3.10, Martial 1.115.2, al.

30. Cf. Catullus 62.39–40: "Vt flos . . . sic uirgo . . ."

31. See Michael S. Silk, *Interaction in Poetic Imagery, with Reference to Early Greek Poetry* (Cambridge: Cambridge University Press, 1974), 100, 102, n. 16, for examples of this collocation, as well as for the terminology used here.

Latin material exercised in the concluding lines (indeed to take "renidet" as a variant of "nitens," "fulgent," and "lucet" is to recontextualize it, to see the whole process as Catullan and Ovidian). Qua anticipatory, its corresponding adjective, "nitidus," can be set alongside the contrasting pair "album" and "rosae."

The closing lines reverse a standard topos. The allusion as it stands makes reference to contexts where feminine beauty is normally praised. The *testimonia* are unanimous on this score, and "decens," a *vox* virtually confined in the Augustan Age to Horace and Ovid, emphasizes the point since it is only used of women.[32] By reversing terminology normally applied to the woman and applying it to the man, the narrator in André's translation equates his own beauty when crowned with flowers to that of the girl who is avoiding him. The ironies of the elderly man vaunting his own beauty are forcefully increased in André's version precisely because of the relevant subtext.

Viewed in terms of the deflection and transformation of lexis, the poem just examined exhibits manipulation at its most persuasively allusive: in the space of ten lines, the reader is encouraged to hunt for allusions that are then subjected to a reversal of the most startling kind. The application of the "female" topos at the close to a male narrator is a clear demarcation of historical distance traveled, evidence that the reader's sympathy is engaged in favor of the translation without owing reverence to the Ovidian *auctoritas* on which it is based. Causal links (Ovid as the origin of the translation) could be said to be laid aside, and simple dependency through *allusio* jettisoned in favor of a form of *aemulatio*. If *variatio* is a sign of translation's tendency to manipulate its classical data, *aemulatio* is the furthest point of such a manipulation, the point at which linguistic play prevents the reader from assuming an undisturbed relationship between text and subtext and challenges him or her to see a different relationship between "original" and "translation." Translation is not just a question of the rehousing and the redeployment of inherited linguistic collocations but one of ambitious rivalry with the texts on which it is supposedly parasitical, subordinate.

The paradox of this position, in the case of Ovidian allusions, is that much of Ovid's material itself is a rewriting of previous elegy or lyric.[33] "The

---

32. A representative selection of *loci* is as follows: Horace *Carm.* 1.4.6–7: "Gratiae decentes / alterno terram quatiunt pede," 1.18.6: "quis non te potius, Bacche pater, teque, decens Venus?"; Ovid *Met.* 12.405–6: "Hylonome, qua nulla decentior inter/semiferos altis habitavit femina silvis"; *Her.* 5.35–36: "Qua Venus et Iuno sumptisque decentior armis/venit."

33. Cf. Kathleen Morgan, *Ovid's Art of Imitation: Propertius in the "Amores"* (Leiden: Brill, 1977); Jean-Marc Frécaut, *L'esprit et l'humour chez Ovide* (Grenoble: Presses Universitaires, 1972).

rewriter rewritten" might be a convenient tag for André's attitude toward Ovid, were it not for the fact that such a tag suggests too sharp and defined an awareness of linguistic strata, as well as a more pervasive, less fleeting Ovidian presence in André than is necessarily the case. Nonetheless, if the techniques of Neo-Latin translation can to any degree be perceived as *aemulatio,* then such techniques will entail the eventual overturning of translation's subordinate position with regard to its original, for *aemulatio* implies centrifugal linguistic motion.[34] "Translation theory was effectively only an outgrowth of imitation theory," Terence Cave writes about vernacular poetics.[35] One might add that, though naturally suggesting a technique of imitation, the very notion of *aemulatio* to which such adventures in subtextual awareness give rise is also a properly translative activity, since sanctioned by no less an authority than Quintilian himself. Quintilian, it will be recalled, had defined the art of the paraphrase as a matter of ambitious rivalry rather than mere translation.[36] By viewing meanings as floating and debatable, Quintilian gives corresponding license to *interpretatio* as a discipline of perpetual transformation through which meanings can be re-created within their own cultural sphere. Under the stimulus of *aemulatio,* Neo-Latin translation can be portrayed as a matter of paraphrase, in the sense of talking alongside its models of inherited diction, not because it necessarily advocates subjecting the *res* of the Greek poem to radical modification in theme or nature, nor because it cultivates anything other than standardized Latin equivalents for Anacreontic meter, but rather because it reshapes the patterns of subtextual reading out of which the *res* are composed. The equivocal relationship in which *aemulatio* implicates the Neo-Latin translation and its subtexts is a version of the struggle between originality and repetition that Thomas Greene finds at work in the imitations of Horace and others:[37] translation enacts the same problematics that beset French Renaissance theory and practice of imitation.

In this translation by André of ode 34, the decisively Ovidian and Catullan overtones are placed in such a way that the translation does not merely mime the technical process involved, does not merely exercise mimetic power on a heterogeneous corpus of classical material, but, by a supreme act of ungrateful reflexivity, alerts the reader to a familiar voice *(vox)* whose echoes are then

---

34. Cf. Luce Guillerm, "L'auteur, les modèles, et le pouvoir ou la topique de la traduction au XVIe siècle en France," *Revue des Sciences Humaines* 52 (1980): 6: "la 'version' est bien le lieu par excellence où observer les éventuels glissements de l'attitude par rapport aux modèles."
35. Cave, *The Cornucopian Text,* 57, discussing Sebillet.
36. Quintilian, *Inst. or.* 10.5.5: "Neque ego paraphrasin esse interpretationem tantum uolo, sed circa eosdem sensus certamen atque aemulationem."
37. Greene, *The Light in Troy,* chapter 4, 54–80 and passim.

compelled to assume an oblique and indirect relationship with the text they come to host. Thus the fusion of disparate lexes implied by *contaminatio* entails a cumulative linguistic activity that unleashes not a controlled ordering and reordering (intelligible as forms of *variatio*) but rather the displacement of interest away from subtexts to the translation itself and its capacity to manipulate successfully the *elocutio* to which it is the heir. The motion is from linguistic subordination to linguistic dominance, from imitative following to emulation, a motion whose prime consequence is the reader's perception of a voice in the text that takes its cue from the rewriting of classical predecessors.

2

At this point a further characteristic of this translation may be commented upon: the high proportion of *sententiae* with which André credits "Anacreon."[38] In a sense such an attitude toward the text might seem to be an inevitable concomitant of André's view of lexis. Just as the classical vocabulary of oratory and comedy is perpetuated by its capacity to appear in texts other than its initial ones, so the fluid, mercurial aspects of the Anacreontic texts—a fluidity that matches the characteristic iambic trimeter line—are fixed, changed into dogmatic statements or reflections on the imponderables of human life. Two points emerge from this. On the one hand, the demonstration of a moralizing strain within the Anacreontea (whether it "actually" exists or not) assimilates the text to the line of classical wisdom that could be excerpted and classified—the chapbook mentality. From this point of view, "Anacreon" is yet a further *exemplum* of the aphoristic and anthologizing traditions to which all

---

38. On the general importance of proverbs and maxims, see the clear account (not only valid for medieval times) in Ernst Robert Curtius, *European Literature and the Latin Middle Ages*, trans. Willard R. Trask, Bollingen Series, no. 36 (New York: Pantheon Books, 1953), *"Sententiae* and *Exempla,"* 57–61. The rhetorical function of the *sententia* is fully discussed by Heinrich Lausberg, *Handbuch der literarischen Rhetorik* 1: secs. 872–79, 2: sec. 1244. The crucial recent book on *exempla* is John D. Lyons, *Exemplum: The Rhetoric of Example in Early Modern France and Italy* (Princeton: Princeton University Press, 1989).

For the Renaissance vogue for *sententiae* (which the Anacreontea thus reinforce), see Verdun-L. Saulnier, "Proverbe et paradoxe du XVe au XVIe siècle: Un aspect majeur de l'antithèse: Moyen Age—Renaissance," in *Pensée humaniste et tradition chrétienne aux XVe et XVIe siècles*, Paris (26 au 30 octobre 1948), Colloques Internationaux du Centre National de la Recherche Scientifique, Sciences Humaines ([Paris]: CNRS, 1950), 87–104; Walter J. Ong, "Commonplace Rhapsody: Ravisius Textor, Zwinger and Shakespeare," in *Classical Influences on European Culture, A.D. 1500–1700*, ed. Robert R. Bolgar (Cambridge: Cambridge University Press, 1976), 91–126, especially 91–95 for further references; Paul Zumthor, "L'épiphonème proverbial," *Revue des Sciences Humaines* 41 (1976): 313–28, and "Tant de lieux comme un," *Etudes Françaises* 13 (1977): 3–10; Lambert Wierenga, "'Sentence' et manipulation: Aspects rhétoriques d'une forme simple," *Neophilologus* 71 (1987): 24–34.

classical authors were susceptible. On the other hand, "the *sententia* . . . was considered as one of the forms of imitating the ancients,"[39] and one has the impression that the philosophy that is being highlighted here is seized upon because it is most evocative of Epicureanism analogous to (for example) that of Horace.

Perhaps the most obvious *loci* within translations for such *sententiae* are beginnings or ends of poems. A poem can be felt to start with a sentential notion or to present such a notion as its conclusion. Consider for instance the opening of ode 26:[40]

"   Simul subit Lyaeus,
"Curae graues quiescunt,
Laetúsque canto, Croesi
Ceu possidens talanta.

["As soon as Lyaeus comes upon me, oppressive cares calm down," and I sing happily, as if I owned the wealth of Croesus.]

Compare the Greek:

Ὅταν ὁ βακχος εἰσέλθῃ,
Εὕδουσιν αἱ μέριμναι,
Δοκῶν δ' ἔχειν τὰ Κροίσου,
Θέλω καλῶς ἀείδειν.

[Whenever Bacchus comes upon me, my cares go to sleep, and, thinking that I have the wealth of Croesus, I want to sing beautifully.]

The proverbializing of the opening alters its relationship to the whole. The Greek envisages a number of indefinite occasions represented by ὅταν and the aorist subjunctive. The Latin renders the condition by "simul" and the indicative and hence exchanges the frequent for the punctual. At the same time, the most generalizing qualities of the opening are emphasized: the statement is strangely depersonalized, an utterance made by an alien voice,[41] of which the

---

39. B.J. Mallet, "Some uses of *sententiae* in Ronsard's Love-Sonnets," *French Studies* 27 (1973): 134.
40. 1556.24; Greek text: 1554.22.
41. Cf. A.-J. Greimas, "Idiotismes, proverbes, dictons," *Cahiers de Lexicologie* 2 (1960): 56, speaking of the tone implied by proverbs and dicta: "on a l'impression que le locuteur abandonne volontairement sa voix et en emprunte une autre pour proférer un segment de la parole qui ne lui appartient pas en propre, qu'il ne fait que citer."

poem following ("Laetúsque canto . . .") is in some sense an appendage designed to exemplify the validity of the utterance. The general, universal, and impersonal precedes the personal and particular.[42] In instances like this, the twin voices of the text—impersonal, then personal—sit in uneasy juxtaposition with each other. It is strange perhaps that the most indubitable proverbial evidence within the poem—"Croesi talanta"[43]—passes almost unnoticed amid the strong light thrown onto the first two lines.

The corresponding case—proverbial utterance as a seal to a text—creates a rather different impression.[44] Ode 52 (1556.45–47; Greek text: 1554.46–48) is a case in point. The context establishes an implicit eroticism: the mention of "uvae" recalls all those contexts in which the vine is an erotic symbol.[45] The poem bears out the implicit promise of its opening lines: a scene of rape stimulated by the effects of drink. Indeed Eros and Bacchus are cited, and their role as controlling agents in this scene is emphasized by capitalization. *Elocutio* is again deployed here to effect: "consopitam" is Endymion's sleep mentioned by Cicero ("consopitus putatur," *Tusc.* 1.38). The Greek ends thus:

Μετὰ γὰρ νέων ὁ βακχος
Μεθύων ἄτακτα παίζει.

[for drunken Bacchus wreaks havoc when he plays with young people.]

Bacchus is traditionally πολυγηθής (merry), φιλοπαίγμων (fun-loving), but here the play is rougher. Drink and disorder are frequently linked with Bacchic rites, and specific associations with sexual license are often introduced.[46] The closing line allegorizes the incident: Bacchus is drunk and impels the young to outrageous behavior. André increases the disorderly conduct:

"Siquidem ebrius Lyaeus
"Petulante cum iuuenta
"Ita ludit insolenter.

---

42. In purely historical terms, one might add that the impersonal would have been regarded as making the personal more acceptable.
43. On Croesus' well-known wealth, see A.S.F. Gow, ed., *Theocritus*, 2 vols. (Cambridge: Cambridge University Press, 1950), *ad Id.* 8.53 ff., supplying examples of Croesus' proverbiality from Greek and Latin literature; *TGL*, s.v. Κροῖσος, "celebratus propter divitias."
44. On this aspect, see Barbara Herrnstein Smith, *Poetic Closure: A Study of How Poems End* (Chicago: University of Chicago Press, 1968).
45. E.g., Ovid *Met.* 13.795; Propertius 3.13.31; Nisbet and Hubbard, *Commentary on Horace "Odes" Book 2, ad Carm.* 2.5.10 give other relevant instances, adding: "Presumably grapes were associated with breasts."
46. Cf., e.g., Horace *Carm.* 1.2.34, 2.12.18, and 19.25–26.

["Since drunken Lyaeus thus plays immoderately with lascivious youth."]

῎Ατακτα is strengthened by its transformation into "insolenter" and "petulante." Thereby the behavior is itself not wholly allegorical, it is no longer the prerogative of Bacchus alone: "insolenter" and "petulans" are equally strong as designators of behavior. The human has the same measure of responsibility as the extrahuman. Note how, after the evenhanded distribution of blame, the sentence becomes ripe for conversion into a generalized comment on drunken conduct. A paradigmatic reading of the text would emphasize how παίζει and "ludit" activate the sensuality implicit in μελάνοχρως and "uvae."[47] In Greek, the agent of such sensuality is Bacchus; supernatural activity is uppermost, supported by the capitalized Eros of previous lines. In Latin, Lyaeus is a metaphorical substitute for wine and drunkenness, a concrete manifestation of the psyche.

At the same time, the *sententia* cannot be regarded as totalizing the content of the poem; the text cannot be held accountable solely to a *sententia* highlighting the role of Bacchus. Even if the Greek original itself asserts prevalent Bacchic influence, to proverbialize such a comment reckons without the position of Eros. For the rape is specifically attributed to the instigation of the god of love:

Ὁ δ' ἔρως ἄωρα θέλγων
Προδότιν γάμων γενέσθαι.

[Love, casting an untimely spell, coaxes her to become a betrayer of marriage.]

῎Αωρα is Eros' equivalent of Bacchus' ἄτακτα: the two agents work as one. Moreover, ἄωρα is right in a sentence commenting on Eros' effect on a woman, since in ἄωρα the ear inevitably hears ἄωρες.[48] In Latin, such implications disappear, ἄωρα being dispersed into "malignus" and "mulier." Further, behind "ludit," as behind παίζει, are evoked by association those contexts in which these verbs qualify erotic activity.[49] But by enclosing his ending within quotation marks, André not only accentuates the responsibility of Bacchus; he excludes the silent presence of Amor, the capacity for wine and lust to inhabit the same or similar vocabulary, as acting with the same or similar effect. The

---

47. Cf. μελανόχρως of women in Theocritus *Id.* 3.35.
48. See *Et. Mag.* s.v.: ῎Αωρες· αἱ γυναῖκες. Similarly, Hesychius: ἄορες· γυναῖκες; and Suda: ἄορες· αἱ γυναῖκες.
49. E.g., Ovid *A.A.* 2.389; Catullus 61.204.

sententia serves to reenforce the lesson[50] and indeed enlarge its field of application only by excluding constituent elements of that lesson; hence the field of application, widened from one viewpoint, is diminished from another. As a translation of the Greek, these lines have the obvious function of underscoring the disorderly behavior inspired by drink and love: to that extent, they support the moral that the *sententia* will attempt to encapsulate. From another standpoint, however, the efflorescence of interpretation that these lines inspire defeats the very purpose for which the *sententia* is set in place, since the *sententia* only partially covers the facts.

No account of these lines can, however, ignore the remarkable outgrowth of meaning in the Latin. The context is again significant:

Ibi eam Cupido mulcens,
Suadet facem malignus
Violare nuptialem.

[There Cupid ill-treats her and persuades her, spiteful as he is, to violate her marriage vows.]

The force of "violare" is underlined by Guy Lee when he says, in another context, "'violare' is a strong word with implications not only of physical violence but of religious desecration and spiritual defilement."[51] As applied to an erotic context, the term is most prominent in Tibullus, who uses it five times in the first book of his *Carmina*.[52] Added to this is "facem nuptialem"—variously extant in classical literature and particularly, perhaps, in the form of Cicero's "faces nuptiales" (*Clu.* 15). "Facem nuptialem" is obviously more colored than the neutral γάμων, while "violare" involves notions of transgression of sacrality more strongly and more strikingly, to judge from its resonances in Tibullus, than are present in προδότιν. To say that this Neo-Latin poem thereby takes on new nuances is to emphasize the linguistic shifts in and between the original and the supposedly derivative translation. The translation tries out the effects of juxtaposing two pieces of terminology drawn from varying contexts. "Facem violare nuptialem" establishes a new linguistic collocation that extends and enhances the Latin language, and it does so by combining the two allusions through a form of linguistic *contaminatio*.

More complex interactions between text and *sententia* are also possible. The examples studied so far orientate the reader's reaction either by presenting

---
50. The status of a *sententia* as *auctoritas* is noted by Curtius, *European Literature,* 57–61.
51. Guy Lee, *Tibullus: "Elegies,"* 2d ed. (Liverpool: Cairns, 1982), 19; and see the further examples from Latin literature collected by Murgatroyd, *Tibullus I ad* 1.3.81–82 and 6.51.
52. Tibullus 1.2.79, 3.81, 6.51, 9.2 and 19.

the poem as an exemplification of a maxim enunciated from the very beginning or by transforming the apparently unexceptional narrative line into a variant on a maxim that serves to clinch the poem.[53] To this basic pattern, others can be added. In ode 15 (1554.14–15),[54] lines 9 and 10 form one of the most evident syntactical patterns; the all but asyndetic contrast between present and future is carried through by the symmetrical metrical positioning of noun (τὸ σή-μερον/τὸ αὔριον) and verb (μέλει/οἶδεν) plus monosyllable (μοι/τίς). This pattern is submerged in André's Latin:

Id curo iam quod instat.
"Cui nota crastina est lux?

[I care for what is at hand. "Who bothers about tomorrow?"]

"Curo" is André's choice in this poem for μέλει, but the rearranged lexical choices of the following line do not implement the more obvious contrastive patterns of the Greek. The most evident manipulation of the Greek lies, however, in the raising of Τὸ δ' αὔριον τίς οἶδεν to the status of a *sententia*. Admittedly, in one sense this manipulation does no more than bring out the maxim latent within the line: classical writers constantly emphasize the unknowability of the future.[55] In this case, however, epistemological uncertainty is highlighted, as if this were in some way the upshot of the poem, without a corresponding highlighting of the exhortation to seize the day. As a result, the *sententia* calls attention to itself by its lack of total integration in the surrounding verbal texture.

This is not the only passage in which such sentiments are present. Ode 41[56] explores similar ideas:

Τί γάρ ἐστί σοι κέρδος
Ὀδυρωμένῳ μερίμνας.
Πόθεν οἴδαμεν τὸ μέλλον.
Ὁ βίος βροτοῖς ἄδηλος.

[What is the point of bewailing your cares? How can we know the future? Human life is uncertain.]

---

53. On this recognized feature of proverbial utterances in literature, see Zumthor, "L'épiphonème proverbial," 324, for the "procès de dispersion" initiated by opening proverbs and the "rassemblement du sens" by closing proverbs.

54. 1556.17.

55. To draw up a list of all the occurrences of this idea in classical literature would be otiose. For a representative conspectus, see Nisbet and Hubbard *ad Carm.* 1.9.13 and 11.8.

56. 1556.37–38; Greek text: 1554.37–38.

These lines are seized upon by André:

"Tibi quid dolore prodest,
"Et confici querelis?
"Quis enim futura nouit?
"Sua cuique vita caeca est.[57]

["What use is worry, or wearing yourself out with cares? Who knows what is going to happen? Each person's life is unforeseeable."]

Here the lines "'Tibi . . . querelis" appear more fully integrated into the rest of the poem: wine as the alleviation of care gives rise to the idea that worry is useless. As such these lines should have a summarizing, retrospective function. The use of μερίμνα ensures that the reader is alive to such a function, looking back to φροντίδας (line 16) and ἄχος (line 14). Although "dolor" quite decidedly fits in with μερίμνα ("dolor," line 10/"angor," line 11/"cura," lines 14, 17), its implications are less summarizing than bound up with the following lines: typographical arrangement ensures that these lines are prominent and that they form a cohesive unit within the body of the poem. From this viewpoint, a causal relationship may seem to be proposed by this aphoristic sequence: to juxtapose these apparently distinct elements and to unify them by typographical distinction is to suggest to the reader that some intrinsic relationship exists between their constituent elements. A causal relationship is perhaps the most obvious sequence to invoke: *because* the future is wholly uncertain, "dolor" and "querelae" are both to no avail. This view assumes that "'Quis . . . est" is to be identified as the major term within the series, an assumption reinforced both by the "enim" of "'Quis enim futura nouit?" and by the adducing of the absolutist phrase "'Sua cuique vita caeca est." This last phrase may appear to be a particular rephrasing of "'Quis enim futura nouit?"; but it is more than that. Where "'Quis enim . . .'" at least maintained logical sequence by the introduction of "enim," "'Sua cuique vita caeca est" maintains no such grammatical continuity. Offering itself as a rewriting of "'Quis . . . nouit," it presents itself not as a question (even a rhetorical question may presume some degree of latitude) but as a statement of unchallenged general truth. It seeks to establish absolute terms against which there is no appeal.

---

57. The very phraseology of this final sentence itself alerts the reader to the presence of a proverb: cf. Tibullus 1.4.77: "gloria cuique sua est," and Murgatroyd *Tibullus I, ad loc.*, citing Plautus *Stich.* 693, Catullus 22.20, Virgil *Aen.* 10.467, al.

In the last example, the phrase "'Sua cuique vita caeca est," although not prominent in the original Greek poem, was elevated to the status of a philosophical tenet consonant with an Epicurean attitude toward life. In other translations, the relationship between the *sententia* and the surrounding text is more problematic. In ode 4,[58] the proverbialization affects lines 7–10 of André's translation:

"Cita nanque currit aetas,
"Rota ceu voluta currus.
"Iacebimúsque puluis
"Leuis ossibus solutis.

["For life races by like a speeding chariot wheel. And we shall lie in our graves, a handful of dust."]

The nature of these lines as a topos (the fleetness of time)[59] makes it perhaps a likely subject for quotation marks. Similar observations may be made about "'Iacebimúsque . . . solutis." The source of interest resides in the lines immediately following the sentential passage:

Lapidi quid addis vnguen?
Quid humi rosas profundis?

[Why are you pouring perfume on the gravestone? Why are you scattering roses on the ground?]

Here too classical topoi are brought into play,[60] but despite their general relevance to the motif of vanity, neither receives the status of *sententia*. Yet these lines might well be candidates for just such a status: they are reflective rather than narrative, their rhetorical question form is often favored by André as a means of introducing *sententiae*,[61] and their content is not markedly different from other passages that do attract quotation marks.[62] The criteria by

---

58. 1556.8–9; Greek text: 1554.4–5.
59. See Nisbet and Hubbard, *Commentary on Horace "Odes" Book 2, ad Carm.* 2.5.13: "currit enim ferox/aetas," and Otto, *Sprichwörter,* s.v. "dies (1)," for the proverbial status of this notion.
60. See Nisbet and Hubbard, *Commentary on Horace "Odes" Book 2, ad Carm.* 2.20.23–24 on the ritual tributes paid to the tomb.
61. E.g., ode 23 (1556.22–23) 11.8–9: "'Quare laboro frustra, / 'Praeoccupóque luctus? / 'Nam si mori necesse est, / 'Quid me iuuabit aurum?"
62. E.g., ode 36 (1556.33) *ad fin.:* "'Nam mortuum teges me / 'Breui mora. Sepultus / 'Nil concupiscit vnquam."

which André identifies *sententiae* and highlights them for the reader's attention are not always logical or consistent. Indeed, they often depend on the translator's interpretation of the poem in front of him. In other words, the translation is not a neutral medium; the reader is presented with poetry that has already been read and interpreted for him.

Ode 25 is a more striking example of the same phenomenon.[63] The theme and its treatment are standard within the collection:

> Mihi bibendo vinum
> Aerumna dormit omnis.
> Ad me quid attinet labor?
> Quid cura, quídve luctus?

[When I drink wine, all my troubles fall asleep. What do I care about anxiety? What do I care about worries and sorrows?]

The first of the *sententiae* sequences is then introduced:

> "Mors me manet, nolim licet.
> "Vitae iuuat quid error?

["Death awaits me, whether I like it or not. Why worry about the uncertainties of life?"]

and the consequent exhortation:

> Ergo merum bibamus,
> Pulchri merum Lyaei.

[Therefore let us drink wine, the wine of beautiful Lyaeus.]

The poem ends with a second sentential sequence:

> "Bibendo nanque vinum
> "Aerumna dormit omnis.

["For when one drinks wine, all one's troubles fall asleep."]

The striking feature here is that the concluding words are an almost verbatim repetition of the opening words. Yet those opening words are not presented as

---

63. 1556.23–24.

containing any gnomic sentiment: the aphorism is created simply by the omission of the personal pronoun *mihi*. While the poem moves satisfyingly from the particular ("mihi bibendo vinum") to the general ("bibendo . . . vinum"), it does also demonstrate that *sententiae* are not subject to precise canons of definition: their presence or not depends on the translator's variable interpretations of his text, and to some extent on his whim.[64]

In other places, the impersonal nature of *sententiae* utterances are given a personalized form. Ode 23 is a prime example:[65]

"   Si prorogare vitam
"Mortalibus valeret,
"Seruare nitar aurum:
"Sumpto appetens vt auro
"Me Parca praeteriret,
. . . .
"Nam si mori necesse est,
"Quid me iuuabit aurum?

["If gold could extend human life, I would strive to store it up, desiring Fate to take the gold and pass me by. . . . For if I have to die, why should I bother about tomorrow?"]

Gold as a corrupter of morals was a standard classical theme[66] and its appearance within the Anacreontea is not unexpected. In the present poem the rejection of gold as being unable to liberate the poet from transience is highlighted by making it part of a proverbializing wisdom. At the same time, such feelings are placed in the mouth of a first-person narrator and the placing of quotation marks around the words presents the experience as being of universal worth. In this case, the two "parts" of the poem are linked by "ergo" (line 12), which draws the conclusion from the premises. Yet the quotation marks distance the utterance from the remainder of the poem, make it external to the other pronouncements of the poem. The first eleven lines—all quoted as *sententiae*—

---

64. Note also the verse "Quid cura, quídve luctus?" Such a sentiment is closely associated with the dispersal of cares and is normally the recipient of quotation marks: this is the case in the very next poem ("'Curae graves quiescunt," ode 26, line 2, 1556.23–24). The reasons for the absence of quotation marks around "Quid cura, quídve luctus?" here seem just as indeterminate as those imposed on the first two lines. A similar case of variability (this time in the choice of dramatic *sententiae*) is noted by Richard Griffiths, *The Dramatic Technique of Antoine de Montchrestien: Rhetoric and Style in French Renaissance Tragedy* (Oxford: Clarendon Press, 1970), 104–5.
65. 1556.22–23.
66. E.g., Horace *Carm.* 3.24.48–49, Tibullus 1.9.17 ff., and *TLL,* s.v. "aurum" 1527.50 ff.

assume a new role, whereby the statements of the poem are not simply the reflections and preferences of an anonymous narrator but timeless arguments about attitudes toward money in the face of inevitable transience.

Even greater manipulations of the narrative *persona* are possible, as becomes clear in the very next translation (ode 24):[67]

"   Mortalis editus sum
"Vitae ad viam terendam:
"Quantúmque iam peregi
"Cursum scio, at latet me
"Quantum viae supersit.

["I was destined to be a mortal to travel on life's highway: I know how much of the journey I have accomplished, but I do not know how much life I still have left."]

Where the previous poem subordinated the predominance of the *persona* to a discursive commentary on gold, here no such subordination takes place. Pronominalization is allowed a central position, but it is a pronominalization of a type unusual in sentential phraseology: "I" appears where "we" or "one" might be expected. The self in this poem is not distinct from the other collective selves implied by the "one" and "we" pronominal forms: on the contrary, the first-person singular here is representative of these collective selves and enacts a destiny that the quotation marks assert to be universal.[68] On this view, there is little or no distinction in meaning between statements uttered by the "ego" in this poem and the abrupt "'Siquidem mori stat omneis" of ode 39. Elsewhere, recognition of the impersonality of this pronoun is accorded: in ode 23, André translates the γένοιτο of line 12 by a hortatory first-person plural ("optamus," 1556.22).

In all the sentential poems cited, the reflections of a narrator on wine and love and transience are transformed into axiomatic statements on the nature of human existence; the "I" of the text is used as a symbol of human frailty, and the reader is invited by André to take note of those instances where such reflections are foregrounded through the introduction of inverted commas. At such moments, the poems depersonalize the narrator in order to make the *ego* utterances assimilable to statements involving "we" or "all." Instead of I/we/all

---

67. 1556.23.
68. Historically, one might perhaps note the influence of the epitaphic tradition in the establishment of an easy fluidity in the use of pronouns.

being distinct entities with individualized reactions, there is a habitual exchange between the particular and the universal. The "I" in André's translations is there not to describe but to prescribe, to elevate the narrative beyond itself, to transform mobility into precept.

It may appear that the two phenomena examined above are unconnected. But this is not so. Taking a cue from André's prefatory letter in which he speaks of "festiuus Anacreon etiam Latinè loquens" (merry Anacreon actually speaking Latin), it may be suggested that both be subsumed under the term *vox,* "word" as well as "voice."[69] The pluralizing lexis and the identification of *sententiae* can both be seen as a desire to locate within the text a natural voice, a *vox,* that will enable the original text to render its message in terms familiar to a contemporary reader. In each case, the desire is to assert a familiarity within the Anacreontic text that will present no uncomfortable problems for the prospective reader. Perhaps the extreme form of such a naturalizing tendency is the "discovery" of *sententiae,* which help to attribute permanent value to Anacreontic verse, since they can be displaced indefinitely from their original context. As a paradoxical result, the voice of their author is the more widely respected the more he is absent from his home (his *locus*). The voice, in order to be appropriated and made known, has to be wrested away from the primary place in which it was originally heard and resited in a locale in which the poet can be given attempted permanency of residence in sentential form. Indeed, the *sententia* owes its distinction to the prominence of the subsequent *loci* in which it has appeared, and to that extent, its power is in direct relation to its appropriations: as Estienne might have argued, Anacreontic *sententiae* command respect because they appear in Horace. Where "Anacreon's" voice is at its most persuasive, it is also at its most impersonal, its most general.

Against this background, the importance of *vox* as "word" can easily be seen. The imitative process appears in reverse. Horace had displaced Anacreontic *sententiae* into his odes; in turn, the translator is allowed to familiarize the Greek by applying a wide range of linguistic devices and registers. The Greek can be made to render different *voces,* often within the confines of a single poem. Where the sentential voice is univocal in its insistence on transience, the voice of *elocutio* is just as insistently plural, not easy to capture in a single framework. As a consequence, "Anacreon" is preserved paradoxically: his lexis is assigned no formal equivalent but is instead translated by vocabulary drawn from the entire range of the Latin language. In André, the move to make

---

69. Cf. Compagnon, *La seconde main,* 149, where *vox* in Latin oratorical writing is defined as "le son (musical), la parole, la langue, le dicton."

"Anacreon" speak Latin, then, necessarily involves a dispersal, a loss of lexical coherence. In order to display the serried richness of Latin diction, the translation must in effect fragment the voices emerging from the Greek. No single voice *(vox)* dominates the translation, because no one set of lexical terms *(voces)* is accorded privileged status.

Hence the ambivalent status of the *sententiae*. Readily identifiable through their typographical prominence, they constitute a layer of seemingly anthologizable and quasi-independent meaning dependent on an equally prominent narrative *ego*. To discover sentential activity is not just to perceive moral purpose or permanent worth in pseudo-Anacreon but to endow him with a character that acts as a point of stasis in a rapidly moving thematic and metrical scheme. *Sententiae* appear to assert a voice in the text that can be naturalized and foregrounded as the bearer of a univocal message. Yet matters are not quite so simple. *Sententiae* were, of course, felt to support the text in which they appeared. However, in André these unified units of sense rely on the same disparate vocabulary characteristic of the rest of the translation: there is no unified diction to support an ostensibly unified message. The profound ambivalence of the *sententiae* is increased when they are situated against the pluralizing lexical strata of the translations. As topoi, *sententiae* are extractable as a separate discourse with wider application than their immediate context; as contextualized elements, they are subject to the same lexical *contaminatio* that is apparent throughout André's translation.

A translation of this kind depends not on utter fidelity to an original but on a series of transformations to the Greek. The translation exists, in fact, as such a series of transformations, by which standardized equivalents are abandoned and any Greek word is susceptible to several translations, all of equal status. The movement is therefore away from lexical unity toward a lexical disparity that frequently affords the maximum contrast between the component elements of an individual poem. However, André's translation is specifically not felt to be a deviant textuality necessarily departing from an originary fullness and operating with diminished lexical resources. The overall impression is, on the contrary, a sense of exuberance, a sense of celebration at the ability of Latin to display its multifaceted, multilayered transpositions of Greek diction. The apparently secondary is characterized by the same fullness as the original. Thus is "Anacreon" *festiuus* indeed, to use André's word.

A technique of this nature implies in André a holistic perception of the target language, not distinguishing between its linguistic elements historically or even generically but at the level of ornamentation: the translation displays the *elocutio* it borrows. A reduced sense of historical process emerges from such a translation as André's because the process is not perceived as having progressed or terminated. The translation relies not on the painful perception of the temporal distance separating two linguistic epochs but on the abolition of such distinctions. In order to better accommodate this constantly transmigratory view of lexis, the translation becomes, for André as for Estienne before him, a *locus,* a bounded space that allows the constant repetition of elements drawn from different and often conflicting linguistic periods and strata of Latinity and whose condition of existence is the willingness to ignore disparities of register, the refusal to stand by a single hard-and-fast view of generic *proprietas.*

Toward the end of the collection, a further poem on the lyre occurs, a complement and extension of ode 1.[70] The very title André gives it—"Homeri lyra"—is indeed evocative of the initial poem with its programmatic stance. That stance has not changed:

Age da lyram mî Homeri,
Vbi chorda abest cruenta.
Age da scyphos sacrarum
(Volo temperare) legum:
Vt humum ebrius lacessam,
Pede verberans soluto.

[Come, give me Homer's lyre, without the bloodthirsty string. Come, give me cups of sacred laws (I want to tune them in), so that I may stamp the ground when drunk, dancing merrily.]

Epic ("chorda . . . cruenta") is rejected and (by implication) the minor works attributed to Homer's authorship embraced. The poem sets the moment of inspiration within the context of drinking: the Horatian and Ovidian "temperare" (*Carm.* 4.3.18, *Ep.* 1.19.28–29; *Met.* 10.108) is enclosed by "scyphos sacrarum / . . . legum." The result of composition under the influence of drink is then given at once and forms the subject of lines 5 and 6. Now taken solely as a translation, "Vt humum ebrius lacessam, / Pede verberans soluto" is far in excess of the Greek μεθύων ὅπως χορεύσω (that I may dance drunkenly) and none of the usual categories of translation is sufficiently precise to encompass it. Taken, however, as an *allusio,* its status as a rewriting of a famous Horatian *locus* (*Carm.* 1.37.1–2: "Nunc est bibendum, nunc pede libero / pulsanda tellus" [Now is the time to drink, now is the time to stamp the ground freely]) is

---

70. 1556.42.

apparent. *Allusio* ensures a different context and a different technique (a technique of *aemulatio*), guaranteed by the inspired madness of the following lines. Here, the singing voice of the poet-narrator ("volo temperare") is now shared by the lyre and most obviously manifested through alliteration and assonance:

Citharáque concinente,
Rabie furens modesta,
Temulenta verba fundam.

[so that, with the singing lyre, and mad with a restrained madness, I may pour out intoxicated words.]

The essential connection with drinking is maintained in the Bacchic vocabulary of "furens" and "temulenta," but despite the reassuring overtones of "rabie ... *modesta,*" the dividing line between high inspiration and chaotic delirium seems uncomfortably thin: the explicit outpouring of "temulenta verba fundam" provokes uncertainty as to whether the words are to be given positive or negative interpretation. Understood in broader terms, this double reading cue is attributable to excess (a form of *copia*): the Neo-Latin translation exceeds its source text by the overdetermination of elements serving to stimulate, as the counterpart of the translator's own *memoria*, the reader's powers of recognition of a classical locution now subject to classicizing manipulation.[71] Excess works not only as a description of a reading cue but also as a wider description of this translation's disregard of classifiable limits, its refusal to remain within manageable theoretical confines. Textual vitality moves in swift succession from *allusio* to *contaminatio* to *aemulatio*. Yet such crossings and recrossings of conceptual boundaries observe no orderly sequence of transmission, no progression accelerating in intensity and in nuanced distance from the source text. A translation by André may reach the point at which it gives privileged status to any particular one of these resources. But the status is temporary and the translation reformulates its emphases. Much as the inflections of Anacreontic voice move from narrator to lyre and back in an endless motion, so the modulations of André's translation achieve temporary crystallization, then pass on.

---

71. Even the rewritten Horatian *locus* in ode 48 is not itself a final version but one of two attempts at a rewriting, the other being "pedibus solum lacessam" (1556.10: the *context* here might also suggest the relevance of "altero terram quatiunt pede" from Horace *Carm.* 1.4.7: in the last analysis, *contaminatio* prevents ascription to a single passage).

CHAPTER 5

Neo-Latin into French: Ronsard from the *Livret de Folastries* to the *Continuations des Amours*

The major task facing Ronsard and Belleau, the vernacular translators of the Anacreontea, is that of adaptation. How can a newly emerged Greek author, once thought consigned to oblivion, be given adequate expression in view of the lexical and metrical resources of the vernacular? For the vernacular does not enjoy the linguistic advantages at the immediate disposal of Neo-Latin translations, where the immense intertextual resources of Latinity derive from the connotations of words created over time, their historical accretions of meaning. Ronsard's reaction to the problem will differ from Belleau's in at least one important respect, since Ronsard never published a translation of "Anacreon" *tout court,* either in full or in part. His translations always appear alongside imitations, in collections where imitations are the prevailing concern. Translation in Ronsard will therefore regularly invite comparison with imitation as two parallel and related approaches to identical material.

Two other issues require preliminary consideration as being broadly indicative of the particular problems in translation that the vernacular, in the person of Ronsard, confronts. The first is a question of Anacreontic style and rhetorical idiom. When transferred to a vernacular context, the discussion of Anacreontic style in which Estienne engages, not always systematically, in the *editio princeps* raises problems of critical awareness. Estienne's choice of Dionysian vocabulary, especially in his preface, associates (implicitly, at least) "Anacreon" with the rhetorical *genus floridum,* the ἀνθηρὸς χαρακτήρ (flowery style), to use an Aristotelian or Theophrastan term for one of the stylistic types that also became standardized in Latin oratorical writing.[1] By this account,

---

1. On this complex subject, see Donald A. Russell, *Criticism in Antiquity* (London: Duck-

Anacreontics are to be considered in the middle class, *floridum* or ἀνθηρός.² A certain amount of critical *contaminatio* is evident even in Estienne's terminology, since his subsequent deployment of the oratorical description ἀφέλεια is associated with Lysias and bucolic, both examples of the *genus tenue* or *humile*. Difficulties increase in the vernacular. It is uncertain whether Ronsard's statements about *beau stille bas* are rhetorical statements in the strict sense of the term. Critics emphasize the contrast in Ronsard's work between "high" and "low" poetic styles without committing themselves to conclusions about the rhetorical status of such styles. Thus Terreaux concludes that in the *Continuations* "les accents doux et gracieux de la lyre téienne succèdent, sans prétention, aux grandes envolées du lyrisme thébain et aux accents élevés des poèmes à Cassandre"³ and that in the imagery of the *Continuations* "le poète use volontiers de comparaisons intimistes ou familières, très souvent d'un aimable caractère agreste et, pour accentuer l'impression de familiarité, de mots ou de tours sans façon . . ."⁴ Laumonier's definition of the "ode légère"—along with which he classifies pseudo-Anacreon—is also suitably broad: "L'Ode légère, qui prend parfois le nom de chanson, est une ode courte, ayant pour sujets, simultanément ou non, la nature extérieure sous ses plus riants aspects, l'amour, le vin, la bonne chère, et d'une façon générale le plaisir des sens."⁵

There is evidence to suggest, then, that *bas* is less an autonomous category with precisely defined contours than an antithesis to the 1550 *Odes* and the 1552 *Amours*, and that it is capable of broadly embracing both *genus floridum* and *genus tenue* material. Ronsard's interest in pseudo-Anacreon, while recall-

---

worth, 1981), chapter 9, "Theories of Style," 129–47; the same author's concise account in the *OCD*, s.v. "Literary Criticism in Antiquity"; and his helpful tabulation of stylistic types, based on Quintilian and pseudo-Plutarch, in *"Longinus,"* xxxvi. G.M.A. Grube, *The Greek and Roman Critics* (London: Methuen, 1965), 107–8, disbelieves the general view that the theory of three styles originated with Theophrastus.

2. Names for the three types vary considerably from one oratorical writer to another. Representatively, Cicero's *Orator* speaks of a plain style ("summissus et humilis," *Or.* 76), a middle style ("uberius . . . robustius," *Or.* 91), and a grand style ("amplus, copiosus, gravis, ornatus," *Or.* 97). For the same categories, Quintilian uses "subtile," "medium" or "floridum," and "grande atque robustum" (*Inst. or.* 12.10.58), while the *rhetorica ad Herennium* proposes "extenuata," "mediocris," "gravis" (*rhet. ad Her.* 4.11).

3. Louis Terreaux, "Le style 'bas' des *Continuations des Amours*," in *Lumières de la Pléiade*, Neuvième stage international d'études humanistes, Tours 1965, De Pétrarque à Descartes, no. 11 (Paris: Vrin, 1966), 341.

4. Terreaux, "Le style 'bas'," 341.

5. Paul Laumonier, *Ronsard poète lyrique: Etude historique et littéraire*, 2d ed. (Paris: Hachette, 1923), 428.

ing oratorical definitions and indebted to them to some degree, cannot in this instance be tied down to sharp contrast in rhetorical practice. Yet this is not to deny all stylistic particularity to vernacular encounters with the Anacreontea. Quite the reverse: Ronsard's recurrent use of the term *doux* (sometimes also *doux-coulant*) in speaking of the Greek poet underlines, in contrast to Pindaric inflation and obscurity, the lightness and musicality of *stille bas* models to be reproduced in the vernacular poet's work,[6] while Belleau's pervasive cultivation of *mignardise* is a constructive attempt to bring out Anacreontic nature or "character."

No small part of the point of such stylistic and generic registers is to direct an audience toward accepted and familiar foci. In terms of audience response to translation, a primary necessity for our vernacular translators (as also for our Neo-Latins) seems to have been to acquaint an expectant audience with the lineaments of the Greek author. The immediate purpose is utilitarian; and its clear implication is that close familiarity with the Greek language in the mid-1550s cannot be assumed beyond a relatively restricted number of *cognoscenti*. But the corollary of this purpose is not that a prospective vernacular audience will automatically require a word-for-word translation in order for this acquaintance to be made. Vernacular polemic against literal renderings before and during the 1550s demonstrates that even such utilitarian purposes would not preclude the cultivation of "literary" style or the deployment of an accepted battery of devices. The flexibility this can tolerate and the sophistication to which it can lead will be apparent from the work of Ronsard, who is more interested in experimentation than in providing a direct account of a Greek idiom. In Belleau's case, the translation of "Anacreon" strictly follows the order of Estienne's edition and is widely acknowledged to be more literal than Ronsard's; but experimentation is not absent by any means. Belleau's translation covers a number of audience expectations. While conveying the nature of Anacreontic poetry without a change in the sequence as published by Estienne, it nonetheless displays a greater thematic interest than a simple transfer of words from one context to another. Ronsard's approach is both more gradual and more demanding, because it is more diverse and less settled in one place. Yet he is engaged upon the same familiarizing enterprise for his readership. In his case, his progressive approach to the Anacreontea is, it will be argued, gathered around a threefold momentum making use of Alexandrian devices previously evident in the Neo-Latin world: *contaminatio, variatio* in

---

6. Cf. Terreaux, "Le style 'bas,'" 341; Laumonier, *Ronsard poète lyrique,* 170–71 for "doux."

the form of *variae interpretationes,* and *allusio.* In other words, questions of Alexandrianism will once again be paramount.

1

The means by which Ronsard was introduced to the Anacreontea have never been established to complete satisfaction. It might be supposed that his acquaintance with this Greek author could not be assumed before 1554 (and thus that his versions were produced quickly between the appearance of Estienne's edition in March and November, the "achevé d'imprimer" for both the *Bocage* and the *Meslanges*), were it not for the fact that scholars have made claims for his early knowledge of this poetry. The claims have differed in boldness, as they have differed in plausibility, and they have been summarized by Silver.[7] Pierre de Nolhac considered that Ronsard had come across Anacreon's name in Planudes' Anthology;[8] he further held that the French poet had come to know "Anacreon" in advance through Dorat or Muret.[9] Laumonier is more tentative, though on three occasions in his thesis, he opts for Muret as the mediator of Anacreontic verse, and he dates this introduction to 1552 and early 1553.[10] Laumonier links "Anacreon" with the Greek Anthology and suggests that the two sets of texts are similar and that Muret introduced Ronsard to the former via the latter:

> [Ronsard] s'était rapproché sensiblement d'Anacréon lui-même, en étudiant et en imitant les épigrammes de l'*Anthologie grecque* à l'instigation et à l'exemple de Muret, c'est-à-dire dans les années 1552 et 1553.[11]

Henri Longnon made bolder claims still:

> Avant de les publier en volume, Henri Estienne avait communiqué à ses amis la plupart des pièces découvertes par lui en 1549. Ronsard connaissait donc Anacréon dès cette époque; la première pièce de lui qui le montre parut en septembre 1552, dans les *Amours.*[12]

---

7. Silver, *The Formative Influences,* 110–17, particularly 110–13.
8. De Nolhac, *Ronsard et l'humanisme,* 108.
9. De Nolhac, *Ronsard et l'humanisme,* 108.
10. Laumonier, *Ronsard poète lyrique,* 121.
11. Laumonier, *Ronsard poète lyrique,* 123.
12. Henri Longnon, *Pierre de Ronsard: Essai de biographie* (Paris: Champion, 1912), 304 n.1.

The pivot here—to which Longnon makes reference—is the sonnet "Ces liens d'or . . ." (*Amours,* 1552, sonnet VI; Lm. IV, 10–11), on which Muret commented in the following year: "La fiction de ce Sonnet, comme l'Autheur mesme m'a dit, est prinse d'vne Ode d'Anacreon encores non imprimée, qu'il a depuis traduite."[13] Since this is an affirmation by the author himself, Silver concluded that Muret cannot personally have been the intermediary for this particular Anacreontic ode.[14] Silver further takes issue with Laumonier's idea that Ronsard may have come to know "Anacreon" through the Anthology. Silver rightly points out that the only epigrams that were shared by the Anthology and the Anacreontea and imitated by Ronsard were *A.P.* 11.47 and 48.[15] These epigrams were conflated by Ronsard into a single poem, "Du grand Turc je n'ay souci" (Lm. V, 79–80). Hutton, assessing independently the presence of the Greek Anthology in Ronsard, finds little evidence for its influence in the early *Amours* collection: there are, he says, many images akin to those found in the Anthology, but nothing specific, nothing directly attributable.[16]

The fact remains that Ronsard did have some early knowledge of this poetry. His imitation in "Ces liens d'or . . ." had appeared eighteen months before the publication of the Anacreontea in 1554. Moreover, there is collateral evidence that Estienne had shown his Anacreon manuscript to others: Vettori, for one, had seen the poem:

> His autem suauissimis politi philosophi versibus addere licet, suaue itidem, lepidumque Anacreontis carmen, quod, cum paucis ab hinc mensibus hac transiret Henricus Stephanus, Roberti filius, probus adolescens, ac liberali doctrina supra aetatem instructus, ipse mihi dedit inuentum a se forte (vt aiebat) in antiqui libri tegmine: venit enim ille ad me domum, & ingenij sui dotibus commendatus, & graui etiam testimonio honestissimi viri ornatus: litteras enim ei ad me dederat Bernardinus Maphaeus Cardinalis, qui studiosos omnes bonarum artium, quarum ipse refertum pectus habet, amplectitur ac fouet. is igitur mihi munusculum hoc, quo magnopere delectatus sum, dedit. Si reliquae autem partes illius similes huic erant, vere potuit Cicero dicere, totam Anacreontis poësin esse amatoriam: confirmatque etiam breuitas numerorum horum, quod

---

13. *Marc-Antoine de Muret, Commentaires au premier livre des "Amours" de Ronsard,* ed. Jacques Chomarat, Marie-Madeleine Fragonard, and Gisèle Mathieu-Castellani, Commentaires de Ronsard, no. 1 (Geneva: Droz, 1985), 4.
14. Silver, *The Formative Influences,* 113.
15. Silver, *The Formative Influences,* 113.
16. Hutton, *The Greek Anthology in France,* 351.

Demetrius de carmine quodam ipsius, inquit. Videri illud, vt erat, temulenti senis.[17]

[Moreover to this extremely pleasant poetry by a cultivated philosopher [Plato, just discussed] one may add a no less pleasant and charming ode by Anacreon. When Henri Estienne, Robert's son, a fine young man and learned beyond his years, was passing through here a few months ago, he himself gave me the ode that he said had been discovered by him by chance in the cover of an old manuscript. He came to my house, recommended by his gifts of intelligence and armed with a solemn recommendation of a most respectable man: for he had been given a letter for me by Cardinal Bernardo Maffei, who cultivates all scholars in the liberal arts, which are close to his heart. Estienne gave me this little present, which caused me great delight. If the rest of Anacreon was like this, Cicero could rightly say that all Anacreon's poetry was love poetry. This is confirmed by the short meter, which Demetrius says about some ode of his: this seems to be by a drunken old man, as he was.]

As Silver says, "we have no ground for rejecting the possibility that the discoverer of 'Anacreon' would have done as much for his country-men."[18] This conclusion is all the more likely since Estienne himself gives indications of it in his note to the reader set before the commentary in the 1554 *Anacreon*. He says that he had first translated a certain number of the odes into French (a translation that is completely unknown) and subsequently into Latin: "eas Anacreontis odas, quas jam antè Gallicas fecerem, in aliquot amicorum gratiam Latinè quoque aggressus sum vertere" (to please some friends, I also undertook a Latin translation of those odes of Anacreon that I previously translated into French).[19] Estienne continues:

Iam verò extrema manu operi imposita, quum eò rem deductam viderem, vt quae meis intimis dicaueram, cum extremis etiam communicanda forent: quo plures huius mei laboris futuri essent participes, eo maiorem cautionem & diligentiam adhibendam mihi existimaui.[20]

---

17. Vettori, *Petri Victorii Variarum Lectionum libri XXXVIII* (Florence: Giunta, 1582), 238–39. The Greek poem is then cited in its entirety. (Vettori's comment originally appeared in the *Variae lectiones* of 1553.)

18. Silver, *The Formative Influences*, 115, and *Ronsard and the Hellenic Renaissance in France: Ronsard and the Grecian Lyre*, 3 vols. (Geneva: Droz, 1981–87), 3:353.

19. 1554.64.

20. 1554.64.

[The finishing touches had already been put to the work, when I saw that matters had reached the stage that the material I had dedicated to my close friends would need to be communicated along with my most recent work. Inasmuch as many of them were to share in this work of mine, I considered that I had to display all the greater care and attention.]

The imparting of some of the odes seems to have taken place when Estienne translated them into French; his friends urged him to provide a Latin version and he may also have shared this version with his acquaintances. The "intimi" are unnamed, but "parmi les 'intimes', on peut, je crois, compter Ronsard."[21] At any rate, this communication will have taken place before 1554, and if we take account of the fact that Ronsard's sonnet "Ces liens d'or . . ." is included in the 1552 edition of the *Amours,* we may push the likely date back to 1552.[22]

The most puzzling feature of this affair is that if Ronsard had a preview of this collection, he did not make greater use of it. Various explanations are possible. Estienne may have allowed his friends to make only brief examination of the collection. In that case, Ronsard would not have had the opportunity to study the poetry in detail, certainly not closely enough to be able subsequently to reproduce their elements in imitation or translation. Of course, there may have been exceptions to this rule. Indeed, Estienne expressly tells us that certain odes were dedicated to his friends, and the friends would no doubt have had access to these poems. This would account for the source of "Ces liens d'or . . . ," taken from the Anacreontic ode 33. There is no evident reason why Ronsard should have chosen this ode in particular for development in his love poetry (others would lend themselves equally well to such treatment); accordingly it seems reasonable to assume that Ronsard was specially associated with this ode or to take this as an indication that he had only the most limited access to the Anacreontea. As further support for this last suggestion, we might note that Ronsard's versions of *A.P.* 11.47 and 48 remain conflated, as they are in Lascaris' Anthology.[23] Estienne, however, had separated them in his edition of "Anacreon";[24] had Ronsard had closer acquaintance with this collection, he would no doubt have followed suit.[25]

---

21. De Nolhac, *Ronsard et l'humanisme,* 109 n. 2. De Nolhac later (119) refers outright to Ronsard's "ami Henri Estienne." Laumonier, *Ronsard poète lyrique,* 121, says simply that Estienne had leaked the Anacreontea prepublication "à son entourage, à ses familiers."
22. And before September 1552, the "achevé d'imprimer" for the *Amours.*
23. As Laumonier points out: Lm. V, 79 n. 1.
24. 1554.14–15 and 15–16 with Σὺ μὲν λέγεις τὰ Θήβης intervening.
25. It is an odd fact, however, that Ronsard did not subsequently separate the pieces after the publication of Estienne's *Anacreon.*

Thus, although the details of the chronology of contact between Estienne and Ronsard can be established with only moderate certainty, the type of poetry to which Ronsard is exposed in the years immediately preceding the *editio princeps* of the Anacreontic poems is nonetheless of prime importance for his reception of these poems. For in Ronsard's work, the Anacreontea emerge into an arena already bounded by defined literary expectations deriving in the first instance from the welter of Latin, Neo-Latin, and Greek material on the same or parallel topics. From that standpoint, Ronsardian Anacreontism in its broadest understanding antedates the publication of Estienne's *Anacreon*. It goes back at the very least to the *Livret de Folastries* of 1553, a work that, Laumonier claims, marked "une étape importante et comme un tournant dans l'évolution du lyrisme ronsardien."[26] The crucial point is, as Laumonier goes on to show, that "les *Folastries* proprement dites correspondent aux pièces légères que les poètes gréco-latins, notamment Catulle, ont écrites en hendécasyllabes."[27] Catullus and his Italian Neo-Latin heirs—particularly Pontano, Marullo, and Flaminio—to whom may be added the Dutchman Secundus, comprise major models for Ronsard, whose work thus forms part of an existing imitative sequence: the past is made continuous with the present by means of an unbroken literary technique. This historical sequence itself does not originate with Catullus, as the presence of Alexandrian epigrams in the *Livret de Folastries* tacitly underlines: Catullus is himself the successor of Alexandrian poetry; he occupies the same place in the chain that will later be taken up first by the Italian Neo-Latins and then by Ronsard.

By the same token, a major stimulus for Ronsard, as Laumonier surmises, came from Muret's lectures on Catullus in 1552, in that they dealt with the Latin poet's "modèles alexandrins et ses imitateurs néo-latins, dont on trouve de multiples échos dans les *Juvenilia* de cet humaniste, publiés au mois de décembre 1552."[28] Over and above considerations of a purely historical nature, it could be added that the very constitution of the *Livret*—Alexandrian, Latin, Neo-Latin—sketches out the same imitative chain displayed in the literature-as-theft paradigm of Estienne and Dorat. In the *Livret* too, historical handing on is treated as a species of imitative descent. But where Estienne makes of this model something approaching a critical language, Ronsard

---

26. Laumonier, *Ronsard poète lyrique*, 93.
27. Laumonier, *Ronsard poète lyrique*, 95.
28. Laumonier, *Ronsard poète lyrique*, 95. Cf. Morrison, "Ronsard and Catullus"; Gaisser, *Catullus and His Renaissance Readers;* Isidore Silver, "Marc-Antoine de Muret et Ronsard," in *Lumières de la Pléiade,* Neuvième stage international d'études humanistes, Tours 1965, De Pétrarque à Descartes, no. 11 (Paris: Vrin, 1966), 33–48.

makes of it a compositional device without any express theoretical terminology. Nonetheless, in the case of both Estienne and Ronsard, the effect is to establish the permanence and stability of a classical *mundus significans* that has lost none of its vitality through spatiotemporal transmission. *Renovatio* in the vernacular is rendered possible to no small degree because it has already taken place in a Neo-Latin milieu where linguistic and generic continuity can be taken for granted. Neo-Latin mediates *renovatio* to Ronsard, as its own *renovatio* vis-à-vis Alexandrianism had been mediated through the classical Latin neoteric and Augustan poets.

Neo-Latin poetry provides therefore a key area of textual transmission and renewal, and Ronsard's links with it are of an extensive and normative kind, part of the "fruitful symbiosis of French poets well aware of previous models."[29] At the same time, the exploitation of Alexandrian epigram in the *Livret de Folastries* represents a preliminary adventure in the "odelette," the particular form that is evolved for the imitation of Anacreontic poetry proper. Indeed, according to Laumonier, "on peut d'autre part considérer la plupart des épigrammes comme des odelettes monostrophiques";[30] more revealing still, we might recall Couat's statement to the effect that in Alexandrian times epigrams had become "des pièces lyriques analogues aux odes d'Anacréon."[31] Without necessarily postulating in Ronsard sharp consciousness of this analogy, one can say that the "Traduction de quelques Epigrammes Grecz" nonetheless provides crucial contact with a genre to which the fortunes of the Anacreontea had been historically and psychologically linked.

Indeed, the impression of linkage is strengthened by the presence among these translations of two Anacreontic odelettes fused into one[32] as well as of a four-line epigram now held to be spurious.[33] The two odelettes, subsequently to be separated in Estienne (odes 15 and 17), had already had a considerable fortune in view of their propagation via the Anthology. Laumonier mentions imitations by Salmon Macrin and Secundus;[34] Hutton gives a more com-

---

29. Ian D. McFarlane, "Pierre de Ronsard and the Neo-Latin Poetry of His Time," *Res Publica Litterarum* 1 (1978): 179; for a broader panorama on this and related issues, see the same author's "Poésie néo-latine et poésie de langue vulgaire à l'époque de la Pléiade," in *Acta Conventus Neo-Latini Lovaniensis*, ed. Joseph IJsewijn and E. Kessler (Louvain: Louvain University Press; Munich: Fink, 1973), 389–403.
30. Laumonier, *Ronsard poète lyrique*, 94.
31. Couat, *La poésie alexandrine*, 173.
32. Lm. V, 79–80.
33. Lm. V, 81 ("Veux tu sçavoir quelle voye"), not in Page, *Further Greek Epigrams*, but discussed by Laumonier, *Ronsard poète lyrique*, 122 n. 3.
34. Laumonier, *Ronsard poète lyrique*, 122 with n. 4; Lm. V, 79 n. 1.

prehensive list still.[35] Ronsard's translation is into heptasyllabic *rimes suivies*. Of the several changes it makes to the Greek, its most radical bears on the mythological reference to Gyges in the well-known opening:

Οὔ μοι μέλει Γύγαο
Τοῦ Σάρδεων ἄνακτος.[36]

[I do not care about Gyges, the king of Sardis.]

These lines become, in Ronsard's 1553 version,

Du grand Turc je n'ay souci
Ny de l'Empereur aussi.

The mythological reference now directly evokes a contemporary political scene, the poet's rejection of which is likewise a rejection of the political themes of the earlier *Odes*, belonging to the rhetorical *genus grave* or *grande*. The harmonics of the earlier *Odes* are considered incompatible with the cultivation of the odelette. In this light, the "Roys" of Ronsard's fourth line have a political and aesthetic reference beyond the historical updating of τυράννους. As a consequence of these changes, the otherwise straightforward *carpe diem* theme of the Greek itself enlarges to accommodate yet another (if more specific) *renovatio*.

The *Livret de Folastries* is a direct introduction to *genus tenue*. Its linguistic practices implement the recommendations of *La deffence et illustration*, which speaks of *renovatio* through such devices as diminutives and compounds.[37] Yet these devices had themselves been long current in Neo-Latin circles: "the predilection for diminutives is greatly furthered by Secundus' *Basia;* the interest in compound words links up with late Latin formations that are developed by the Neo-Latins."[38] Neo-Latin practice may also have influenced Ronsard's liking for the present participles, gerunds, and gerundives.[39]

---

35. Hutton, *The Greek Anthology in France,* 747, ad A.P. 11.47 and 48.
36. 1554.14.
37. On compounds, see Du Bellay, *La deffence et illustration,* 2.6, 137 with n. 3, and Silver's argument, *Ronsard's General Theory of Poetry,* 90–92, in favor of viewing "composer" as "the typically Greek (and Latin) process of creating compound words." A text such as the Anacreontea, with its inbuilt reliance on compounds, lends itself well, of course, to poetic *renovatio* of the kind envisaged by Du Bellay.
38. McFarlane, "Pierre de Ronsard," 181.
39. McFarlane, "Pierre de Ronsard," 181.

Ronsard appears, then, as a lynchpin between the worlds of Neo-Latin poetry, humanist teaching, and commentary, on the one hand, and, on the other, the vernacular attempts to renew a classical *mundus significans* in an entirely different context. In order to facilitate the transfer, the passage across time, Ronsard specifically envisages a number of intermediaries. Publicly, he is willing to acknowledge Latin neoterics and elegists, as in the apostrophe to Muret from the "Isles Fortunées" of 1553, enumerating the authors that Muret is to read to the assembled "Brigade" in that Utopian realm:

Divin Muret, tu nous liras Catulle,
Ovide, Galle, & Properce, & Tibulle,
Ou tu joindras au Sistre Teïen
Le vers mignard du harpeur Lesbien.[40]

Anacreon and Alcaeus, antonomastically represented as "Sistre Teïen" and "harpeur Lesbien" respectively, are associated with the lighter side of poetic writing, to a degree that is subsequently brought out by Ronsard in the starker contrasts of an elegy to Chretophle de Choiseul:

Me loüe qui vouldra les repliz recourbez
Des torrens de Pindare en profond enbourbez,
Obscurs, rudes, facheux, & ses chansons congnues,
. . . .
Anacreon me plaist, le doux Anacreon![41]

Pindar and Anacreon play out the desired change from high to low style, author and style going hand in hand. This idea is more expressly spelled out in the poem "A son livre" (1556), the conclusion to the *Nouvelle Continuation des Amours,* where the lighter vein of Latin elegiac poetry is set against the very different lyrical poetry of Pindar in the specific domain of love poetry.[42] The distinctions prolong the tactical change to "un beau stille bas" initiated by the *Livret de Folastries,* fed by Neo-Latin as well as classical Latin sources, and

---
40. Lm. V, 188, lines 201–4.
41. Lm. VIII, 356, lines 79–81, 83.
42. Lm. VII, 315–25, especially 324, lines 169–82.

reinforced by the appearance of Estienne's edition of the Anacreontea in March 1554.[43]

2

Four Ronsardian collections progressively assimilate Anacreontic material: the *Bocage* and *Meslanges* of 1554 and 1555, and the two *Continuations des Amours* of 1555–56. Each collection will exploit overlapping aspects of Anacreontic idiom, though the *Continuations* have a more sharply defined preference for amorous themes alone. With characteristic vigor, Ronsard made use of the Anacreontic poems as soon as they appeared in 1554. Unlike any of the other translators of pseudo-Anacreon under consideration, he juxtaposes translations alongside imitations in such a way as to render distinctions between them difficult to establish. The first of these collections, the *Bocage,* will, like the *Livret de Folastries* before it, exploit a quantity and variety of small-scale poetry that precludes any favored position for the Anacreontea as such. Its poetry is more or less formally grouped: votive and epitaphic epigrams (Lm. VI, 14–18, numbered I–VI; and 20–44); love sonnets (*id.,* 45–57, numbered I–XII); "blasons" (*id.,* 83–97); odelettes and other shorter odes (*id.,* 102–25); and finally the "Traduction de quelques épigrammes grecs" reprinted from the *Livret de Folastries* (*id.,* 126–27). As elsewhere in these early collections, the *Bocage* designates purely Anacreontic material by the title "odelette." In part, this title is for the sake of clarity; in part, it is by contrast with the large-scale Pindaric and Horatian odes of previous years. However this may be, the polemical stance that the choice of odelette implies was eventually abandoned, since the odelettes, with rare exceptions, are retitled "odes" from 1560 onward: by this time, no doubt, Ronsard was no longer so immediately associated with *genus grave* Pindaric material. In the thirteen new poems in the Anacreontic odelette section of the *Bocage,* metrical innovation matches lexical polyvocality, and as with the generic strata of the *Bocage* as a whole, metrical schemes are grouped. The first, third, and very last poems are heptasyllabic;[44] the second, fourth, fifth, and sixth octosyllabic;[45] and the remaining six alexandrines.[46]

---

43. Laumonier argued that Estienne's edition was published in March 1554 (*Ronsard poète lyrique,* 121; repeated in Lm. VI, 176 n. 1). His argument is based on the presence of Panjas in the "Odelette à Corydon" (Lm. VI, 175): Panjas left for Rome in April 1554 as secretary to Cardinal Georges d'Armagnac.
44. Lm. VI, 102–3, 105–7, 122–25.
45. Lm. VI, 103–4 and 107–11.
46. Lm. VI, 112–21.

A suitable means of approach to this collection can be made through the "Odelette à Jan Nicot de Nimes" (Lm. VI, 115), a piece in alexandrines that Laumonier terms a paraphrase of the Anacreontic ode 2 (1554.2).[47] It has a companion in the Neo-Latin version of the ode done by Du Bellay in hendecasyllables.[48] Both the vernacular and the Neo-Latin odes are concerned with the harmonious balance of direct and indirect objects dependent on the verb ἔδωκεν (gave). Ronsard constructs all the complements in his first eight lines around the perfect tense "a donné," alleviating the monotony of *enumeratio* by the alternate interweaving of juxtaposed complements ("des cornes aus toreaus," "Aus poissons le noüer," "aus lievres la vitesse," "aus lions des dens") and expanded explanatory noun clauses ("la crampe du pié pour armes aus chevaus," "aux aigles l'adresse / De bien voler par l'aer," "Aus serpens le venin qui recellent dedans / Les peaus de leur gencive").[49] The broader rhythms of the alexandrine allow these effects of acceleration and deceleration, which are then summarized in the balanced doublets of the final lines, where Nature gives women beauty

... pour leur servir en lieu
De haches, & de dars, de lance & d'espieu

—the isocola corresponding to the clausulae of

Ἀντ' ἀσπίδων ἁπασῶν,
Ἀντ' ἐγχέων ἁπάντων.

[instead of any shields, instead of any swords.]

This technique is carried through to the *pointe* of the finale, where it is made possible by the introduction of an extraneous clausula—

Car la beauté, Nicot, d'une plaisante dame
Surmonte hommes & Dieus, les armes & la flame.

---

47. Lm. VI, 115 n. 2.
48. Joachim du Bellay, *Oeuvres poétiques,* vol. 7, *Oeuvres latines, Poemata,* ed. Geneviève Demerson, Société des textes français modernes, no. 179 (Paris: Nizet, 1984), "De amoris uiolentia, ex Anacreonte," 159–61. The poem is put in context by Ian D. McFarlane, "Joachim du Bellay's *Liber amorum*," *L'Esprit Créateur* 19, no. 3 (1979): 56–65, especially 61.
49. This last example is not found at all in the Greek.

—whereas the Greek has minimum regularity:

Νικᾷ δὲ καὶ σίδηρον
Καὶ πῦρ καλή τις οὖσα.

[a beautiful woman vanquishes both fire and sword.]

In Kelly's language, Ronsard maintains the démarche[50] of the original, using a remotivated, dynamic structure and lexis. Only rarely is there a dynamically equivalent lexis, as in the cultural adaptation "De haches, & de dars, de lances & d'espieu" (line 10), even more emphatically obvious in the 1584 variant: "De pistoles, de dars."

Du Bellay's contrasting version equally maintains démarche and its use of hendecasyllables could be seen as a formal structure equivalent to the isometrics of the original. The choice of hendecasyllables is itself proof of cultural adaptation, a recognition and exploitation of Catullus that ties the Anacreontic ode to a specific Latin past. While heptasyllables restrict the clausal and rhythmical expansion on which Ronsard relied, such innovation is not altogether ruled out. Thus Du Bellay carefully pivots his version on the complementary alternation of the verbs "dedit" (lines 1, 2, and 8) and "fecit" (lines 3 and 6), which occupy respectively penultimate and initial *sedes* at each occurrence. Latin accidence, furthermore, allows greater flexibility in the disposition of adjectives, verbs, and objects without ever losing sight of grammatical dependency: hence the inversions and interweaving of the opening lines ("Frontem cornigeram dedit iuuencis / Natura, alitibus dedit uolatum" [Nature gave bullocks a horned head, and gave birds the power of flight]), or the string of adjectives and nouns following the factitive construction ("Fecit cornipedes equos, fugaces / Auritos lepores, natatilesque / Pisces . . ." [it made horses horn-footed, long-eared hares timorous, and fish able to swim]). Within a modulated structure, however, Du Bellay develops a dynamic lexis. The pivotal positioning of verbs has already been commented upon, introducing as it does grammatical regularity to the Greek's disparate *enumeratio*. To it may be added the preference for compound adjectives, as in "frontem cornigeram" (line 1), "cornipedes equos" (line 3), and "leones . . . magnanimos" (lines 5–

---

50. Louis G. Kelly, *The True Interpreter: A History of Translation Theory and Practice in the West* (Oxford: Blackwell, 1979), 158–59, 162 ff. Defined by Kelly as "the expressive priorities of phrase or sentence as signalled by word order, grammatical linkage, rhythm and semantic thrust" (158), démarche is closer to what Norton terms the *rerum ordo* as opposed to the *verborum ordo* (for this pair, see *Ideology and Language,* 38). The major advantage in using démarche lies in its mobile, nonstatic sense of the text.

6), none of which has any counterpart in the Greek, but which were extensively exploited in Neo-Latin circles under the stimulus of Catullan experimentation in the same area. Taken together with the shifting modulations in verbal construction (whose repetition exhibits a modest Catullan influence), these more exuberant lexical innovations are the counterpart of the overlapping layers of doublets or associated pairs characteristic of Ronsard's *renovatio* of this ode.[51]

The ability of Neo-Latin to vitalize poetic structure and lexis—either separately or together—is not totally shared by vernacular Anacreontics. For one thing, by reason of its links with a classical past, Neo-Latin is able to have easy recourse to *allusio* to a degree unknown in vernacular circles, where lexis has to be created through calque rather than through appeal to an inherited tradition. This recourse is clear from Ronsard's version of ode 2, which it would be more correct to call a metalinguistic paraphrase than a translation, inasmuch as the Greek itself gives rise to the epexegetic clausulae and expansive doublets: the additions talk from within the original rather than talking about it or alongside it from without. To counterbalance this inbuilt deficiency, the vernacular "Anacreon," in Ronsard's hands, correspondingly pays closer attention to structural renewal. Lexical renewal is in the first instance a facet of structural renewal, a fact that is most immediately apparent in the variety of metrical and rhythmical schemes employed.

The results of this show through in the three Corydon odes (Lm. VI, 102–3, 103–4, 105–7; nos. 25, 4, and 36 in Estienne, 1554.21–22, 4–5, and 32–33), given coherent organization by Ronsard's dedication to an apostrophized Virgilian protagonist, Corydon. This principle itself suggests a unified focal presentation of a sort endorsed by the Anacreontic odes themselves in other instances. The principle is continued by the choice of a heptasyllabic line in two out of three poems and the prevalent use of *rimes plates*.[52] These features bear larger witness to the degree to which a new version can exert specific pressures either globally or on the individual stages of narrative progression, as in the "Odelette à luy mesmes." Ronsard's articulation of the narrative into

---

51. In place of "doublets," Paulo Valesio, *Novantiqua: Rhetorics as a Contemporary Theory* (Bloomington: Indiana University Press, 1980), 42, prefers the term "synonymic dittology," defining it as "the expression of a given semantic nucleus through two (less frequently, three or more) synonymous words or phrases." He remarks that this device "is well known in Classical Latin, and in the European literary languages from their earliest stages . . . to at least the end of the Renaissance" (42).

52. *Rimes plates* exclusively in "Odelette à Corydon" (Lm. VI, 102–3) and "Odelette à lui mesme" (Lm. VI, 105–7); a mixture of *rimes plates* and *rimes embrassées* in "Odelette à luy mesmes" (Lm. VI, 103–4: the scheme is aabccb, with appropriate modifications over succeeding stanzas).

rhythmically delineated sections highlights grammatical structure, particularly in his liking for complex sentences with multiple subordinate clauses that replace the coordinated syntax of the source language. As a result, Ronsard's opening stanza makes the narrator its principal focus, with "Amour" now appearing as the instrument of his wishes. The pattern is standardized in the poem, as in the third stanza, which collapses three separate Greek sentences into one, highlighting once again the narratorial "je." As an adjunct to this remotivated démarche, a firmer temporal structure in French lends clearer perspective to the poem's argument: "apres nostre heure funeste," "tandis que je suis en vie," and "Avant que la Parque blesmie / M'envoye aus eternelles nuits" are more elaborately worked and hence more emphatically positioned than their briefer Greek equivalents. Lexical renewal is used to aid a dynamic structure that modulates between alternating perspective (narrator, Eros, narrator, Eros) and a single central perspective (narrator). Added to this are anaphora or anadiplosis ("Je veus . . . / Et veus . . . ," lines 2–3; "avecq' la tace pleine, / Et avecq'elle," lines 22–23) and parallelisms, regular or inverted ("De me parfumer . . . / Et de me couronner . . . ," lines 17–18; ". . . d'encens . . . on parfume, / . . . on . . . verse des odeurs," lines 14–15), features conventionally associated with Anacreontic diction. It is within this context that more subtle modulations occur, as, for example, the heightened sensuality in the portrait of Love as a serving-boy ("Amour . . . / . . . / . . . my-nu me verse du vin," lines 3, 6) or the change of image (life as river in place of life as chariot, lines 7–9).

Compared with the quiet rearrangement of démarche in which this poem engages and the poised syntax of its grammatical units, the two odelettes flanking this ode inaugurate more radical disruptions. As Laumonier notes, the second of these poems, "Odelette à lui mesme" (Lm. VI, 105–7), "est une 'contamination' d'odes anacréontiques et d'odes horatiennes."[53] He adds that its opening is a transposed imitation of the Anacreontic ode 36 (1554.32–33). Recognition of this process is perhaps most plausibly triggered not by the poem's opening sequence but by the later restatement of the sequence with its pointed questions:

 É que sert l'estudier,
 Sinon de nous ennuier,
 Et soing dessus soing acroistre
 A nous.

---

53. Lm. VI, 105 n. 1.

Neo-Latin into French 171

The equivalence hides modulated allusions involving a reversal of viewpoint ("l'estudier" for διδάσκεις [you teach]; "nous ennuier" for λόγων . . . / Τῶν μηδὲν ὠφελούντων [words of no value]). On this recognizable kernel, the initial sequence works larger changes:

J'ay l'esprit tout ennuié
D'avoir trop estudié
Les Phenomenes d'Arate.

"Tout ennuié" and "trop estudié" are later reechoed in "nous ennuier" and "l'estudier." This syntactical repetition constitutes a fixed reference against which the poem's thematic reworkings can be measured. Thus the cultural reference in τοὺς νόμους . . . / Καὶ ῥητόρων ἀνάγκας (the laws . . . and rules of orators) is replaced by an equivalent reference, this time to Aratus' *Phenomena,* the epitome of pedantic boredom (note that one Hellenistic text is mentioned, and read, within an imitation of another). From the outset, a string of thematic units emerges—the call to outdoor play (lines 4–5), the opposition of bookishness and living (lines 6–8), cares attributed to study (lines 9–10), human transience (lines 12–16).

These numerous distinctions of theme between source text and target text are a sign of analogous distinctions between translation and imitation: none of the new themes violates the generic propriety *(decorum, proprietas)* of the Anacreontea, but equally none of them arises directly out of the ode under consideration. Furthermore, where Ronsard's poem does take up its subtext—in the call to drinking—is paradoxically the point of entry of extensive Horatian imitation (lines 17ff.). An asymmetrical relation is established between theme and its expression in lyric, initiating the *contaminatio* of which Laumonier speaks. The closing lines likewise contribute to this *contaminatio:*

Je veus boire sans repos,
De peur que la maladie
Un de ces jours ne me die,
Me hapant à l'impourveu,
Meurs gallant, c'est assés beu.

The thematic coherence of this passage and its consistent follow-up of the symposiastic details of the previous lines conceal the fact that it alludes neither to Horace nor to the Anacreontic ode 36, but to a completely different Anacreontic poem, ode 15 (1554.14–15):

Καὶ πῖνε καὶ κύβευε,
Καὶ σπένδε τῷ Λυαίῳ,
Μὴ νοῦσος ἤν τις ἔλθῃ,
Λέγῃ σε μὴ δεῖ πίνειν.

[Drink, play dice, and pour libations to Lyaeus, lest some disease should come and say you must not drink.]

The greater circumstantial detail of the French ("Un de ces jours," "Me hapant à l'impourveu") increases the hypotyposis of a scene whose final line anticipates strangely Time's cry to the beleaguered narrator in Baudelaire's "L'Horloge": "Meurs, vieux lâche, il est trop tard."

A poem of this nature is a characteristic attempt on Ronsard's part to adapt the linguistic resources of the vernacular to devices common to, and imported from, the Neo-Latin tradition. In this case, the specific device is *contaminatio*. It is achieved by transcending the restricted framework of the Anacreontic ode and, while preserving thematic constants, moving with steady progression to equivalent Horatian material and then to an appropriate finale drawn from elsewhere in the Anacreontea. Precisely because of the careful observance of genre, the impression is one of the unified coexistence of perceptibly similar discourses, any or all of which can be drawn into play concurrently. This impression of centripetality is reinforced by the revolving movement of the themes, characteristically stated and then repeated with amplification or other adjustment to perspective; the poem returns upon itself at the same time as it gathers momentum. This occurs in each of the three sections of which the poem is composed (Anacreontic, Horatian, Anacreontic) and sets up a persistent cross-rhythm providing a further mode of connection between the potentially segmented sections of the fifty-line odelette. In this way, the ambiguities that *contaminatio* can throw up between lexis, structure or theme, and their positioning (ambiguities exploited, it should be emphasized, with high success by Neo-Latin translators) are here smoothed away, leaving disparity vanquished and an orderly conveying of information conducted on a number of fronts. It is true that the thematic repetitions can—as in the Anacreontea themselves—become wearisome and too familiar. Nonetheless, there is, in the last analysis, nothing to disrupt or defer the accomplishment of pattern in this poem, nothing to unsettle the reader's sense of the priority of unity.

The creation of pattern achieves a degree of integration in ode 36 for which parallels do not always exist in Estienne's and André's translations. *Contaminatio,* here in Ronsard, bears on the relationship between structural sections rather than on individual lexical choices. The reader's perception of the poem's workings depends crucially on the formal reminiscence of ode 36, two versions of which are offered to him by Ronsard in the first dozen lines. The allusions do not present any extraordinary difficulty of identification, either initially or subsequently, yet they must be identified for the reader to be able to gauge the distance between the ambitions of the present poem and a translation of the same. Large-scale *contaminatio* must be founded upon *allusio* as a reading aid. However, in those places where allusions are too slack or too volatile to be established and perceived with any true degree of precision, then the identity of the poem may remain identities, its configuration composed of several thematic strands recognizable in general but not in particular. At such times, the poem is cut free from specificities of reference and moves further out into the broader, if vaguer, field labeled imitation.

A pertinent example of exactly this type of poem is the "Odelette à Corydon" (Lm. VI, 102–3). With perhaps greater reassurance than the poem warrants in view of the processes involved, Laumonier sees it as "imitée largement"[54] from the Anacreontic ode 25 (1554.21–22). Admittedly, this description goes some way, but not far enough, in acknowledging the breadth of the poem's position, the multiple demands that it could make on an accomplished reader. Laumonier's attribution is plainly based on Ronsard's use of "endormir" in the third line of the poem:

Corydon, verse sans fin
Dedans mon verre du vin,
A fin qu'endormir je face
Un procés qui me tirace
Le coeur & l'ame plus fort,
Qu'un limier un sanglier mort.

"Endormir" corresponds to the εὕδουσιν in Εὕδουσιν αἱ μέριμναι (cares go to sleep), with a change of predicate from cares to the image of the lawsuit. And although the imperative and the scene of lines 1 and 2 are frequent throughout the Anacreontic collection, the tenor of these lines is most noticeably close to ode 26 (1554.22), the companion piece to Ὅταν πίνω τὸν οἶνον (when I drink wine). Here, Εὕδουσιν αἱ μέριμναι recurs (line 2), followed a little later by the command Φέρε μοι κύπελλον ὦ παῖ (bring me a goblet, boy) (line 8). This last locution itself has a number of counterparts, including Ἐμοὶ κύπελλον ὦ παῖ, / Μελιχρὸν οἶνον ἡδὺν / Ἐγκεράσας, φόρησον (Mix the sweet, honey-

---
54. Lm. VI, 102 n. 2.

colored wine and bring me the goblet, boy) (ode 38, 1554.34) and Δὸς ὕδωρ, βάλ' οἶνον ὦ παῖ (Give me water and put in wine, boy) (ode 36, 1554.33). With greater pertinence still, the Greek "model" for the very next odelette imagines Love serving the narrator with the words: Ὁ δ' Ἔρως . . . / Μέθυ μοι διακονείτω (Let Eros serve me wine).[55] The similarity of the French version in both passages opens the possibility that "Corydon, verse sans fin / Dedans mon verre du vin" may constitute a reworking of these Greek lines, displaced into the preceding poem.

The difficult-to-pinpoint quality of these verses is equally reflected in the whole ode. Those elements readily attached to ode 25 ("Jamais peine ne souci / Ne feront que je me dueille" from Τί μοι πόνων, τί μοι γόων / Τί μοι μέλει μεριμνῶν [What do I care about troubles, distress, or worries?]; and "Aussi bien vueille ou non vueille / . . . / Il fault que je meure un jour" from Θανεῖν με δεῖ, κἂν μὴ θέλω [I have to die, even if I do not want to]) are juxtaposed with nonstandardized motifs, such as the image of the lawsuit and the express desire for death once youth is over (lines 13–18). In general terms, the use of refrain and the fitful, almost inconsequential movement from one theme to the next make the démarche of the poem utterly familiar to the reader of the Anacreontea. By contrast, the poem also enacts discontinuous leaps, making it impossible to plot other than multiple relationships between itself and the numerous possible subtexts that support and sustain it. The poem lives out, or almost lives out, an existence parallel to these subtexts, its fidelity to experimentation taking precedence over the duty to supply for the reader unmistakable lexical stepping-stones in the form of reading cues. As with Estienne's version of ode 35, subtextual purchase upon the poem is offered and then withdrawn, as the poem engages in the larger task of fusing previously unrelated thematic strands.

The *Bocage* therefore provides substantial evidence of Ronsard's concerted efforts to make Anacreontic idiom accessible to the reader. The Corydon odes in particular seem to have been conceived as a coherent unit, corresponding in form and intention to the selection of Greek epigrams reprinted in this collection from the *Livret de Folastries*.[56] These epigrams, expressly credited by Ronsard with the title of translation, provide a comparable body of material illustrating the constraints of form and the writer's response to them. Commentators normally suggest that translation constitutes a domain of exploration or a propaedeutic, before the writer moves into the higher realm of imitation. Even

---

55. 1554.4.
56. Lm. VI, 126–27; originally contained in V, 77–91.

a cursory glance shows that, here as elsewhere in Ronsard, the relation between the two areas is not adequately described as incomplete to finished: the dividing line is by no means so clearly defined. Constantly Ronsard's ventures in imitation and translation bring about a breakdown of tidy delineations. More than his public polemical position would suggest, Ronsard's published work is more generous and willing to hold open, simultaneously, distinct categories and so suggest their complicity rather than their antagonism.

Such is likewise the case with the Greek epigrams in the *Bocage,* which constitute an instructive complement to Ronsard's treatment of Anacreontics proper and a reminder that Anacreontics themselves are part of a wider scheme that they help to make viable. Their proliferation of rhythmic, metrical, or lexical forms is a microcosm of the experimentation at work in the *Bocage* as a whole. In metrical terms, the prevalence of *rimes plates* in five out of the seven translations[57] could perhaps be portrayed as an attempt to establish a formal counterpart to the elegiac distich typical of the Greek epigram. Only two constitute permutations on this scheme, the brief Lucillius four-liner done into *rimes embrassées* and the twelve-liner from Palladas done into *rimes croisées.* Verse form is a little more varied: four poems choose octosyllables (nos. IV–VII); the other three heptasyllables (no. III, Lucillius), decasyllables (no. II, Posidippus), and alexandrines (no. I, Palladas). Within this formal framework, a number of other effects are possible. Thus the anonymous *A.P.* 11.203 (Lm. VI, 127, no. VII = V, 89, no. XV) prefigures the recommendations of Ronsard's preface to the 1565 *Abbregé de l'art poëtique* in using a variety of technical terms.[58] In this example, no modulation occurs at all: strict equivalents have to be found to match the technicality of the Greek. Elsewhere, modulation can be necessitated by grammatical structure, as in Ronsard's version of Palladas' epigram *A.P.* 9.394 (Lm. VI, 127, no. VI = V, 87, no. XII) where the change from the masculine Χρυσέ to the feminine "Richesse" automatically entails other parallel modifications: πάτερ to "mere" and υἱέ to "fille." Apart from lexical or grammatical alteration, a further body of effects bears on vocalic play. The extensive alliterations and polyptota of Palladas *A.P.* 11.349 (Lm. VI, 127, no. V = V, 86, no. XI) highlight the rift between the external and internal knowledge. Ronsard makes the demonstration through verbal and vocalic positioning. The enjambment in

---

57. These are numbers I (Palladas), II (Posidippus), IV (Ammianus), VI (Palladas), VII (Anonymous). This follows the reordered numbering of the *Bocage,* different from that of the *Livret de Folastries.*

58. See Laumonier's note *ad* Lm. V, 89, line 12.

Di moy, pourquoy mesures tu
Tout ce monde qui nous enserre?

juxtaposes the man and his ambition, "tu" and "tout," but the similarity of sound does nothing to facilitate the passage from microcosm to macrocosm or to accommodate the fulfillment of the ambition. Quite the reverse: the argument specifically divides what metrical technique seems to join. In addition, Ronsard presses the point of the epigram home by means of increased affectivity. Hence the regularity of ὀλίγον πηλὸν τοῦ σώματος (that little lump of clay, the body), picking up the earlier σῶμα . . . ὀλίγον (little body), is transposed into the heavily negative "De ton corps la fangeuse ordure," where "fangeuse ordure" is hendiadys to πηλόν. So too in the very opening question, the balanced restraint of ἐξ ὀλίγης γαίης σῶμα φέρων ὀλίγον (bearing a little body made out of a small amount of earth) becomes

. . . un petit cors vestu
D'un si petit monceau de terre.

"Monceau de terre" is, in semiotic terms, negatively coded; and the geometer is tied firmly back to clay and human frailty by the pointed metaphor at "vestu," so introducing straightaway hidden topoi—human nakedness as an emblem of transience and the human body as composed of the clay to which it returns.

The longest epigram in the sequence ("De Posidippe," Lm. VI, 126 = Lm. V, 77–78) is also one of the most popular in the Renaissance, *A.P.* 9.359.[59] Like the "Odelette à Jan Nicot de Nimes," this epigram uses its fuller decasyllabic line to chart a more expansive narrative, a self-defeating *enumeratio* that poisons every remedy to and blocks every escape from the unrelieved gloom it describes. In spite of the expansiveness of the narrative, Ronsard's poem does not deny the constraints of theme and idea that the original imposes upon it. Indeed a central point of contact is maintained—the asyndeton that is a marked feature of the middle section of this epigram's brusque examination of the human condition. The mutually canceling antitheses are brought into intellectual opposition and rhythmic conjunction in the penultimate and final lines, in which the choices for human happiness are reduced to just two:

---

59. On this epigram, see in general A.S.F. Gow and Denys L. Page, eds., *The Greek Anthology: Hellenistic Epigrams*, 2 vols. (Cambridge: Cambridge University Press, 1965), 2:501–2; and for its popularity, Hutton, *The Greek Anthology in France*, 701.

. . . ou bien jamais de n'estre,
Ou de mourir si tost qu'on vient de naistre.

Coming into life and passing from it are indissolubly linked, "N'estre" and "naistre" are two syllables, yet the ear is aware of a single sound, a vocalic homoeoteleuton. Beginning and end, life and death, close back upon each other, cutting out the narrative middle with its frustrated maneuvers designed to evade conclusion. The poem describes a circle, returning at the end to its point of departure; and the question posed at the outset is answered punningly in the rhyme of the close.

The discharge of rhetorical and thematic energies with which this version by Ronsard ends is thus at one with Posidippus' epigram itself. The translation's exhaustion, reducing to zero all the viable options for happiness, observes, not transgresses, the equal and equivalent depletions of the original: the original and its translation close at the same point, drawn together, not propelled apart, by the release of their respective linguistic energies. It might almost be a definition of translated pieces of this kind that their manipulations respect the circumference of the poems transmitted to them. A suitably vivid contrast to this position can be obtained by the simple juxtaposition of the "Odelette à Corydon," whose restless eccentric motion—out and away from the easily definable—is embodied in the intransigent, un-Anacreontic (or even anti-Anacreontic) image of the snared boar. The ode will not return to reposeful coincidence with any of its subtexts, or indeed with any Anacreontic poem. If the "Odelette à Corydon" dramatizes a state after the onset of *contaminatio,* the Posidippus translation dramatizes the opposite state—a state before *contaminatio* that allows the unhampered concentration on the minutiae of renewal at the level of vocabulaic positioning, lexical preference, or metrical patterning.

The adventures on which the epigram translations are launched are far from being static formulas susceptible of mechanical application in the sphere of Anacreontic poetry proper. The passage between these related types of poetry is not conditioned by neutral or automatic transfer; on the contrary, the process is constantly dynamic and in a constant state of reevaluation and change. Ronsard willingly envisages different intensities of lexical, rhythmic, or syntactical innovation and renovation from poem to poem or from one group of poems to the next. This is why a hard-and-fast definition of distinctions between translation and imitation proves so difficult to supply: if the two categories do not exactly collapse into each other, they nevertheless affect each other in such a way as to increase rather than decrease our sense of their fluid overlap. In particular, distinctions between them cannot be elaborated on the basis of formal titles alone: to categorize the three odelettes to Corydon as imitations by contrast with the "Traduction de quelques épigrammes grecs" would be a tempting analytical convenience that disregards, for instance, the contrastive gradations in subtextual deviation within the Corydon poems themselves or the reevaluation of narrative beginnings, middles, and ends entailed by the assonantal compression of "n'estre" and "naistre" in the Posidippus epigram.

Even though translation is persistently used in the *Bocage* to reach beyond itself, this is not, of course, to suggest that no criteria whatsoever emerge from this collection or that all Ronsard's Anacreontic poems so successfully avoid systematic categorization as to constitute no more than unindividuated fluctuations. Indeed, a striking aspect of this collection is the self-appraisal by which it maintains an active interest in its own operations, the results of which are then in turn offered to the reader. Prominent among the criteria of assessment on display is the sheer degree of willed departure from recognizable subtexts. This departure can be greatly accelerated or severely reduced by the presence or absence of *contaminatio*. In vernacular circumstances, a poem is most likely to be described as an imitation if its degree of *contaminatio*—its assimilation of multiple intertextual echoes—is heightened and as a translation if its degree of *contaminatio* is diminished. As a conclusion, even an interim and provisional one, this is in marked contrast to the normal assumptions of Neo-Latin translators in whose work *contaminatio* is a habitual and integral feature of inherited language and technique and cannot necessarily be set up as a template for distinctions of the kind operating in the vernacular. The reasons for this could justifiably be said to be historical. If the vernacular cannot rely on the linguistic sedimentation or allusive resonances of Latinity, then it must make more substantial reference to a subtext; in other words, the individual unit of subtextual recognition will be larger, not smaller. As a result—to revert to an earlier argument—a great deal depends on the preservation of démarche, even allowing for Ronsard's distinct preference for an animated, vital structure capable of overall flexibility. The point at which flexibility masters the text totally is also the point of a change in formal status for the text in question. When flexibility pushes the source text too far out of sight by a lack of particularity in theme, motif, or phraseology, the result has fewer, rather than greater, chances of being a translation. In view of their narrow thematic range, the Anacreontea are peculiarly vulnerable to such erasure of distinguishing marks. Where this erasure occurs in vernacular writers, the demarcation lines between translation and imitation are also subject to review. There is nothing rigid about this; indeed, classification may ultimately depend on an all-too-subjective weighing of factors. Even then, the outcome may be just as open as the catch-all title "ode" by which Ronsard comes to view his own productions in the Anacreontic genre.

3

In terms of the relation between translation and imitation, the evidence of the *Bocage* very much suggests the flexibility of the two realms. This flexibility had, to some degree at least, surfaced through the corresponding problem of the link between epigrams and Anacreontics. The way in which the epigrams precede and then foster and nourish Anacreontics, before in turn allowing themselves to be acted upon by Anacreontics, lends credence to Couat's contention that epigrams were held to be virtually small-scale odes in their own right, so putting the connection between the two genres on a more solid basis. Couat himself limits his statement to Alexandrian times alone. And while there is no conclusive evidence that French practitioners of Anacreontics formally grasped this principle, the circumstantial evidence is such as to support the historical extension of these remarks to cover the practical reaction of Ronsard to the introduction of Anacreontic material. Ronsard's reaction will, moreover, be all the more intelligible if it is also understood as the product of an imitation-orientated view of literary history expounded by Jean Dorat.

Epigrams recur alongside the Anacreontea in the *Meslanges,* issued in 1555 but with an "achevé d'imprimer" of 22 November 1554. In this second collection, composed close in date to the *Bocage,* the proportion of Anacreontea has risen to the point at which they give an altogether distinctive shape to the new collection. The increased importance enjoyed by the Anacreontea is signaled from the very threshold of the collection by a version of the familiar *recusatio* of ode 1.[60] In this case, the topos it retraces encloses a summary version of Ronsardian poetic ambitions to date; history and rhetoric intersect and function in respect to the particular trajectory of an individual poet:

Naguiere chanter je voulois
Comme Francus au bord Gaulois
Avecq'sa troupe vint descendre:
Mais mon luc, pincé de mon doi,
Ne vouloit en depit de moi
Que chanter Amour, & Cassandre.[61]

---

60. "A sa lyre," Lm. VI, 133–34.
61. "A sa lyre," Lm. VI, 133, lines 1–6.

Cassandre defines "chanter Amour," much as Francus and his exploits are contemporary ventures to rival Virgil, strengthening a nationalist mythology about the descent of the French monarchy from wandering Trojans. A narrative of changed strings and altered poetic forms then duly and expansively occupies the body of the poem. But in the coda the poem suddenly fails to confirm (or confirms only on specified conditions) its own previous preferences and refusals:

> Or adieu doncq', pauvre Francus,
> Ta gloire, sous tes murs veinqus,
> Se cachera toujours pressée,
> Si à ton neveu, nostre Roi,
> Tu ne dis qu'en l'honneur de toi
> Il face ma Lyre crossée.[62]

Poetry needs patronage: the brutal facts of everyday existence erupt into the poem, making Francus' destiny dependent on economic necessities and no longer on carefully balanced shifts in generic style. Insofar as these lines rewrite and displace the opening, they reveal poetic choice to be determined by the money available and enact a more pressing form of *captatio benevolentiae,* in which a graceful aversion from epic becomes a threat to dismiss a historicizing enterprise unless adequate financial support is forthcoming. Aware of the rhetorical figures it fields and the choices they imply, "A sa lyre" is able simultaneously to endorse and refute the literary tradition it introduces.

The aim of a poem of this kind is not so much to dismiss the *Meslanges* before the collection has got underway as to illustrate in particularly condensed and charged form the pressures and conflicts that the collection is called upon to confront. In the central instance of classicizing traditions, this means that the opening poem points out the heterogeneity that the name *Meslanges* implies. Perspectives do not, however, always shift quite so rapidly as in "A sa lyre." The overall purpose is not to confuse the reader (even though he or she may rightly feel some measure of uncertainty as to the elusive stance of the introductory poem) but rather to adumbrate multiple avenues of approach to the Anacreontic genre. To some degree, the *Bocage* had already anticipated this position in its invited comparisons between, for example, such an Anacreontic poem as the "Ode, ou Songe à François de Revergat" (Lm. VI, 122–24) and the diptych "Odelette au somme" and "Odelette à l'amour" (Lm. VI, 109 and 110–11). In effect, simultaneous ingress of this kind is a form of *variae interpreta-*

---

62. "A sa lyre," Lm. VI, 134, lines 19–24.

tiones, a constructed vernacular analogue to the doubles with which the Anacreontea abound.[63] In addition to the already established practice of *contaminatio* seen in the *Bocage,* the *Meslanges* will greatly multiply the opportunities for changes of perspective inherent in *variae interpretationes,* while at the same time giving them orderly presentation by the introduction of a common stratum of sympotic and love themes to which the Anacreontic odes will be related. Bacchus and Venus as mythological figures or poetic symbols or themes dominate the 1555 *Meslanges.*[64] As the "Odelette à Corydon" (Lm. VI, 174–76) makes clear, Bacchus is the central representative of "Anacreon's" sympotic aspect, corresponding to which are Venus and the erotic strain:

> A toi, gentil Anacreon,
> Doit son plesir le biberon,
> Et Bacus te doit ses bouteilles,
> Amour, son compagnon, te doit,
> Venus, & Silene qui boit
> L'esté, dessous l'ombre des treilles.
>
> (lines 31–36)

Set in a poem that is itself a *contaminatio* of Horatian and Anacreontic sympotic and *carpe diem* motifs, this summary of the poem's main themes and ideas also serves to celebrate the revival of learning[65] and so details a new outlook on the purely generic and rhetorical considerations of "A sa lyre."

The "Odelette, ou plus tost Folie" (Lm. VI, 243–44) is subtitled "Traduitte d'Anacreon Poete Grec." This title was to be resolved into the ambiguous description "Odelette prise d'Anacreon" in the second edition of the *Meslanges* later in 1555, while, from 1560 onward, it became no more than "Ode," sharing the same descriptive fate as the majority of Ronsard's Anacreontic poems. The change in perception does not, in this case, correspond to a subsequent extension or contraction of the text. Lexically, its most marked features

---

63. In this case, then, the term *variae interpretationes* denotes not multiple translations but multiple versions of the same theme.

64. For complementary considerations on Bacchic power in various senses, see Terence Cave, "The Triumph of Bacchus and Its Interpretation in the French Renaissance: Ronsard's 'Hinne de Bacus'," in *Humanism in France at the End of the Middle Ages and in the Early Renaissance,* ed. Anthony Levi (Manchester: Manchester University Press, 1970), 249–70; and the same author's "Ronsard's Bacchic Poetry: From the 'Bacchanales' to the 'Hymne de l'automne'," *L'Esprit Créateur* 10 (1970): 104–16.

65. Compare the immediately preceding lines: "Verse donq, & reverse encor / Dedans cette grand coupe d'or, / Je vois boire à Henry Estienne, / Qui des enfers nous a rendu / Du vieil Anacreon perdu / La douce Lyre Teïenne."

are the doublets or triplets that reproduce formally this standardized Anacreontic feature. If these reduplications can be located anywhere, it is in the dual role allotted to Bacchus:

> Lors que Bacus entre chés moy,
> Je sen le soing, je sen l'émoy
> S'endormir.

"Entre chés moy" physically of a person entering a room or metaphorically of wine entering the body: the double status of Bacchus as character or figurative metonym activates the textual dynamic manifested in the spacious but controlled grammar of the poem, first by doubling ("Je sen le soing, je sen l'émoy"), then by tripling ("plus d'or, / Plus d'argent, & plus de thesor"), then by the longer isocola of the second stanza. Bacchic energy is harnessed, but it remains "folie" capable of bypassing the constraints imposed on it. A characteristic Ronsardian restlessness is incarnated in a figure whose properties elude thematic definition. If Bacchus is one form of this restlessness, Venus is another. They do, of course, comprise complementary activities on the scale of neoplatonic "fureur"; the term "folie" in the "Odelette"—an important Ronsardian gloss on the poem's subject matter and activities—points to an awareness of sketching a theoretical grasp of textual events. Even so, a full-blown theory remains no more than fragmentary, no more than outlined or hinted at.

Such a poem as "Odelette à Olivier de Magny" (Lm. VI, 256–58) employs the same ample rhetoric as the "Odelette ou . . . Folie" but takes no serious account of formal theoretical positions. Ronsard's history of his loves (from ode 32, 1554.29–30) is a controlled *enumeratio,* channeling the vastness of the poet's adventures into an octosyllabic catalog framed on the imperative "Conte." This reordered version of the Anacreontic ode unfolds its extended narrative with cool sobriety and is not compromised by the *adunaton* that artificially closes off the catalog and represents the impossibility of giving an adequate account of the poet's loves even in considerably expanded poetic form and grammatical syntax. Yet the loves are recorded, to some degree at least; the impulsive, disorderly patterns of erotic behavior respond and are subject to a measure of formalization. In terms of translation and imitation also, Ronsard's preservation of démarche and the absence of *contaminatio* makes this poem deserving of something less clear-cut than the simple imitative label that Laumonier wishes to pin on it.[66] It is a poem that negotiates a midcourse between two types of analytical nomenclature. In its simultaneous support for

---

66. See Laumonier's note, Lm. VI, 256 n. 2.

orderly narrative and its respect for untamed erotic experience, it similarly occupies a place midway between the bound Love of the poem "Les Muses lierent un jour" (from ode 30, 1554.27–28; Lm. VI, 253–55), who is infallibly constrained to aesthetic discipline—

>   Courage donques, Amoureux,
>   Vous ne serés plus langoureux,
>   Amour n'oseroit par ses ruses
>   Plus faillir à vous presenter
>   Des vers, quand vous voudrés chanter,
>   Puis qu'il est prisonnier des Muses.
>   (lines 19–24)

—and the unruly child of "La belle Venus un jour" (Lm. VI, 202–4), who successfully evades aesthetic conformity and, taking the offensive, compels the poet to sing not of high lyric but of erotic adventure:

>   ... alors
>   J'obliai tous les acors
>   De ma lyre dedaignée,
>   Pour retenir en leur lieu
>   L'autre chanson que ce Dieu
>   M'avoit par coeur enseignée.
>   (lines 43–48)

Neither bound nor free, neither pliant translation nor measured imitation, the "Odelette à Olivier de Magny" gives evidence of a balanced respect for erotic energies and their encapsulation in literary form. Overt criticism remains potential rather than fully actualized, just as the "Odelette ou . . . Folie" bordered on the dithyrambic lyricism of sympotic mania without totally giving way to it.

Such measured balances and tones do not always characterize the *Meslanges*. Indeed, the two "programmatic" odes just touched upon ("Les Muses lierent un jour" and "La belle Venus un jour") offer sharply polarized visions of how a textual erotics might look. In a sense, these two poems do no more than elaborate the positions adopted by different classical authors (pseudo-Anacreon and Bion respectively). But the similarity of the material suggests rather a desire to present contrasting perspectives, thus maintaining the collection in a state of permanent evolution, almost agitation. The willed nature of the contrasts between "Anacreon" and Bion is clarified by the subsidiary contrast between the condition of the Bion ode and the Anacreontic-inspired "A sa lyre," in that its closing topos of the dismissal of epic reappears, in displaced form, in "La belle Venus un jour," while "A sa lyre" itself turns aside to comment upon the whole process of writing literature.

This idea—the demise of literature—recurs in the antithetical poems "Ode à Jacques de Rubampré" (Lm. VI, 195–97) and the odelette "Ah, si l'or pouvoit alonger" (Lm. VI, 260–61). As Laumonier remarks,[67] the former poem, despite its second edition specification "prise d'Anacreon," is a reworking of a variety of Anacreontic material: here (as often) the strength of the *contaminatio* is such as to block easy ascription. Laumonier might have added that the *contaminatio* does not constitute an end in itself but serves as a springboard for a lament on the extinction of literary culture and the irrevocable transience of language. Anacreon is named along with other Greek lyric poets as the victim of this gnawing erosion (lines 17–20), in the light of which a poet of the French vernacular has little or no chance of survival (lines 25–28). The poet then asserts his own (sardonic) preferences in favor of a life spent in business or standing "davant un Senat pourpré / Pour de l'argent sa langue vendre" (lines 31–32)—better by far than following

> . . . l'ocieux train
> De cette pauvre Caliope,
> Qui toujours fait mourir de faim
> Les meilleurs chantres de sa trope.
>
>   (lines 33–36)

The point is un-Anacreontic: the starveling fate of the poet, common elsewhere in Ronsard, is not a cause for thematic concern in the Anacreontea.[68] In the comparable ode, "Ah, si l'or pouvoit alonger," the subtext is plainly recognizable, but the conclusion is, by contrast, steadfastly anti-Anacreontic:

> Il vaut donques mieux s'adonner
> A feuilleter toujours un livre,
> Qui plustost que l'or peut donner,
> Maugré la mort, un second vivre.
>
>   (lines 13–16)

---

67. Lm. VI, 196 n. 1.
68. The *locus classicus* is the "Hymne de l'or," Lm. VIII, 179–205. *Paupertas,* defined as either indigence or simple insufficiency, *was* a theme of Hellenistic epigram, as is pointed out by Giuseppe Giangrande, "Sympotic Literature and Epigram," 135–39. Further references can be gleaned from Wimmel, *Kallimachos in Rom,* Stichwortindex, s.v. "paupertas."

The distance between this and the Greek equivalent is easily measured by evoking the source text (1554.20–21):

Ἐμοὶ γένοιτο πίνειν,
Πιόντι δ' οἶνον ἡδὺν,
Ἐμοῖς φίλοις συνεῖναι,
Ἐν δ' ἁπαλαῖσι κοίταις
Τελεῖν τὰν ἀφροδίταν.

[let me drink, and drinking sweet wine, be with my friends and on soft beds carry out the rites of Aphrodite.]

To a greater or lesser degree, both French poems are as opposed to their source texts as they are to each other. As they range and match themselves against the tradition that gives them birth, the poems throw up the deflections in tone or circumstance that can turn imitation into estrangement or comfort. The relation to the predecessor can be antagonistic or agonistic.

Thus the latent energies of the Bacchic ode and the "folie" that it exemplifies, or the equilibrium of *enumeratio* and *adunaton* in the Magny poem, are transferred into and activated through the thematic proliferation of Ronsardian *variae interpretationes*. Such doublings are not meek adjustments to versification or vocabulaic practice; they affect the very nature of the ode and the values it advocates. Not all poems in the collection feel obliged by the same constraints as the Magny ode. Indeed, the "Odelette à sa jeune maitresse" (Lm. VI, 259–60)[69] reverses these acquired notions of what control might mean. Here, erotic mastery is not a metaphor for the shaping of material but for sexual contest and the subjugation of woman by man. These ideas are carried by an increase in the vocabulary of physical contact ("Tu ne veus pas que l'on te touche," "si je t'avoi sous ma main," "Bien tost je t'aurois mis le frain," lines 5, 6, and 8), including an overt gloss on the nature of the subject matter:

Puis te voltant à toute bride
Soudain je te ferois au cours,
Et te piquant serois ton guide
Dans la carriere des Amours.

(lines 9–12)

---

69. This odelette is one of the rare instances of poems drawn from Estienne's appendix to the Anacreontea: Πῶλε Θρηικίη (1554.57–58).

The magnified erotic play of Ronsard's version anticipates the final distance between rider and filly and allows the discharge of energies before the conclusion denounces these lines as pure hypothesis. In the "Odelette: 'Le boyteus mari de Venus'" (Lm. VI, 229–30), the glosses of the final lines push the "démarche of the imitation even further away from the Anacreontic ode 45—

> Vrayment tu sentiras un jour
> Combien leur pointure est amere,
> Quand d'elles blessé dans le coeur,
> Toi qui fais tant du belliqueur,
> Languiras au sein de ma mere.
>
> (lines 14–18)

The swelling of démarche looks beyond its immediate context and, through its anticipation of the love of Mars and Venus, imagines versions of Anacreontic poetry worked upon by erotic energy and deflected by it.

A surge of erotic energy can pass from one poem to another in a sequence of *variae interpretationes,* modifying the sequence as it goes by contiguous momentum. A prime example of just this lateral transaction and disruption is to be seen in the ode "Quand je veux en amours prendre mes passe-tems" (Lm. VI, 198–99). It is a twenty-line reworking in alexandrines of the Anacreontic ode 11, with greater attention to circumstantial detail and incorporating the proverbial "volentiers bon cheval ne devint jamais rosse," a quotation from Sophocles that recurs in Erasmus and in Estienne's preface to the *Anacreon.*[70] Its companion piece is just as easily recognizable, the odelette based on the analogous poem Μή με φύγης (ode 34; Lm. VI, 255–56). Its departures from its guiding Anacreontic text are announced at the very beginning, where are mentioned the apparently casual, parallel images of head and face, lily and rose, man and woman—

> Pourtant si j'ay le chef plus blanc
> Que n'est d'un liz la fleur eclose,
> Et toi le visage plus franc
> Que n'est le bouton d'une rose,
>
> (lines 1–4)

—that are intertwined at the end, following the Greek, as a discreet indication of sexual contact:

---

70. Lm. VI, 198 n. 2.

Ne sçais tu pas, toi qui me fuis,
Que, pour bien faire une couronne
Ou quelque beau bouquet, d'un liz
Toujours la rose on environne?

(lines 9–12)

The discretion of image is in contrast to the spirited assertion of the middle section of the poem:

Si j'ay la teste blanche en haut,
J'ay en bas la queüe bien franche.

(lines 7–8)

The last hemistich puzzles Laumonier: "cet hémistiche n'est pas dans la pièce grecque."[71] This criticism is not strictly true: Τἀμὰ φίλτρα (my love-charms) is an obvious equivalent. More allusively, the affinities are with an earlier poem, unidentified by Laumonier despite Ronsard's later attribution to Dorat. In the "Odelette à Jane" (Lm. VI, 164), the mistress, noticing the poet's white hair, plucks it out:

Come s'un cheveu blanc ou noir
Pour baiser eust quelque pouvoir.

(lines 5–6)

But Jane is mistaken, the poet insists:

Un cheveul blanc est assés fort
Au seul baiser, pourveu que point
Tu ne vueilles de l'autre point.

(lines 8–10)

The intensified eroticism of "la queüe bien franche" has all the collected energy of "l'autre point," invested with a power to erupt and disrupt, turning the Anacreontic poem into an allusion to a (Neo-Latin?) poem on the same subject, indeed within the same sequence. Quotation here is self-quotation, allusion is self-allusion, and *contaminatio* is the result of a cumulative thematic reading. The Anacreontic tradition is reshaped not just by the action of a past poem on a contemporary poem, or even by the action of one contemporary author on

---
71. Lm. VI, 255 n. 3.

another, but by the action of the contemporary author upon himself. Ronsard's ode shades its own account of Μή με φύγῃς by its analogous, but no longer distinct, account of the "Odelette à Jane," so producing the inverse of the precise checks on eroticism to be found in the "Ode à Olivier de Magny." Emanating not from the model but from the imitation, reading-activated energy deflects the ode along a path unforeseen by the mimetic enterprise: the ode is waylaid and significantly determined by one of its own kind. The *Meslanges* have become the source of their own mimetic opportunities.

These poems on the aging poet do not exemplify merely local instances of a mystery with its solution to match. The type of concern they embody can be given voice, in the most symbolically direct of fashions, in the several dialogue poems in the *Meslanges*. These intersect with the Anacreontea in the shape of the "Ode de la Colombelle" (Lm. VI, 220–23), a dialogue between Cassandre and the dove. Its own dialogue with the Anacreontic Ἐρασμίη πέλεια (ode 9, 1554.8–10) is an exchange also with concurrent, non-Anacreontic versions. To that extent, the poem's awareness of its differences is of prime importance to the specificity and individuality of its task. The dove's message is for Cassandre, not Bathyllus, and its sender is Ronsard, not "Anacreon." The independent interlocutor of the Greek is eliminated. Geographical setting is equally the object of *aggiornamento,* "Vandomois" (line 23) appearing instead of the presumed Hellenistic setting of the original. The self-conscious redesigning of character and place betokens a larger shaping of the whole into a Petrarchist avowal of love. Ronsard will never serve any other than Cassandre (lines 17–20); the dove is commissioned to soften the lady's "fierté" (lines 26–27); the dove herself becomes a "douce mignonne" (line 46), loved by the poet since they are both in captivity (lines 47–55). In one way, this poem is the confirmation of the argument of other Anacreontic "bird" poetry in the *Meslanges:* elsewhere, a "babillarde Arondelle" wakes the poet as he lays dreaming of the embrace with Cassandre (Lm. VI, 230–31, line 1), and the springtime return of the swallow engenders lengthy metaphorical imagery of Love raising his nestlings in the poet's heart (Lm. VI, 199–201). This broad heterogeneity only throws into sharper relief the affinities and contrasts with the other two dialogues. Both are "débats" and thus fully concordant with the medieval tradition. But the first, "Ode en dialogue des yeux et de son coeur" (Lm. VI, 250–53), allies the stock-in-trade of the "débat" with imitation of Petrarch;[72] whereas the "Ode en dialogue, L'Espérance et Ronsard" (Lm. VI, 261–66) adopts a solution similar to that of the "Ode de la Columbelle," in that the

---

72. Laumonier, *Ronsard poète lyrique,* 485–86, gives details.

transition from a dialogue between Hope and Ronsard to a three-way conversation between Hope, Ronsard, and Cassandre acts out equivalent temporal and aesthetic transitions, an etiology of imitation, from medieval to Renaissance form.

The impetus locatable in sympotic or erotic energy, Bacchus or Venus, of itself brings a double focus that allows the mind or the text to be taken beyond itself. In Ronsard's Bacchic poetry proper, this doubling produces a twofold narrative, marked off by the use of dithyrambs or such devices as interjections, repetitions, or disjunctive syntax. Such double-layered narrative can sometimes be assigned to the influence of "folie," a term whose appearance in the "Odelette ou . . . Folie" is a residual effect of neoplatonism. But residual the term is: the *Meslanges* point away from rather than toward a supporting neoplatonic idiom. Indeed, when Love accuses the poet of being "sot" and having "la teste fole" in "La belle Venus un jour" (Lm. VI, 203, lines 25, 27), this event takes place specifically before possession by Love and indicates no supernatural state. Elsewhere, as in the "Hinne de Bacus," where Bacchic fury is manifest, it is syncretically blended with classical elements, so that no one element stands alone: syncretism entails polyvocality, a recourse to more than one classical text brought to bear on the subject under consideration. Syncretism and polyvocality might almost be considered normative procedures in the *Meslanges,* a way of describing the refracted character of this collection, which lives through its multiple avenues of approach, its desire to keep in the field competing versions of *genus tenue* material. Bacchus and Venus are themselves part of, not divorced from, these multiple perspectives. They focus central ideas of the *Meslanges* but are not special hermeneutic keys.

Even between the (at first sight) similar outlooks of the *Bocage* and the *Meslanges,* the imitative position has been rethought and reformulated; new configurations of arrangement and emphasis have entered into consideration. Most noticeable from this angle is the refusal of the *Meslanges* to fall into a master pattern of presentation whereby the reader is invited to make comparison across as well as between the thematic groupings of odes, sonnets, and epigrams. By contrast with this orderly transmission of information, the *Meslanges* will inevitably appear to be disorganized, sometimes having local patterns of coherence to propose, more often relying on the reader's capacity to deduce from the convergent and divergent narratives before him or her. The consequence of this opening up of new inroads, these fresh broachings of access, is an evolving work, ultimately open-ended and offering no particular thread by which the reader may travel through the collection. Yet for all that, Ronsard's aim is not to disorientate or bewilder the reader but to warn the reader that the *Meslanges* will live out their title in their preference for diversity and reformulation. Working with Anacreontic material means, for Ronsard, examining, testing, trying out its compatibility with other types of analogous material. In these circumstances, polyvocality is an inevitability.

One of the most compelling phenomena, then, in the *Meslanges,* is the rich suggestiveness arising from this matching of material. However, in order for this to occur at all, there needs to be a catalyst facilitating the absorption of "Anacreon" and the transmission of the rediscovered poet to the Renaissance scene, a breaching of historical epochs through the selection of a close aesthetic analogue. Unsurprisingly, a determinant role is played here by Horace, "l'Anacréon latin," as Laumonier called him.[73] It is of central significance from this standpoint that the welcoming of "Anacreon" in the "Odelette à Corydon" ("Je vois boire à Henry Estienne," Lm. VI, 175, line 27) is squarely situated within an ode making considerable use of Horatian material in order to associate symposium with a celebration of the confraternity of the "Brigade" and to associate these in turn with the return of a classical author from the dead. "Anacreon" in this poem is read through a Horatian grid, a fortune also shared, to a greater or lesser degree, by Panyassis (Lm. VI, 172–74) and Mimnermus (Lm. VI, 191–94). It might also be noted that the "Ode à P. Paschal" (Lm. VI, 161–62), with its twofold Horatian inspiration, opens with a defense of the narrator's devotion to love poetry in a manner strongly reminiscent of the numerous rearrangements of the Anacreontic ode 1 recurrent in the *Meslanges.* While not all the Anacreontic odes hinge on this supporting Horatian reading, it is true nonetheless that the majority of Ronsard's versions are positioned in respect to the Latin lyric poet. Similar observations could be made about Catullus, though here the influence is less sustained, more sporadic.

Thus, as with the Neo-Latins, "Anacreon" *redivivus* in the vernacular lives through intermediaries. The very choice of these intermediaries itself shows Neo-Latin influence, insinuated as a recognition of and respect for Anacreontic *proprietas;* Ronsard grafts fresh subject matter onto a stem firmly rooted in the tradition of Salmon Macrin and Joannes Secundus. "Anacreon" is assigned a place by comparison with a major line of Latinity with claims on historical continuity. But in addition to being animated, "Anacreon" is also invested with animating power: the *Meslanges* create out of "Anacreon" a new source of *energeia* whose resources are subsequently demonstrated in the capacity to reinvigorate adjacent areas of text and traditional aesthetic forms with new

---

73. Laumonier, *Ronsard poète lyrique,* 617. Cf. De Nolhac, *Ronsard et l'humanisme,* 33: "tout ce qu'il [Ronsard] empruntera à l'Anacréon d'Henri Estienne . . . , le chantre de Lydie le lui a déjà révélé."

intention and purpose. The Anacreontea are both the object of renewal and the further instrument of renewal, held in place by cross-threaded references to epigram, elegy, and lyric, yet also reaching out to interanimate Medieval, Neo-Latin, and Latin.

Translation and imitation are, on this model, conceived as Protean entities unrestrained by boundaries or demarcations. The particular foci for this unbounded activity in the *Meslanges* are Bacchus and Venus, who accordingly become metaphors, in some sort, for translative energy. Sympotic and erotic spillage is seen most clearly in *variae interpretationes,* for the latter insist on a view of translation and imitation emphasizing the dynamic evolution of a text, a perpetual mobilizing and remobilizing of linguistic and thematic forces, with a corresponding inability for these forces to settle into an invariable set of constants or coordinates. The Anacreontea, in Ronsard's hands, are engaged in producing new poetic texts rather than passively conforming to a standardized model of poetic behavior. As Ronsard carries Anacreontic idiom forward into later collections, its restlessness finds embodiment, its character receives translation, in new combinations of aesthetic shape and flexible form. Ronsard's wish simultaneously to integrate and to exploit continues.

4

The *Continuation des Amours* (1555) and the *Nouvelle Continuation des Amours* (1556) have more than one connection with the Anacreontea. They do, of course, contain Anacreontic material. On this occasion, however, they substitute for the manifold contours endemic to the title and practice of the *Meslanges* a single aesthetic object for investigation and adventure: the peasant girl Marie, a deliberate contrast to the courtly Cassandre and therefore a symbol more than an instigator of vernacular *stille bas*. In a sense, the two new love collections pick up and formalize the love poems of the *Meslanges* with their noticeably lighter tone. From another angle, these collections transfer into a new dimension the erotic overflow discharged through and beyond the *Meslanges*. The *Continuations* will rewrite the *Meslanges* from a specific aspect, incorporating as they do so this transposed charge of eroticism.

The whole problem of writing love poetry, together with the very status of the collection before us, is raised in the initial sonnet of the *Continuation des Amours* (Lm. VII, 115–16). It is a *recusatio* in a now familiar vein, bearing comparison with the corresponding poem in the *Meslanges,* yet independently modeled and with no visible Anacreontic input. The contrasts its strikes with the mythological obscurity of the 1552 *Amours* are elaborated in greater detail in "A son livre" (Lm. VII, 315–25), the epilogue to the *Nouvelle Continuation,* which became the opening poem of the *Second Livre des Amours* in the first collected edition of 1560. Here, the argument in favor of rejecting Petrarch and cultivating a new style in love poetry is conducted both at the conceptual level and at the "realistic" level of putative autobiography—the poet's meeting with the girl from Anjou (VII, 323, lines 159f.) following immediately on from his complaints about the haughty behavior of Cassandre (lines 151f.). In a famous passage, the generic inferences are then drawn; "l'humeur Pindarique" of high lyric is incompatible with love poetry:

> . . . les amours ne se souspirent pas
> D'un vers hautement grave, ains d'un beau stille bas,
> Populaire & plaisant, ainsi qu'a fait Tibulle,
> L'ingenieux Ovide, & le docte Catulle.
>
> (lines 173–76)

Shortly afterward, the preferences are reinforced by calling for a "mignard & dous stille" without "enfleure ny fard" (line 179). From the writers of classical antiquity to the classicizing writer of Renaissance France, historical continuity is once more ensured by virtue of rhetorical style. The move to a "natural" idiom is constructed as an antithetical comparison between the discourses of separate historical epochs (Greek lyric and Latin elegy) framed within the "autobiographical" antithesis of Cassandre and Marie. The "high" and "low" styles are historicized through embodiment in specified literary predecessors and then brought to intersection and particular exemplification in fresh tensions deriving from the "personal" experience of the contemporary poet.

In this embedding of current poetic needs within a complex of rhetorical and historical layers, "Anacreon" has no individual part to play. He does not so much represent an autonomous poetic stance as feed into the preexistent requirements of love poetry. "Anacreon" enriches texture rather than creating new texts; he supports and fosters rather than initiates the application of *genus tenue* to an entire sequence of love poetry. Unsurprisingly, then, the greatest incidence of Anacreontics comes in the guise of allusions.[74] In the *Bocage* and the *Meslanges,* a considerable measure of oscillation is perceptible between imitation and translation. In some cases, identification is certain; for a large number of other cases, it is nothing like as straightforward as Laumonier's tidy

---

74. A glance at Belleau's 1560 commentary on the *Second Livre des Amours* confirms this fact: see *Remy Belleau, Commentaire au second livre des "Amours" de Ronsard,* ed. Marie-Madeleine Fontaine and François Lecercle, Commentaires de Ronsard, 2 (Geneva: Droz, 1986).

labeling suggests. In the *Continuations,* however, the move to *allusio* weights the balance in favor of imitation. The Anacreontea have ceased to occupy and inform large areas of textual surface. Their claim over large segments of typographical space is relinquished, and they move to a subliminal position where they exist as stimuli to a by now acquired familiarity with the characteristics of their idiom.

As if to highlight this change in status, Ronsard includes recognizable elements of translation and imitation for purposes of both contrast and identification. Thus the new input of epigram translations, "Traduction de quelques épigrammes grecs, sur la Jenisse d'aerain de Myron excellentement bien gravée" (Lm. VII, 201–3), is an exercise in *variae interpretationes* more conspicuous than any in the *Bocage* or *Meslanges* and also more tonally and metrically limited than the corresponding Anthology translations in the *Livret de Folastries.* In conjunction with the epigrams stand, on one hand, a virtual translation[75] of ode 14 into alexandrine verse and sonnet form (Lm. VII, 117) and, on the other, two poems specifically designated "imitation d'Anacreon" (Lm. VII, 193 and 195–96) but whose imitative properties are so ill defined that even Laumonier is driven to labeling them paraphrases.[76] All these poems do nothing to enlarge our sense of Ronsard's handling of the idiom of translation or to redraw the lines between translation, paraphrase, and imitation or tighten and sharpen their contours. They are too few in number and too ill organized to complete such undertakings with any degree of adequacy. What they can do is to mesh with the thematic projects of adjacent poems—a task fulfilled without difficulty by a wide range of Anacreontic verse. Rather than serving as independent units of meaning in their own right, they are to be seen as performing the same function as *allusio;* they are allusions writ large, extended into typographical space; allusions with their full text appended, something to which allusions themselves can only motion.

By comparison with the *contaminatio*-based allusions of the *Bocage,* which are predominantly thematic rather than lexical, the allusions of the *Continuations* are lexical as well as thematic and can frequently be reminiscent of quotations, though without the verbal exactness and proximity to the original that quotation requires. In both collections, allusions are also the prerogative of imitation alone. It would not be inconceivable for a vernacular translation to engage in quotation or allusion (Belleau will afford a salient instance), but it would normally be a comparatively restricted phenomenon: vernacular transla-

---

75. This qualified ascription ("presque une traduction") is Belleau's: *Commentaire,* fol. 14ᵛ.
76. Lm. VII, 193 n. 1 and 195 n. 4.

tion, if it is to remain purely a translation, cannot tolerate the large-scale capture by composite voices that is the norm in Neo-Latin translation. Typical of these observations is the sonnet "J'ayme la fleur de Mars . . ." from the *Nouvelle Continuation* (Lm. VII, 255–56). Belleau identifies the second line as Anacreontic:[77]

> J'ayme la fleur de Mars, j'ayme la belle Rose,
> L'une qui est sacrée à Venus la deesse,
> L'autre qui a le nom de ma belle maistresse,
> Pour qui ne nuict ne jour en paix je ne repose.
>
> (lines 1–4)

The line is an allusion rather than a quotation: the rose is variously the rose of the loves (ode 5, 1554.5), Aphrodite's delight (ode 53, 1554.48),[78] and Love's flower (ode 53, *loc. cit.*), in addition to being dedicated to the Muses and Bacchus (ode 53, 1554.48, 50). The amorphous content of the Greek poem now disappears (to survive, perhaps, only in the *enumeratio* of Ronsard's sonnet) and the line enters into witty erotic and mythological play. The mention of Mars and Venus brings in the topos of the association and conflict of Love and War,[79] but to Venus is now added the narrator's mistress. Marie's name, though never once mentioned, is assonantally similar to that of Mars, and the link between the two is further strengthened since the "violette de Mars" was, according to Cotgrave's testimony,[80] also called the "violette de Marie." Marie is the cause of the poet's turbulence, his conflicting emotions, which are recorded in the Petrarchist phraseology of the fourth line. Poet and lady play as contemporary counterparts to the two classical figures, Mars and Venus, who are themselves allegories of the state of love.

Elsewhere, "Anacreon" may have less individual prominence but cooperates with other classical authors and motifs. The image of the gnat in the sonnet "Amour se vint cacher dans les yeux de Cassandre" (*Continuation,* sonnet LVI; Lm. VII, 173–74)[81] is in the first instance from Apollonius of Rhodes *Argonautica* 3.275–77, where Love, hiding in the folds of Jason's cloak in order

---

77. Belleau, *Commentaire,* fol. 38ᵛ.
78. Both these examples are quoted by Belleau, *Commentaire,* fol. 38ᵛ. For further notes on this poem, consult Ronsard, *Pierre de Ronsard: Les Amours,* ed. Henri Weber and Catherine Weber (Paris: Garnier, 1963), 645–46, *ad* sonnet XV.
79. *Pace* Laumonier (Lm. VII, 255 n. 1), who interprets "Mars" solely as a reference to the month.
80. Cited by Laumonier, Lm. VII, 255 n. 3.
81. Cf. also Weber, *Ronsard: Les Amours,* 632–33, *ad* sonnet LVI.

to shoot arrows into Medea's eyes, rises into the air like a gnat that stings cattle. This image can equally well be found in the Anacreontic ode 3. One Alexandrian author follows another, as, pivoting on the shared image, Ronsard models his second quatrain and the opening line of the first tercet on the Anacreontic model:

> Il élongna ses mains, & feit son arc estendre
> En croissant, qui se courbe aus premiers jours du mois,
> Puis me lascha le trait, contre qui le harnois
> D'Achille, ni d'Hector ne se pourroit defendre.
> Apres qu'il m'eut blessé, en riant s'en volla.
>
> (lines 5–9)

The poet stung by love is also the duped Anacreontic narrator who pities the rain-soaked child only to be wounded by his arrow: these overtones underpin the eleventh line of the present poem ("Mais toutesfois au coeur me demoura la playe"), which begins the coda. The reference to the corselet of Achilles and Hector brings in another possible Anacreontic reference, to ode 14 where Love and the lover do battle, in preparation for which the lover takes up arms and armor like Achilles (1554.13–14). Yet this poem too ends with the lover's defeat. The god of love changes himself into a missile, lodges in the lover's heart, and so vanquishes him; and the lover is left with the despairing reflection that external struggle is useless if the true battle lies within. The subtexts here create not only the argument of the piece but also, in all three cases, the impact of the conclusion. The poem works by concatenation, one subtext triggering off another with associated pertinence, all emphasizing the destructiveness of love and thus consonant with the sonnet's *pointe:* "le remede est la mort."

In this sonnet, "Anacreon" does not have sole dominance but is nonetheless of sufficient centrality to achieve individual importance. The sonnet "Marie, vous avés la joue aussi vermeille" (Lm. VII, 126–27) has similarly expressed Anacreontic debts, but the other subtextual possibilities are so dense, the *contaminatio* so great, that these debts are all but lost in the general current of allusions.[82] Indeed, in its multiplicity of references, it might almost be a history of the reception of the Anacreontea. Thus the eighth line—

> Pithon vous feit la vois à nulle autre pareille

---

82. These allusions are recorded by Belleau, *Commentaire,* fols. 11r–12r, and Weber, *Ronsard: Les Amours,* 616, *ad* sonnet X.

is both Anacreontic—

Γράφε χεῖλος οἷα Πειθοῦς,
Προκαλούμενον φίλημα[83]

[paint her lips, like Persuasion's, inviting a kiss]

—and Marullan—

Mellita comitante dicta Suada.[84]

[with sweet persuasion accompanying her words.]

From the same page of the Anacreontic poem come lines 1 and 2:

Marie, vous avés la joue aussi vermeille
Qu'une rose de Mai.
Γράφε ῥῖνα καὶ παρειὰς,
Ῥόδα τῷ γάλακτι μίξας.

[paint her nose and cheeks, by mixing roses and cream.]

But the idea is such a commonplace of classical love poetry that unequivocal and univocal ascription would be impossible and misleading. The *descriptio* of Marie is in fact so grounded in the constitutive traditions that even a partial account of this poem would have to include Molza for the image of the bee moulding honey on the mistress' lips, Ariosto for the breasts as milky hills, Homer for the descriptions of Juno's arms and Aurora's hand. The image of Love leaving his arrows in Marie's eyes likewise unites the Graeco-Latin and Petrarchist traditions in a way that would equally be capable of inexhaustible exemplification. Brought to bear on a single aesthetic object, these allusions reveal varying degrees of integration and assimilation. In some cases, they refer to specific and identifiable subtexts; in others (as, for example, the opening lines), they refer less to an individual subtext than to a topos enshrined within the literary tradition as a whole and traceable in a variety of classical and contemporary writers. Yet there is no sense of rival claims or of voices competing for the reader's attention. On the contrary, the allusions work in conjunc-

---

83. Ode 28, 1554.24.
84. Marullus *Epig.* 4.13.15.

tion and fuse into a coherent impression of the tradition for which they stand. As commonly in Estienne's commentary, this poem by Ronsard sets up interpretants for "Anacreon," establishing affinities for his themes and ideas, with the result that "Anacreon's" individual voice melts into and emerges from a polyphony of concomitant voices and associated literary texts. "Anacreon" becomes a voice among voices.

The integrative strategies sketched here in respect to *allusio* do not, of course, preclude other approaches in the *Continuations*. Allusion is itself a facet of imitation, but a facet in which the subtext does not occupy the same measure of space or individual prominence as an imitative lingering over a single poem. Such lingerings, such attentions to individual pieces, do occur: the sonnet "Douce, belle, gentille, & bien fleurente Rose" (Lm. VII, 184–85) would be one such example, a rewriting of certain elements from Στεφανηφόρου μετ' ἦρος (1554.48–50). But widespread imitation of this nature is by no means as prevalent in the two *Continuations* as it was in the *Meslanges*. What is so striking, in fact, is that Anacreontic themes can blend so successfully with the concerns of these collections that, in extreme instances, as in "Marie, vous avés la joue . . . ," the individuality of Anacreontic voice is lost and the subject relevant in a general way rather than with any particular informing intent for the twists and turns of the poem. The intensity of erasure or submersion apparent in this instance is unusual elsewhere but symptomatic of the degree of integration to which "Anacreon" can be susceptible in this collection.

Through a variety of techniques elaborated over successive collections and years, Ronsard progressively assimilates the new Anacreontic material furnished by Estienne's *editio princeps*. Ronsard's criteria for evaluation recall closely those prevalent in Neo-Latin circles, *beau stille bas* being therefore a commonsense counterpart of *genus tenue*. But to suggest such a proximity is not to believe in banal influence or mechanical transfer from one poetic idiom or circle to another. As usual, Ronsard avoids typecasting and invests the Anacreontic data with dynamic force. Innovation and variety, not static reproduction, are the hallmarks of his experiments in the "ode légère." Formally speaking, there is no concerted attempt on Ronsard's part to create an analogous lexicon for Anacreontics. No particular vocabulary is selected and cultivated as a counterpart for a perceived character or *proprietas* of the Greek poetry. This distinguishes Ronsard from Belleau and (to a lesser extent) from the Neo-Latins. Ronsard's preferences seem to be for mobility of form and flexibility of structure; words are empowered as energy. Glyn Norton's analyses of precisely the concept of "énergie" or *energeia* show that these terms testify to "the intuition that words can reanimate a past that is dead, a text that is absent."[85] *Energeia* is *actio*,[86] words a form of action, the power of a translation or an imitation to convey with minimum loss the entirely different *mundus significans* of the source text. Translation and imitation are part of a single process, intent on seeking out and encapsulating the dynamisms of the Anacreontea through the equivalent dynamisms of French. Yet, as Norton further points out, this notion of "énergie" carries within it its own contradictions. The source text cannot simply be transferred, or translated in the simplest sense of the word: "translation is calibrated on an act of irremediable transformation."[87] The source text is constantly elusive, never capturable with any finality or certainty, and yet simultaneously patient of attempts to give it renewed voice and form. On every occasion, translation and imitation must begin afresh.

In terms of an overall scheme, the trajectory of "Anacreon's" absorption into Ronsard's work is along a spectrum moving from *contaminatio* and *variae interpretationes* to *allusio*. The initial identification and contextualization of "Anacreon" by reference to epigram, elegy, or lyric correspond to *contaminatio*. The rediscovered Greek author is combined with comparable writers or genres. The launching out into independent poetic activity is manifested through *variae interpretationes,* with the Anacreontea taking on percussive force, a measurable and modifying impact on the surrounding textual fabric. *Allusio* works as a qualified instance of this scheme, since either it carries out local rather than global modifications or it harmonizes with the other strata of the poem and does not exclusively shape its given context. However, despite the apparent linearity of this trajectory, these processes are not mutually exclusive. *Allusio* can overlap with certain types of *contaminatio* poem, where there is a high incidence of non-Anacreontic material. Again, the *Continuations* contain examples of *variae interpretationes* in the same way as the *Meslanges,* so it is impossible to compartmentalize these techniques and tie them down easily to specific collections: some measure of overlap will occur even where general tendencies can be discerned.

If the relationship between the Ronsardian collections is plotted as a function of imitation and translation, the general pattern is not progressive but oscillating. Each collection considered contains both to differing extents. To some degree, translation acts as an agent of transmission, relaying the basic lineaments of the Anacreontic poem and normally preserving its *rerum ordo* (démarche), even if modifying the *verborum ordo*. Imitation, by contrast, can

---

85. Norton, *Ideology and Language,* 260.
86. Borrowing Estienne's definition, *TGL, apud* Norton, *Ideology and Language,* 263.
87. Norton, *Ideology and Language,* 261.

rework the poem's data through bearing on either the *verborum ordo* or the *rerum ordo* or both. The reworking of *rerum ordo* is precisely what is in evidence in imitative *contaminatio,* when Anacreontic texts are brought into confrontation and fusion with other texts drawn from other traditions. The reworking of *verborum ordo* is what happens in *allusio;* but if the reworking is too radical, then the *allusio* loses its perceptibility and the reader his purchase on the text. Thus *contaminatio* and *allusio* are features of imitation, whereas *variae interpretationes* can be indifferently within either sphere or indeed a mixture of the two.

In Anacreontics as in other domains, Ronsard's commitment is open-ended. It does not terminate with our *terminus ad quem* of 1556, though admittedly the greatest number of occurrences in his work tend to be early rather than late. In any case, the total assimilation detectable in the *Continuations* continues with *allusio* as dominant technique: the Anacreontea never again shape an entire collection, as was the case with the *Meslanges.* Imitation likewise remains Ronsard's major preoccupation and with it a desire to exercise the maximum degree of integration. Translation is implicit in many of Ronsard's operations, but it more usually occurs in the sense of transfer or transmission and in response to questions of how best to convey Anacreontics in French—what parallels can be used, what combinations are possible. For Ronsard, "Anacreon" *redivivus* is "Anacreon's" voice matched with equal force in the vernacular, resonant power transformed into resonant power. Ronsard ultimately places this capacity for transformation in the ambit of imitation; Remy Belleau will include imitation and transformation within the practice of translation.

CHAPTER 6

Inspiration, Metamorphosis: Belleau's *Odes d'Anacreon Teien*

Of those in Ronsard's circle of friends and acquaintances, only Remy Belleau immediately took up the challenge of "Anacreon" by producing a complete translation of the Odes.[1] The first edition appeared in 1556, in three slightly different printings.[2] The third edition appeared in 1572–73, the fourth in 1574; thereafter editions appeared in 1577 and 1578. There is no trace of a second edition of 1567.[3]

There is some evidence, then, of the moderate popularity of Belleau's version. Ronsard, whose interest in pseudo-Anacreon precedes Belleau's, wrote a relatively lengthy liminary poem to the *editio princeps* of the translation.[4] Dedicating the poem to Chretophle de Choiseul, Ronsard celebrates polemically the renewal of learning in France, listing in the process the conspicuous characteristics of Anacreontic idiom: love and wine, personified as Venus and Bacchus, are associated with the hedonistic life and then further with song and dance (lines 61–69). In particular, "Anacreon" *redivivus* is representative of the transition from one poetic style to another, from the "repliz recourbez . . . / Obscurs, rudes, facheux" of Pindar to the "doux stille":

Non pas d'un vers enflé plain d'arrogance haute,
Obscur, masqué, broüillé d'un tas d'inventions

---

1. Belleau translates all fifty-five Anacreontic odes printed by Estienne. Among the additional material supplied by Estienne, he translates only the famous Sapphic ode, Φαίνεταί μοι (M.-L. I, 46).

2. Quoted by Maurice F. Verdier, "Les introuvables éditions des 'Odes d'Anacréon' (Rémy Belleau)," *Bibliothèque d'Humanisme et Renaissance* 33 (1971): 360.

3. Verdier, "Les introuvables éditions," 361.

4. This poem was later collected in the *Second Livre des Hymnes* and is reproduced both in Lm. VIII, 351–58, and in Belleau's *Odes d'Anacréon*, ed. O'Brien and Cameron.

> Qui font peur aux lisans, mais par descriptions
> Douces, & doucement coulantes d'un doux stille,
> Propres au naturel de Venus la gentille.
>
> (lines 70–74)

Aside from the conventional assertion of *renovatio,* then, "Anacreon" appears expressly in Ronsard as the effect of a transition, a move to another poetic mode, the outcome of a rhetorical style: Ronsard is here sketching out an inchoate metapoetics of the passage, to use Mary Ann Caws' expression.[5] At the same time this new translation is vindicated as an authentic poetic production by reference to theories of source and inspiration: Belleau has found a new path to the springs of Helicon (lines 55–56), symbol of renewal, or is by implication a truly inspired poet, by contrast with those shadowy doubles, the "serfs imitateurs"

> . . . qui ne sçavoient que nostre poësie
> Est un don qui ne tombe en toute fantasie,
> Un don venant de Dieu, que par force on ne peut
> Aquerir si le Ciel de grace ne le veut.
>
> (lines 25–28)

The sacrality of poetic inspiration in this passage, the gift of Heaven, foreshadows the later evocation of the poet's ascent to Helicon: both are images of elevation, linking inspiration to high places and heightened states.

As might no doubt be expected in a liminary poem, Ronsard's reading of Belleau is distinctly positive, generating imagery of renewal, inspiration, and transition, which is then further adduced as evidence of the worth of the translator's own "naturel" aided by "fureur." A somewhat different picture emerges, however, if one turns to the "Ode à Rémy Belleau" (Lm. VII, 311–13), written for the *Nouvelle Continuation des Amours* of 1556. This poem might almost be a spiritual as well as a chronological companion to the liminary piece, since it systematically invokes and overturns the propositions advanced in the "Elégie à Chr. de Choiseul." Access to Helicon is now restricted only to the scholarly rather than to those who "s'alie[nt] / De Bacchus & de sa compaigne" (lines 17–18); and although Belleau is admitted to the company of the studious ("estudier / comme tu fais . . . ," lines 16–17), his cultivation of "Bacchus & . . . sa compaigne" and the broadly negative overtones of the

---

5. Mary Ann Caws, *A Metapoetics of the Passage: Architextures in Surrealism and After* (Hanover and London: University Press of New England, 1981).

poem as a whole make his inclusion in their number less than unambiguously felt. Ronsard takes the argument further by asserting that Bacchus combined immoderately with Venus is suspect (lines 19–21)—a reversal of one of the basic Anacreontic thematic patterns. More importantly, wine without water is equally ruinous (lines 29–30); immoderate wine drinking, Ronsard implies, is not an automatic guarantee of inspiration. The paradoxical alliance of Bacchus and water is a classical motif usually occurring in love contexts and so might well seem highly appropriate to Anacreontic concerns. When applied to the poem in hand, however, this motif becomes no longer an anodyne adjunct to the previous imagery of the springs of Helicon, but it tempers Bacchic with aquatic intoxication to produce a new variant on the classical debate over wine and water as rival means of inspiration.[6] With greater specificity, the motif reinforces the well-known opening lines of this poem:

Tu es un trop sec biberon
Pour un tourneur d'Anacreon,
Belleau . . .

(lines 1–3)

Laumonier warns against taking these words in an unduly solemn sense.[7] However, over and above any jocularity of tone, Ronsard is signaling the precarious nature of the translator's enterprise, emphasizing that Bacchic indulgence is not synonymous with fullness, that inspiration runs close to insufficiency. His remark not only points to a discrepancy between a theme (inspiration) and its implications (reproduction) but does so in one of the images of bodily activity (drinking) comparable to the imagery of incorporation that Du Bellay offers as an analogy for the process of imitation in *La deffence et illustration*.[8] Viewed in this light, the preference for sympotic hedonism advocated by the Anacreontea can be seen not just as a preference for a scheme of life but as an awareness of the importance of inspiration as a poetic issue. And the many ways in which Belleau tackles this issue, the variety of approaches that he suggests, are an indication of his concern with questions of inspiration and the problems of relating translation to them.

---

6. The debate is fully documented in the *testimonia* to Cratinus, frag. 203, in Rudolf Kassel and Colin Austin, eds., *Poetae comici graeci*, vol. 4, *Aristophon-Crobylus* (Berlin and New York: De Gruyter, 1983), 226–27.
7. Laumonier, *Ronsard poète lyrique*, 163.
8. Du Bellay, *La deffence et illustration*, 1.7, especially 42–43.

1

In the literary tradition, the link between drinking and inspiration had been standardized in the neoplatonic doctrine of the four furies, one of which was Bacchus.[9] Demerson points out[10] that a neoplatonizing "fureur" is a thematic constant throughout Belleau's work, though there is no suggestion of total adherence to the philosophical values it represents. In Belleau's Anacreontic translations, Bacchic "fureur" can be linked expressly with its companion, prophetic "fury" and, by implication, to erotic "fury," as in ode 13 (M.-L. I, 15–16). In the cognate form of "rage," the idea recurs in ode 31 (M.-L. I, 28), where the initial commonplace connection of drink as release from care is modulated, via the ambiguous pivotal term "furieux," to a statement about the relationship of drink to another paranormal state, madness, with its representative classical *exempla*. Bacchic "douce rage" is now specifically analogous to a state in which the mind is taken beyond itself, so that, by the time the poem reaches its concluding line, the trajectory that the argument has plotted—leaving behind simple intoxication and rejecting the negative associations of madness—allows the reader to measure retrospectively the full distance between "J'é vouloir d'entrer en furie" and its preceding near-synonym and refrain "Je veux devenir furieux." Possibly the most potent instance of the thematic network of which "fureur" is a part lies in ode 54 (M.-L. I, 45), where the various characteristics of Anacreontism are attributed to a narrator-*persona:*

> Un vieillard encor bien apris,
> De bien parler, et de bien boire,
> Et qui de fureur et de gloire
> Encor' quelque fois est espris.
>
> (lines 13–16)

Eloquence, drink, and madness are the features that this French translation shares with its Greek original. Yet the emphases have been subtly altered. "Bien parler" seems to evoke "ars bene dicendi" as a description of classical rhetoric and thus conjures up the tradition of Latin eloquence. Yet that tradition is now redefined; "bien parler" requires "bien boire"; intoxication is necessary

---

9. Among the substantial literature on this topic, the fundamental work is still Robert V. Merrill with Robert J. Clements, *Platonism in French Renaissance Poetry* (New York: New York University Press, 1957), especially chapter 6, "The Four Furies," 118–44.

10. Guy Demerson, "Poétique de la métamorphose chez Remy Belleau," in *Poétiques de la métamorphose* (Saint-Etienne: Université de Saint-Etienne, 1981), 135.

for a properly eloquent productivity. This modification in turn can be linked to the term "gloire," the most glaring example of Belleau's rehandling of the Anacreontic ode. A loaded term, recalling the Pléiade's explicit desire for fame ("de gloire / . . . espris"),[11] "gloire" functions, therefore, as an indirect endorsement of Pléiade attitudes toward precisely the type of aesthetic and cultural renewal that this translation itself represents.

Despite the overall coherence of such ideas in these poems, there is nevertheless no suggestion of an established currency of neoplatonic values providing an infallible key to the relative positions of inspiration and intoxication in Belleau's translation. On other occasions—as, for example, in odes 25 and 26—wine simply alleviates care and is celebrated as such; there is no real possibility of attaching this theme to the broader question of inspiration that is openly supposed by the use of the terminology "fureur," "furie," and "rage." If a common thread exists between the otherwise discontinuous thematics of this poetry, it is to be found in the sympotic theme of transformation or expansive transfer from one state to another, which wine is taken to motivate and facilitate. Drink is the catalyst serving now as the focus, now as the starting point for a series of wide-ranging reflections. Such transformation can be variously recorded as metamorphosis of the self or of the *inamorata* under the spur of desire, as transmutation that is the effect of the practice of translation; or as ambivalence that questions the borderline separating translation from imitation. Thus Belleau places at the heart of his concerns a principle of inherent mobility that mediates the passage between two different discourses.

To understand, therefore, the fully paradoxical nature of Ronsard's remarks, it must be realized that Belleau is consistently drawn to precisely that stratum of Anacreontic poetry that deals with the changes brought about by the onset of Bacchic control. A number of odes in his translation chart the passage between two psychological states and invest this moment of transfer with considerable thematic significance.[12] One characteristic attitude toward drinking in Belleau is to celebrate it as a moment of multiple generation, perceived as a power to work transformation and impart energy. In this category, ode 39 (M.-L. I, 33; 1554.35–36) is a typical example. The moment of drinking is expressly connected with celebration and poetic exercise:

---

11. See Françoise Joukovsky, *La gloire dans la poésie française et néolatine du XVIe siècle (des Rhétoriqueurs à Agrippa d'Aubigné)*, Travaux d'Humanisme et Renaissance, no. 102 (Geneva: Droz, 1969), 277–78, for Belleau himself.

12. So odes 13 (M.-L. I, 15–16), 14 (M.-L. I, 16–17), 20 (M.-L. I, 20), 26 (M.-L. I, 23–24), 27 (M.-L. I, 24), 31 (M.-L. I, 28), 36 (M.-L. I, 31), 38 (M.-L. I, 32–33), 39 (M.-L. I, 33), 41 (M.-L. I, 34–35), 47 (M.-L. I, 39), 48 (M.-L. I, 39), 52 (M.-L. I, 42–43).

Quand je boi de ce bon vin,
Soudain je sens ma poitrine
Qui veut commencer un hymne
Aux Muses, tropeau divin.

(lines 1–4)

The experience is shortly afterward interpreted as a Bacchic "ravissement" ("ce bon Dieu / . . . / Me ravist," lines 9, 12), thus expanding into the realm of neoplatonic theory ("ravist" corresponds to δονέει [rouses], devoid of any such overtones); later still, a hymn to Kupris is undertaken (interpreted by Belleau as an *inamorata* not the goddess). At each stage in the Greek ode, the refrain ῞Οτ' ἐγὼ πίω τὸν οἶνον (when I drink wine) generates some new activity in which the narrator engages. The sections are less clearly marked in French because the refrain is either suppressed or appears in variant form ("quand j'é bien beu," line 12; "Quand je boi," line 25). Yet the basic point is maintained: the poem catches the narrator at the point at which he undergoes multiple transformations under the influence of wine. And this moment of expansive metamorphosis is equally apparent at the lexical level. The transformations of the narrator are paralleled by the transformations of the narrative, notably in the expansion of noun and adjective or noun and noun compounds. Thus "Tous mes ennuis, et mes maux, / Et mes plaintes langoreuses" (lines 5–6) stands for μέριμναι / Πολυφρόντιδές τε βουλαί (worries and fretful deliberations), "les aleines souflantes / Des dous Zephirs, odorantes" (lines 10–11) for Πολυανθέσιν . . . ἐν αὔραις (in fragrant breezes), and "ma Cytherée, / . . . mon coeur, ma sucrée" (lines 18–19) for κούρην / . . . Κύπριν (girl . . . Aphrodite, a misinterpretation of the Greek). The magnification of the narrative seeks to replicate linguistically the onset of inspiration. Such expansiveness itself implies not a direct mirroring of the original but a centrifugal action with its characteristic shifts. Hence there is no concerted effort on Belleau's part to tease out the dense allusions behind λιγαίνειν (to sing), ἁλικτύπος (roaring over the sea), or πολυανθής (fragrant) or to create linguistic equivalents for them, as our Neo-Latins do. His translation sets up its own patterns of affinity, as, for example, "Des dous Zephyrs" echoing back in "De la vie, les douceurs" (line 16; poetic song is at one with Nature's song); or the isocola of "Et sur mon chef je le plante, / Puis sus ma lyre je chante" (lines 14–15) with the contrasting play in "sur" and "sus"; or again the *rimes embrassées* that establish a rhythmical continuity for a series of repeated actions (rhyme in French replaces refrain in Greek).

An extension of the transforming effect of wine that imitates exuberant activity is the moment of birth or emergence. This is evident in the second of the rose poems, "Les louanges de la rose" (M.-L. I, 43–44). The fact that the flower is dedicated to Bacchus allows it to be brought within the same thematic purview as other Bacchic poems. Here too, coming into being is treated as a form of metamorphosis and is attended by the same stylistic expansiveness present in "Du plaisir de boire." The etiological myth of the rose's origin is announced in Greek by the single line Φέρε δὴ φυὴν λέγωμεν (come, let us tell of its birth). Belleau marks the importance of the event by lexical extension:

> Or sus donc chantons sa naissance,
> Et comme elle a premierement
> En terre pris acroissement.
>
> (lines 40–42)

Only the first line strictly corresponds to the Greek: it is the telltale "premierement" in the second line that points to Belleau's fascination with the nascent. The swelling of the narrative is a measure of the importance of the event, narrative growth being the counterpart of organic growth. In this light, the use of noun doublets in the early part of the poem presages the event to follow and alerts the reader to its importance: "la bouche sacree / Et la douce aleine des Dieux" (lines 8–9) for θεῶν ἄημα (breath of the gods), "Le baiser, et la mignardise, / De Venus" (lines 15–16) for ἀφροδίσιόν τ' ἄθυρμα (delight of Aphrodite), "la seulle entreprise / Et le soing des Poettes vanteurs" (lines 16–17) for μέλημα μύθοις (object of attention in poetry).

More important still, the etiology of the rose is conveyed in terms that make its coming into being synonymous not merely with narrative expansion but with the actualization of a particular kind of lexis: *mignardise*. Indeed, the birth of Venus, referred to directly afterward, is itself a *mignard* event:

> . . . Venus encor rousoiante
> Dessus l'eccume blanchissante
> Apparut au meillieu de l'eau.
>
> (lines 43–45)

The *mignardise* detectable in the present participles spreads equally to the rose itself, of which Venus is in some sort a mythological anticipation; the rose is expressly the "mignardise / De Venus" and what is grown is precisely a *mignard* object fashioned out of the doublets and expansions that compose this poem. The point is made with even greater clarity in the first rose poem (M.-L. I, 10–11), whose terminology is more overtly *mignard:* here the rose is "l'honneur des fleurettes" (line 8) and "des Dieux, les Amourettes" (line 10). Yet the objective is similar in both cases: the moment of emergence is an emergence into a particular kind of diction and a particular poetic outlook.

In the sphere of drink and drink-motivated thematics, then, we can build up a response to Ronsard's comment about Belleau by appealing to the process of transformation that the text is made to undergo, thus thematizing inspiration as process. In addition to its status as thematic vehicle, transformation in this poem also plots a certain itinerary out of the past into the present, an emergence into a new lexical configuration defined as *mignardise;* the rose's origin is lost in a mythological past that saw the birth of Aphrodite and Athena, but the passage of time can be breached and the essence of the Anacreontea made intelligible by means of a specific contemporary poetic idiom. Just as the Anacreontea themselves frequently rewrite grave mythological stories in a lighter vein, so now Belleau's translation in turn rewrites this lighter vein in order to accommodate it to the current vogue for *mignardise.* It thereby repeats what it takes to be the authentic idiom of the Greek poems themselves, as can be seen from the following extract from the 1574 dedicatory letter to Jules Grassot in which "naiveté" and "mignardise" compose two types of Anacreontic "character":

> Car ne restant de luy [Anacreon] que quelque petis fragmens espandus çà et là, il y a dixhuit ans, qu'aporté d'Italie, il commença à prendre l'air de la France: moy en ce mesme temps, essayant à rendre en nostre langue, la naiveté, et mignardise des Grecs, pour coup d'essay, je fis chois de cest Auteur. (M.-L. I, 4)

Mignardise here acts, if not as a full-fledged theoretical term in the strict sense, at least as an active textual principle. It can tentatively be compared (from the critical standpoint) to the Alexandrian λεπτότης as an index of the lightness of *stille bas;* or (from the practical standpoint) to Estienne's term πίνος as an indication of stylistic veneer and incrustation. In terms of rhetorical *proprietas,* at any rate, the uniform choice of *mignardise*—much more rigidly enforced in Belleau than in Ronsard—suggests alignment with a perceived vocabulaic *decorum* of the sort that emerges with much greater infrequency in the Neo-Latin translators of pseudo-Anacreon.

Belleau's translation characteristically is neither a word-for-word translation nor a paraphrase. Like the rose itself, the translation exists in the space between recognizability and deviation and enacts the particular configuration that will hold the two together. The act of translation, for Belleau, constantly

Inspiration, Metamorphosis 209

highlights some moment of transformation as a paradigm for his attitude toward the Anacreontic Greek. The endless reworking of this theme in his *Odes d'Anacreon Teien* and the numerous approaches that he suggests and plots have to be balanced against the fact that the very theme of transformation implies a move away from the original. If Estienne and André commonly deal with this problem by linguistic devices that Greene classes as exploitative,[13] in that they usually emphasize the presiding presence of *contaminatio,* Belleau's vernacular version is neither fully exploitative nor fully heuristic.[14] To be recognizable as heuristic, a version must advertise its *clinamen,*[15] its swerving aside from the master text. Instead, Belleau creates a hybrid form, situated somewhere between the two. His translation proclaims its distance from the classical text and its adherence to a contemporary fashion or idiom, while nonetheless labeling this distancing as an authentic reading of the Greek author. The relation Belleau takes up with "Anacreon" is, one might say, proximity-in-distance, an indirection modifying any notion of direct transfer that the idea of translation might, straightforwardly, be assumed to have. Deviation away from thus becomes compatible, in Belleau, with deviation back toward. Or to use more traditional terms: in order to be faithful, translation must be faithless.

Inspiration and its practical manifestations can be approached from another angle, complementary to the first. The vital issue here is the notion of sound and its cognate notions, such as voice and rhythm.[16] *Mignard* objects themselves can be literally given a tongue, as in the case of the dove poem (M.-L. I, 12–14), where the bird's talkative nature articulates the very *mignardise* that characterizes both the dove itself and the poet's love, Bathyllus. Here, the poem, through the dove as intermediary, motivates its own *stille bas* and its links with love. In terms of techniques that act as markers to the reader, one primary way of developing this relation of proximity-in-distance is, it has been seen, through what can be termed lexical extrusion—the swelling of the narrative frame by elements that are not alien to the thought of the original, even if they do not strictly appear in that original. Its counterpart is lexical excision: the translation does not develop synonyms or parallels, as markers to the creative energy that the text encourages, but rather resolutely omits or strips

---

13. Greene, *The Light in Troy,* 39.
14. Greene, *The Light in Troy,* 40. The definitions used here for "exploitative" and "heuristic" are both taken from Greene.
15. The term is Harold Bloom's: see *The Anxiety of Influence: A Theory of Poetry* (New York: Oxford University Press, 1973), chapter 1, "*Clinamen* or poetic misprision," 19–45.
16. In the corresponding area of verse schemes, Belleau establishes metrical norms by his clear preference for octosyllables (32 out of 55 odes), followed by heptasyllables (18 odes). Four odes (nos. 13, 26, 37, 50) are hexasyllabic; one (no. 23) a medley of four- and six-syllable lines.

away strata of the original in order to throw into stronger relief chosen events or turns of phrase.

Among numerous available examples of this phenomenon, Belleau's octosyllabic version of ode 6 (M.-L. I, 11; 1554.6–7) is typical in the meager importance it accords to the details of its Greek counterpart. In the translation's opening lines, ἁβρὰ γελῶντες (laughing gently) disappears into the anemic "d'une façon gentille"; κροτάφοισι, πλοκάμοις, and θύρσους are excised completely. They are replaced by a renewed attention to song and dance:

> . . . la fille aiant le Lierre,
> Fredonnant dessus sa Guiterre,
> Dance d'un pié mignardelet.
>
> (lines 4–6)

The Greek girl has delicate ankles (χλιδανόσφυρος, a *hapax*); in French, her "pié mignardelet" makes her as much an object of *mignardise* as the rose quoted earlier, while the steps of her dance associated with song evoke the imitative patterns and rhythms of the translation itself. The lines immediately following then concentrate on song and playing as a complement to song and dance:

> Puis qu'un jeune garçon accorde
> Aux douces voix, sa douce corde,
> Joüant les sons les plus mignars.
>
> (lines 7–9)

The recurrent adjective ("mignars"/"mignardelet") identifies the relevant poetic register. Yet the rhythmical density of the second passage moves beyond a straightforward reemphasizing of a particular literary style and points insistently to the colorful poetic surface as the place where sound is produced: hence the contrast between two types of "c" and the alliance of singing and playing carried on the repetition of "douce," whose diphthong later recurs in "poussant," just as the vowel combinations in "garçon" will reappear in inverted order in "sons . . . mignars." This analysis could no doubt be taken even further, but it is clear that *mignard* renovation in these lines is allied to and perceptible through an increase in surface ornament. At another level, if the poem's indulgence in vocalic play can be seen as significant of the broader threefold alliance of sound, voice, and song and hence of the characteristics of inspiration, nonetheless the cultivation of nontransmissible features, such as rhythm and rhyme, points firmly to a textual surface as the place of renewal and locates this renewal in kaleidoscopic shifts in verbal fabric, exemplified here in the harmonies of the youth's voice and playing. In other hands this emphasis on texture might be taken as a manifesto for a closer approximation between translation and original. Here Belleau shows no concern for literalism, no desire to circumscribe the Greek text ever more tightly. His interest in sound pattern is in fact the counterpart of his interest in renewal of the surface fabric and the verbal designs that can be printed upon it through the medium of translation. The *décalage* in this poem between the exfoliation of meaning and the efflorescence of rhyme is precisely the space in which translation grows and operates, proclaiming its divergence from the Greek text as the paradoxical condition of its continued fidelity to the "naiveté, et mignardise des Grecs."

Attention to sound and song is thus of central importance to the concept of inspiration, whose etymology moreover ties it to the kindred area of breath production.[17] Thus Ronsard's observation about wine and inspiration comes to encompass a larger lexical and conceptual area, focusing on the idea of a voice natural to poetry. Earlier, the Anacreontea had been assimilated to a pervasive *mignardise* as a mark of their "true" nature. Now a further dimension is opened up, emphasizing the authentic sound that Belleau's translation characterizes itself as embodying and illustrating in response to the originary sounds of Anacreontic lyric. Local occurrences of the motif, as exemplified in the ode just considered, are amplified elsewhere, most notably through the rhetorical device of *recusatio,* widely used to illustrate the moment of shifting from inauthentic to authentic productivity, and Belleau takes advantage of such moments to underscore the new sound that his translation will make.

This idea surfaces, in association with related notions, in ode 48, a *recusatio* that rejects Homeric epic and implicitly states a preference for the Homeric *genera minora.* Extrusion by synonyms and doublets is evident throughout Belleau's short octosyllabic version (M.-L. I, 39; 1554.43). Particularly noticeable for our purposes is the second half of the poem:

> Affin qu'yvre de ce breuvage,
> Espoinçonné de douce rage,
> Dessous les accordz babillardz,
> Et sous les fredons de ma lyre,
> Je dançe, et je vous puisse dire

---

17. The issues are dealt with by Cave, *The Cornucopian Text,* 125–56.

En buvant cent contes gaillardz.

(lines 7–12)

The lyre is explicitly personified as having a tongue ("babillardz") and the theme is coupled to the kindred areas of wine and drink through a version of rapturous possession ("Espoinçonné de douce rage"), itself a stereotype for inspiration. Drink, song, and dance all combine to stimulate the narrative outpouring envisaged at the close ("cent contes gaillardz"); and these activities are both the source and the product of such productivity, whose very numerousness and eloquence are in some sense testimonies to the authenticity of the elements that inspire it (the notation of number is absent from the Greek). Similarly, the term "gaillard" notably characterizes the stories as emanating from an elderly narrator whose hallmark this epithet is, but it once again identifies this form as a further element in a *mignard* series, since "gaillard" frequently occurs with "mignard" or "folastre."

If in ode 48 sound and song are part of a larger more generalized thematics, in ode 42 (M.-L. I, 35–36) they achieve greater individual prominence. The ode proceeds on the principle of intrusion as well as extrusion. Where extrusion elaborates on some element already present in the thought of the passage, intrusion starts from the opposite position—the introduction into the passage at large, or the syntagm in particular, of some feature originally alien to it. In ode 42, it is "chanter" and its lexical associates that operate intrusively and extrusively. Lines 3 and 4 initiate the process; the Greek reads as follows (1554.39):

Φιλέω δ' ὅταν ἐφήβου
Μετὰ συμπότου λυρίζω.

[I love it when I play the lyre with a youth as my drinking companion.]

Extrusion and intrusion are brought to bear on λυρίζω:

Sous ma lyre chanteresse,
Aux dous accens de ma vois . . .

(lines 4–5)

The first line in French is simply an extended version of the Greek verb, transposed into a prepositional phrase. The second, by contrast, is intrusive: it corresponds to nothing in the immediate syntagm or in the broader context. Yet in its obtrusive prominence, it articulates a number of thematic constants, notably in that it binds together the singing lyre and the singing voice (they now form a single unit), reinforces the attribution of harmonizing abilities to encomiasts and symposiasts (the "garçon" of ode 6 provides an obvious companion), and promotes the idea of the voice of poetry. The same idea is pursued a little later in "ce que plus je desire / C'est de chanter, et de rire" (line 8), where "chanter" is a partial translation of ἀθύρειν, whose *sensus proprius* ("play an instrument") is transferred metonymically from object to person, from instrument to symposiast—the transfer being in retrospect prepared by the association of human and instrumental song in lines 3 and 4. The final lines take up and recapitulate both these passages and all these issues. In the 1574 edition of the *Odes d'Anacreon Teien,* these lines read as follows:

Dançans sous les chans mignons
De ma lyre, et de mes sons.

(lines 21–22)

"Sons" is a member of a doublet indicating (extrusively) the sounds of the lyre itself or indicating (intrusively) the tones of the narrator's voice—a variant, therefore, on the earlier "doux accens de ma vois." "Chants" is the mediating term, previously applied equally to the symposiast ("je desire . . . chanter") as to the lyre ("lyre chanteresse"); while "mignons," like "mignars" in ode 6, imprints the syntagm with the λεπτότης that "mignardise" claims as its own.

The technique of these odes—6, 48, and 42—is equally indebted to transformation, inasmuch as the interrelated topics of sound, voice, and song double as theoretical topoi designating inspiration, and this in turn is inevitably linked with *mignardise* as the authentic contemporary instance of such inspiration. But perhaps the most allusive and compact term by which to designate the problem of inspiration is "contresonner," the verb that occurs in the very opening translation (M.-L. I, 7–8) to describe the activity of translation itself:

Et ja commençois à dire
D'un haut stille, la grandeur
D'Hercule, et de son labeur:
Mais tousjours elle fredonne
L'Amour qu'elle contresonne.

(lines 8–12)

"Haut stille" derives from conventional Renaissance rhetorical terminology; yet here it takes on an added topicality, in that it evokes the "grave" Pindaric and Horatian poetry of Ronsard's early odes, which that poet had himself rejected in favor of a *beau stille bas.* Belleau's poem openly marks the transition to a new poetic mode by appeal to a recognizable idiom that had equally been the subject of contemporary controversy. In this light, "mignarder," placed earlier in the translation ("Mais ma lyre ne s'accorde / Qu'à mignarder une corde / Pour l'Amour tant seullement," lines 3–5), alerts the reader to the nature of this new mode; while the tenor of the two opening lines—

Volontiers je chanterois
Les faitz guerriers de noz Rois

—marks a departure from that celebration of Valois' political achievements that had formed an important part of Ronsard's early work. This version by Belleau itself looks like a rehearsal of Ronsard's own version of ode 1 from the 1554 *Meslanges:* the same references to the political themes of the odes recur, and to the "high" style in which such themes were couched. Belleau repeats Ronsard's *recusatio,* both because it represents his own attitude with regard to Ronsard and because it represents a formal affirmation of the value of *stille bas.* In the space of a few lines, Belleau presents his own version as simultaneously repetition and variation, shaped by and wary of the influence of his eminent contemporary. While recalling the parallel endeavors of Ronsard in the same genre, the potential problems involved in Belleau's rewriting of poetic idiom can be focused by the term "contresonner," an exact translation of ἀντεφώνει that catches both the desire to sing counter—to move against a prevailing idiom and so produce something new—and the danger this action runs of producing something wayward; departure from an established idiom is not in itself a guarantee of authenticity. Inasmuch as it embodies an ambition and a dilemma, the verb *contresonner* is related to a further term that Belleau puts into play, *contrefaire,* with its dual implications of imitation and counterfeiting.[18] The movement toward the authentic runs the risk of falling into the

---

18. *Contrefaire* is put to wide strategic use. Thus in "Le pourtrait de Bathylle" (M.-L. I, 25–27), its problematic focusing of Nature and Art is displaced into the analogous area of speech (the living) and silence (the represented); Bathyllus must be Nature even though he is Art: "Bref, si bien la [la bouche] contrefaisant, / Qu'elle devise en se taisant" (I, 26). Elsewhere—to instance selectively from the *Petites Inventions*—*contrefaire* designates the wings of the butterfly, which appear to be painted, thus inverting the hierarchy of Nature over Art (I, 50), so that the "pinceau" represents through "vn feint image" the "viue peinture" of Nature (I, 59: the authentic comes alive through the counterfeit; or again the "ombre" that adds dark colors to Nature's picture (I, 65): the artistry of the shadow is a subdivision of the artistry of Nature). Finally, the *Bergerie* makes use of *contrefaire* in the context of the tapestries and tableaux whose deliberately enhanced

inauthentic, and Belleau's translation moves along the ambiguous borderline where the apparent opposites meet and confront each other.

2

In the selection of poems so far considered, an implicit response to Ronsard's comment about inspiration brings with it cognate problems of renewal and authenticity. Inspiration itself implies transformation, the poem's ability to transmute its given material, which is in turn guaranteed by the τίνος of *mignardise*. As a counterpart to such renewal of the verbal surface, authenticity can equally be located in the sound that the poem produces: as well as being a local indication of the variety of rhyme schemes exploited, this feature also acts more broadly as evidence of the lyric quality to which this translation corresponds in its authentic sound. This endorsement of the authentic production can equally be located, as in the last two examples, in a first-person narrator, a *persona* who serves to coordinate the diverse activities predicated of him. It is "Anacreon" who authenticates the diverse modes of inspiration scattered thematically throughout the translation. The narrative first-person becomes a convenient means of assembling the cluster of terms composing the inspirational thematics: song, dance, voice, drink above all.

Nonetheless, despite the coherence of Belleau's approaches, it must be emphasized that the problematic that Ronsard's question opens does not receive unambiguous resolution. An interest in metamorphosis as theme as well as technique precludes a solution of this kind. Its potentially double-sided nature, directly expressed in Ronsard's reading of inspiration as fullness and deficiency, can also be measured in the use of *contresonner*, thematically ambiguous because of the role that Ronsard himself will come to play in Belleau's translation. Belleau's reaction to Ronsard thus enriches and complicates issues of inspiration and its associated values and plots a new aesthetic trajectory for his translation of "Anacreon." Earlier, the choice of *mignardise* and the creation of a contained lexical pluralism had turned Belleau's translation simultaneously away from and back to the classical ancestor, so plotting an irregular course between present and past, a double detour back and forth. This process is now repeated in respect to Ronsard. The allusions in ode 1 to "haut

---

"vraisemblance" facilitates the crossing of the primary and secondary levels of narrative (cf., e.g., I, 247, where the distinction between "contrefaits" and "viuans" eventually collapses, or I, 288, where ladies-in-waiting disguised as shepherdesses are further disguised as the mythological figures of the Parcae).

stille" and to the "faictz guerriers de noz Rois" are allusions to the work of an individual as well as to a genre, so that Belleau's "contresonner" suggests an ambiguous relation to a presence that is nonetheless crucial for the understanding of his translation. Ronsard is the further "sound" emanating from Belleau's work, and he has double-edged status: the "high" lyric of Ronsard's *Odes* and their political subject matter are rejected, while echoes, snatches, and fragments of Ronsardian song are nonetheless retained.

On one hand, indications of Ronsardian presence can sometimes be of the most direct kind. Thus ode 9 (M.-L. I, 12–14) closes with a reversion to Ronsardian quotation, as an admission that such quotation constitutes its own vital voice—". . . plus babillarde / Qu'une corneille jazarde / Tu m'as faitte . . ." (lines 41–43; M.-L. I, 14)—retaining the simile, but transposing the adjectives, of Ronsard's ". . . plus jazarde / Qu'une corneille babillarde" (Lm. VI, 223, lines 57–58). Similar remarks can be made about ode 16 (M.-L. I, 17–18), where the translator is captured as much by his poetic contemporary as by the mistress (compare Belleau's final line ". . . la cause de ma prise," line 10, with Ronsard's ". . . a causé ma prise," Lm. VII, 193, line 10, or again ode 33 (M.-L. I, 29–30), in which "nichée" and "bechée" (lines 15, 16) are the Ronsardian referents (compare Lm. VI, 200, lines 21 and 24). These manifestations of intertextual voice in so direct and barely manipulated a form suggest recoverable presence, actualized through the vehicle of the translation.

At the other extreme, Ronsardian "voice" sounds distantly, in the form of allusive *imitatio*. This is the case with Belleau's use of compound adjectives. This stylistic feature is standard throughout the Anacreontic Greek. Uncommon in the vernacular, equivalents had been developed and exploited most particularly by Ronsard in his Pindaric odes in 1550. Belleau is more sparing of their use but nonetheless follows Ronsard and early Pléiade use in adopting the practice. Thus in the six odes that demonstrate the feature, "Dieu porte-laurier" (M.-L. I, 16) is an antonomasia replacing δαφνηφόροιο Φοίβου (Apollo who bears the laurel) (ode 13, 1554.13); "Bacchus . . . / Le deli-soing, le chasse-peine" (M.-L. I, 24) corresponds to ὁ λυσίφρων, ὁ λυαῖος (Bacchus who liberates the mind) (ode 27, 1554.22); "Oreste au pie-blanc" (M.-L. I, 28) translates literally λευκόπους Ὀρέστης (white-footed Orestes) (ode 31, 1554.28) but is juxtaposed with "Le tumere . . . / Alcmaion" (M.-L. I, 28), a transposition of the participial phrase τὰς μητέρας κτανόντες (killing their mothers) (1554.28); Bacchus is "ce bon pere porte-lance, / . . . ce bon Bacchus trouve-dance" (M.-L. I, 34, 35) in response to Διονύσου / Φιλοπαίγμονος χορείας (dances of pleasure-loving Bacchus) (ode 41, 1554.38–39); while the cicada is, like her Greek counterpart, "terre-née, / Aime-chanson" (M.-L. I,

37; γηγενής, φίλυμνε [earth-born, song-loving], ode 42, 1554.40). Finally, "dous-coulant" in ode 22 (M.-L. I, 21) is important enough to merit fuller commentary later. A degree of verbal ingenuity is already apparent in these transpositions, which are far from presenting uniformly literal transcriptions of the Greek.

In general terms, then, Ronsard appears in Belleau's translation in the form of quotation or allusion, more rarely as imitation. Such quotation requires a considerable degree of perceptibility on the reader's part, since its presence is not often extensive and is frequently limited to a few words embedded in the poem structure. Ronsard's "Odelette à Jan Nicot de Nimes" (Lm. VI, 115), for example, is written in alexandrines, while Belleau's corresponding ode (ode 2, M.-L. I, 8) is written in octosyllables. The greater space at Ronsard's disposal is taken up with alternating expansion and contraction of elements ("Aus poissons le noüer" compared with "aux aigles l'adresse / De bien voler par l'aer," or "aus lievres la vitesse" compared with "Aus serpens le venin qui recellent dedans / Les peaus de leur gencive"). This rhythm of contraction and acceleration is not open to Belleau—except at one point, where greater expansiveness is clearly not a reflection of choices in Greek:

Nature a donné . . .

. . . .

. . . aux hommes d'estre prudens:
Et n'estant plus en sa puissance
Donner aux femmes la prudence,
Que leur at elle presenté?

(lines 1, 6–9)

The Greek is as pithy as ever:

Τοῖς ἀνδράσι φρόνημα.
Γυναιξὶν οὐκ ἔτ' εἶχεν.
Τί οὖν δίδωσι;

[To men Nature gave thoughtfulness. It still had nothing for women. What did it give them?]

It is Ronsard who is the model for such expansiveness:

La Nature a donné . . .

. . . .
A l'homme la sagesse, & n'ayant plus puissance
De donner comme à l'homme aus femmes la prudence.

And the choice of verb and noun in the final line—

La seulle Beauté dont la femme
Surmonte l'acier et la flamme.

(lines 11–12)

—clinches the contact, looking back to Ronsard's

Car la beauté, Nicot, d'une plaisante dame
Surmonte hommes & Dieus, les armes & la flame.

The point at which Belleau's translation allows itself greatest expansiveness is exactly the point at which it admits Ronsard's interpretation of the Greek. Ronsard's own imitative paradigms are now viewed as a literary object in their own right, inviting incorporation into a new aesthetic medium through whose focus they are then reperceived.

Exemplification of this phenomenon is given by critics who have devoted space to Belleau,[19] but there is rarely, if ever, any attempt to specify the differences as well as the similarities between the two writers. Yet a significant feature of the use of quotation is its resurfacing within a renewed context, which thus gives rise to the clash of similarity and dissimilarity. Ode 4 (M.-L. I, 9–10) is a typical example of this clash. Its contacts with Ronsard (Lm. VI, 103–4) are well advertised: the verbs "trousse" (line 5), "roule" (line 8), and "parfume" (lines 13, 17) all have Ronsardian counterparts, reaching particular density toward the middle of the poem. Belleau writes:

Aussi bien ne restera pas
Chose de nous qui soit plus chere

---

19. The standard critical references are Henri Chamard, *Histoire de la Pléiade*, 4 vols. (Paris: Didier, 1939–40), 2:87–95; Alexandre Eckhardt, *Remy Belleau: sa vie—sa "Bergerie," étude historique et critique* (Budapest: Németh, 1917), chapter 5, "Belleau disciple de Ronsard," 164–75, especially 164–68 for pseudo-Anacreon; Marcel Raymond, *L'influence de Ronsard sur la poésie française*, Bibliothèque littéraire de la Renaissance, n.s., no. 14, 2 vols. (Paris: Champion, 1927), I, chapter 6, "Ronsard et Belleau," 167–95, especially 172–73; Silver, *The Formative Influences*, 234–41. Belleau's references to Ronsard are detailed in *Odes d'Anacréon*, ed. O'Brien and Cameron.

> Qu'un peu de cendre, et de poudriere
> De nos os, apres le trespas.
>
> (lines 9–12)

recalling Ronsard's:

> Et apres nostre heure funeste,
> De nous en la tombe ne reste
> Qu'un peu de cendre de nos ôs.

The main verb and most particularly the phrase "un peu de cendre . . . / De nos os" seal the quotation and thus the similarity. But equally striking is Belleau's mode of reformulation—the expansion of "un peu de cendre de nos ôs" into a doublet and the introduction of the ironic "Chose de nous qui soit plus chere." Although both poems are octosyllabic, Belleau's liking for expansion produces a longer poem.

These local differences of emphasis are, moreover, significant of wider disparities. In particular, Belleau characteristically fuses internal and external, human and natural, through a shared sense of movement:

> Sur tous les arbres j'é desir
> Le Myrte, et l'Alisier choisir
> Pour boire à leur ombre mouvant,
> Et veus qu'Amour d'un fil de soie
> Trousse sa robbe qui ondoie
> Dessus l'espaule, en me servant.
>
> (lines 1–6)

Absent from both Anacreontic Greek and Ronsard's French, "ondoye" certainly, "mouuant" plausibly, are metaphorical appropriations from the sphere of water: man and nature dissolve in a fluid medium of exchange, metaphor inducing and enabling metamorphosis. The metaphor once established, its sensual appeal is further extended by shifting to an adjacent metonym—the olfactory. This sequence, also developed by Ronsard, includes "parfumer," "encens," "odeurs," and "parfume," in such a way as to bring "lis" (line 15) and "fleurs" (line 18) into the ambit of sense perception: the placing of "lis" and "fleurs" next to the extended metaphorical sequence joins and separates the flower from its scent, allowing the nouns to hover on the edge of metaphorical engagement from which they are nonetheless formally excluded:

> Donq que nous sert de parfumer
> Les tombes d'encens, et semer
> La terre de lis et d'odeurs?
> J'aime trop mieux durant ma vie,
> Qu'on me parfume, et qu'on me plie
> Sur la teste, un chapeau de fleurs.
>
> (lines 13–18)

Sense and argument work against each other, dividing man and nature while simultaneously suggesting their interextensibility. "Parfumer" is the shared verb, extended from human ("proper") to nonhuman ("figurative"), thus reversing the earlier motion from "mouvant" to "ondoye." The cluster of satellite terms enforces the parallel ("parfumer . . . semer" reflected by "parfume . . . plie"), but the sensuous exchange is restricted by the argument that refuses to connect the two areas. The metaphor is created and yet its characteristic telescoping of different linguistic spheres is denied by the very argument into which it is inserted.

Metaphor and argument stand even further apart in the final lines, with their discovery of activities that defy the onward pull of life into death and that are heralded by a triple "avant que" that seeks to maximize deferral:

> Avant qu'entre les morts je balle,
> Là bas sur la rive infernalle
> Je veus espandre mon soucy.
>
> (lines 22–24)

"Je balle" contrasts with the earlier "galoppent" and "roule" (". . . galoppent noz jours / Comme un char qui roule tousjours," lines 7–8), while "espandre," more polyvalent than σκεδάσαι (to scatter), evokes and counters "semer . . . de lis" (lines 14–15). "Baller" and "espandre" as terms of motion are now independently focused around the *persona* of the narrator, viewed as a separate entity from the engulfing forces of nature. As the argument progresses, the initial harmony between man and nature is revoked and finally dismantled, while the preference for hedonistic life that continues even into death is played out in terms of the relationship between the constituent elements of metaphor. More broadly, this drama itself is representative of the poem's attitude toward quotation from Ronsard. Transferred from Ronsard's own briefer, more disparate poem, and integrated into a larger sequence dealing with the potential coalescence and division of interrelated topics (metaphor, metamorphosis, life, death, movement), the quotations are advertised but never dominate. Belleau foregrounds Ronsardian quotations in order to measure his distance from their original context and their creator.

This enterprise, productive of sound and countersound, dependence on and independence of Ronsard, could be exemplified many times over in Belleau's Anacreontic translations. The most succinct and emblematic exposition of this position is ode 24, "De vivre gaiment" (M.-L. I, 22; 1554.21). Its partner is a Ronsardian imitation (specifically named as such by him: Lm. VII, 195-96). It is the middle of Belleau's poem that invites especial subtextual awareness:

Loing de moi fuiez tristesse,
Fuiez ennuiz et detresse,
Loing de moi fuiez vous tous,
Je n'ay que faire avec vous!

(lines 7–10)

The allusion is to these lines by Ronsard:

Pour-ce fuiés vous-en, esmoi,
Qui rongés mon coeur à tous cous,
Fuiés vous-en bien loing de moi,
Je n'ai que faire avecques vous.

(Lm. VII, 196, lines 9–12)

The point of contact between the two vernacular poets is clearest in the last two lines quoted. Over the four lines as a whole, this contact is highlighted by Belleau's insistent repetition of "fuiez," marking the subtext with a particular clarity.[20] The threefold repetition of "fuiez" is also combined with threefold amplification of φροντίδες (worries): Ronsard's term "esmoi" begets Belleau's "tristesse," "ennuis," and "detresse," but as synonyms and alternatives circling both the Greek original and the French imitation. Yet the point of intersection with Ronsard is also a point of deviation. The substitution of a group of plain synonyms for Ronsard's emphatic personification "esmoi, / Qui rongés mon coeur à tous cous" is both a closer approximation to the sparse original and an invitation to lexical inventiveness (albeit not in this case of a very high order).

---

20. Both versions represent a great amplification of the Greek diction: Μέθετέ με φροντίδες, / Μηδέν μοι καὶ ὑμῖν ἔστω.

A further point of proximity lies in the lines immediately preceding the middle of the poem. Ronsard gives an amplified development:

> Je cognois bien les ans que j'ay,
> Mais ceus qui me doivent venir,
> Bons ou mauvais, je ne les sçai,
> Ny quand mon age doit finir.
>
> (Lm. VII, 196, lines 5–8)

Belleau's proximity is to Ronsard:

> Je cognois combien j'é d'age,
> Mais làs! je ne puis sçavoir
> Les ans que je dois avoir.
>
> (lines 4–6)

Neither poet carries through the imagery of the original with its standardized terminology of life as a journey, βιότου τρίβον ὁδεύειν (to journey on life's highway), παρῆλθον (I traveled), δραμεῖν (to run). Or rather both vernacular poets measure the time, rather than the distance, traveled, substituting a temporal image for a spatial one. It is Belleau who marks both his awareness that the Greek imagery exists ("faire le chemin / De ce trop soudain voyage") and his decision to abandon this type of imagery and move to imagery of another type exploited by Ronsard.

As it emerges from this example, one of the most marked features of Belleau's work is the way in which Greek text and contemporary version by Ronsard are parallel "sources" to be combined or divided at will. Belleau's translation exists as what Genette christens a palimpsest,[21] a place of transformation where the two texts are brought face to face, to be superimposed, reworked, and modified according to new tensions. Belleau's work, in part, represents Ronsard's work, which had itself re-presented the Anacreontic original. In so doing, it provides a tacit admission of Ronsard's status, which it indirectly endorses, acknowledging in the contemporary the authority normally accorded the ancient. Recapturing the past now becomes a question of rewriting a modern as the supreme model of achievement. Where humanist translators, such as Estienne and André, constantly thematize their proximity

---

21. Gérard Genette, *Palimpsestes: La littérature au second degré,* Poétique (Paris: Seuil, 1982).

and distance from the Greek text through the double-edged status of Ovid or Horace, in Belleau the transition from past to present, subtext to surface text, is mediated through Ronsard, who provides a further set of linguistic criteria against which Belleau's version has to be plotted. In that sense, Belleau's version itself exists as a hybrid, supplying a vernacular version of *contaminatio* by opening itself to the presence of Ronsard and allowing the contemporary the power to shape and re-model that the Neo-Latin translators of "Anacreon" regularly attribute to Augustan forebears. Belleau's *contaminatio* is therefore significantly different from that of Ronsard studied in the previous chapter: where Ronsard had ranged widely and eclectically over Italian Neo-Latins, as well as the *Florilegia* of Stobaeus and Turnèbe, Belleau sets aside this diversity in order to privilege a single national poet.

One further group of cases has to be noted. Here, Ronsard as practical source of inspiration is joined to the theme of inspiration-as-drunkenness; thus ode 26 (M.-L. I, 23–24; 1554.22) reads:

Aussi tost mon esmoi
S'endort, que dedans moi
Dedans moi est entrée
Cette liqueur sacrée.

(lines 1–4)

This is Ronsard:

Lors que Bacus entre chés moy
Je sen le soing, je sen l'émoy
S'endormir.

(Lm. VI, 243, lines 1–3)

Repetitio of a specific noun and verb collocation ("émoy / S'endormir") is combined with *variatio* of "je sen . . . je sen" to produce "dedans moy/Dedans moy," this type of repetition being felt by vernacular poets to be germane to sympotic poetry in general and Bacchic poetry in particular.[22] This opening indeed serves as a frame to which the corresponding Ronsardian edge is found at the close—

---

22. For a parallel instance, see Ronsard's 1553 "Dithyrambes à la pompe du bouc de Jodelle" (Lm. V, 53–76).

Mieux vaut se coucher yvre,
Que mort sans plus revivre,

(lines 21–22)

—standing in the corresponding position to Ronsard's

Il vaut mieux yvre se coucher
Dans le lit, que mort dans la tombe.

(Lm. VI, 244, lines 17–18)

This frame defines a literary space in which both the Anacreontic and the Ronsardian texts are subject to manipulation. Ronsard employs lexical doublets or triplets that grow out of the dithyrambic repetitions at the beginning of the poem: "j'ay plus d'or, / Plus d'argent, & plus de thesor," "Mide . . . Croese," "je fui les honneurs, / . . . les estats . . . / . . . je foule à terre" (Lm. VI, 244). Belleau adopts a less symmetrical approach to the material. He resorts to an archaism ("De Croese la chevance"); a hendiadys ("Tout aplat je m'estens / Sur le ventre, et je prens / Un tortis de lierre" for κισσοστεφὴς δὲ κεῖμαι [I lie down crowned with ivy]); and a Ronsardian quotation ("Un tortis de lierre") closely followed by a variation on the same ("Sous le pié je le metz" in place of "je foule à terre"). Here as elsewhere, Belleau's poetry takes its stand in the interstices between two possible versions, two possible alternatives—a fidelity to the Greek text that implies simple transfer, and a more ambitious transformation of Ronsard.

To that extent, a translation of this kind is formally equivalent to the ecphrasistic poems, where the frame is prominently displayed. It is no surprise, therefore, that it is precisely in ecphrasistic translation that Ronsardian influence is most strongly foregrounded. Marcel Raymond was the first to point out the similarities between Ronsard's "Elegie à Janet Peintre du Roi" (Lm. VI, 152–60) and Belleau's "Le portrait de sa Maistresse" from the *Bergerie* (M.-L. I, 260–64).[23] Despite the fact that this poem stands outside Belleau's Anacreontic translations as formally constituted, its findings are of sufficient importance to justify devoting space to it.

Two stages can be discerned in Belleau's incorporation of Ronsard into the "Portrait de sa Maistresse." The first, most elementary stage, is that of direct quotation. A clear example is one of the poet's numerous apostrophes to the painter—

---

23. Raymond, *L'influence de Ronsard*, 188–90. For an appreciation of a particular kind of pictural quality in Ronsard's poems, see Richard A. Sayce, "Ronsard and Mannerism: The *Elegie à Janet*," *L'Esprit Créateur* 6 (1966): 234–49.

> Mon Dieu, mon Dieu ie ne sçay plus
> Où i'en suis.
>
> (M.-L. I, 262)

—being Ronsard's

> Je ne sçay plus, mon Janet, où j'en suis.
>
> (Lm. VI, 157, line 123)

Almost immediately, however, this category fuses into the second, in which extensive quotation is present in perceptible though modified form, as in

> Mais, mon Dieu, ie ne sçauroy feindre
> De quel pinceau tu pourras peindre
> Ses beaux yeux.
>
> (M.-L. I, 261)

representing

> Mais las! mon Dieu, mon Dieu je ne sai pas
> Par quel moien, ni comment, tu peindras
> . . . .
> De ses beaus yeus la grace naturelle.
>
> (Lm. VI, 154, lines 47–48, 50)

In this last example, the tendency of Ronsardian elements to be fragmented into smaller units now becomes apparent, to the point at which it is individual words only that indicate to the reader the presence of the informing subtext. Thus Belleau bids the painter treat his mistress' hair in this way:

> Fay, Peintre, que le crespe d'or
> Qui ses beaux cheueux represente
> En ce tableau, souefuement sente
> La mesme odeur.
>
> (M.-L. I, 260)

"Represente," "sente," and "la mesme odeur" all derive from Ronsard's own version:

> Fai luy premier les cheveus ondelés

. . . .
Qui de couleur le cedre representent,
Ou les demesle, & que libres ils sentent
Dans le tableau, si par art tu le peus,
La mesme odeur de ses propres cheveux.

(Lm. VI, 152–53, lines 11, 13–16)

Similarly, in the description of the chin—

. . . ce menton fosselu,
Poli, grasselu, pommelu,

(M.-L. I, 263)

—the first adjective and the last are Ronsardian (". . . son menton au meillieu fosselu / . . . le bout en rondeur pommelu," Lm. VI, 157, lines 111–12). In these instances, the importance of Ronsard depends on his position in the *repetitio-variatio* spectrum. Actual quotation maximizes *repetitio;* partial quotation emphasizes *variatio*. Often the same passage will be evidence of both categories, as in the description of the hair, which highlights the remanipulation to which the Ronsardian context has been subjected. The process to which such passages bear witness is the motion from translation to imitation, from transposition to independent modeling.

The quotations from Ronsard have, moreover, to be set alongside a further, indeed more extensively developed, idiom in this poem. This idiom belongs to Belleau himself, since large tracts of the poem are verbatim quotations from Belleau's translation of odes 28 and 29, the two Anacreontic poems on the beloved.[24] The "Portrait," then, consists of segments of translation directly

---

24. The instances are as follows:

"Maistresse"	M.-L. I, 260–64	Ode 28	Ode 29
p. 260	"Sus donc . . . son absence"	I, 24	
	"Frisez, retors"		I, 26
p. 261	"Mais sur tout . . . la nature"	I, 25	
	"à fin aussi . . . on desespere"		I, 26
p. 262	"Bref, si bien . . . en se taisant"		I, 26
p. 263	"sur la branche . . . iaunastre peau"		I, 26
	"Où toutes les graces . . . volees"	I, 25	
p. 264	"vn accoustrement / D'vn crespe" and "vesture . . . membres accomplis"	I, 25	
	"Il suffit" and "ie la voy, c'est elle . . . à moy"	I, 25	

transferred into a new medium without being subject to the internal lexical manipulations characteristic of Belleau's treatment of Ronsardian idiom.[25] The juxtaposition of quotation and self-quotation is particularly clear in the closing lines, where this juxtaposition is at its most intense:

> Il suffit, Peintre, oste la main,
> Oste, ie la voy tout à plain.
> Ha, mon Dieu, ie la voy, c'est elle,
> Et possible est que la cruelle
> Par la peinture que ie voy
> Parlera doucement à moy.
>
> (M.-L. I, 264)

Here Belleau's transfer of his own translation encloses a direct quotation from Ronsard ("ha mon Dieu je la voy," Lm. VI, 160, line 191), a modulation of Ronsard ("oste la main" for "Leve tes mains," Lm. VI, *loc. cit.*), and an invention of his own ("ie la voy tout à plain"). These closing lines could be said to summarize the various techniques employed in the poem—quotation, self-quotation, transfer, and invention—all of which define further variants on the intertextual processes initially apparent in Belleau's Anacreontic translation, in that the present poem substitutes Ronsard and Belleau himself (two contemporary presences) for "Anacreon" and Ronsard.

In all the cases mentioned except one, the linguistic devices can be regarded as versions of *repetitio*. They undergo some degree of transformation bearing on form, content, or subtext, but no single transformation bears radically on all three of these elements. In one major instance, however, an emphasis on form over content combined with a shared rhetorical function highlights imitation of the Ronsardian text. This major instance is the image. The palpable predecessor here is Ronsard himself, whose extensive similes are an expansion of the more concise imagery of the Greek text. Whereas the appearance of Belleau's own translation in a modified context is the extreme point of *repetitio*—the point at which quotation turns back on itself and becomes self-quotation—

The parallels were noted by Marty-Laveaux himself, who, however, mistakenly asserted that the "Portrait de sa Maistresse" was "le développement de la traduction d'une des *Odes d'Anacreon*" (M.-L. I, 353 n. 164). Delacourcelle, in her edition of the earlier *Bergerie* of 1565, *La Bergerie: texte de l'édition de 1565* (Geneva: Droz, 1954), 82 n. 1, rectifies the error but provides no further details. Precise line references are given in Belleau's *Odes* d'Anacréon, O'Brien and Cameron, ed.

25. There are occasional minor substitutions, as for example "rousoye" (M.-L. I, 263) for "launoye" of the original (M.-L. I, 26), "courber leur vouture" (M.-L. I, 261) for "perdre leur vouture" (M.-L. I, 25). The substitutions are so rare that they do not invalidate the general point.

the Ronsard-inspired imagery is the extreme point of *variatio,* the point at which it transposes into imitation. In both poets, the images are placed in direct apposition to the part of the body on which they comment. Identity of positioning and of figure (though not of form or of content) invites the parallel with Ronsard to be pressed home, although Belleau substitutes octosyllables for Ronsard's decasyllables. Ronsard's poem maintains its link with the original Greek poem by the nature of its similes, a large number of which are classical either in inspiration or in allusion.[26] Belleau's network of imagery concentrates instead on a second series of affinities originally elaborated by Ronsard's poem: the beloved as a landscape. Ronsard and Belleau alike develop the standard Greek imagery of roses, lilies, and carnations. More extensive imagery is also evident: the mistress' delicately veined neck ("ce rameau albâtre") is to breathe

> D'vn doux & mignard tremblement,
> Comme on voit sous vn petit vent
> Tremblotter l'herbe mi-panchee
> Du pié passager non touchee.
>
> (M.-L. I, 263)

Or again, her hair floats freely "sur son tetin mignonnement," half hiding her majestic forehead like the crescent moon hidden by a cloud, or

> . . . sous le pampre verdissant
> Rougir le raisin pourprissant
> Et prendre couleur sous l'ombrage
> De son frais & pampreux fueillage.
>
> (M.-L. I, 260)

The description of these bodily parts as "mignard" and "mignon" points in fact to the nature of the undertaking: this exercise in imitation is an exercise in *mignardise,* as the frequent occurrences of this term and its related adjective and adverb make clear, combined with the usual preference for diminutives and multiple adjectives and a greater emphasis on the sensuous appreciation of the woman.

---

26. Lm. VI, 153, lines 19–22; 154, lines 57–64 (two similes juxtaposed); 159, lines 170–74 (two similes juxtaposed). These are similes not appearing in either of the Greek originals: the total number of classical similes would be far higher.

Imitation in this poem is imitation of a poetic idiom that Belleau acknowledges in his own writing and discerns in that of Ronsard. Yet equally striking is Belleau's constant crossing of the frames of reference; and this version of *contaminatio* operates at several levels. Imitation is a primary example of it, in that *mignardise* elicits quotation and self-quotation, imitation of an imitation, and incorporation of a translation. This *contaminatio* of linguistic categories can also be taken to be a dimension of the problem of Art and Nature: styles and genres extraneous to an imitation now appear within it, redrawing the lines between the internal and the external, direct translation and indirect imitation. Indeed, the poem is expressly framed by a title and a prologue that are directly indebted to the idiom of translation. Yet the distance traveled by this poem in respect of imitated idiom is visible from the coda, where translation and imitation are juxtaposed: the frame itself is modified by the same forces that affect the remainder of the poem.

The same idea is thematized in terms of speech and silence. Its first appearance is through the incorporation of a segment of Belleau's translation of the Anacreontic poem on Bathyllus:

Bref, si bien la contrefaisant
Qu'elle deuise en se taisant.

(M.-L. I, 262)

The change from Bathyllus to the mistress is also a change in status for these lines, a transposed translation that speaks its own identity ("deuise") while submerging ("en se taisant") this linguistic status in favor of its new context. This process is taken to still greater lengths at the close of the poem:

Ha, mon Dieu, ie la voy, c'est elle,
Et possible est que la cruelle
Par la peinture que ie voy
Parlera doucement à moy.

(M.-L. I, 264)

The recognition of the lady ("ie la voy, c'est elle") is recognition of a pictorial event ("Par la peinture que ie voy"). And the speech with which the portrait may be endowed coincides with the incorporated quotations from Ronsard and the incorporated self-quotation from Belleau's own previous work. Literature as palimpsest is at its clearest, and the hybrid nature of this portrait is nowhere more apparent than at this, its closing point. At just the point when Art and

Nature are blurred by the assertion that the picture is coming to life, an analogous equivocation is similarly apparent in linguistic frames by which the poem is enclosed: quotation and self-quotation, imitation of an imitation, and transposition of a translation, Belleau's "Portrait de sa Maistresse" stands ambivalently between two conceptual categories.

What the "Portrait" principally highlights is the process of *inventio* itself, construed both as the technique of discovering suitable material and as inventiveness, a capacity for blending or transforming this material. *Inventio* as theme is matched by two other major concerns: the relationship between the twin contemporary forms of Ronsard and Belleau, and the wavering frontier between painting and reality. All three can be viewed as implying a double frame, superimposed within the poem so as to promote maximum convergence between normally distinct domains like writer and painter, seer and seen, subtext and surface text, contemporary and ancestral. Starting from this basis, a further group of Anacreontic translations in Belleau will investigate the duplicitous rhetorical power of metamorphosis itself. Metamorphosis now takes the field as protagonist, agent as well as theme.

3

The ambivalences that hold true for the "Portrait" can be extended to the other ecphrases. In "La façon d'un bassin d'argent" (M.-L. I, 41–42), it is the enallage of the tenses that serves the same purpose of blurring the distinctions between inside and outside. In this case, the enallage allows the figure on the bowl to stand in the same temporal perspective as the spectator:

> Ainsi tire et repousse l'onde,
> Avecques les flotz vagabonde,
> Ja ja le tetin pourprissant,
> Et ja l'ivoire blanchissant
> De son col, la vague surpasse,
> Et paroist dans l'humide trace,
> Comme les lis entortillés
> Entre la rose et les oeilletz.
>
> (lines 19–26)

The anaphoric "Ja ja . . . / Et ja . . ." fulfills the same role as "c'est elle" in the "Portrait" poem (M.-L. I, 25; 264), both marking the "presentness" of the scene, increasing the hypotyposis, but here with the added feature of pointing to the emergent or nascent that Jean Braybrook[27] identifies as a particular interest of Belleau's. And what emerges into this particular "humide trace" is in all essentials a petrarchist lady seized at the very moment of her emergence, caught between her formal properties ("l'ivoire" having specific petrarchist resonances for a contemporary audience) and sensuous appeal, conveyed by the delicate shades of contrasting color ("pourprissant," "blanchissant") and the overriding sense of movement ("tire et repousse," "vagabonde"). Venus' proximity to the type of the petrarchist lady is emphasized by their shared *mignardise,* with which the poem ends:

Puis elle aprochant le rivage
Esgaie son coeur gentement
En souriant folastrement.

(M.-L. I, 42; lines 36–38)

The Greek balances γελῶσα (laughing) against the neutral νήχεται (swims). Belleau's French ends with "folastrement," a sign that Venus is indeed defined by the epithets and adverbs of *mignardise,* whose "doux-coulant" nature is symbolized by the "humide trace" over which she travels. At the same time, her visual impact is increased, recalling the analogous characterization of the mistress in the *Bergerie* "Portrait." Both Venus and the *Bergerie* mistress have a shared fictiveness and a shared "vraisemblance." Riding ashore, carried to the very edges of the bowl and of the narrative (understanding "rivage" metonymically), Venus similarly stands out from the vessel on which she is engraved: the frame enclosing her dissolves, and the spectator and Venus find themselves on the same level. The tactic of situating a character outside his or her own restraining boundaries is in essence an exacerbated form of metalepsis. "Personnages échappés d'un tableau," as Genette demonstrates,[28] are one of a series of such "jeux" that

> . . . manifestent par l'intensité de leurs efforts l'importance de la limite qu'ils s'ingénient à franchir au mépris de la vraisemblance, *et qui est précisément la narration (ou la représentation) elle-même.*[29]

The lady is outside and inside the frame; she is real and yet an artistic trick; and the reader's perspective swivels ambivalently between these two perspectives.

---

27. Jean Braybrook, "Remy Belleau and the Figure of the Artist," *French Studies* 37 (1983): 4.
28. Gérard Genette, "Discours du récit," in *Figures III,* Poétique (Paris: Seuil, 1972), 245.
29. Genette, "Discours du récit," 245 (Genette's emphasis).

A familiar variant on this idiom is the mirror poem, as can be seen from the translation of ode 20 (M.-L. I, 20), Belleau's title for which, "Qu'il se voudroit voir transformé en tout ce qui touche sa maistresse," is indicative of its content. The metamorphic perspective is immediately apparent from the opening lines, where transformation is centralized through the introduction on two occasions of the verb "changea." Thus Belleau's poem is not so much a misunderstanding, and hence a mistranslation, as a rewriting of the original prefiguring the remainder of the poem, where the narrator turns from classical myth to his own desired metamorphoses. In contrast to the reported actions enshrined in myth (neither certain fact nor simple fiction), the transformations of the narrator are couched in the hypothetical subjunctive:

Or' que pleust aux Dieux que je fusse
Ton miroüer, afin que je peusse
Te mirant dedans moi, te voir.

(lines 7–9)

The Greek has the narrator as the object of the lady's gaze (ὅπως ἀεὶ βλέπῃς με [so that you may always look at me]). Belleau reverses the perspective: the narrator now acts as a mirror internalizing the lady as his desired object of possession. It is the lady who is now the object and the objective, but despite the optimism that the mirror image implies, the objective cannot be directly attained but has to be mediated through a further series of objects. Desire multiplies the objects and impels the narrator into the expansive transformations, yet without reducing the distance between narrator and lady; narrative metamorphosis increases the number of objects associated with the lady without attaining the lady herself. In the meantime, the narratorial subject is himself dispersed through constant translation into these objects, which touch or adorn the lady's body. He exists only through such transformations. And if the series ultimately brings the objective no nearer, it nonetheless increases noticeably the sensuous attraction of the lady:

Ou le parfum, et la civette,
Pour emmusquer ta peau douillette,
Ou le voile de ton tetin,
Ou de ton col la perle fine,
Qui pend sur ta blanche poitrine . . .

(lines 13–17)

Amplificatio, in these lines, is a function of the overall mimesis-inducing desire, attempting to swell the narrative into closer proximity with its desired objective, to diminish the gap between lover and lady. Desire induces mimesis and it is manifested in the objects through which the lover channels his erotic energies. Indeed, the poem lives solely by the metamorphoses it recounts; and it explores not the lady as final end to which the lover is drawn but the manifold objects receptive to the narrator's passion.

In the poems considered so far, the allurements of pictorial or specular representation have been symbolized by the allurements of a female figure whose seductiveness is located in her general physical attractions or, more specifically, in her gaze, her smile, or her voice. One of the paradoxical features of Belleau's position as it emerges from the last example is an intensification of the sensuousness of the beloved, yet without a correspondingly greater proximity to her. The reality of the woman is coextensive with the reality of the desire projected onto her by the narrator-lover. There is no true specularity because the allurements are created rather than reflected. Yet a third type of spatial poem is exploited by Belleau and this falls under the heading of *locus amoenus.* The link between the beloved, desire, and landscape is clearly shown by the incomplete ode 49 (M.-L. I, 39–40), which Belleau specifically entitles "Le portrait d'un païsage":

Sus Peintre fai moi un beau païsage,
Où les cités portent visage
Gaillard, honneste, et valereux:
Et si la table permet ores,
Trace les passions encores
Et les arrestz des amoureux.

(lines 1–6)

The "beau païsage" is Belleau's own interpellated gloss on the subject of this poem, just as "passions" represents an interpretation, as opposed to "arrests des amoureux," a straightforward equivalent of νόμους φιλούντων (decrees of lovers). The poem does no more than establish the point, but once established it receives greater exploration in ode 22 (M.-L. I, 21; 1554.19–20). Here, desire and a charged sensuality relate to another beloved, Bathyllus:

Παρὰ τὴν σκιὰν Βάθυλλε
Κάθισον, καλὸν τὸ δένδρον.
Ἀπαλὰς σίει δὲ χαίτας

Μαλακωτάτῳ κλαδίσκῳ.
Παρὰ δ' αὐτῷ ἐρεθίζει
Πηγὴ ῥέουσα πειθοῦς.

[Sit down in the shade, Bathyllus, the tree is beautiful. It shakes its soft hair on a most delicate branch. By it babbles a spring flowing with persuasion.]

This produces

Fai moi pres ce jouvenceau
Un ombrageus arbrisseau,
Afin que sa tresse blonde
Soit au branle vagabonde
De ses rameaux tendreletz:
Fai pres de luy crespeletz
Les replis d'une fontaine
Dous-coulant parmy la plaine.

(lines 1–8)

As Giangrande remarks, "Bathyllus is, by way of a metaphor, visualised as a tree."[30] The figurative effects are more complex than this bare statement allows. Ἁπαλὰς σίει . . . χαίτας, a standardized classical collocation, is literal to Bathyllus,[31] metaphorical to trees,[32] and metonymic to beauty (καλὸν τὸ δένδρον). Belleau reorganizes this figural nexus through his version "tresse blonde," where the shared term (for trees and beloveds) is "tresse." The introduction of "blonde," however, limits the application to Bathyllus, whose "tresse blonde" is then in nonetheless direct parallel to the "branle . . . / De ses rameaux tendreletz"; the boy's golden hair and the trees' new shoots are fused together, in French as in Greek. Μαλακός and the preceding ἁπαλός, when viewed retrospectively, belong both to the human and to the natural worlds[33]

---

30. Giuseppe Giangrande, "On the Text of the Anacreontea," *Quaderni Urbinati di Cultura Classica* 19 (1975): 185. Rosenmeyer, *The Poetics of Imitation,* 199 n. 89, signals West's view that the nature imagery of this poem constitutes a sexual allegory.

31. The proper use of χαίτη is widely exemplified in the LSJ, s.v. For combinations involving σείω (-ομαι) + χαίτη, see Aristophanes *Lys.* 1312, Euripides *Cyc.* 75, *Med.* 1191.

32. See the neat example quoted in the LSJ, s.v. χαίτη from Hesiod *Scut.* 299: ὄρχος σειόμενος φύλλοισι; for χαίτη in a botanical sense, see Theocritus *Id.* 6.16.

33. Μαλακός can refer to "things subject to touch" (LSJ, s.v. I): thus Homer *Od.* 5.72, *Il.* 14.349; and of skin or flesh, Euripides *Med.* 1403, Xenophon *Mem.* 3.10.1.

and so mediate and strengthen Giangrande's observation that Bathyllus is visualized as a tree.

In French, by contrast, the figurative fusion of the two worlds is activated later and in a different sphere. It is "vagabonde" that captures hair and tree as a single movement, thereby also bringing into conjunction "tresse blonde" and "rameaux tendreletz," with "tendreletz" overdetermined with respect to Bathyllus, as μαλακός had been. At the same time, "vagabonde" also anticipates "fontaine" following, just as "crespeletz / Les replis d'une fontaine" depends for its metaphorical intelligibility on the preceding "tresse blonde" of Bathyllus. Hair and water serve as metaphorical terms for each other, as echoes elsewhere in Belleau can help to make clear: in the description of Bathyllus' hair in ode 29 (M.-L. I, 26), the boy has "poil meslé, / Frizé, retors, et crespelé" that is allowed to "errer en ondes, / A lentour du col vagabondes," thus confirming that metamorphosis in the present translation affects both terms of comparison and eventually erases distinctions between literal and figurative. The fusion of hair and water is not simply a means of insisting on a pervasive metamorphosis that is here represented in the process of operating its characteristic transformations. More specifically, the metamorphosis is linguistic, representing the point of collapse when tenor and vehicle are no longer distinguishable. A notable telltale sign in this respect is the term "douscoulant," predicated of the spring and a common metonym for *mignardise*.[34] In this light, the diminutive in "crespeletz" is an effect of such a style, which can be seen to extend to the whole poem, embracing the countryside ("rameaux tendreletz," "crespeletz / . . . replis") as well as Bathyllus himself ("jouvenceau"). Bathyllus, tree, spring—all three major elements in this passage are thus the exemplification of a chosen poetic idiom.

Who, seeing such a καταγώγιον, could pass it by? asks the Greek in conclusion. Belleau's equivalent, "pourpris," similarly suggests an enclosure; but in his translation there is nothing formally enclosed, merely a wordscape invested by *mignardise* that, supported by dense figuration, persistently blurs all frontiers, whether between man and nature, water and tree, or literal and metaphorical. The enclosure bounds a poem in which boundaries have collapsed; and the French translator's comment—

---

34. For a neat encapsulation of this point, cf. Belleau's "Le Pinceau" (*Petites Inventions*, M.-L. I, 58–60), which closes with the following appeal to the dedicatee, Georges Bombas: "Vueilles ce Pinceau remouiller / Dedans la belle eau qui distile / Tant doucement de ton dous stile": "dous stile" here encompasses the world of writing as well as painting and, by the rapprochement of poet and artist, points to the pun in "belle eau."

> Voiant cest heureux pourpris
> Dieux! qui n'en seroit espris!
>
> (lines 8–10)

—is both an indication that this erotic desire here suffuses a landscape that is indistinguishable from a bodyscape and more particularly a characterization of the reader's own desiring reception of the Anacreontic poems. Reading itself is a form of desire, in its willingness to breach, on invitation, the walls separating a classical past from a classical present, or to invest art ("mignardise") with the authority of nature ("naiveté"), or to credit metamorphosis with precisely that power of radical transformation that translation requires. As a metaphor for just such a transaction between text and reader, this poem, or at least Belleau's translation of it, exhibits the rhetorical devices enabling this transaction to occur.

A further area of equivocation in Belleau's translations is that of dream. The contrast between dream and reality is a standard one and to it Belleau adds an essential link with love; all Belleau's "songes" are also "songes amoureux." On occasion, the habitual contrast between dream and its referent is exploited directly, as in ode 8 (M.-L. I, 12), a "songe amoureux" that verges on the "baiser" but draws away when the dream evaporates:

> En sommeillant je m'approuche
> Pour les baiser.
>
> (lines 10–11)

"Sommeillant" and "baiser" are drawn close together by the syntax of the sentence, then definitely separated by the narrative context:

> . . . je les voi
> S'escarter soudain de moi.
>
> (lines 11–12)

The dream remains only a dream, unactualized. But it is the narrator's comment on his dream that is of prime importance:

> Ainsi pipé de mansonge,
> Je me rendors sus mon songe,
> Pour assopir mon esmoi.
>
> (lines 13–15)

The "mensonge/songe" rhyme is common elsewhere in French poetry, particularly in the later Ronsard;[35] and as in Ronsard, the narrator, though fully conscious of the deceptive nature of his dream, nonetheless plunges back into the dream. In Ronsard, the tone is one of self-conscious realization of the gap between desire and its fulfillment and one of a deliberate keeping apart of the two poles. In this Belleau poem, emotional significance is reinvested in the dream, primarily as a means of consolation. Yet behind this it seems that dream is exploited precisely for the ambiguity it brings, the possibility it offers of giving at least partially what reality denies totally—the contact with "fillettes." Dream allows a potential reshaping of reality in terms that reality itself denies; so that the status of dream is promoted for its malleability, even if its content is openly acknowledged to be deceptive.

In the "Songe de l'Amour" (ode 44, M.-L. I, 37), the idea of Love pursuing the narrator introduces an element not present in the Greek:

Je sçai qu'Amour m'a mis au plonge
De cent cruautés, mais helas!
De la plus part, il est possible
D'en eschapper, mais impossible,
Que je ne meure entre voz bras.

(lines 12–16)

The final line is a purely petrarchist equivalent for συνδεθῆναι, one of two images of binding (the other being πλακέντα): the Greek envisages neither the hyperbole nor the apostrophe to the external addressee, never named but presumed to be the mistress. Yet precisely this apostrophe entails the revision of the dream narrative: the allegorical conflict of Love and the lover is itself allegorical of the conflict between the sexes—a double and doubled metaphor. For Eros, now read the mistress; and the vocabulary of sexual conquest, which Belleau elaborates at some length, can now be interpreted as the double of the contest between love and the narrator:

Or que sa plante prisonniere
Fust d'un plon pendant, toutesfois
Il me devance, il me surmonte,

---

35. Lm. XVII², 244, I.54, lines 11, 14 ("mensonge/songe"); 264–65, II.23 (dream acknowledged as fallacious, but embraced); 293, II.52, lines 11, 14 ("mensonge/songe"). These examples are all taken from another collection of love poetry, the *Sonets pour Helene*.

> Et en fin tellement me donte,
> Qu'esclave me fist de ses loix.
>
> (lines 6–10)

Dimensions assume importance: the horizontal chase "parmi la plaine" and the vertical ascendancy of Love over the narrator-lover ("il me surmonte"), followed by the downward plunging of the narrator into the cruelties of love ("Amour m'a mis au plonge / De cent cruautés"). And this importance is part of the extended metaphor, which does not simply act as narrative *amplificatio* but favors the doubling of Eros/narrator and beloved/lover, until the final line with its further doubled reference in "meure," compressing two levels of erotic conflict, metaphorical in both cases but with the additional petrarchist conceitfulness. The two levels are brought into and taken out of phase by the identity and the dissimilarity of reference. The doublings in this poem affect not so much the content of the dream as its interpretation and reference. Because interpretation is double, reference is similarly double: a "literal" conflict between poet and beloved is metaphorically expressed as an amorous battle between poet and Love, yet this only emerges in the final line, which then gives the first conflict the status of an allegory. The literal appears not in its own right but in the context of dream and within dream as a metaphor within a metaphor.

4

Although metamorphosis, in Belleau's *Odes d'Anacreon Teien,* is not synonymous with a theoretical principle but represents a number of wide-ranging effects for which it is a collective term, these effects are nevertheless capable of a high degree of formalization. The primary importance of metamorphosis lies in the fact that its textuality is compatible with the textualities of gaps and distances. Gaps and distances are naturally endemic to the spatial metaphor present in the notion of translation, while, in a temporal sense, translation must also deal with its own removal from its source and the consequent discrepancy between two cultures historically distanced. In Belleau, metamorphosis as technique and theme cuts across the line demarcating spatiotemporal distance and proximity. On the widest possible view, metamorphosis opens up and emphasizes gaps between Greek and French as a means of foregrounding the *renovatio* that metamorphosis itself undertakes to carry out. In that sense, each poem in Belleau's translation is part of an overall sequential narrative in which coherence and variety are the keynotes, sanctioned by the transformational processes inherent in translation. Each separate translation is a new attempt at renewal, and the total distance between the two idioms of French and Greek is only perceptible to the reader as the collection is read in its entirety, each translation succeeding each. Endowed with the power of creating gaps and distances, metamorphosis is also capable of dissolving them, in a making solvent of tensions, as when Bathyllus and tree, man and nature, merge in the *tertium comparationis* of water.

Metamorphosis, therefore, provides two interpretations of the spatiotemporal problematic confronting translation as a genre, plotting out the difficulties that time and space imply only to gather them back in episodes that overcome such difficulties. The concept of metamorphosis is central to a theory of translation, inasmuch as it openly acknowledges the slippages and discontinuities inherent in the attempt to translate one language into another: translation necessarily implies transformation and transposition, rather than simply a neutral transfer. The very variety of thematic strata in Belleau is thus consonant with a larger notion of language and its operations in the practice of translation. Over against this are metaphorical approaches to the issue of representation, thematized variously as the relationship between a painting and its frame, landscape and desire, dream and fulfillment. In these areas, the action of metamorphosis is traceable in the blurring of frames and lines of demarcation that keep such areas apart. This type of metamorphic poem in Belleau is less a point of separation or division than a point of convergence and ambivalent interchange.

It must be emphasized that these two approaches do not operate in total isolation from each other; a single poem can frequently be read along both axes. Nor are these axes regarded by Belleau as mutually exclusive, even though their implications provide different solutions for the same problem. This move is typical of Belleau, as a number of critics imply. Thus Demerson points out that metamorphosis for Belleau can be either turbulence or repose;[36] while Jean Braybrook finds him pursuing problems of authentic and fake artistry or seeing dreams as containing truth and falsehood in unquantifiable doses.[37] It seems clear that what interests Belleau is not a fixed and settled set of determined referents capable of being read off as a barometer to his views of translation or history or the classical text. He appears more fascinated by the innately restless qualities of metamorphosis itself, as central generator of meanings.

Following on from Ronsard's reading of inspiration in Belleau, therefore,

---

36. Demerson, "Poétique de la métamorphose," 137.
37. Braybrook, "Remy Belleau," especially 3 ff., 6.

Belleau's own reading of Ronsard thus internalizes his contemporary as central to the very debates in which his translation engages. Ronsard's comment no longer exists outside Belleau's translation but can be situated within a whole series of complementary inquiries that ultimately provide no formal, unequivocal answers to the problems they confront. Curiously enough, Ronsard himself gives impetus to this process, since his introduction into a sequence of pre-established antinomies (past and present, classical and contemporary, translation and imitation) disrupts and distorts the tidy geometry composed by these pairs. At this as at other levels, the released energies of translation under the central stimulus of metamorphosis push Belleau's work beyond purely formal definitions and into a realm in which the very nature of translation itself is perceived to depend on a careful plotting of, and transaction between, ostensibly exclusive terms.

Translating "Anacreon": Reflections in Conclusion

All our chosen translators face, at the outset, the brute problem of Greek words to be translated into Latin or French. Among Neo-Latin translators, the predominant technique employed is *allusio*. This highlights microcontext—the lexical unit that comprises any particular translated statement. *Allusio* can make reference to a known classical context that does or does not have relevance for a reading of the contemporary Renaissance context; and the classical phrase may appear as it exists in its original context or in some recognizably varied form. The variety of such allusions, and their accompanying lexicon, is a striking feature of Neo-Latin translation. Several reasons may account for this. One argument would emphasize that the Neo-Latin tradition assimilates all linguistic strata in such a way as to maximize the degree of allusion and simultaneously to ornament discourse with the broadest range of contrasting, rare, or striking vocabulary. Estienne's reliance on *allusio* in his commentary provides cogent support for this view, as does the comparable activity of another Anacreontic practitioner, J.C. Scaliger.[1] For both these authors *allusio* is normative and Estienne therefore appears to be doing no more than giving shape and expression to contemporary literary expectations.

This argument envisages a layering of the text according to historical criteria: the strata reflect, though in a haphazard rather than in an ordered way, a historical dimension, a consciousness of antiquity incorporated into the translation. An argument of this kind is really an extension of the process of identifying allusions. It would gain strong corroboration from Estienne's prin-

---

1. Cf. Michel Magnien, "Anacréon, Ronsard et J.-C. Scaliger," in *Mélanges sur la littérature de la Renaissance à la mémoire de V.-L. Saulnier,* Travaux d'Humanisme et Renaissance, no. 202 (Geneva: Droz, 1984), 407 n. 42: "Scaliger emprunte aussi abondamment à Plaute, Ovide, Martial leurs mots rares."

ciple of literary theft or plagiarism, with its open acknowledgment of the motivating presence of one author within another. Whether chronological evidence of this nature impinged as strongly on André must remain conjectural. One notes his strong liking for Plautine vocabulary (more marked in André than in Estienne); whether this constitutes a form of historical consciousness is difficult to ascertain. André may well read "Anacreon" with the same degree of literary acuity as Estienne, but the evidence of his translation is too disparate for positive conclusions to be drawn.

Firmer ground is reached with the concept of specific *allusio* underpinning generic requirements. Both Estienne and André display something of the liking for participles and diminutives that are a hallmark of the *mignard* style derived from Catullus. Estienne and André would not be the first humanist poets to appeal to a Catullan idiom, but they use it as a springboard for the creation of a style to convey not just Anacreontic lightness but also its parody, its irony, and its comedy. Even here, this style is not uniformly distributed, nor does it work to the exclusion of other notions of stylistic *decorum,* most notably lyric or elegiac strains equally discernible (and not infrequently crucially operative) in these Neo-Latin translations of "Anacreon."

That at least two types of stylistic *decorum* emerge from this Neo-Latin practice, functioning together but asymmetrically to cover sometimes the same, sometimes quite different, areas of tone, inflection, and stylistic need, is itself indicative of the extent to which Estienne and André favor *contaminatio.* It is a technique similarly favored in vernacular circles (who may have adopted it under Neo-Latin influence), but the distinctions between the two domains are noticeable. In Neo-Latin Anacreontic translation, *contaminatio* is a function of *allusio* and the ally of *imitatio,* and it entails plurivocality of diction. The trigger for this process might almost be given by Estienne's analysis of Horace. His analysis conceals the fact that they exist multiply in Horace's work itself— not in presentable concatenation, but in composite imitation or indeed translation. The counterpart of what Nancy Struever terms the continuity in change of *imitatio* is *contaminatio*'s diversity in continuity.[2] In a Neo-Latin translation, the tendency is to accentuate centrifugality, which results in the breakup of total homogeneity of diction: hence it is possible to construct two models of diction—a Catullan-based model and a lyric or elegiac model—for Anacreontic *decorum.*

Transposed across different literary genres, the *contaminatio* principle re-

---

2. Struever, *The Language of History in the Renaissance,* 193.

mains actively the same, but its manifestation changes. Thus *contaminatio* in Estienne's humanist commentary blends the philological with the exegetical, the restitution of the authentic reading through the resolution of *cruces* with the elucidation of literary parallels, references, and echoes. Again, in the sphere of vernacular Anacreontics, the nearest to the Neo-Latin position on *contaminatio* is to be seen in Belleau, where there is a sleight of hand involved in using Ronsard to rechart questions of translation and imitation. Ronsard's own work gives the more usual state of affairs: the quantity of echoes and resonances contained in a vernacular *contaminatio* determines whether any particular piece is to be classified as an imitation or a translation. Yet perhaps this is too simple and too crude: Ronsard excels in leaving the reader in perplexity as to where along the translation-imitation spectrum he or she is being placed, and the removal of all paratextual aids ("imitation d'Anacréon," "traduit d'Anacréon") increases the potential interpenetration of two domains that are in any case closely related. Whereas Belleau makes ambivalence the object of persistent thematizing, Ronsard makes it a radical experience of categorization: his categories are nothing if not mobile.

That mobility is written into the very nature and project of translation. "To translate," apart from being a description of a literary practice, is also a verb of motion, in which Muret's term "transmarinus" stands both for the carrying over of alien discourse into a new context and onto a new surface and the transfer of the author himself, his rebirth and reemergence within a renewed setting: "Anacreon" *redux* and *redivivus*. Two general metaphors govern these connected transfers. The first is that of translation as *locus*. The use of this term to designate the translated poem as a receptacle for the display of lexis offers a number of advantages. Not least among these advantages is that it purposely highlights the work of translation as an agent of continuous transmission, relocating Latin diction in order to accommodate the appearance of a newly published Greek author. Thus translation as *locus* ties in with Estienne's image of the diachronic descent of imitation, units of an author traveling from one place to the next, in this case one translation to the next. Such relocation is provisional, reflecting the provisionality of translation itself: translation as *locus* is empty, diction is mobile, the production of linguistic possibilities in translation potentially infinite. Hence also the importance of ecphrastic portrait poems such as odes 28 and 29. Since the material for the "Portrait de sa Maistresse" had already partly appeared in Belleau's translation of these two Anacreontic odes and in Ronsard's "Elegie à Janet," there is no clearer example of the translation's mobility and its potential for dispersal and reassembling. And what Belleau supplies on one preeminent occasion, Ronsard makes his general rule. Ronsard typically allows no more than a minimum of typographical stability to his translations; in subsequent editions, the dedicatee may change, the title and order change, variants invade the text itself.

Other types of description of translation's objectives are also to be found in the translators. In retrospect, it seems plain that Estienne's treatment of "Anacreon" in his commentary aims to assert a series of analogies by which "Anacreon" can be recognized and assimilated to familiar schemes of literary response. In addition, Estienne's recourse to Dionysian terminology, there and in his preface, envisages a rhetorical norm, the *genus floridum,* but one whose stylistic specificity is sufficiently broad to encompass the heteroclite nature of his translation. For if Estienne's stated positions appear to be conducive to a sustained view of "Anacreon," his translation does not by any means straightforwardly respond to his overt principles. As the notion of theft hints, there is a lawlessness, a disseminative force, about his translation, not totally obedient to stylistic or generic norms.[3] Rhetorical prescriptions, when carried over into his translation, do not necessarily coalesce into an abiding stylistic impression.

In other translators, further devices are evoked to bestow abstract pattern on agglomerations of translated words and to convey what might be taken as Anacreontic character. One striking instance of this practice is the thick veneer of *mignardise* covering Belleau's *Odes d'Anacreon Teien.* Few of Belleau's translations are without the hallmarks of this style, the ubiquitous diminutives and present participles whose superabundance Weber describes caustically as "la déformation mignarde."[4] For Belleau, individual character is rhetorical χαρακτήρ: the personality of "Anacreon" is a function of an oratorical device, the λεπτὸς χαρακτήρ, *genus tenue.* "Character" exists as a creation of style. Indeed, the presence of *mignardise* is so strong in Belleau that it brings about a virtual collapse of the objects it describes: the homogeneity of this vocabulary, compounded by the thematic or phraseological similarity of large numbers of the Anacreontic poems, almost erases the contours dividing one poem from another. In associating Anacreontics with *mignardise,* Belleau achieves a type of λεπτότης reminiscent of Alexandrian poetry. Moreover, he gathers the diverse sympotic and hedonistic thematic strands around a related narrative *persona,* identifiable as "Anacreon." The notion of an authorial "presence" in the work is a common enough sixteenth-century view of translation. It occurs

---

3. Cf. Jacques Derrida, "La dissemination," in *La dissemination,* Tel Quel (Paris: Seuil, 1972), 321–407.

4. Weber, *La création poétique au XVIe siècle en France,* 258.

in Montaigne[5] and, within these Anacreontic translations, in Belleau and André, who both attribute to this Greek poetry a "voice." It is an idea that has hidden links with the notion of *locus:* translation is the place where the poet speaks.[6] In André, voice is sentential voice, an abstracted sound; an attribute of the poetry primarily and only secondarily of a narrator-poet. What is crucial for André is that Anacreontic voice conveys a message, that the author communicates a didactic purpose.[7]

If Anacreontic translation calls into question neat distinctions between translation and imitation, the overall conclusion cannot be that none exists. As one commentator remarks,[8] the relationship between the two domains is too uncertain to permit such a conclusion; the desire either to separate definitively or to join definitively is too polarized a desire. So, while Estienne can cite (with no detectable tone of disapproval) Horace's "translation" of Anacreontic or Alcaean phraseology and while his own "honestè furari" could apply equally well to humanist translation as to imitation, at other times he can state quite categorically: "Sed aliud est imitari, aliud, interpretari" (but it is one thing to imitate, another to translate).[9] The remark is symptomatic, as is Ronsard's attribution and subsequent cancellation of the description, "Traduit d'Anacréon." As a counterbalance to the textual subtleties he or she is called upon to identify, several obvious features remind the reader of "Anacreon" that he or she has before him a translation and not an imitation. Meter is one such element, acting as a norm to less quantifiable innovations. Metrical adventurousness is relatively slight when compared with verbal or thematic retexturing. Hexa-, hepta-, and octosyllables are common in vernacular translators, iambic dimeter among Neo-Latins. Ronsard is, almost inevitably, the exception to these rules, with his excursions into decasyllable and alexandrine. Even he, however, in common with the other translators, seeks to create a meter comparable with the original; and in order to guide the reader as to the type of

---

5. Cf. apropos of Montaigne's translation of Sebond, Antoine Compagnon, "Montaigne: De la traduction des autres à la traduction de soi," *Littérature* 55 (1984): 42: "le livre est personnifié; mots et choses confondues, il est l'expression d'une personnalité."

6. In "L'herméneutique ancienne: Les mots et les idées," *Poétique* 6 (1975): 291–300, Jean Pépin demonstrates that the classical term ἑρμηνεία covers both "discours, parole, élocution" (292) and translation (294–96).

7. At this level, André's *sententiae* are evidence of didactic purpose, of *prodesse* that a work should provide in addition to *delectare.* His translation itself encourages further transfer, the removal of highlighted phrases to serve as embellishment to new discourse.

8. Theo Hermans, "Images of Translation: Metaphor and Imagery in the Renaissance Discourse on Translation," in *The Manipulation of Literature: Studies in Literary Translation* (London: Croom Helm, 1985), 103.

9. *Moschi, Bionis, Theocriti . . . idyllia aliquot,* [Giij^r].

poetry he or she is facing, Ronsard gives it (in the beginning, at least) the title "odelette." More broadly speaking, the imitative techniques summarized above occur within the framework of the poem. Neither the reworking of *allusio* nor Belleau's metatextual glosses require alteration to the *rerum ordo* in order to perform their distinctive tasks, though they may indeed suggest insights into the original not manifestly present in the *res* of the original. Where the *rerum ordo* is more violently disturbed, as is common in Ronsard, it becomes proportionately more difficult to decide on a poem's status. By contrast, any of the characteristic translative techniques may well require modification to the *verborum ordo*. Doublets and synonyms are permissible devices, particularly common in vernacular translation; and what is lost in a correspondence theory of translation can be replaced in a compensation theory of translation. Once again, however, if even the word order of the original evaporates, difficulties attend classification.

On balance, what these Neo-Latin and vernacular translators of "Anacreon" do present is not at bottom so much a single-minded justification of the conventional theoretical position that translation is (a form of) imitation (so Sebillet and Peletier), as a belief, however strained or contradictory, in what Sebillet's mirror image has to offer. What this image does not offer is an image of the perfect reflection of the past in the present: translators are too aware that, as Peletier puts it, "il né sé peùt feré."[10] Even Sebillet himself covertly admits as much by the wording of his advice to the translator—to put as much of his author into his translation as a mirror would allow: this advice conjures an image of partiality that does not so much recall a pro-Ciceronian fixity as an anti-Ciceronian Erasmian acculturation or acclimatization. Two languages will never correspond. The senses are destined ever to circle in paraphrastic play, yet the balances can be weighted through a series of feints that the translations nonetheless do not conceal but purposely show for what they are by the comparison of version with original or version with version. Such feints produce the stratification and rich texturing that is the translated text; they envisage, singly or severally, assimilation to an individual author (Horace), to a genre (epigram), to a register (Catullan; comic), to a style *(mignardise),* to a tropological scheme *(enargeia,* metaphor); and they are entailed in the endeavor to make "Anacreon" not just *redux,* but *redivivus.*

---

10. Peletier du Mans, *Art poëtique,* 111.

Appendix

Concordance of Estienne's *Editio Princeps* with Selected
Modern Editions of the Anacreontea

Page	Estienne *Editio Princeps* 1554 Ode*	Incipit	West (Teubner 1984, 1993²) Number	Campbell** (Loeb 1988) Number
1–2	1	Θέλω λέγειν 'Ατρείδας	23	23
2	2	Θύσις κέρατα ταύροις	24	24
2–4	3	Μεσονυκτίοις	33	33
4–5	4	Ἐπὶ μυρσίναις	32	32
5–6	5	Τὸ ῥόδον τὸ τῶν ἐρώτων	44	44
6–7	6	Στεφάνους μὲν κροτάφοισι	43	43
7	7	Ὑακινθίνῃ με ῥάβδῳ	31	31
7–8	8	Διὰ νυκτὸς ἐγκαθεύδων	37	37
8–10	9	Ἐρασμίη πέλεια	15	15
10–11	10	Ἔρωτα κήρινόν τις	11	11
11–12	11	Λέγουσιν αἱ γυναῖκες	7	7
12	12	Τί σοι θέλεις	10	10
12–13	13	Οἱ μὲν καλὴν Κυβήβην	12	12
13–14	14	Θέλω θέλω φιλῆσαι	13	13

*Estienne does not number the odes. The numbering adopted here (and throughout this book) simply follows the poems of the *editio princeps* in order.

**In addition to Campbell, there is a further translation of the Anacreontic odes into English in appendix C of Patricia A. Rosenmeyer, *The Poetics of Imitation: Anacreon and the Anacreontic Tradition* (Cambridge and New York: Cambridge University Press, 1992).

Page	Ode	Estienne Editio Princeps 1554 Incipit	West (Teubner 1984, 1993²) Number	Campbell (Loeb 1988) Number
14–15	15	Οὔ μοι μέλει Γύγαο	8	8
15	16	Σὺ μὲν λέγεις	26	26
15–16	17	Τὸν ἄργυρον τορεύσας	4	4
16–17	18	Καλὴ τέχνα τορεύσον	5	5
17–18	19	Ἡ γῆ μέλαινα πίνει	21	21
18–19	20	Ἡ Ταντάλου	22	22
19	21	Δότε μοι	18, 1–9	18, 1–9
19–20	22	Παρὰ τὴν σκιὴν	18, 10–17	18, 10–17
20–21	23	Ὁ πλοῦτος	36	36
21	24	Ἐπειδὴ βροτὸς ἐτέχθην	40	40
21–22	25	Ὅταν πίνω	45	45
22	26	Ὅταν ὁ βάκχος	48	48
22–23	27	Τοῦ Διὸς ὁ παῖς	49	49
23–25	28	Ἄγε ζωγράφων ἄριστε	16	16
25–27	29	Γράφε μοι Βάθυλλον	17	17
27–28	30	Αἱ μοῦσαι	19	19
28–29	31	Ἄφες με τοὺς θέους	9	9
29–30	32	Εἰ φύλλα πάντα	14	14
30–31	33	Σὺ μὲν φίλη χελιδὼν	25	25
31–32	34	Μή με φύγῃς	51	51
32	35	Ὁ ταῦρος οὗτος	54	54
32–33	36	Τί με τοὺς νόμους	52, 52A	52A, 52B
33–34	37	Ἴδε πῶς	46	46
34–35	38	Ἐγὼ γέρων μέν εἰμι	47	47
35–36	39	Ὅτ' ἐγὼ πίω	50	50
36–37	40	Ἔρως ποτ' ἐν ῥόδοισι	35	35
37–40	41	Ἱλαροὶ πίωμεν	38	38
38–39	42	Ποθέω μὲν Διονύσου	42	42
39–40	43	Μακαρίζομέν σε τέττιξ	34	34
40–41	44	Ἐδοκοῦν ὄναρ τροχάζειν	30	30
41–42	45	Ὁ ἀνὴρ ὁ τῆς Κυθήρης	28	28
42–43	46	Χαλεπὸν τὸ μὴ φιλῆσαι	29, 29A	29
43	47	Φιλῶ γέροντα τερπνὸν	39	39
43	48	Δότε μοι λύρην Ὁμήρου	2	2
44	49	Ἄγε ζωγράφων ἄριστε	3	3
44–45	50	Ὁ τὸν ἐν πότοις	56	56

Appendix

Page	Estienne *Editio Princeps* 1554 Ode	Incipit	West (Teubner 1984, 1993²) Number	Campbell (Loeb 1988) Number
45–46	51	Ἆρα τις τόρευσε	57	57
46–48	52	Τὸν μελανοχρῶτα βότρυν	59	59
48–50	53	Στεφανηφόρου μετ' ἦρος	55	55
50–51	54	Ὅτ' ἐγὼ νέοις ὁμιλοῦν	53	53
51	55	Ἐν ἰσχίοις	27	27

Bibliography

André, Elie, trans. *Anacreontis Teii antiquissimi poëtae lyrici Odae, ab Helio Andrea Latinae factae, ad clariss. virum Petrum Montaureum Consiliarium, & Bibliothecarium Regium.* Paris: Robert Estienne and Guillaume Morel, 1556.

Angenot, Marc. "Présupposé, topos, idéologème." *Etudes Françaises* 13 (1977): 11–34.

Armstrong, Elizabeth. *Robert Estienne, Royal Printer: An Historical Study of the Elder Stephanus.* Rev. ed. Oxford: Clarendon Press, 1986.

———. "Les rapports d'Henri Estienne avec les membres de sa famille restés ou redevenus catholiques." In *Henri Estienne,* 43–53. Cahiers V.-L. Saulnier, no. 5. Paris: Presses de l'E.N.S. de Jeunes Filles, 1988.

Atkins, John W. *Literary Criticism in Antiquity: A Sketch of Its Development.* 2 vols. London: Methuen 1952.

Barthes, Roland. "L'effet de réel." In *Le bruissement de la langue,* 167–74. Paris: Seuil, 1984.

———. "L'ancienne rhétorique: Aide-mémoire." In *L'aventure sémiologique,* 85–165. Paris: Seuil, 1985.

Baumann, Michael. *Die Anakreonteen in englischen Übersetzungen: Ein Beitrag zur Rezeptionsgeschichte der anacreontischen Sammlung.* Studien zum Fortwirken des Antike, no. 7. Heidelberg: Winter, 1974.

Bauschatz, Cathleen M. "Montaigne's Conception of Reading in the Context of Renaissance Poetics." In *The Reader in the Text,* edited by Susan Suleiman and Inge Crosman, 264–92. Princeton: Princeton University Press, 1980.

Beckby, Hermann, ed. *Anthologia Graeca.* 4 vols. Munich: Heimeran, 1957–58.

Belleau, Remy. *Oeuvres poétiques de Remy Belleau.* Edited by Charles Marty-Laveaux. 2 vols. La Pléiade françoise. Paris: Lemerre, 1878.

———. *La Bergerie: Texte de l'édition de 1565.* Edited by Doris Delacourcelle. Geneva: Droz, 1954.

———. *Remy Belleau, Commentaire au second livre des "Amours" de Ronsard.* Edited by Marie-Madeleine Fontaine and François Lecercle. Commentaires de Ronsard, no. 2. Geneva: Droz, 1986.

———. *Odes d'Anacréon.* Edited by John O'Brien and Keith Cameron. Paris: Champion, forthcoming.

Bellenger, Yvonne. "Les poètes français et la peinture: La ressemblance comme critère

esthétique au XVIe siècle." In *Mélanges Franco Simone,* Bibliothèque Franco Simone, no. 4, 1:427–48. Geneva: Slatkine, 1980.
Bentley, Jerry H. *Humanists and Holy Writ: New Testament Scholarship in the Renaissance.* Princeton: Princeton University Press, 1983.
Bergk, Theodor. *Griechische Literaturgeschichte.* 2 vols. Berlin: Weidmann, 1883.
Beugnot, Bernard. "Florilèges et *polyantheae:* Diffusion et statut du lieu commun à l'époque classique." *Etudes Françaises* 13 (1977): 119–41.
Bloom, Harold. *The Anxiety of Influence: A Theory of Poetry.* New York: Oxford University Press, 1973.
Bolgar, Robert R. *The Classical Heritage and Its Beneficiaries.* Cambridge: Cambridge University Press, 1954.
Bonner, Stephen F. *Dionysius of Halicarnassus: A Study in the Development of Critical Method.* Cambridge: Cambridge University Press, 1939.
Braybrook, Jean. "Remy Belleau and the Figure of the Artist." *French Studies* 37 (1983): 1–16.
Brioso Sánchez, Máximo. *Anacreontea: Un ensayo para su datación.* Salamanca: Colegio Trilingue de la Universidad, 1970.

———. "Aportaciones al problema de la métrica griega tardía." *Estudios Clásicos* 16 (1972): 95–138.

———. "Las Anacreónticas y su división estrófica." *Cuadernos de Filología Clásica* 4 (1972): 427–40.

———. "¿Otra consagración poética? Anacreóntica primera." *Emerita* 47 (1979): 1–9.

———. *Anacreónticas: Texto revisado y traducido.* Madrid: Consejo Superior de Investigaciones Científicos, 1981.
Brodeau, Jean. *Ioannis Brodaei Turonensis Miscellaneorum libri sex. In quibus, praeter alia scitu dignissima, plurimi optimorum autorum tam Latinorum quàm Graecorum loci, uel deprauati hactenus restituuntur, uel multo quàm antea à quoquam est factum rectius explicantur.* Basel: Oporinus, [1555].
Brooks, Peter. *Reading for the Plot: Design and Intention in Narrative.* Oxford: Clarendon Press, 1984.
Buck, August. *Die Rezeption der Antike in den romanischen Literaturen der Renaissance.* Berlin: Schmidt, 1976.

———. *Die Rezeption der Antike: Zum Problem der Kontinuität zwischen Mittelalter und Renaissance.* Hamburg: Hauswedell, 1981.
Buck, August, and Otto Herding, eds. *Der Kommentar in der Renaissance.* Deutsche Forschungsgemeinschaft, Kommission für Humanismusforschung, Mitteilung 1. Bonn and Bad Godesburg: Boldt, [1975].
Bullock, Anthony. "Tibullus and the Alexandrians." *Proceedings of the Cambridge Philological Society,* n.s., 19 (1973): 71–89.
Bundy, Elroy T. "The 'Quarrel between Kallimachos and Apollonios' Part I: The Epilogue of Kallimachos's 'Hymn to Apollo.'" *California Studies in Classical Antiquity* 5 (1972): 39–94.
Bunker, Ruth. *A Bibliographical Study of the Greek Works and Translations Published in France during the Renaissance: The Decade 1540–1550.* New York: Columbia University Press, 1939.

Burke, U. Peter. *The Renaissance Sense of the Past.* Documents of Modern History. London: Arnold, 1969.

Cairns, Francis. *Generic Composition in Greek and Latin Poetry.* Edinburgh: Edinburgh University Press, 1972.

———. *Tibullus: A Hellenistic Poet at Rome.* Cambridge: Cambridge University Press, 1979.

Cameron, Alan. *The Greek Anthology from Meleager to Planudes.* Oxford: Clarendon Press, 1993.

Campbell, David, trans. and ed. *Greek Lyric.* Vol. 2, *Anacreon, Anacreontea, Choral Lyric from Olympus to Alcman.* Loeb Classical Library. Cambridge, Mass.: Harvard University Press; London: Heinemann, 1988.

Castor, Grahame. *Pléiade Poetics: A Study in Sixteenth-Century Terminology and Thought.* Cambridge: Cambridge University Press, 1964.

Cave, Terence. "Ronsard's Bacchic Poetry: From the 'Bacchanales' to the 'Hymne de l'automne.'" *L'Esprit Créateur* 10 (1970): 104–16.

———. "The Triumph of Bacchus and Its Interpretation in the French Renaissance: Ronsard's 'Hinne de Bacus.'" In *Humanism in France at the End of the Middle Ages and in the Early Renaissance,* edited by Anthony Levi, 249–70. Manchester: Manchester University Press, 1970.

———. "Copia and Cornucopia." In *French Renaissance Studies 1540–70: Humanism and the Encyclopedia,* edited by Peter Sharratt, 52–69. Edinburgh: Edinburgh University Press, 1976.

———. "*Enargeia:* Erasmus and the Rhetoric of Presence in the Sixteenth Century." In *The French Renaissance Mind: Studies Presented to W.G. Moore,* edited by Barbara C. Bowen, 5–19. *L'Esprit Créateur* 16, no. 4 (1976).

———. *The Cornucopian Text: Problems of Writing in the French Renaissance.* Oxford: Clarendon Press, 1979.

———. "The Mimesis of Reading in the French Renaissance." In *Mimesis: From Mirror to Method,* edited by John D. Lyons and Stephen G. Nichols, 149–65. Hanover and London: University Press of New England, 1982.

Caws, Mary Ann. *A Metapoetics of the Passage: Architextures in Surrealism and After.* Hanover and London: University Press of New England, 1981.

Céard, Jean. "Les transformations du genre du commentaire." In *L'automne de la Renaissance, 1580–1630,* edited by Jean Lafond and André Stegmann, 101–15. Paris: Vrin, 1981.

Chamard, Henri. *Histoire de la Pléiade.* 4 vols. Paris: Didier, 1939–40.

Chambers, Ross. "Commentary in Literary Texts." *Critical Inquiry* 5 (1978–79): 323–37.

Charles, Michel. *Rhétorique de la lecture.* Poétique. Paris: Seuil, 1977.

———. "Bibliothèques." *Poétique* 33 (1978): 1–28.

———. *L'arbre et la source.* Poétique. Paris: Seuil, 1985.

Chavy, Paul. "Les traductions humanistes au début de la Renaissance: Traductions médiévales, traductions modernes." *Canadian Review of Comparative Literature* 8, no. 2 (1981): 284–306.

———. *Traducteurs d'autrefois, Moyen Age et Renaissance: Dictionnaire des traduc-*

teurs et de la littérature traduite en ancien et moyen français, 842–1600. Paris: Champion, 1988.

Chomarat, Jacques, ed. *Prosateurs latins en France au XVIe siècle.* Paris: Presses de l'Université de Paris-Sorbonne, 1987.

Cicero. *Ciceronis poetica fragmenta.* Edited by Antonio Traglia. 2 vols. Testi per Esercitazioni Accademiche, no. 1. Rome: Gismondi, 1950.

———. *Epistulae ad familiares.* Edited by D.R. Shackleton Bailey. Vol. 1, *62–47 B.C.* Cambridge Classical Texts and Commentaries, no. 16. Cambridge: Cambridge University Press, 1977.

Clausen, Wendel V. "Callimachus and Roman Poetry." *Greek, Roman, and Byzantine Studies* 5 (1964): 181–96.

———. "Catullus and Callimachus." *Harvard Studies in Classical Philology* 74 (1970): 85–94.

Clément, H. *Henri Estienne et son oeuvre française: Etude d'histoire littéraire et de philologie.* Paris: Picard, 1898.

Clements, Robert J. *Critical Theory and Practice of the Pléiade.* Harvard Studies in the Romance Languages, no. 18. 1942. Reprint, New York: Octagon Books, 1970.

Compagnon, Antoine. *La seconde main ou le travail de la citation.* Paris: Seuil, 1979.

———. "Montaigne: De la traduction des autres à la traduction de soi." *Littérature* 55 (1984): 37–44.

Couat, Auguste. *La poésie alexandrine sous les trois premiers Ptolémées (324–222 av. J.-C.).* Paris: Hachette, 1882.

Croiset, Alfred. *Histoire de la littérature grecque.* 2d ed. Vol. 2, *Lyrisme—Premiers Prosateurs. Hérodote.* Paris: Fontemoing, 1898.

Crusius, Otto. "Zu den Anacreonteen." *Philologus* 47, n.s., 1 (1889): 235–41.

Curtius, Ernst Robert. *European Literature and the Latin Middle Ages.* Translated by Willard R. Trask. Bollinger Series, no. 36. New York: Pantheon Books, 1953.

D'Amico, John. *Theory and Practice in Renaissance Textual Criticism: Beatus Rhenanus between Conjecture and History.* Berkeley and Los Angeles: University of California Press, 1988.

Davis, Natalie Zemon. *Society and Culture in Early Modern France.* Stanford: Stanford University Press, 1975.

Delboulle, Achille. *Anacréon et les poèmes anacréontiques: Texte grec avec les traductions et imitations des poètes du XVIe siècle.* Le Havre: Lemale, 1891.

Delcourt, Marie. *Etude sur les traductions des tragiques grecs et latins en France depuis la Renaissance.* Brussels: Lamertin, 1925.

Demerson, Geneviève. *Dorat en son temps: Culture classique et présence au monde.* Héritages, no. 1. Clermont-Ferrand: Adosa, 1983.

———. "Joachim du Bellay traducteur de lui-même." In *Neo-Latin and the Vernacular in Renaissance France,* edited by Grahame Castor and Terence Cave, 113–28. Oxford: Clarendon Press, 1984.

Demerson, Guy. "Poétique de la métamorphose chez Remy Belleau." In *Poétiques de la métamorphose,* 125–42. Saint-Etienne: Université de Saint-Etienne, 1981.

Denis, J. "Pseudo-Anacréon." *Bulletin mensuel de la Faculté des Lettres de Caen* 6 (1885): 196–206.

De Nolhac, Pierre. *La bibliothèque de Fulvio Orsini: Contributions à l'histoire des*

collections d'Italie et à l'étude de la Renaissance. Bibliothèque de l'Ecole des Hautes Etudes, no. 64. Paris: Vieweg, 1887.
———. *Ronsard et l'humanisme.* Bibliothèque de l'Ecole des Hautes Etudes, no. 227. 1921. Reprint, Paris: Champion, 1966.
Derrida, Jacques. *Tel Quel: Théorie d'ensemble (choix).* Points. Paris: Seuil, 1968.
———. *La dissémination.* Tel Quel. Paris: Seuil, 1972.
———. *L'oreille de l'autre: Otobiographies, transferts, traductions.* Textes et débats avec Jacques Derrida. Edited by Claude Lévesque and Christie V. McDonald. Montreal: VLB, 1982.
———. "Des tours de Babel." In *Difference in Translation,* edited by Joseph F. Graham, 209–48. Ithaca and London: Cornell University Press, 1985.
De Saussure, Ferdinand. *Cours de linguistique générale.* 1915. Reprint, Paris: Payot, 1972.
Des Autelz, Guillaume. *Replique de Guillaume des Autelz, aux furieuses defenses de Louis Meigret. Avec la Suite du Repos de Lautheur.* Lyon: De Tournes and Gazeau, 1551.
Desgraves, Louis. *Elie Vinet, humaniste de Bordeaux (1509–1587): Vie, bibliographie, correspondance, bibliothèque.* Travaux d'Humanisme et Renaissance, no. 156. Geneva: Droz, 1977.
D'Estrebay, Jacques-Louis. *Aristotelis Stagiritae Politica ab Iacobo Lodoico Strebaeo à Graeco conuersa.* Paris: Roigny, 1549.
———. *Xenophontis philosophici et historici clarissimi Opera, quae quidem Gręcè extant, omnia, partim iam olim, partim nunc primùm, hominum doctissimorum diligentia, in latinam linguam conuersa.* Basel: Isingrinius, 1553.
Dezeimeris, Reinhold. *De la renaissance des lettres à Bordeaux au XVIe siècle.* 1864. Reprint, Geneva: Slatkine, 1970.
Dihle, Albrecht. "The Poem on the Cicada." *Harvard Studies in Classical Philology* 71 (1966): 107–13.
Dionisotti, Carlotta. "Polybius and the Royal Professor." In *Tria Corda: Scritti in onore di Arnaldo Momigliano,* edited by E. Gabba, 179–99. Como: Edizioni New Press, 1983.
———. "From Stephanus to Du Cange: Glossary Stories." *Revue d'Histoire des Textes* 14–15 (1984–85): 303–36.
———. "Claude de Seyssel." In *Ancient Historiography and the Antiquarian,* edited by M.H. Crawford and C. Ligota. London: Warburg Institute, forthcoming.
———. "Hellenismus." In *The Vocabulary of Teaching and Research, 1350–1550,* edited by O. Weijers. Forthcoming.
Dionisotti, Carlotta, and Anthony Grafton, eds. *The Uses of Greek and Latin: Historical Essays.* Warburg Institute Surveys, no. 16. London: Warburg Institute, 1988.
Dionysius of Halicarnassus. *Dionysii Halicarnassei De compositione, seu orationis partium apta inter se collocatione, ad Rufum. Eiusdem, Artis rhetoricae capita quaedam, ad Echeratem. Item quo genere dicendi sit vsus Thucydides, ad Ammaeum.* Paris: Robert Estienne, 1547.
———. *Dionysii Halicarnassei opuscula.* Edited by Hermann Usener and Ludwig Radermacher. 2 vols. Leipzig: Teubner, 1904–29.
Dorat, Jean. *Ioannis Aurati Lemovicis poetae et interpretis regij Poëmatia.* Paris: Linocer, 1586.

———. *Les odes latines*. Edited by Geneviève Demerson. Clermont-Ferrand: Faculté des Lettres et Sciences Humaines de l'Université de Clermont-Ferrand II, 1979.
Dover, Kenneth J., ed. *Theocritus: Select Poems*. London: Macmillan, 1971.
Du Bellay, Joachim. *La deffence et illustration de la langue françoyse*, edited by Henri Chamard. Société des textes français modernes. 1948. Reprint, Paris: Didier, 1970.
———. *Oeuvres poétiques*. Vol. 7, *Oeuvres latines, Poemata*, edited by Geneviève Demerson. Société des textes français modernes, no. 179. Paris: Nizet, 1984.
Dupèbe, Jean. "Documents sur Jean Dorat." *Bibliothèque d'Humanisme et Renaissance* 50 (1988): 707–14.
Easterling, Patricia E. "Before Palaeography: Notes on Early Descriptions and Datings of Greek Manuscripts." *Studia Codicologica* 124 (1977): 179–87.
Easterling, Patricia E., and Bernard Knox, eds. *The Cambridge History of Classical Literature*. Vol. 1, *Greek Literature*. Cambridge: Cambridge University Press, 1985.
Eckhardt, Alexandre. *Remy Belleau: Sa vie—sa "Bergerie," étude historique et critique*. Budapest: Németh, 1917.
Edmonds, J.M., trans. and ed. *Elegy and Iambus*. Vol. 2, *Being the Remains of all the Greek Elegiac and Iambic Poets from Callinus to Crates excepting the Choliambic Writers, with the Anacreontea*. Loeb Classical Library. London: Heinemann; New York: Putnam, 1931.
England, E.B. "H. Stephens's *vetustissima exemplaria*." *Classical Review* 8 (1894): 196–97.
Erasmus, Desiderius. *De copia verborum ac rerum*. Edited by Betty I. Knott. Vol. 1.6 of *Opera omnia Desiderii Erasmi Roterodami*. Amsterdam and New York: North-Holland, 1988.
Estienne, Henri, ed. *Anacreontis Teij odae. Ab Henrico Stephano luce à Latinitate nunc primùm donatae*. Paris: Henri Estienne, 1554.
———. *Dionysii Halicarnassei responsio ad Gn. Pompeij epistolam, in qua ille de reprehenso ab eo Platonis stylo conquerebatur. Eiusdem ad Ammaeum epistola*. Paris: Charles Estienne, 1554.
———. *Moschi, Bionis, Theocriti, elegantissimorum poetarum idyllia aliquot, ab Henrico Stephano Latina facta. Eiusdem carmina non diuersi ab illis argumenti*. Venice: Paolo Manuzio, 1555.
———. *Anacreontis et aliorum Lyricorum aliquot poëtarum Odae. In easdem Henr. Stephani Obseruationes*. Paris: Guillaume Morel and Robert Estienne, 1556.
———. *Moschi, Bionis, Theocriti, elegantissimorum poetarum idyllia aliquot, ab Henrico Stephano Latina facta. Eiusdem carmina non diuersi ab illis argumenti*. Paris: Robert Estienne, 1556.
———. *Athenagorae Atheniensis philosophi Christiani apologia pro Christianis, ad imperatores Antoninum & Commodum. Eiusdem, De resurrectione mortuorum*. [Geneva]: Henri Estienne, 1557.
———. *Pindari Olympia, Pythia, Nemea, Isthmia. Caeterorum octo Lyricorum carmina, Alcaei, Sapphus, Stesichori, Ibyci, Anacreontis, Bacchylidis, Simonidis, Alcmanis, nonnulla etiam aliorum*. [Geneva]: Henri Estienne, 1560.
———. *Pindari Olympia, Pythia, Nemea, Isthmia. Caeterorum octo Lyricorum carmina, Alcaei, Sapphus, Stesichori, Ibyci, Anacreontis, Bacchylidis, Simonidis, Alcmanis, nonnulla etiam aliorum. Editio II. Graecolatina H. Steph. recognitione*

quorundam interpretationis locorum, & accessione lyricorum carminum locupletata. 2 vols. [Geneva]: Henri Estienne, 1566.

———. *Florilegium diuersorum epigrammatum ueterum, in septem libros diuisum, magno epigrammatum numero & duobus indicibus auctum* [Geneva]: Henri Estienne, 1566.

———. *Poetae Graeci principes heroici carminis, & alii nonnulli.* [Geneva]: Henri Estienne, 1566.

———. *Pindari Olympia, Pythia, Nemea, Isthmia. Caeterorum octo Lyricorum carmina, Alcaei, Sapphus, Stesichori, Ibyci, Anacreontis, Bacchylidis, Simonidis, Alcmanis, nonnulla etiam aliorum. Omnia Graecè & Latinè.* 2 vols. Antwerp: Plantin, 1567.

———. *Pindari Olympia, Pythia, Nemea, Isthmia. Caeterorum octo Lyricorum carmina, Alcaei, Sapphus, Stesichori, Ibyci, Anacreontis, Bacchylidis, Simonidis, Alcmanis, nonnulla etiam aliorum. Editio III. Graecolatina H. Steph. recognitione quorundam interpretationis locorum, & accessione lyricorum carminum locupletata.* 2 vols. [Geneva]: Henri Estienne, 1586.

———. *Henri Estienne.* Cahiers V.-L. Saulnier, 5. Paris: Presses de l'E.N.S. de Jeunes Filles, 1988.

Ferguson, Margaret. *Trials of Desire: Renaissance Defenses of Poetry.* New Haven: Yale University Press, 1983.

Feugère, Léon. *Essai sur la vie et les ouvrages d'Henri Estienne suivi d'une étude sur Scévole de Sainte-Marthe.* Paris: Delalain, 1883.

Firmin Didot, Ambroise. *Notice sur Anacréon.* Paris: Firmin Didot, 1864.

François, Michel. *Le Cardinal François de Tournon: Homme d'état, diplomate, mécène et humaniste (1489–1562).* Bibliothèque des Ecoles Françaises d'Athènes et de Rome, no. 173. Paris: De Brocard, 1951.

Fraser, P. *Ptolemaic Alexandria.* 3 vols. Oxford: Clarendon Press, 1972.

Frécaut, Jean-Marc. *L'esprit et l'humour chez Ovide.* Grenoble: Presses Universitaires, 1972.

Fumaroli, Marc. *L'âge de l'éloquence: Rhétorique et "res literaria" de la Renaissance au seuil de l'époque classique.* Geneva: Droz, 1980.

Gaisser, Julia Haig. *Catullus and His Renaissance Readers.* Oxford: Clarendon Press, 1993.

Garavini, Fausta, ed. *Michel de Montaigne: Journal de voyage.* Collection Folio. Paris: Gallimard, 1983.

Genette, Gérard. "Discours du récit." In *Figures III,* 67–273. Poétique. Paris: Seuil, 1972.

———. *Palimpsestes: La littérature au second degré.* Poétique. Paris: Seuil, 1982.

Gentili, Bruno, ed. *Anacreon.* Rome: Ateneo, 1958.

———. "Anacreontea nelle critica antica e moderna." *Cultura e Scuola* 1 (1961): 52–57.

Giangrande, Giuseppe. "*Arte Allusiva* and Alexandrian Epic Poetry." *Classical Quarterly,* n.s., 17 (1967): 85–97.

———. Review of *Recherches sur le poème Mégara,* by T. Breitenstein. *Classical Review,* n.s., 18 (1968): 163–65.

———. "Sympotic Literature and Epigram." In *L'épigramme grecque,* 93–177. En-

tretiens sur l'Antiquité classique, no. 14. Vandoeuvres-Geneva: Fondation Hardt, 1968.
———. "Hellenistic Poetry and Homer." *Antiquité Classique* 39 (1970): 46–77.
———. "Gli epigrammi alessandrini come arte allusiva." *Quaderni Urbinati di Cultura Classica* 15 (1973): 7–31.
———. "Los tópicos helenísticos en la elegía latina." *Emerita* 42 (1974): 1–36.
———. "On the Text of the Anacreontea." *Quaderni Urbinati di Cultura Classica* 19 (1975): 177–210.
———. "Hellenistic Topoi in Ovid's 'Amores.'" *Museum Philologicum Londiniense* 4 (1981): 25–51.
Ginsberg, Ellen S. "Change and Permanence in the French Renaissance: Muret and Ronsard." *Journal of Medieval and Renaissance Studies* 16 (1986): 91–102.
———. "Peregrinations of the Kiss: Thematic Relationships between Neo-Latin and French Poetry in the Sixteenth Century." In *Acta Conventus Neo-Latini Sanctandreani,* edited by Ian D. McFarlane, 331–42. Binghampton: MRTS, 1986.
Gmelin, Hermann. "Das Princip der Imitatio in den romanischen Literaturen der Renaissance." *Romanische Forschungen* 46 (1932): 85–360.
Gow, A.S.F., ed. *Theocritus.* 2 vols. Cambridge: Cambridge University Press, 1952.
Gow, A.S.F., and Denys L. Page, eds. *The Greek Anthology: Hellenistic Epigrams.* 2 vols. Cambridge: Cambridge University Press, 1965.
———. *The Greek Anthology: The Garland of Philip.* 2 vols. Cambridge: Cambridge University Press, 1968.
Goyet, Francis. "*Imitatio* ou intertextualité? (Riffaterre revisited)." *Poétique* 71 (1987): 313–20.
———, ed. *Traités de poétique et de rhétorique de la Renaissance.* Paris: Livre de Poche, 1990.
Grafton, Anthony T. *Joseph Scaliger: A Study in the History of Classical Scholarship.* Vol. 1, *Textual Criticism and Exegesis.* Oxford Warburg Studies. Oxford: Clarendon Press, 1983.
———. "The Availability of Ancient Works." In *The Cambridge History of Renaissance Philosophy,* edited by Charles B. Schmitt, Quentin Skinner, and Eckhard Kessler, 767–91. Cambridge: Cambridge University Press, 1988.
———. *Forgers and Critics: Creativity and Duplicity in Western Scholarship.* Princeton: Princeton University Press, 1990.
———. *Defenders of the Text: The Traditions of Scholarship in an Age of Science, 1450–1800.* Cambridge, Mass., and London: Harvard University Press, 1991.
———. *Joseph Scaliger: A Study in the History of Classical Scholarship.* Vol. 2, *Historical Chronology.* Oxford Warburg Studies. Oxford: Clarendon Press, 1993.
Grafton, Anthony T., and Lisa Jardine. *From Humanism to the Humanities: Education and the Liberal Arts in Fifteenth- and Sixteenth-Century Europe.* London: Duckworth, 1986.
Greene, Thomas M. *The Light in Troy: Imitation and Discovery in Renaissance Poetry.* New Haven and London: Yale University Press, 1982.
———. *The Vulnerable Text: Essays on Renaissance Literature.* New York: Columbia University Press, 1986.

Greimas, A.-J. "Idiotismes, proverbes, dictons." *Cahiers de Lexicologie* 2 (1960): 41–61.

Griffin, Robert. "The French Renaissance Commonplace and Literary Context: An Example." *Neophilologus* 54 (1970): 258–61.

Griffiths, Richard. *The Dramatic Technique of Antoine de Montchrestien: Rhetoric and Style in French Renaissance Tragedy.* Oxford: Clarendon Press, 1970.

Grube, G.M.A. *The Greek and Roman Critics.* London: Methuen, 1965.

Guillerm, Luce. "L'auteur, les modèles, et le pouvoir ou la topique de la traduction au XVIe siècle en France." *Revue des Sciences Humaines* 52 (1980): 5–31.

———. "L'intertextualité démontée: le discours sur la traduction." *Littérature* 55 (1984): 54–63.

———. *Sujet de l'écriture et traduction autour de 1540.* Paris: Aux Amateurs de Livres, 1988.

Hamon, Philippe. *Introduction à l'analyse du descriptif. Langue, linguistique, communication.* Paris: Hachette, 1981.

Hampton, Timothy. *Writing from History: The Rhetoric of Exemplarity in Renaissance Literature.* Ithaca and London: Cornell University Press, 1990.

Hanssen, F. "Zur Kritik der Pseudoanakreontea." *Philologus* 46 (1888): 445–57.

Hennebert, Frédéric. *Histoire des traductions françaises d'auteurs grecs et latins pendant le XVIe et le XVIIe siècles.* [Gand]: n.p., [1858].

Hermans, Theo. "Images of Translation: Metaphor and Imagery in the Renaissance Discourse on Translation." In *The Manipulation of Literature: Studies in Literary Translation,* 103–35. London: Croom Helm, 1985.

Herter, Hans. *Kallimachos und Homer: Ein Beitrag zur Interpretation des Hymnos auf Artemis.* In *Kleine Schriften,* edited by E. Vogt, 371–416. Munich: Fink, 1975.

Hutchison, G.O. *Hellenistic Poetry.* Oxford: Clarendon Press, 1988.

Hutton, James. *The Greek Anthology in Italy to the Year 1800.* Cornell Studies in English, no. 23. Ithaca: Cornell University Press, 1935.

———. *The Greek Anthology in France and in the Latin Writers of the Netherlands to the Year 1800.* Cornell Studies in Classical Philology, no. 28. Ithaca: Cornell University Press, 1946.

———. *Essays on Renaissance Poetry.* Edited by Rita Guerlac. Ithaca and London: Cornell University Press, 1980.

———. *Themes of Peace in Renaissance Poetry.* Edited by Rita Guerlac. Ithaca and London: Cornell University Press, 1984.

IJsewijn, Joseph. *Companion to Neo-Latin Studies.* Amsterdam: North-Holland, 1977.

Ishigami-Iagolnitzer, Mitchiko, ed. *Les humanistes et l'antiquité grecque.* Paris: Editions du CNRS, 1989.

Jacobsen, E. *Translation, a Traditional Craft: An Introductory Sketch with a Study of Marlowe's "Elegies."* Classica et Medievalia, Dissertationes, no. 6. Copenhagen: Gyldendal, 1958.

Jacobson, Roman. "On Linguistic Aspects of Translation." In *On Translation,* edited by Reuben Brower, 232–39. Harvard Studies in Comparative Literature, no. 23. Cambridge, Mass.: Harvard University Press, 1959.

Jardine, Lisa. *Erasmus, Man of Letters: The Construction of Charisma in Print.* Princeton: Princeton University Press, 1993.

Jeanneret, Michel. "Les oeuvres d'art dans 'La Bergerie' de Belleau." *Revue d'Histoire Littéraire de la France* 70 (1970): 1–13.

———. "La lecture en question: Sur quelques prologues comiques du seizième siècle." *French Forum* 14, no. 3 (1989): 279–89.

———. "Préfaces, commentaires et programmation de la lecture: L'exemple des *Métamorphoses*." In *Les commentaires et la naissance de la critique littéraire: France, Italie, XIVe–XVIe siècles,* edited by Gisèle Mathieu-Castellani and Michel Plaisance, 31–39. Paris: Aux Amateurs de Livres, 1990.

———. "Commentary on Fiction, Fiction as Commentary." *The South Atlantic Quarterly* 91, no. 4 (1992): 909–28.

———. "L'exégèse à la Renaissance." *Le défi des signes,* 21–31. Orléans: Paradigme, 1994.

Jehasse, Jean. *La renaissance de la critique: L'essor de l'humanisme érudit de 1560 à 1614.* Saint-Etienne: Université de Saint-Etienne, 1976.

———. "De la critique humaniste à la critique littéraire: Henri II Estienne." In *Les commentaires et la naissance de la critique littéraire: France, Italie, XIVe–XVIe siècles,* edited by Gisèle Mathieu-Castellani and Michel Plaisance, 205–10. Paris: Aux Amateurs de Livres, 1990.

Jerome, Saint. *Saint Jérôme: Lettres.* Edited and translated by Jérôme Labourt. Paris: Belles Lettres, 1953.

Joukovsky, Françoise. *La gloire dans la poésie française et néolatine du XVIe siècle (des Rhétoriqueurs à Agrippa d'Aubigné).* Travaux d'Humanisme et Renaissance, no. 102. Geneva: Droz, 1969.

———. *Le bel objet: Les paradis artificiels de la Pléiade.* Paris: Champion, 1991.

Kahn, Victoria. *Rhetoric, Prudence, and Skepticism in the Renaissance.* Ithaca and London: Cornell University Press, 1985.

———. "Humanism and the Resistance to Theory." In *Literary Theory/Renaissance Texts,* edited by Patricia Parker and David Quint, 373–96. Baltimore and London: Johns Hopkins University Press, 1986.

Kambyllis, Athanasios. *Die Dichterweihe und ihre Symbolik: Untersuchungen zu Hesiodos, Kallimachos, Properz und Ennius.* Heidelberg: 1965.

Kassel, Rudolf, and Colin Austin, eds. *Poetae comici graeci.* Vol. 4, *Aristophon-Crobylus.* Berlin and New York: De Gruyter, 1983.

Kegel, W.J.H.F. "Anacreon en de Anacreontea: En merkwaardige receptiegeschiedenis." *Lampas* 13 (1980): 372–88.

Kelly, Louis G. *The True Interpreter: A History of Translation Theory and Practice in the West.* Oxford: Blackwell, 1979.

Kennedy, George, ed. *The Cambridge History of Literary Criticism.* Vol. 1, *Classical Criticism.* Cambridge: Cambridge University Press, 1989.

Kenney, Edward J. "The Character of Humanist Philology." In *Classical Influences on European Culture,* A.D. *500–1500,* edited by Robert R. Bolgar, 119–28. Cambridge: Cambridge University Press, 1971.

———. *The Classical Text: Aspects of Editing in the Age of the Printed Book.* Sather Classical Lectures, no. 44. Berkeley: University of California Press, 1974.

Kirkwood, G.M., ed. *Poetry and Poetics from Ancient Greece to the Renaissance:*

Studies in Honor of James Hutton. Ithaca and London: Cornell University Press, 1975.

Kloepfer, Rolf. *Die Theorie der literarischen Übersetzung.* Freiburger Schriften zur romanischen Philologie, no. 12. Munich: Fink, 1967.

Kretschmer, F.A. "The 'res/verba' Dichotomy and 'copia' in Renaissance Translation." *Renaissance and Reformation* 11 (1975): 24–29.

Kroll, Wilhelm. *Studien zum Verständnis der römischen Literatur.* Stuttgart: Mezler, 1924.

Labarbe, Jules. "Un curieux phénomène littéraire, l'anacréontisme." *Bulletin de la classe des Lettres de l'Académie Royale de Belgique* 68 (1982): 146–81.

Lambin, Denys. *Aristotelis De moribus ad Nicomachum libri decem. Nunc primum è Graeco & Latinè & fideliter, quod vtrunque querebantur omnes praestitisse adhuc neminem, à Dionysio Lambino expressi.* Venice: Valgrisi, 1558.

———. *Dionys. Lambini, litterarum Graecarum doctoris, et earundem Latini interpretis regii, De utilitate linguae Graecae, & recta Graecorum Latinè interpretandorum ratione, oratio.* Paris: Bienné, 1572.

Larwill, Paul H. *La théorie de la traduction au début de la Renaissance (d'après les traductions imprimées en France entre 1477 et 1527).* Munich: Wolf, 1934.

Lattimore, Richmond. *Themes in Greek and Latin Epitaphs.* Illinois Studies in Language and Literature, vol. 28, nos. 1–2. Urbana: University of Illinois Press, 1942.

Laumonier, Paul. *Ronsard poète lyrique: Etude historique et littéraire.* 2d ed. Paris: Hachette, 1923.

Lausberg, Heinrich. *Handbuch der literarischen Rhetorik: Eine Grundlegung der Literaturwissenschaft.* 2 vols. Munich: Hueber, 1960.

Lebègue, Raymond. "Horace en France pendant la Renaissance." *Humanisme et Renaissance* 3 (1936): 141–64, 289–308, 384–419.

———. "Les traductions en France pendant la Renaissance." In *Association Guillaume Budé: Actes du congrès de Strasbourg, 20–22 avril 1938.* 362–377. Paris: Belles Lettres, 1939.

Lee, Guy. *Tibullus "Elegies."* 2d ed. Liverpool: Cairns, 1982.

Lee, Rensselaer W. *"Ut pictura poesis": The Humanistic Theory of Painting.* Norton Library, no. 399. New York: Norton, 1967.

Lefevere, André. *Translating Poetry: Seven Strategies and a Blueprint.* Approaches to Translation Studies, no. 3. Assen: Van Gorcum, 1975.

Lefkowitz, Mary R. "The Quarrel between Callimachus and Apollonius." *Zeitschrift für Papyrologie und Epigraphik* 40 (1980): 1–19.

Legrand, Philippe-Ernest. *Etude sur Théocrite.* Bibliothèque des Ecoles Françaises d'Athènes et de Rome, no. 79. Paris: Fontemoing, 1898.

Levarie, Janet. "Renaissance Anacreontics." *Comparative Literature* 25 (1973): 22–39.

Lindsay, W.M. *The Codex Turnebi of Plautus.* 1898. Reprint, Hildesheim: Olms, 1972.

Lobel, Edgar, and Denys L. Page, eds. *Poetarum Lesbiorum Fragmenta.* Oxford: Clarendon Press, 1955.

Longeon, Claude, ed. *Premiers combats pour la langue française.* Paris: Livre de poche, 1989.

Longnon, Henri. *Pierre de Ronsard: Essai de biographie.* Paris: Champion, 1912.

Ludwig, Walther. "Die Kunst der Variation im hellenistischen Liebesepigramm." In *L'épigramme grecque,* 299–348. Entretiens sur l'Antiquité classique, no. 14. Vandoeuvres-Geneva: Fondation Hardt, 1968.

———. "The Catullan Style in Neo-Latin Poetry." In *Latin Poetry and the Classical Tradition: Essays in Medieval and Renaissance Literature,* edited by Peter Godman and Oswyn Murray, 183–97. Oxford: Clarendon Press, 1990.

Lyons, John D. *Exemplum: The Rhetoric of Example in Early Modern France and Italy.* Princeton: Princeton University Press, 1989.

Maclean, Ian. *Interpretation and Meaning in the Renaissance: The Case of Law.* Ideas in Context. Cambridge: Cambridge University Press, 1992.

Magnien, Michel. "Anacréon, Ronsard et J.-C. Scaliger." In *Mélanges sur la littérature de la Renaissance à la mémoire de V.-L. Saulnier,* 399–410. Travaux d'Humanisme et Renaissance, no. 202. Geneva: Droz, 1984.

Mallet, B.J. "Some Uses of *sententiae* in Ronsard's Love-Sonnets." *French Studies* 27 (1973): 134–50.

Margolin, Jean-Claude. "La rhétorique d'Aphthonius et son influence au XVIe siècle." In *Colloque sur la rhétorique,* edited by R. Chevalier, 239–69. Paris: Belles Lettres, 1979.

Marullus. *Michaelis Marulli Carmina.* Edited by Alessandro Perosa. Bibliotheca scriptorum latinorum mediae et recentioris aetatis, no. 4. Turin: Thesaurus Mundi, [1951].

Mathieu-Castellani, Gisèle. *Les thèmes amoureux dans la poésie française (1570–1600).* Paris: Klincksieck, 1975.

———. "Intertextualité et allusion: Le régime allusif chez Ronsard." *Littérature* 55 (1984): 24–36.

Mathieu-Castellani, Gisèle, and Michel Plaisance, eds. *Les commentaires et la naissance de la critique littéraire: France, Italie, XIVe–XVIe siècles.* Paris: Aux Amateurs de Livres, 1990.

McClelland, John. "Lieu commun et poésie à la Renaissance." *Etudes Françaises* 13 (1977): 53–70.

McFarlane, Ian D. "Poésie néo-latine et poésie de langue vulgaire à l'époque de la Pléiade." In *Acta Conventus Neo-Latini Lovaniensis,* edited by Joseph IJsewijn and E. Kessler, 389–403. Louvain: Louvain University Press; Munich: Fink, 1973.

———. "Reflections on Ravisius Textor's *Specimen Epithetorum.*" In *Classical Influences on European Culture, A.D. 1500–1700,* edited by Robert R. Bolgar, 81–90. Cambridge: Cambridge University Press, 1976.

———. "Pierre de Ronsard and the Neo-Latin Poetry of His Time." *Res Publica Litterarum* 1 (1978): 177–205.

———. "Joachim du Bellay's *Liber amorum.*" *L'Esprit Créateur* 19, no. 3 (1979): 56–65.

Meerhoff, Kees. *Rhétorique et poétique au XVIe siècle en France: Du Bellay, Ramus et les autres.* Leiden: Brill, 1986.

Meleuc, Serge. "Structure de la maxime." *Langages* 13 (1969): 69–100.

Merrill, Robert V., with Robert J. Clements. *Platonism in French Renaissance Poetry.* New York: New York University Press, 1957.

Meschonnic, Henri. *Pour la poétique.* Vol. 2, *Epistémologie de l'écriture, poétique de la traduction.* Le Chemin. Paris: Gallimard, 1973.

Michelangeli, Luigi A. *Anacreonte e la sua fortuna nei secoli.* Bologna: Zanichelli, 1922.

Morgan, Kathleen. *Ovid's Art of Imitation: Propertius in the "Amores."* Leiden: Brill, 1977.

Morrison, Mary. "Catullus in the Neo-Latin Poetry of France before 1550." *Bibliothèque d'Humanisme et Renaissance* 17 (1955): 365–94.

———. "Ronsard and Catullus: The Influence of the Teaching of Marc-Antoine de Muret." *Bibliothèque d'Humanisme et Renaissance* 18 (1956): 240–74.

———. "Catullus and the Poetry of the Renaissance in France." *Bibliothèque d'Humanisme et Renaissance* 25 (1963): 25–56.

Müller, R. *Motivkatalog der römischen Elegie: Eine Untersuchung zur Poetik der Römer.* Zürich: Juris, 1952.

Mund-Dopchie, Monique. "Le premier travail français sur Eschyle: Le 'Prométhée enchaîné' de Jean Dorat." *Les Lettres Romanes* 30 (1976): 262–74.

———. *La survie d'Eschyle à la Renaissance: Editions, traductions, commentaires, et imitations.* Louvain: Peeters, 1984.

Murarasu, D. *La poésie néo-latine et la renaissance des lettres antiques en France (1500–1549).* Paris: Gamber, 1928.

Muret, Marc-Antoine de. *M.A. Mureti Iuuenilia.* Paris: Veuve Maurice de la Porte, 1553.

———. *Catullus et in eum Commentarius M. Antonii Mureti.* Venice: Paolo Manuzio, 1554.

———. *M. Antonii Mureti Opera omnia, ex MSS. aucta et emendata, cum breui annotatione Davidis Ruhnkenii.* 4 vols. Leiden: Luchtmans, 1789.

———. *Marc-Antoine de Muret, Commentaires au premier livre des "Amours" de Ronsard.* Edited by Jacques Chomarat, Marie-Madeleine Fragonard, and Gisèle Mathieu-Castellani. Commentaires de Ronsard, no. 1. Geneva: Droz, 1985.

Murgatroyd, Paul. *Tibullus I: A Commentary on the First Book of the Elegies of Albius Tibullus.* Pietermaritzburg: University of Natal Press, 1980.

Murphy, James, ed. *Renaissance Eloquence: Studies in the Theory and Practice of Renaissance Rhetoric.* Berkeley and Los Angeles: University of California Press, 1983.

Nemer, Monique. "La traduction au XVIe siècle: Contrôle et transformation du discours." *Cahiers de l'U.E.R. Froissart* 2 (1977): 30–44.

Nisbet, R.G.M., and Margaret Hubbard, eds. *A Commentary on Horace "Odes" Book 1.* Oxford: Clarendon Press, 1975.

———. *A Commentary on Horace "Odes" Book 2.* Oxford: Clarendon Press, 1978.

Nissen, Theodor. *Die byzantinischen Anakreonteen.* Sitzungsberichte der Bayerischen Akademie der Wissenschaften, philosophisch-historischen Abteilung, no. 3. Munich: Verlag der Bayerischen Wissenschaften and Beck, 1940.

Norton, Glyn P. "Translation Theory in Renaissance France: Etienne Dolet and the Rhetorical Tradition." *Renaissance and Reformation* 10 (1974): 1–13.

———. "Translation Theory in Renaissance France: The Poetic Controversy." *Renaissance and Reformation* 11 (1975): 30–44.

———. "Humanist Foundations of Translation Theory (1400–1450): A Study of the Dynamics of the Word." *Canadian Review of Comparative Literature* 8, no. 2 (1981): 173–203.

———. "La notion de *phrasis* dans la traduction française de la Renaissance." *Réforme Humanisme Renaissance* 15, no. 1 (1982): 102–8.

———. "*Fidus interpres:* A Philological Contribution to the Philosophy of Translation in Renaissance France." In *Neo-Latin and the Vernacular in Renaissance France,* edited by Terence Cave and Grahame Castor, 227–51. Oxford: Clarendon Press, 1984.

———. *The Ideology and Language of Translation in Renaissance France and Their Humanist Antecedents.* Travaux d'Humanisme et Renaissance, no. 201. Geneva: Droz, 1984.

———. "The Politics of Translation in Early Renaissance France: Confrontations of Policy and Theory during the Reign of Francis I." In *Die literarische Übersetzung: Fallstudien zu ihrer Kulturgeschichte,* edited by Brigitte Schultze and A.P. Frank, 1–13. Berlin: Schmidt, 1987.

O'Brien, John. "Translation, Philology, and Polemic in Denys Lambin's 'Nicomachean Ethics' of 1558." *Renaissance Studies* 3, no. 3 (1989): 267–89.

———. "Ronsard, Belleau, and Renvoisy." *Early Music History* 13 (1994): 199–215.

Ong, Walter J. "Commonplace Rhapsody: Ravisius Textor, Zwinger and Shakespeare." In *Classical Influences on European Culture,* A.D. *1500–1700,* edited by Robert R. Bolgar, 91–126. Cambridge: Cambridge University Press, 1976.

Orsini, Fulvio. *Carmina novem illustrium feminarum, Sapphus Erinnae Myrus Myrtidis Corinnae Telesillae Praxillae Nossidis Anytae et Lyricorum Alcmanis Stesichori Alcaei Ibyci Anacreontis Simonidis Bacchylidis Elegiae Tyrtaei, & Mimnermi. Bucolica Bionis & Moschi. Ex bibliotheca Fulvii Orsini Romani.* Antwerp: Plantin, 1568.

Otto, A. *Die Sprichwörter und sprichwörtlichen Redensarten der Römer.* Leipzig: Teubner, 1890.

Page, Denys L., ed. *Sappho and Alcaeus: An Introduction to the Study of Ancient Lesbian Poetry.* Oxford: Clarendon Press, 1955.

———. *Poetae melici graeci.* Oxford: Clarendon Press, 1962.

———. *Supplementum Lyricis Graecis.* Oxford: Clarendon Press, 1974.

———. *Further Greek Epigrams.* Cambridge: Cambridge University Press, 1981.

Parker, Patricia, and David Quint, eds. *Literary Theory/Renaissance Texts.* Baltimore and London: Johns Hopkins University Press, 1986.

Pasquali, Giorgio. *Storia della tradizione e critica del testo.* 2d ed. Florence: Le Monnier, 1952.

Patterson, Annabel M. *Hermogenes and the Renaissance: Seven Ideas of Style.* Princeton: Princeton University Press, 1970.

Peletier, Jacques du Mans. *Art poëtique.* Edited by André Boulanger. Publications de la Faculté des Lettres de l'Université de Strasbourg, no. 53. Paris: Belles Lettres, 1930.

Pépin, Jean. "L'herméneutique ancienne: Les mots et les idées." *Poétique* 6 (1975): 291–300.

Périon, Joachim. *Ioachimi Perionii Benedict. Cormoeriaceni De optimo genere interpretandi, In Aristotelis X. libros ethicorum, siue De moribus, à se latinitate donatos, Commentarij.* Paris: De Colines, 1540.

Pfeiffer, Rudolf. "The Future of Studies in the Field of Hellenistic Poetry." *Journal of Hellenic Studies* 75 (1955): 69–73.

———. "Dichter und Philologen im französichen Humanismus." *Antike und Abenland* 7 (1958): 73–83.

———. "Von den geschichlichen Begegnungen der kritischen Philologie mit dem Humanismus: Eine Skizze." In *Ausgewählte Schriften: Aufsätze und Vorträge zur griechischen Dichtung und zum Humanismus,* edited by Winfried Bühler, 159–74. Munich: Beck, 1960.

———. *History of Classical Scholarship from the Beginnings to the End of the Hellenistic Age.* Oxford: Clarendon Press, 1968.

———. *History of Classical Scholarship from 1300 to 1850.* Oxford: Clarendon Press, 1976.

Pichon, Réné. *Index Verborum Amatoriorum.* 1902. Reprint, Hildesheim: Olms, 1966.

Pigman, G.W. "Imitation and the Renaissance Sense of the Past: The Reception of Erasmus's *Ciceronianus.*" *Journal of Medieval and Renaissance Studies* 9, no. 2 (1979): 155–77.

———. "Versions of Imitation in the Renaissance." *Renaissance Quarterly* 33, no. 1 (1980): 1–32.

———. "Neo-Latin Imitation of the Latin Classics." In *Latin Poetry and the Classical Tradition: Essays in Medieval and Renaissance Literature,* edited by Peter Godman and Oswyn Murray, 199–210. Oxford: Clarendon Press, 1990.

Porcher, Jean. "La *Théologie Naturelle* et les théories de la traduction au XVIe siècle." In *Oeuvres complètes de Michel de Montaigne,* edited by A. Armaingaud, vol. 10, *La "Théologie Naturelle" de Raymond Sebon, II,* 447–79. Paris: Conard, 1935.

Pot, Olivier. *Inspiration et mélancholie: L'épistémologie poétique dans les "Amours" de Ronsard.* Travaux d'Humanisme et Renaissance, no. 240. Geneva: Droz, 1990.

Potez, Henri. "Deux années de la Renaissance (d'après une correspondance inédite)." *Revue d'Histoire Littéraire de la France* 13 (1906): 458–98, 658–92.

Potez, Henri, and François Préchac, eds. *Lettres galantes de Denys Lambin, 1552–54.* Paris: Vrin, 1941.

Preisendanz, Carl, ed. *Carmina Anacreontea e Bybl. Nat. Par. Cod. Gr. Suppl. 384 post Val. Rosium tertium edidit Carolus Preisendanz.* Leipzig: Teubner, 1912.

Puelma Piwonka, Mario. *Lucilius und Kallimachos: Zur Geschichte einer Gattung der hellenistisch-römischen Poesie.* Frankfurt am Main: Klostermann, [1949].

Py, Albert. *Imitation et Renaissance dans la poésie de Ronsard.* Histoire des idées et critique littéraire, no. 228. Geneva: Droz, 1984.

Quint, David. *Origin and Originality in Renaissance Literature.* New Haven: Yale University Press, 1983.

Randone, Giovanni. *Anacreonte e l'anacreontismo.* N.p.: Manfede, n.d.

Raymond, Marcel. *L'influence de Ronsard sur la poésie française.* Bibliothèque littéraire de la Renaissance, n.s., no. 14. 2 vols. Paris: Champion, 1927.

Reed, A.W. "John Clements and His Books." *The Library,* 4th ser., no. 6 (1926): 329–39.

Reiff, Arno. *Interpretatio, imitatio, aemulatio: Begriff und Vorstellung literarischer Abhängigkeit bei den Römern.* [Düsseldorf]: n.p., 1959.

Reitzenstein, Erich. "Zur Stiltheorie des Kallimachos." In *Festschrift Richard Reitzenstein.* 23–69. Leipzig and Berlin: Teubner, 1931.

Reitzenstein, Richard. *Epigramm und Skolion: Ein Beitrag zur Geschichte der alexandrinischen Dichtung.* Giessen: Ricker, 1893.

Renouard, A.A. *Annales de l'imprimerie des Estienne ou histoire de la famille des Estienne et de ses éditions.* 2d ed. Paris: Renouard, 1843.

Reverdin, Olivier. *Les premiers cours de grec au Collège de France ou l'enseignement de Pierre Danès d'après un document inédit.* Paris: Presses Universitaires de France, 1984.

———. "Henri Estienne à Genève." In *Henri Estienne,* 21–42. Cahiers V.-L. Saulnier, no. 5. Paris: Presses de l'E.N.S. de Jeunes Filles, 1988.

Reynolds, Leighton D., ed. *Texts and Transmissions: A Survey of the Latin Classics.* Corrected ed. Oxford: Clarendon Press, 1990.

Reynolds, Leighton D., and Nigel G. Wilson. *Scribes and Scholars: A Guide to the Transmission of Greek and Latin Literature.* 3d ed. Oxford: Clarendon Press, 1991.

Rice, Eugene F. *St. Jerome in the Renaissance.* Baltimore and London: Johns Hopkins University Press, 1985.

Riffaterre, Michael. *Essais de stylistique structurale.* Edited by Daniel Delas. Nouvelle bibliothèque scientifique. Paris: Flammarion, 1971.

———. *Semiotics of Poetry.* University Paperbacks, no. 684. London: Methuen, 1978.

———. "L'explication des faits littéraires." In *La production du texte.* Paris: Seuil, 1979.

———. "Un faux problème: L'érosion intertextuelle." In *Le signe et le texte: Etudes sur l'écriture au XVIe siècle en France,* edited by Lawrence D. Kritzman, 51–59. Lexington, Ky.: French Forum, 1990.

Rigolot, François. *Le Texte de la Renaissance: Des Rhétoriqueurs à Montaigne.* Geneva: Droz, 1982.

———. "Introduction à l'étude du 'commentataire': L'exemple de la Renaissance." In *Les commentaires et la naissance de la critique littéraire: France, Italie, XIVe–XVIe siècles,* edited by Gisèle Mathieu-Castellani and Michel Plaisance, 51–62. Paris: Aux Amateurs de Livres, 1990.

Rizzo, Silvia. *Il lessico filologico degli umanisti.* Sussidi eruditi, no. 26. Rome: Edizioni di storia e letteratura, 1973.

Robortello, Francesco. *Francesci Robortelli Utinensis, De arte sive ratione corrigendi antiquorum libros disputatio.* In Gaspar Schoppe, *De arte criticâ; & praecipue, de alterâ ejus parte emendatrice, Quaenam ratio in Latinis scriptoribus ex ingenio emendandis observari debeat; commentariolus.* Amsterdam: Pluymer, 1662.

Ronsard, Pierre de. *Oeuvres complètes.* Edited by Paul Laumonier; Raymond Lebègue and Isidore Silver. 20 vols. Paris: Hachette; Droz; Didier, 1914–75.

———. *Piene de Ronsard: Les Amours.* Edited by Henri Weber and Catherine Weber. Paris: Garnier, 1963.

Rose, Valentin, ed. *Anacreontis Teii quae vocantur συμποσιακὰ ἡμιάμβια ex Anthologiae Palatinae volumine altero nunc Pariensiensi post Henricum Stephanum et Josephum Spalleti tertium edita a Valentino Rose.* 2d ed. Leipzig: Teubner, 1876.

Rosenmeyer, Patricia A. *The Poetics of Imitation: Anacreon and the Anacreontic Tradition.* Cambridge and New York: Cambridge University Press, 1992.

Rubio y Lluch, Antonio. *Estudio crítico-bibliográfico sobre Anacreonte y la coleccion*

anacreóntica y su influencia en la literatura antigua y moderna. Barcelona: Subirana, 1879.
Russell, Donald A. "Literary Criticism in Antiquity." In *The Oxford Classical Dictionary,* 2d ed., edited by N.G.L. Hammond and H.H. Scullard, 611–12. Oxford: Clarendon Press, 1978.
———. *De imitatione.* In *Creative Imitation and Latin Literature.* Edited by David West and Tony Woodman, 1–16. Cambridge: Cambridge University Press, 1979.
———. *Criticism in Antiquity.* London: Duckworth, 1981.
———, ed. *"Longinus": On the Sublime.* Corrected ed. Oxford: Clarendon Press, 1970.
Sainte-Beuve, Charles A. "Anacréon, *Odes,* traduites en vers français avec le texte en regard, par M. Veissier-Descombes." In *Oeuvres,* vol. 1, *"Premiers Lundis," début des "Portraits littéraires,"* edited by Maxime Leroy, 217–22. Bibliothèque de la Pléiade. Paris: Gallimard, 1956.
Sandys, John E. *A History of Classical Scholarship.* 3 vols. Cambridge: Cambridge University Press, 1903–8.
Saulnier, Verdun-L. "Proverbe et paradoxe du XVe au XVIe siècle. Un aspect majeur de l'antithèse: Moyen Age—Renaissance." In *Pensée humaniste et tradition chrétienne aux XVe et XVIe siècles,* 87–104. Paris (26 au 30 octobre 1948). Colloques internationaux du Centre National de la Recherche Scientifique. Sciences Humaines. [Paris]: CNRS, 1950.
Sayce, Richard A. "Ronsard and Mannerism: The *Elegie à Janet.*" *L'Esprit Créateur* 6 (1966): 234–49.
Scaglione, Aldo. *The Classical Theory of Composition from Its Origins to the Present: A Historical Survey.* Chapel Hill: University of North Carolina Press, 1972.
Schmid, Wilhelm, and Otto Stählin. *Geschichte der griechischen Literatur.* Vol. 1, *Die griechische Literatur vor der attischen Hegemonie.* Munich: Beck, 1929.
Schmitt, Charles B. *Aristotle and the Renaissance.* Cambridge, Mass., and London: Harvard University Press, 1983.
Schmitt, Charles B., and Quentin Skinner. *The Cambridge History of Renaissance Philosophy.* Cambridge: Cambridge University Press, 1988.
Schreiber, Fred. *The Estienne: An Annotated Catalogue of 300 Highlights of Their Various Presses.* New York: Schreiber, 1982.
Schwarz, Werner. *Principles and Problems of Biblical Translation: Some Reformation Controversies and Their Background.* Cambridge: Cambridge University Press, 1955.
Screech, Michael A. "Greek in the Collège Trilingue of Paris and the Collegium Trilingue at Louvain: A propos of Professor Reverdin's Lecture at the Collège de France." *Bibliothèque d'Humanisme et Renaissance* 48 (1986): 85–90.
Sebillet, Thomas. *Art poétique françois.* Edited by Félix Gaiffe. Revised and updated by Francis Goyet. Société des textes français modernes. Paris: Nizet, 1988.
Secundus, Joannes. *Les baisers et l'épithalame, suivi des odes et des élégies.* Translated by Maurice Rat. Paris: Garnier, 1938.
Sharratt, Peter. "Ronsard et Pindare: Un écho de la voix de Dorat." *Bibliothèque d'Humanisme et Renaissance* 39 (1977): 97–114.
———. "The Role of the Writer and the Uses of Literary Critical Theory in the Prefaces to the Editions of the Classics in Sixteenth-Century France." In *Acta Conventus*

Neo-Latini Turonensis, edited by Jean-Claude Margolin, 1249–56. Paris: Vrin, 1980.

Siegel, Jerrold E. *Rhetoric and Philosophy in Renaissance Humanism.* Princeton: Princeton University Press, 1968.

Silk, Michael S. *Interaction in Poetic Imagery, with Special Reference to Early Greek Poetry.* Cambridge: Cambridge University Press, 1974.

Silver, Isidore. "Marc-Antoine de Muret et Ronsard." In *Lumières de la Pléiade,* 33–48. Neuvième stage international d'études humanistes, Tours 1965. De Pétrarque à Descartes, no. 11. Paris: Vrin, 1966.

———. *The Intellectual Evolution of Ronsard.* Vol. 1, *The Formative Influences.* St. Louis: Washington University Press, 1969.

———. *The Intellectual Evolution of Ronsard.* Vol. 2, *Ronsard's General Theory of Poetry.* St. Louis: Washington University Press, 1973.

———. *Ronsard and the Hellenic Renaissance in France: Ronsard and the Grecian Lyre.* 3 vols. Geneva: Droz, 1981–87.

Sintenis, K. "Zur Ehrenerklärung für H. Stephanus." *Philologus* 1 (1846): 134–42.

Sitzler, Jakob. *Anthologie aus den Lyrikern der Griechen.* Vol. 2, *Die melischen und chorischen Dichter.* Leipzig: Teubner, 1898.

———. "Zu den Anakreonteen." *Wochenschrift für klassiche Philologie* 1913: cols. 809–14, 847–61.

Smith, Barbara Herrnstein. *Poetic Closure: A Study of How Poems End.* Chicago: University of Chicago Press, 1968.

Spengel, Leonhard von. *Rhetores graeci.* 3 vols. Leipzig: Teubner, 1853–56.

Steiner, George. *After Babel: Aspects of Language and Translation.* London: Oxford University Press, 1975.

Stemplinger, Eduard. *Das Plagiat in der griechischen Literatur.* Leipzig and Berlin: Teubner, 1912.

Stierle, Karlheinz. "L'histoire comme exemple, l'exemple comme histoire." *Poétique* 10 (1972): 176–98.

———. "Les lieux du commentaire." In *Les commentaires et la naissance de la critique littéraire: France, Italie, XIVe–XVIe siècles,* edited by Gisèle Mathieu-Castellani and Michel Plaisance, 19–29. Paris: Aux Amateurs de Livres, 1990.

Struever, Nancy. *The Language of History in the Renaissance: Rhetoric and Historical Consciousness in Florentine Humanism.* Princeton: Princeton University Press, 1970.

Taccone, Vittorio. *Le anacreontiche: studio critico filologico.* N.p.: Acireale, 1898.

Tarán, Sonya L. *The Art of Variation in the Hellenistic Epigram.* Columbia Studies in the Classical Tradition, no. 9. Leiden: Brill, 1979.

Terreaux, Louis. "Le style 'bas' des *Continuations des Amours.*" In *Lumières de la Pléiade,* 313–42. Neuvième stage international d'études humanistes, Tours 1965. De Pétrarque à Descartes, no. 11. Paris: Vrin, 1966.

Tilley, Arthur. "Henri Estienne." *Classical Review* 8 (1894): 251.

Timpanaro, Sebastiano. *La genesi del metodo del Lachmann.* 2d ed. Padua: Liviana, 1985.

Trapp, Joseph B. "The Conformity of Greek and the Vernacular: The History of a Renaissance Theory of Languages." In *Classical Influences on European Culture, A.D. 500–1500,* edited by Robert R. Bolgar, 239–44. Cambridge: Cambridge University Press, 1971.
Tyrell, R. "The *Bacchae* of Euripides." *Classical Review* 8 (1894): 294–96.
Valesio, Paolo. "The Virtues of Traducement: Sketch of a Theory of Translation." *Semiotica* 18, no. 1 (1976): 1–96.
———. *Novantiqua: Rhetorics as a Contemporary Theory.* Bloomington: Indiana University Press, 1980.
Van Tieghem, Paul. *La littérature latine de la Renaissance: Etude d'histoire littéraire européenne.* Paris: Droz, 1944.
Verdier, Maurice F. "Les introuvables éditions des 'Odes d'Anacréon' (Rémy Belleau)." *Bibliothèque d'Humanisme et Renaissance* 33 (1971): 359–63.
Vettori, Pier. *Petri Victorii Variarum Lectionum libri XXXVIII.* Florence: Giunta, 1582.
Vickers, Brian. "Rhetorical and Anti-Rhetorical Tropes: On Writing the History of *elocutio.*" *Comparative Criticism* 3 (1981): 105–32.
———. *In Defence of Rhetoric.* Oxford: Clarendon Press, 1988.
Vida, Marco Girolamo. *The "De arte poetica" of Marco Girolamo Vida.* Edited by Ralph G. Williams. New York: Columbia University Press, 1976.
Waswo, Richard. *Language and Meaning in the Renaissance.* Princeton: Princeton University Press, 1987.
Weber, Henri. *La création poétique au XVIe siècle en France de Maurice Scève à Agrippa d'Aubigné.* Paris: Nizet, 1955.
Weinberg, Bernard. *Critical Prefaces of the French Renaissance.* Northwestern University Studies, Humanities Series, no. 20. Evanston: Northwestern University Press, 1950.
Welcker, F.G. "Anacreon." Review of *Anacreontis carminum reliquiae,* by T. Bergk. *Rheinisches Museum für Philologie* 3 (1835): 269–314.
Wells, Margaret Brady. "What Did Du Bellay Understand by 'Translation'?" *Forum for Modern Language Studies* 16 (1980): 175–85.
West, Martin L. *Greek Metre.* Oxford: Clarendon Press, 1982.
———. "Problems in the Anacreontea." *Classical Quarterly* 34 (1984): 206–21.
———. "The *Anacreontea.*" In *Sympotica: A Symposium on the "Symposion,"* edited by Oswyn Murray, 272–76. Oxford: Clarendon Press, 1990.
———, ed. *Carmina Anacreontea.* 1984. 2d ed. Leipzig: Teubner, 1993.
Wierenga, Lambert. "'Sentence' et manipulation: Aspects rhétoriques d'une forme simple." *Neophilologus* 71 (1987): 24–34.
Wilamowitz-Moellendorff, Ulrich von. *Hellenistiche Dichtung in der Zeit des Kallimachos.* 2 vols. Berlin: Weidmann, 1924.
———. *History of Classical Scholarship.* Edited by Hugh Lloyd-Jones. London: Duckworth, 1982.
Wilson, Dudley B. *Descriptive Poetry in France from Blason to Baroque.* Manchester: Manchester University Press; New York: Barnes and Noble, 1967.
Wilson, Nigel. *Scholars of Byzantium.* London: Duckworth, 1983.

———. *From Byzantium to Italy: Greek Studies in the Italian Renaissance.* London: Duckworth, 1992.

Wimmel, Walter. *Kallimachos in Rom: Die Nachfolge seines apologetischen Dichtens in der Augusterzeit.* Hermes Einzelschriften, no. 16. Wiesbaden: Steiner, 1960.

Worth, Valerie. *Practising Translation in Renaissance France: The Example of Etienne Dolet.* Oxford: Clarendon Press, 1988.

Young, Margaret M.L. *Guillaume des Autelz: A Study of His Life and Work.* Travaux d'Humanisme et Renaissance, no. 48. Geneva: Droz, 1961.

Zanker, Graham. "Enargeia in the Ancient Criticism of Poetry." *Rheinisches Museum,* n.s., 124 (1981): 297–311.

———. *Realism in Alexandrian Poetry: A Literature and Its Audience.* London: Croom Helm, 1987.

Zetzel, James E.G. *Latin Textual Criticism in Antiquity.* New York: Arno, 1981.

———. "Catullus, Ennius, and the Poetics of Allusion." *Illinois Classical Studies* 8 (1983): 251–66.

———. "Re-creating the Canon: Augustan Poetry and the Alexandrian Past." *Critical Inquiry* 10, no. 1 (1983): 83–105.

Zumthor, Paul. "L'épiphonème proverbial." *Revue des Sciences Humaines* 41 (1976): 313–28.

———. "Tant de lieux comme un." *Etudes Françaises* 13 (1977): 3–10.

Index

Aactio, 198
Adunaton, 182, 185
Adversaria, 9
Aemulatio, 47, 67, 82, 85, 138–39, 154
Aeschines, 49
Agathias Scholasticus, 98n.11, 111
Agustín, Antonio, 5
Alcaeus, 25–29, 31, 165, 245
Alexandrianism, 80–82, 85, 87, 158, 162, 163
Allegory, 237
Allusio, 38, 40, 42, 43, 80, 81, 84–88, 101, 103, 107, 129, 130, 132, 138, 153–54, 158, 169, 173, 193, 197, 198, 199, 241–42, 246
Amplificatio, 63, 101, 111, 116, 122, 233, 238
Anacreon, 23–25, 31–33, 38, 104, 165
Anadiplosis, 170
Anaphora, 170, 230
André, Elie, 3, 27, 91, 99–101, 120, 125–54, 209, 222, 242, 245
Aneau, Barthelemy, 54n.10
Apollonius of Rhodes, 194–95
Apostrophe, 237
Aratus, 171
Ariosto, 196
Aristophanes, 30
Aristotle, 37n.78, 38n.80, 53–58
Armstrong, Elizabeth, 5n.1
Asyndeton, 176
Auctoritas, 86, 138, 144n.50
Austin, Colin. *See* Kassel, Rudolf

Baif, Jean-Antoine de, 8
Barthes, Roland, 116, 120
Bathos, 115
Bathyllus, 188, 233–35, 239
Baudelaire, 172
Baumann, Michael, 20n.49
Belleau, Remy, 155, 157, 192n.74, 193, 194, 195n.82, 197, 199, 201–40, 243, 244, 245, 246
Bellenger, Yvonne, 116n.41
Bentley, Jerry H., 51n.3
Bergk, Theodor, 75
Bion, 183–84
Blason, 117
Bloom, Harold, 209n.15
Bolgar, Robert R., 62n.29
Braybrook, Jean, 231, 239
Brioso Sánchez, Máximo, 74
Brodeau, Jean, 9–12
Brooks, Peter, 83
Bruni, Leonardo, 54
Buck, August, 92n.3
Bundy, Elroy T., 95n.6
Burke, U. Peter, 86n.97

Cairns, Francis, 85n.95
Callimachus, 95n.6
Cameron, Alan, 14n.27
Campbell, David, 1, 75nn. 69, 71
Captatio benevolentiae, 180
Carpe diem, 181
Cassandre, 188, 189, 191, 192, 194
Castigationes, 9, 48

Index

Castor, Grahame, 70n.51, 72n.62
Catullus, 2, 80, 129, 134, 135, 136–37, 162, 168–69, 190, 242, 246
Cave, Terence, 62n.29, 63n.34, 66, 70n.51, 121nn. 58, 59, 139, 181n.64, 211n.17
Caws, Mary Ann, 202
Chamard, Henri, 218n.19
Chavy, Paul, 65n.35
Choiseul, Chretophle de, 165, 201
Cicero, 30, 38n.81, 49–60, 71, 73, 74, 113, 114, 121, 133, 142
Clausen, Wendel V., 76n.78
Clement, John, 14, 15
Clements, Robert J., 71n.58
Clinamen, 209
Collège de Coqueret, 9
Collège du Cardinal Lemoine, 9
Compagnon, Antoine, 151n.69, 245n.5
Contaminatio, 23, 35–36, 37, 43, 85, 87, 101, 102, 104, 106, 107, 129, 140, 144, 152, 154, 156, 157, 171–73, 177, 178, 181, 184, 187, 193, 195, 198, 199, 209, 223, 229, 242–43
Copia, 49, 63, 64, 121, 129, 135, 154
Corrado, Ludovico, 59
Couat, Auguste, 76, 163, 179
Croesus, 142
Crux (cruces), 6, 58, 110, 243
Curtius, Ernst Robert, 140n.38, 144n.50

Débat, 188
Decorum, 56, 59, 74, 171, 208, 242
Delacourcelle, Doris, 226n.24
Della Casa, Giovanni, 13
Démarche, 168, 170, 174, 178, 182, 186, 198
Demerson, Guy, 204n.10, 239
Demetrius, 37n.78, 38n.80
Demosthenes, 49
De Nolhac, Pierre, 12n.22, 20n.50, 44n.93, 47, 158, 161n.21, 190
Derrida, Jacques, 84, 244n.3
De Saussure, Ferdinand, 83–84
Des Autelz, Guillaume, 72–73, 74
Desgraves, Louis, 125n.2

D'Estrebay, Jacques-Louis, 54–56
Dezeimeris, Reinhold, 125n.2
Dionisotti, Carlotta, 7n.9
Dionysius of Halicarnassus, 15, 32–34, 36, 38, 244
Dispositio, 107, 120
Divinatio, 6, 22, 55, 60, 78, 95, 110
Dolet, Etienne, 53, 64–67
Dorat, Jean, 2, 8, 44–45, 47, 158, 162, 179, 187
Doux (-coulant), 157, 217, 231, 235
Dover, Kenneth J., 116n.37
Du Bellay, Joachim, 8, 69–74, 167–69, 203

Easterling, Patricia E., 12n.20
Eckhardt, Alexandre, 218n.19
Ecphrasis (descriptio), 115–20, 196, 224, 230–31, 243
Edmonds, J.M., 1, 75n.71
Elocutio, 51, 116, 119, 122, 126, 127, 128, 130, 132, 133, 140, 142, 151, 152
Emendatio, 5
  ope codicum, 12, 17, 21, 22
  ope ingenii, 17, 22
Enallage, 230
Enargeia, 117–18, 130, 190, 246
Energeia, 197–98
England, E.B., 19n.47
Ennius, 45
Enumeratio, 167, 168, 176, 182, 185, 194
Erasmus, Desiderius, 62–64, 74, 84, 186, 246
Estienne, Henri, 2, 3, 5, 13–17, 18–19, 22–41, 43–44, 45, 46, 47, 48, 76–81, 84, 86, 87, 91–124, 136, 151, 157, 158, 159, 160, 161, 162, 163, 172, 174, 186, 190, 197, 209, 222, 241, 242, 243, 244, 245
Estienne I, Robert, 32, 47
Estienne II, Robert, 125
Euripides, 7
Eusebius, 52
Exemplum(a), 108, 140, 204

Facilitas, 64
Faerno, Gabriele, 5
Farnese, Alessandro, 21
Ferguson, Margaret, 70n.51
Feugère, Léon, 13n.23, 32n.67
Fides, 18–19, 21, 22
Flaminio, 162
François, Michel, 57n.18
Francus, 180
Fraser, P., 95n.6
Frécaut, Jean-Marc, 138n.33
Fumaroli, Marc, 49n.1

Gaisser, Julia Haig, 9n.13, 80n.85, 162n.28
Gellius, Aulus, 108–10
Genette, Gérard, 222n.21, 231
Genus floridum, 155–56, 244
Genus grave or *grande,* 164, 166
Genus humile or *tenue,* 59, 156, 164, 189, 192, 197, 244
Giangrande, Giuseppe, 81, 82n.88, 106n.24, 135n.25, 184n.68, 234–35
Gow, A.S.F., 142n.43, 176n.59
Goyet, Francis, 39n.82, 54n.10, 65n.37, 67n.42
Grafton, Anthony T., 5, 6, 9n.14, 22n.58, 44n.93, 48, 53n.8, 57n.15
Grassot, Jules, 208
Greek Anthology, 2, 77, 78, 79, 80, 98n.11, 108–10, 158, 159, 161, 162, 163, 175, 193
Greene, Thomas M., 40, 70n.51, 83, 85–86, 120–21, 122, 126n.5, 129n.12, 139, 209
Greimas, A.-J., 141n.41
Griffiths, Richard, 149n.64
Grube, G.M.A., 156n.1
Guillerm, Luce, 65n.35, 139n.34

Hamon, Philippe, 116, 117n.4
Helicon, 202, 203
Herding, Otto. *See* August Buck
Hermans, Theo, 245n.8
Hermogenes, 36, 38
Herter, Hans, 81n.86

Hesiod, 45
Homer, 45, 106, 135, 153, 196, 211
Homoeoteleuton, 177
Horace, 6, 9, 22–31, 35, 37, 38, 39, 40, 48, 52, 79, 84, 86, 98, 99–101, 105, 126, 130, 153, 171, 190, 214, 223, 242, 246
Hubbard, Margaret. *See* Nisbet, R.G.M.
Hutchison, G.O., 76n.78
Hutton, James, 13n.23, 80, 102n.18, 130n.17, 159, 176n.59
Hyperbole, 237
Hypotyposis, 116, 172, 230

Imitatio, 37, 40–43, 77, 78, 87, 103, 216, 242
Intention, 73
Interpretatio, 23, 139
Inventio, 121, 230
Isocolon, 115, 182, 206
Isocrates, 34n.72

Jacobsen, E., 63n.33
Jeanneret, Michel, 92n.3
Jerome, St., 51–52, 53, 55, 73
Joukovsky, Françoise, 205n.11

Kambyllis, Athanasios, 41n.85
Kassel, Rudolf, 203n.6
Kelly, Louis, 168
Kenney, Edward J., 17n.39, 18n.44, 19, 21n.57
Kloepfer, Rolf, 51n.4
Kroll, Wilhelm, 42, 85n.95

Lambin, Denys, 56–60, 74
Larwill, Paul H., 64n.35, 88
Laumonier, Paul, 156, 157n.6, 158, 162, 163, 166n.43, 167, 182, 184, 187, 188n.72, 190, 192, 193, 203
Lausberg, Heinrich, 115n.37, 140n.38
Lebègue, Raymond, 9n.12, 64n.35
Lee, Guy, 144
Lee, Rensselaer W., 116n.41
Lefèvre d'Etaples, Jacques, 54
Lefkowitz, Mary R., 95n.6

Legrand, Philippe-Ernest, 85n.95
Lindsay, W.M., 12n.21
Lobel, Edgar, 25n.62, 27n.64
Locus, 38, 116, 119, 120, 121, 128, 129, 141, 151, 153, 243, 245
Locus amoenus, 233
"Longinus," 37n.78
Longnon, Henri, 158
Lucretius, 37n.78
Ludwig, Walther, 82
Lyons, John D., 140n.38
Lysias, 33, 34, 36, 38, 156

Magnien, Michel, 241n.1
Mallet, B.J., 141n.39
Marie, 191–97
Marullus, 80, 120n.54, 123, 162, 196
Mathieu-Castellani, Gisèle, 87–88, 92n.3, 117n.44
McFarlane, Ian D., 102n.16, 163n.29, 164nn. 38, 39, 167n.48
Meerhoff, Kees, 54n.10
Memoria, 49, 64, 154
Merrill, Robert V., 204n.9
Meschonnic, Henri, 90
Metaphor, 185, 188, 219–21, 234–36, 237, 238, 246
Meter, 75, 104, 114, 139, 140, 145, 164, 166, 167–69, 175, 182, 186, 193, 206, 209n.16, 210, 211, 217, 219, 228, 245
Metonym, 182, 213, 219, 231, 234, 235
Mignardise, 102, 135, 157, 192, 207–8, 210, 211, 212, 213, 215, 228, 229, 231, 235, 242, 244, 246
Mimnermus, 79, 86, 190
Molza, 196
Montaigne, Michel de, 18n.44, 245
Montdoré, Pierre de, 125
Morgan, Kathleen, 138n.33
Morrison, Mary, 9n.13, 80n.85, 162n.28
Müller, R., 96n.8
Mundus significans, 83, 84, 163, 165, 198
Muret, Marc-Antoine de, 6, 7, 8, 9, 12, 13, 22, 30, 39, 43, 48, 59, 60, 158, 159, 162, 165, 243

Murgatroyd, Paul, 135n.26, 144n.51, 146n.57

Nemer, Monique, 65n.35
Neoplatonism, 189, 204, 205, 206
Nisbet, R.G.M., 126n.5, 142n.45, 145n.55, 147nn. 59, 60
Nissen, Theodor, 75n.70
Norton, Glyn P., 3n.7, 49n.1, 53nn. 6–8, 54n.9, 60n.25, 64n.35, 70n.51, 71, 72nn. 61–62, 95, 197–98

O'Brien, John, 57n.15, 201n.4, 218n.19, 226n.24
Ode légère, 2, 156, 197
Ong, Walter J., 140n.38
Ordo
  rerum, 168n.50, 198–99, 246
  verborum, 168n.50, 198–99, 246
Orsini, Fulvio, 2, 5, 20–22
Otto, A., 137n.29
Ovid, 77, 79, 96–98, 101, 102–4, 106, 127, 136–39, 153, 223

Page, Denys L., 24nn. 59–61, 80n.84
Palladas, 79, 132–33, 175
Panyassis, 190
Peletier du Mans, Jacques, 67–69, 74, 246
Pépin, Jean, 245n.6
Périon, Joachim, 53–60, 74
Persona, 76, 150, 204, 220, 244
Petrarch, Petrarchism, 188, 192, 196, 231, 237, 238
Pfeiffer, Rudolf, 6n.6, 16, 75n.73, 74, 76n.77, 95n.6
Pichon, Réné, 106n.24
Pigman, G.W., 44n.92, 70n.53, 86n.97
Pindar, 26, 29, 31–33, 157, 165, 166, 192, 201, 213, 216
Plagiarism *(furtum)*, 41–48
Plato, 34, 60
Plautus, 112, 114, 127, 128, 131–32, 134, 242
Pléiade, 2, 9, 39, 190, 205, 216
Plutarch, 33n.71

Pointe, 167, 195
Politian (Angelo Poliziano), 5, 6, 9, 10, 11, 18
Polyptoton, 115, 175
Pontano, 80, 123, 162
Porcher, Jean, 89n.107
Posidippus, 175, 176–77, 178
Potez, Henri, 57n.15
Preisendanz, Carl, 14nn. 26–28, 15
Pronunciatio, 49
Proprietas, 102, 118, 127, 128, 153, 171, 190, 197, 208
Puelma Piwonka, Mario, 41n.85, 95n.6
Py, Albert, 3n.8

Quellenforschung, 6
Quintilian, 35, 37, 38, 60–64, 72, 74, 121, 127n.10, 139

Radermacher, Ludwig. *See* Usener, Hermann
Ravisius Textor, 98, 126n.7
Raymond, Marcel, 218n.19, 224
Recensio, 5, 6, 77
Recusatio, 95, 105, 126, 127, 179, 191, 211, 214
Reed, A.W., 14n.27
Reeve, Michael D., 50n.2
Reiff, Arno, 61n.28
Reitzenstein, Erich, 41n.85
Reitzenstein, Richard, 77n.80
Renovatio, 40–41, 80, 86, 122–23, 163, 164, 169, 202, 238
Repetitio, 83–84, 87, 103, 105, 107, 108, 109, 122–23, 223, 226, 227
Res, 4, 50, 54, 56, 67, 73, 89, 121, 139, 246
Reverdin, Olivier, 5n.1
Reynolds, Leighton D., 11n.19, 50n.2
Rice, Eugene F., 51n.4
Riffaterre, Michael, 39n.82, 103n.19
Robortello, Francesco, 2, 17–20
Ronsard, Pierre de, 2, 8, 155–99, 201–3, 208, 211, 214, 215–30, 239–40, 243, 244, 245, 246
Rose, Valentin, 14nn. 26–28, 15

Rosenmeyer, Patricia A., 1, 14n.27, 74, 96n.8, 106n.24, 132n.22, 135n.25, 234n.30
Russell, Donald A., 42nn. 86, 91, 155n.1

Sainte-Beuve, Charles A., 1, 2
Salmon Macrin, Jean, 163, 190
Sapinus, Baptista, 9, 10
Sappho, 31–33
Saulnier, Verdun-L., 140n.38
Sayce, Richard A., 224n.23
Scaliger, Joseph Justus, 11
Scaliger, Julius Caesar, 241
Schmitt, Charles B., 53n.8, 54n.10, 57n.17
Schwarz, Werner, 51n.3
Sebillet, Thomas, 65–69, 73, 74, 246
Secundus, Joannes, 80, 120n.54, 123, 162, 163, 164, 190
Sententia (sentence, sens), 4, 50, 54, 73, 89, 140–54
Silk, Michael S., 137n.31
Silver, Isidore, 9n.13, 13n.23, 47, 57n.15, 65n.35, 158, 159, 160, 162n.28, 218n.19
Sintenis, K., 19n.47
Sitzler, Jakob, 75n.71, 76
Smith, Barbara Herrnstein, 142n.44
Socrates, 33–34
Somnia amoris (songes amoureux), 101, 236–38
Sophocles, 186
Steiner, George, 4n.9, 73n.67
Stemplinger, Eduard, 42
Stille bas, 156, 157, 165, 191, 197, 208, 214
Stobaeus, 223
Struever, Nancy, 40–41, 242

Tarán, Sonya L., 82n.88
Terence, 113, 131–32
Terreaux, Louis, 156, 157n.6
Theocritus, 36–37, 77, 112, 113–15
Thesaurus, 121–24
Thucydides, 33

Tibullus, 144
Tilley, Arthur, 19n.47
Timpanaro, Sebastiano, 12n.20
Toussain, Jacques, 6
Translation
  acculturation, 84, 164, 246
  balance, 50, 64
  compensation theory, 51, 64, 73, 105, 246
  correspondence theory, 246
  excision, 209–10
  exploitative, 209
  extrusion, 209, 212–13
  heuristic, 209
  "innutrition," 70
  internalization, 65, 66, 70
  intrusion, 212–13
  propaedeutic, 49, 74, 174
  reflection, 3, 66, 68
  rivalry, 61–62
  spatio-temporality, 3–4, 74, 85, 86, 116, 122, 124, 138, 153, 238
  transfer, 3–4, 23, 29, 61, 67, 68, 74, 155
  transposition (transformation), 122, 123, 139, 205
Translatio poesis, 3
Translatio studii, 3, 22, 83
Turnèbe, Adrien, 11–13, 59, 223
Tyrell, R.Y., 19n.47

Usener, Hermann, 33n.69

Valesio, Paolo, 89, 169n.51
Variae interpretationes, 98, 101, 103, 105, 107, 158, 180–81, 185, 186, 191, 193, 198, 199
Variae lectiones, 9, 48
Variatio, 81–87, 98, 101, 102, 103, 105, 107, 108, 115, 122–23, 137, 138, 140, 157, 223, 226, 228
Verbum(a), 4, 50, 54, 56, 67, 73, 89, 121
Verdier, Maurice F., 201nn. 2, 3
Vettori, Pier, 5, 10, 11, 15, 18, 59, 159–60
Vida, Marco Girolamo, 45–47
Virgil, 45, 72, 73, 106, 119
Vox (voces), 117, 136, 138, 139, 150–51
Vraisemblance, 118, 214n.18, 231

Weber, Henri, 99n.12, 194nn. 78, 81, 195n.82, 244
Weinberg, Bernard, 64n.35, 65n.36
Welcker, F.G., 76n.77
Wells, Margaret Brady, 71, 72nn. 62–63, 73nn. 66–68, 89n.105
West, Martin L., 1, 14nn. 25, 28, 15, 75, 126n.6
Wierenga, Lambert, 140n.38
Wilson, Dudley B., 117n.45
Wilson, Nigel, 11n.19
Wimmel, Walter, 41n.85, 95n.6, 184n.68
Worth, Valerie, 65n.35

Xenophon, 38, 55, 60

Young, Margaret M.L., 72

Zetzel, James E.G., 76n.78
Ziegler, K., 42
Zumthor, Paul, 140n.38, 145n.53